Modern Computer Architecture and Organization

Learn x86, ARM, and RISC-V architectures and the design of smartphones, PCs, and cloud servers

Jim Ledin

BIRMINGHAM—MUMBAI

Modern Computer Architecture and Organization

Commissioning Editor: Kunal Chaudhari
Acquisition Editor: Denim Pinto
Senior Editor: Afshaan Khan
Content Development Editor: Tiksha Lad
Technical Editor: Gaurav Gala
Copy Editor: Safis Editing
Project Coordinator: Francy Puthiry
Proofreader: Safis Editing
Indexer: Pratik Shirodkar
Production Designer: Aparna Bhagat

First published: April 2020

Production reference: 1290420

Published by Packt Publishing Ltd.
Livery Place
35 Livery Street
Birmingham
B3 2PB, UK.

ISBN 978-1-83898-439-7

www.packt.com

Packt.com

Subscribe to our online digital library for full access to over 7,000 books and videos, as well as industry leading tools to help you plan your personal development and advance your career. For more information, please visit our website.

Why subscribe?

- Spend less time learning and more time coding with practical eBooks and Videos from over 4,000 industry professionals

- Improve your learning with Skill Plans built especially for you

- Get a free eBook or video every month

- Fully searchable for easy access to vital information

- Copy and paste, print, and bookmark content

Did you know that Packt offers eBook versions of every book published, with PDF and ePub files available? You can upgrade to the eBook version at packt.com and as a print book customer, you are entitled to a discount on the eBook copy. Get in touch with us at customercare@packtpub.com for more details.

At www.packt.com, you can also read a collection of free technical articles, sign up for a range of free newsletters, and receive exclusive discounts and offers on Packt books and eBooks.

Contributors

About the author

Jim Ledin is the CEO of Ledin Engineering, Inc. Jim is an expert in embedded software and hardware design, development, and testing. He is also accomplished in embedded system cybersecurity assessment and penetration testing. He has a B.S. degree in aerospace engineering from Iowa State University and an M.S. degree in electrical and computer engineering from Georgia Institute of Technology. Jim is a registered professional electrical engineer in California, a **Certified Information System Security Professional (CISSP)**, a **Certified Ethical Hacker (CEH)**, and a **Certified Penetration Tester (CPT)**.

About the reviewer

Roger Spears has over 15 years' experience in the academic field and over 20 years' experience in IT. He has a B.S. in technology from Bowling Green State University and an M.S. in information assurance, specializing in network defense, from Capella University. He has developed and facilitated individual courses for networking, programming, and databases. He was a member of the Protect and Detect working group on the National Cyberwatch Center Curriculum Standards Panel for the Cybersecurity Foundation Series. Roger has been awarded over $750,000 in cybersecurity grants from the government for various academic and industrial customers. He holds certificates from Microsoft and Oracle. He also holds a CCNA and CySA+ certification.

> *I would like to acknowledge my wife (Leann) and children (Maverick and Sierra) for providing me the opportunity to grow with them and for the freedom to pursue various academic and vocational endeavors. Your understanding and tolerance meant more than I can say with words.*

Packt is searching for authors like you

If you're interested in becoming an author for Packt, please visit authors. packtpub.com and apply today. We have worked with thousands of developers and tech professionals, just like you, to help them share their insight with the global tech community. You can make a general application, apply for a specific hot topic that we are recruiting an author for, or submit your own idea.

Table of Contents

3

Processor Elements

4

Computer System Components

5

Hardware-Software Interface

6

Specialized Computing Domains

Section 2:
Processor Architectures and Instruction Sets

7
Processor and Memory Architectures

8
Performance-Enhancing Techniques

9
Specialized Processor Extensions

10

Modern Processor Architectures and Instruction Sets

11

The RISC-V Architecture and Instruction Set

Section 3: Applications of Computer Architecture

12
Processor Virtualization

13
Domain-Specific Computer Architectures

Other Books You May Enjoy

Index

Preface

This book presents the key technologies and components employed in modern processor and computer architectures and discusses how various architectural decisions result in computer configurations optimized for specific needs.

To understate the situation quite drastically, modern computers are complicated devices. Yet, when viewed in a hierarchical manner, the functions of each level of complexity become clear. We will cover a great many topics in these chapters and will only have the space to explore each of them to a limited degree. My goal is to provide a coherent introduction to each important technology and subsystem you might find in a modern computing device and explain its relationship to other system components.

I will not be providing a lengthy list of references for further reading. The Internet is your friend in this regard. If you can manage to bypass the clamor of political and social media argumentation on the Internet, you will find yourself in an enormous, cool, quiet library containing a vast quantity of accumulated human knowledge. Learn to use the advanced features of your favorite search engine. Also, learn to differentiate high-quality information from uninformed opinion. Check multiple sources if you have any doubts about the information you're finding. Consider the source: if you are looking for information about an Intel processor, search for documentation published by Intel.

By the end of this book, you will have gained a strong grasp of the computer architectures currently used in a wide variety of digital systems. You will also have developed an understanding of the relevant trends in architectural technology currently underway, as well as some possibly disruptive advances in the coming years that may drastically influence the architectural development of computing systems.

Who this book is for

This book is intended for software developers, computer engineering students, system designers, computer science professionals, reverse engineers, and anyone else seeking to understand the architecture and design principles underlying all types of modern computer systems from tiny embedded devices to smartphones to warehouse-sized cloud server farms. Readers will also explore the directions these technologies are likely to take in the coming years. A general understanding of computer processors is helpful but is not required.

What this book covers

The information in this book is presented in the following sequence:

Chapter 1, Introducing Computer Architecture, begins with a brief history of automated computing devices and describes the significant technological advances that drove leaps in capability. This is followed by a discussion of Moore's law, with an assessment of its applicability over previous decades and the implications for the future. The basic concepts of computer architecture are introduced in the context of the 6502 microprocessor.

Chapter 2, Digital Logic, introduces transistors as switching elements and explains their use in constructing logic gates. We will then see how flip-flops and registers are developed by combining simple gates. The concept of sequential logic, meaning logic that contains state information, is introduced, and the chapter ends with a discussion of clocked digital circuits.

Chapter 3, Processor Elements, begins with a conceptual description of a generic processor. We will examine the concepts of the instruction set, register set, and instruction loading, decoding, execution, and sequencing. Memory load and store operations are also discussed. The chapter includes a description of branching instructions and their use in looping and conditional processing. Some practical considerations are introduced that lead to the necessity for interrupt processing and I/O operations.

Chapter 4, Computer System Components, discusses computer memory and its interface to the processor, including multilevel caching. I/O requirements including interrupt handling, buffering, and dedicated I/O processors are described. We will discuss some specific requirements for I/O devices including the keyboard and mouse, the video display, and the network interface. The chapter ends with descriptive examples of these components in modern computer applications, including smart mobile devices, personal computers, gaming systems, cloud servers, and dedicated machine learning systems.

Chapter 5, Hardware-Software Interface, discusses the implementation of the high-level services a computer operating system must provide, including disk I/O, network communications, and interactions with users. This chapter describes the software layers that implement these features starting at the level of the processor instruction set and registers. Operating system functions, including booting, multiprocessing, and multithreading, are also described.

Chapter 6, Specialized Computing Domains, explores domains of computing that tend to be less directly visible to most users, including real-time systems, digital signal processing, and GPU processing. We will discuss the unique requirements associated with each of these domains and look at examples of modern devices implementing these features.

Chapter 7, Processor and Memory Architectures, takes an in-depth look at modern processor architectures, including the von Neumann, Harvard, and modified Harvard variants. The chapter discusses the implementation of paged virtual memory. The practical implementation of memory management functionality within the computer architecture is introduced and the functions of the memory management unit are described.

Chapter 8, Performance-Enhancing Techniques, discusses a number of performance-enhancing techniques used routinely to reach peak execution speed in real-world computer systems. The most important techniques for improving system performance, including the use of cache memory, instruction pipelining, instruction parallelism, and SIMD processing, are the subjects of this chapter.

Chapter 9, Specialized Processor Extensions, focuses on extensions commonly implemented at the processor instruction set level to provide additional system capabilities beyond generic data processing requirements. The extensions presented include privileged processor modes, floating-point mathematics, power management, and system security management.

Chapter 10, Modern Processor Architectures and Instruction Sets, examines the architectures and instruction set features of modern processor designs including the x86, x64, and ARM processors. One challenge that arises when producing a family of processors over several decades is the need to maintain backward compatibility with code written for earlier-generation processors. The need for legacy support tends to increase the complexity of the later-generation processors. This chapter will examine some of the attributes of these processor architectures that result from supporting legacy requirements.

Chapter 11, The RISC-V Architecture and Instruction Set, introduces the exciting new RISC-V (pronounced *risk five*) processor architecture and its instruction set. RISC-V is a completely open source, free-to-use specification for a reduced instruction set computer architecture. A complete user-mode (non-privileged) instruction set specification has been released and a number of hardware implementations of this architecture are currently available. Work is ongoing to develop specifications for a number of instruction set extensions. This chapter covers the features and variants available in the RISC-V architecture and introduces the RISC-V instruction set. We will also discuss the applications of the RISC-V architecture in mobile devices, personal computers, and servers.

Chapter 12, Processor Virtualization, introduces the concepts involved in processor virtualization and explains the many benefits resulting from the use of virtualization. The chapter includes examples of virtualization based on open source tools and operating systems. These tools enable the execution of instruction-set-accurate representations of various computer architectures and operating systems on a general-purpose computer. We will also discuss the benefits of virtualization in the development and deployment of real-world software applications.

Chapter 13, Domain-Specific Computer Architectures, brings together the topics discussed in previous chapters to develop an approach for architecting a computer system design to meet unique user requirements. We will discuss some specific application categories, including mobile devices, personal computers, gaming systems, Internet search engines, and neural networks.

Chapter 14, Future Directions in Computer Architectures, looks at the road ahead for computer architectures. This chapter reviews the significant advances and ongoing trends that have resulted in the current state of computer architectures and extrapolates these trends in possible future directions. Potentially disruptive technologies are discussed that could alter the path of future computer architectures. In closing, I will propose some approaches for professional development for the computer architect that should result in a future-tolerant skill set.

To get the most out of this book

Each chapter in this book includes a set of exercises at the end. To get the most from the book, and to cement some of the more challenging concepts in your mind, I recommend you try to work through each exercise. Complete solutions to all exercises are provided in the book and are available online at `https://github.com/PacktPublishing/ Modern-Computer-Architecture-and-Organization`.

In case there's an update to the code examples and answers to the exercises, updates will appear on the existing GitHub repository.

We also have other code bundles from our rich catalog of books and videos available at `https://github.com/PacktPublishing/`. Check them out!

Code in Action

Code in Action videos for this book can be viewed at (`https://bit.ly/2UWc6Ov`). Code in Action videos provide dynamic demonstrations of many of the examples and exercises from this book.

Conventions used

There are a number of text conventions used throughout this book.

`Code in text`: Indicates code words in text, database table names, folder names, filenames, file extensions, pathnames, dummy URLs, user input, and Twitter handles. Here is an example: "Subtraction using the `SBC` instruction tends to be a bit more confusing to novice 6502 assembly language programmers."

A block of code is set as follows:

```
; Add four bytes together using immediate addressing mode
LDA #$04
CLC
ADC #$03
ADC #$02
ADC #$01
```

Any command-line input or output is written as follows:

```
C:\>bcdedit

Windows Boot Manager
--------------------
identifier              {bootmgr}
```

Bold: Indicates a new term, an important word, or words that you see onscreen. Here is an example: "Because there are now four sets, the **Set** field in the physical address reduces to two bits and the **Tag** field increases to 24 bits."

> **Tips or important notes**
> Appear like this.

Get in touch

Any errors in this book are the fault of the author, me. I appreciate receiving feedback on the book including bug reports on the contents. Please submit bug reports on GitHub at https://github.com/PacktPublishing/Modern-Computer-Architecture-and-Organization/issues. Feedback from readers is always welcome.

As necessary, errata will be made available online at https://github.com/PacktPublishing/Modern-Computer-Architecture-and-Organization.

Piracy: If you come across any illegal copies of this work in any form on the Internet, we would be grateful if you would provide us with the location address or website name. Please contact us at `copyright@packt.com` with a link to the material.

If you are interested in becoming an author: If there is a topic that you have expertise in and you are interested in either writing or contributing to a book, please visit `authors.packtpub.com`.

Reviews

Please leave a review. Once you have read and used this book, I ask you to leave a review on the site that you purchased it from. Potential readers can then see and use your unbiased opinion to make purchase decisions. Thank you!

For more information about Packt, please visit `packt.com`.

Section 1: Fundamentals of Computer Architecture

In this section, we will begin at the transistor level and work our way up to the computer system level. You will develop an understanding of the key components of modern computer architectures.

This section comprises the following chapters:

- *Chapter 1, Introducing Computer Architecture*
- *Chapter 2, Digital Logic*
- *Chapter 3, Processor Elements*
- *Chapter 4, Computer System Components*
- *Chapter 5, Hardware–Software Interface*
- *Chapter 6, Specialized Computing Domains*

1
Introducing Computer Architecture

The architecture of automated computing devices has evolved from mechanical systems constructed nearly two centuries ago to the broad array of modern electronic computing technologies we use directly and indirectly every day. Along the way, there have been stretches of incremental technological improvement interspersed with disruptive advances that have drastically altered the trajectory of the industry. These trends can be expected to continue into the future.

In past decades, the 1980s, for example, students and technical professionals eager to learn about computing devices had a limited range of subject matter available for this purpose. If they had a computer of their own, it might have been an IBM PC or an Apple II. If they worked for an organization with a computing facility, they might have used an IBM mainframe or a Digital Equipment Corporation VAX minicomputer. These examples, and a limited number of similar systems, encompassed most people's exposure to computer systems of the time.

Today, numerous specialized computing architectures exist to address widely varying user needs. We carry miniature computers in our pockets and purses that can place phone calls, record video, and function as full participants on the Internet. Personal computers remain popular in a format outwardly similar to the PCs of past decades. Today's PCs, however, are orders of magnitude more capable than the first generations of PCs in terms of computing power, memory size, disk space, graphics performance, and communication capability.

Companies offering web services to hundreds of millions of users construct vast warehouses filled with thousands of closely coordinated computer systems capable of responding to a constant stream of requests with extraordinary speed and precision. Machine learning systems are trained through the analysis of enormous quantities of data to perform complex activities, such as driving automobiles.

This chapter begins by presenting a few key historical computing devices and the leaps in technology associated with them. This chapter will examine modern-day trends related to technological advances and introduce the basic concepts of computer architecture, including a close look at the 6502 microprocessor. These topics will be covered:

- The evolution of automated computing devices
- Moore's law
- Computer architecture

The evolution of automated computing devices

This section reviews some classic machines from the history of automated computing devices and focuses on the major advances each embodied. Babbage's Analytical Engine is included here because of the many leaps of genius contained in its design. The other systems are discussed because they embodied significant technological advances and performed substantial real-world work over their lifetimes.

Charles Babbage's Analytical Engine

Although a working model of the Analytical Engine was never constructed, the detailed notes Charles Babbage developed from 1834 until his death in 1871 described a computing architecture that appeared to be both workable and complete. The Analytical Engine was intended to serve as a general-purpose programmable computing device. The design was entirely mechanical and was to be constructed largely of brass. It was designed to be driven by a shaft powered by a steam engine.

Borrowing from the punched cards of the Jacquard loom, the rotating studded barrels used in music boxes, and the technology of his earlier Difference Engine (also never completed in his lifetime, and more of a specialized calculating device than a computer), the Analytical Engine design was, otherwise, Babbage's original creation.

Unlike most modern computers, the Analytical Engine represented numbers in signed decimal form. The decision to use base-10 numbers rather than the base-2 logic of most modern computers was the result of a fundamental difference between mechanical technology and digital electronics. It is straightforward to construct mechanical wheels with ten positions, so Babbage chose the human-compatible base-10 format because it was not significantly more technically challenging than using some other number base. Simple digital circuits, on the other hand, are not capable of maintaining ten different states with the ease of a mechanical wheel.

All numbers in the Analytical Engine consisted of 40 decimal digits. The large number of digits was likely selected to reduce problems with numerical overflow. The Analytical Engine did not support floating-point mathematics.

Each number was stored on a vertical axis containing 40 wheels, with each wheel capable of resting in ten positions corresponding to the digits 0-9. A 41st number wheel contained the sign: any even number on this wheel represented a positive sign and any odd number represented a negative sign. The Analytical Engine axis was somewhat analogous to the register used in modern processors except the readout of an axis was destructive. If it was necessary to retain an axis's value after it had been read, another axis had to store a copy of the value. Numbers were transferred from one axis to another, or used in computations, by engaging a gear with each digit wheel and rotating the wheel to read out the numerical value. The axes serving as system memory were referred to collectively as the *store*.

The addition of two numbers used a process somewhat similar to the method of addition taught to schoolchildren. Assume a number stored on one axis, let's call it the addend, was to be added to a number on another axis, let's call it the accumulator. The machine would connect each addend digit wheel to the corresponding accumulator digit wheel through a train of gears. It would then simultaneously rotate each addend digit downward to zero while driving the accumulator digit an equivalent rotation in the increasing direction. If an accumulator digit wrapped around from nine to zero, the next most significant accumulator digit would increment by one. This carry operation would propagate across as many digits as needed (think of adding 1 to 999,999). By the end of the process, the addend axis would hold the value zero and the accumulator axis would hold the sum of the two numbers. The propagation of carries from one digit to the next was the most mechanically complex part of the addition process.

Operations in the Analytical Engine were sequenced by music box-like rotating barrels in a construct called the *mill*, which is analogous to the processing component of a modern CPU. Each Analytical Engine instruction was encoded in a vertical row of locations on the barrel where the presence or absence of a stud at a particular location either engaged a section of the Engine's machinery or left the state of that section unchanged. Based on Babbage's hypothesized execution speed, the addition of two 40-digit numbers, including the propagation of carries, would take about three seconds.

Babbage conceived several important concepts for the Engine that remain relevant today. His design supported a degree of parallel processing that accelerated the computation of series of values for output as numerical tables. Mathematical operations such as addition supported a form of pipelining, in which sequential operations on different data values overlapped in time.

Babbage was well aware of the complexities associated with mechanical devices such as friction, gear backlash, and wear over time. To prevent errors caused by these effects, the Engine incorporated mechanisms called *lockings* that were applied during data transfers across axes. The lockings forced the number wheels into valid positions and prevented accumulated errors from allowing a wheel to drift to an incorrect value. The use of lockings is analogous to the amplification of potentially weak input signals to produce stronger outputs by the digital logic gates in modern processors.

The Analytical Engine was programmed using punched cards and supported branching operations and nested loops. The most complex program for the Analytical Engine was developed by Ada Lovelace to compute the Bernoulli numbers.

Babbage constructed a trial model of a portion of the Analytical Engine mill, which is currently on display at the Science Museum in London.

ENIAC

ENIAC, the Electronic Numerical Integrator and Computer, was completed in 1945 and was the first programmable general-purpose electronic computer. The system consumed 150 kilowatts of electricity, occupied 1,800 square feet of floor space, and weighed 27 tons.

The design was based on vacuum tubes, diodes, and relays. ENIAC contained over 17,000 vacuum tubes that functioned as switching elements. Similar to the Analytical Engine, it used base-10 representation of ten-digit decimal numbers implemented using ten-position ring counters (the ring counter will be discussed in *Chapter 2, Digital Logic*). Input data was received from an IBM punch-card reader and the output of computations was sent to a card punch machine.

The ENIAC architecture was capable of complex sequences of processing steps including loops, branches, and subroutines. The system had 20 ten-digit accumulators that were similar to registers in modern computers. However, it did not initially have any memory storage beyond the accumulators. If intermediate values were required for use in later computations, they had to be written to punch cards and read back in when needed. ENIAC could perform about 385 multiplications per second.

ENIAC programs consisted of plugboard wiring and switch-based function tables. Programming the system was an arduous process that often took the team of talented female programmers weeks to complete. Reliability was a problem, as vacuum tubes failed regularly, requiring troubleshooting on a day-to-day basis to isolate and replace failed tubes.

In 1948, ENIAC was improved by adding the ability to program the system via punch cards rather than plugboards. This improvement greatly enhanced the speed with which programs could be developed. As a consultant for this upgrade, John von Neumann proposed a processing architecture based on a single memory region containing program instructions and data, a processing component with an arithmetic logic unit and registers, and a control unit with an instruction register and a program counter. Many modern processors continue to implement this general structure, now known as the von Neumann architecture.

Early applications of ENIAC included analyses related to the development of the hydrogen bomb and the computation of firing tables for long-range artillery.

IBM PC

In the years following the construction of ENIAC, several technological breakthroughs resulted in remarkable advances in computer architectures:

- The invention of the transistor in 1947 by John Bardeen, Walter Brattain, and William Shockley delivered a vast improvement over the vacuum tube technology prevalent at the time. Transistors were faster, smaller, consumed less power, and, once production processes had been sufficiently optimized, were much more reliable than the failure-prone tubes.

- The commercialization of integrated circuits in 1958, led by Jack Kilby of Texas Instruments, began the process of combining large numbers of formerly discrete components onto a single chip of silicon.

- In 1971, Intel began production of the first commercially available microprocessor, the Intel 4004. The 4004 was intended for use in electronic calculators and was specialized to operate on 4-bit binary coded decimal digits.

From the humble beginning of the Intel 4004, microprocessor technology advanced rapidly over the ensuing decade by packing increasing numbers of circuit elements onto each chip and expanding the capabilities of the microprocessors implemented on the chips.

The 8088 microprocessor

IBM released the IBM PC in 1981. The original PC contained an Intel 8088 microprocessor running at a clock frequency of 4.77 MHz and featured 16 KB of RAM, expandable to 256 KB. It included one or, optionally, two floppy disk drives. A color monitor was also available. Later versions of the PC supported more memory, but because portions of the address space had been reserved for video memory and read-only memory, the architecture could support a maximum of 640 KB of RAM.

The 8088 contained fourteen 16-bit registers. Four were general purpose registers (AX, BX, CX, and DX.) Four were memory segment registers (CS, DS, SS, and ES) that extended the address space to 20 bits. Segment addressing functioned by adding a 16-bit segment register value, shifted left by four bit positions, to a 16-bit offset contained in an instruction to produce a physical memory address within a one megabyte range.

The remaining 8088 registers were the **Stack Pointer (SP)**, the **Base Pointer (BP)**, the **Source Index (SI)**, the **Destination Index (DI)**, the **Instruction Pointer (IP)**, and the **Status Flags (FLAGS)**. Modern x86 processers employ an architecture remarkably similar to this register set (*Chapter 10, Modern Processor Architectures and Instruction Sets*, will cover the details of the x86 architecture). The most obvious differences between the 8088 and x86 are the extension of the register widths to 32 bits in x86 and the addition of a pair of segment registers (FS and GS) that are used today primarily as data pointers in multithreaded operating systems.

The 8088 had an external data bus width of 8 bits, which meant it took two bus cycles to read or write a 16-bit value. This was a performance downgrade compared to the earlier 8086 processor, which employed a 16-bit external bus. However, the use of the 8-bit bus made the PC more economical to produce and provided compatibility with lower-cost 8-bit peripheral devices. This cost-sensitive design approach helped to reduce the purchase price of the PC to a level accessible to more potential customers.

Program memory and data memory shared the same address space, and the 8088 accessed memory over a single bus. In other words, the 8088 implemented the von Neumann architecture. The 8088 instruction set included instructions for data movement, arithmetic, logical operations, string manipulation, control transfer (conditional and unconditional jumps and subroutine call and return), input/output, and additional miscellaneous functions. The processor required about 15 clock cycles per instruction on average, resulting in an execution speed of 0.3 **million instructions per second (MIPS)**.

The 8088 supported nine distinct modes for addressing memory. This variety of modes was needed to efficiently implement methods for accessing a single item at a time as well as for iterating through sequences of data.

The segment registers in the 8088 architecture provided a clever way to expand the range of addressable memory without increasing the length of most instructions referencing memory locations. Each segment register allowed access to a 64-kilobyte block of memory beginning at a physical memory address defined at a multiple of 16 bytes. In other words, the 16-bit segment register represented a 20-bit base address with the lower four bits set to zero. Instructions could then reference any location within the 64-kilobyte segment using a 16-bit offset from the address defined by the segment register.

The CS register selected the code segment location in memory and was used in fetching instructions and performing jumps and subroutine calls and returns. The DS register defined the data segment location for use by instructions involving the transfer of data to and from memory. The SS register set the stack segment location, which was used for local memory allocation within subroutines and for storing subroutine return addresses.

Programs that required less than 64-kilobyte in each of the code, data, and stack segments could ignore the segment registers entirely because those registers could be set once at program startup (compilers would do this automatically) and remain unchanged through execution. Easy!

Things got quite a bit more complicated when a program's data size increased beyond 64-kilobyte. Compilers for the 8088 architecture distinguished between *near* and *far* references to memory. A near pointer represented a 16-bit offset from the current segment register base address. A far pointer contained 32 bits of addressing information: a 16-bit segment register value and a 16-bit offset. Far pointers obviously required 16 bits of extra data memory and they required additional processing time. Making a single memory access using a far pointer involved the following steps:

1. Save the current segment register contents to a temporary location.
2. Load the new segment value into the register.
3. Access the data (read or write as needed) using an offset from the segment base.
4. Restore the original segment register value.

When using far pointers, it was possible to declare data objects (for example, an array of characters) up to 64 KB in size. If you needed a larger structure, you had to work out how to break it into chunks no larger than 64 KB and manage them yourself. As a result of these segment register manipulations, programs that required extensive access to data larger than 64 KB were susceptible to code size bloat and slower execution.

The IBM PC motherboard also contained a socket for an optional Intel 8087 floating-point coprocessor. The designers of the 8087 invented data formats and processing rules for 32-bit and 64-bit floating point numbers that became enshrined in 1985 as the IEEE 754 floating-point standard, which remains in near-universal use today. The 8087 could perform about 50,000 floating-point operations per second. We will look at floating-point processors in detail in *Chapter 9, Specialized Processor Extensions*.

The 80286 and 80386 microprocessors

The second generation of the IBM PC, the PC AT, was released in 1984. **AT** stood for **Advanced Technology** and referred to several significant enhancements over the original PC that mostly resulted from the use of the Intel 80286 processor.

Like the 8088, the 80286 was a 16-bit processor, and it maintained backward compatibility with the 8088: 8088 code could run unmodified on the 80286. The 80286 had a 16-bit data bus and 24 address lines supporting a 16-megabyte address space. The external data bus width was 16 bits, improving data access performance over the 8-bit bus of the 8088. The instruction execution rate (instructions per clock cycle) was about double the 8088 in many applications. This meant that at the same clock speed the 80286 would be twice as fast as the 8088. The original PC AT clocked the processor at 6 MHz and a later version operated at 8 MHz. The 6 MHz variant of the 80286 achieved an instruction execution rate of about 0.9 MIPS.

The 80286 implemented a protected virtual address mode intended to support multiuser operating systems and multitasking. In protected mode, the processor enforced memory protection to ensure one user's programs could not interfere with the operating system or with other users' programs. This groundbreaking technological advance remained little used for many years, mainly because of the prohibitive cost of adding sufficient memory to a computer system to make it useful in a multiuser, multitasking context.

The next generation of the x86 processor line was the 80386, introduced in 1985. The 80386 was a 32-bit processor with support for a flat 32-bit memory model in protected mode. The flat memory model allowed programmers to address up to 4 GB directly, without the need to manipulate segment registers. Compaq introduced an IBM PC-compatible personal computer based on the 80386 called the DeskPro in 1986. The DeskPro shipped with a version of Microsoft Windows targeted to the 80386 architecture.

The 80386 maintained a large degree of backward compatibility with the 80286 and 8088 processors. The design implemented in the 80386 remains the current standard x86 architecture. Much more about this architecture will be covered in *Chapter 10, Modern Processor Architectures and Instruction Sets.*

The initial version of the 80386 was clocked at 33 MHz and achieved about 11.4 MIPS. Modern implementations of the x86 architecture run several hundred times faster than the original as the result of higher clock speeds, performance enhancements such as extensive use of cache memory, and more efficient instruction execution at the hardware level.

The iPhone

In 2007, Steve Jobs introduced the iPhone to a world that had no idea it had any use for such a device. The iPhone built upon previous revolutionary advances from Apple Computer including the Macintosh computer in 1984 and the iPod music player in 2001. The iPhone combined the functions of the iPod, a mobile telephone, and an Internet-connected computer.

The iPhone did away with the hardware keyboard that was common on smartphones of the time and replaced it with a touchscreen capable of displaying an on-screen keyboard or any other type of user interface. The screen was driven by the user's fingers and supported multi-finger gestures for actions such as zooming a photo.

The iPhone ran the OS X operating system, the same OS used on the flagship Macintosh computers of the time. This decision immediately enabled the iPhone to support a vast range of applications already developed for Macs and empowered software developers to rapidly introduce new applications tailored to the iPhone, once Apple began allowing third-party application development.

The iPhone 1 had a 3.5" screen with a resolution of 320x480 pixels. It was 0.46 inches thick (thinner than other smartphones), had a 2-megapixel camera built in, and weighed 4.8 oz. A proximity sensor detected when the phone was held to the user's ear and turned off screen illumination and touchscreen sensing during calls. It had an ambient light sensor to automatically set the screen brightness and an accelerometer detected whether the screen was being held in portrait or landscape orientation.

The iPhone 1 included 128 MB of RAM, 4 GB, 8 GB, or 16 GB of flash memory, and supported **Global System for Mobile communications (GSM)** cellular communication, Wi-Fi (802.11b/g), and Bluetooth.

In contrast to the abundance of openly available information about the IBM PC, Apple was notoriously reticent about releasing the architectural details of the iPhone's construction. Apple released no information about the processor or other internal components of the first iPhone, simply calling it a closed system.

Despite the lack of official information from Apple, other parties have enthusiastically torn down the various iPhone models and attempted to identify the phone's components and how they interconnect. Software sleuths have devised various tests to attempt to determine the specific processor model and other digital devices implemented in the iPhone. These reverse engineering efforts are subject to error, so descriptions of the iPhone architecture in this section should be taken with a grain of salt.

The iPhone 1 processor was a 32-bit ARM11 manufactured by Samsung running at 412 MHz. The ARM11 was an improved variant of previous generation ARM processors and included an 8-stage instruction pipeline and support for **Single Instruction-Multiple Data (SIMD)** processing to improve audio and video performance. The ARM processor architecture will be discussed further in *Chapter 10, Modern Processor Architectures and Instruction Sets*.

The iPhone 1 was powered by a 3.7V lithium-ion polymer battery. The battery was not intended to be replaceable, and Apple estimated it would lose about 20 percent of its original capacity after 400 charge and discharge cycles. Apple quoted up to 250 hours of standby time and 8 hours of talk time on a single charge.

Six months after the iPhone was introduced, *Time* magazine named the iPhone the "Invention of the Year" for 2007. In 2017, *Time* ranked the *50 Most Influential Gadgets of All Time*. The iPhone topped the list.

Moore's law

For those working in the rapidly advancing field of computer technology, it is a significant challenge to make plans for the future. This is true whether the goal is to plot your own career path or for a giant semiconductor corporation to identify optimal R&D investments. No one can ever be completely sure what the next leap in technology will be, what effects from it will ripple across the industry and its users, or when it will happen. One technique that has proven useful in this difficult environment is to develop a rule of thumb, or empirical law, based on experience.

Gordon Moore co-founded Fairchild Semiconductor in 1957 and was later the chairman and CEO of Intel. In 1965, Moore published an article in *Electronics* magazine in which he offered his prediction of the changes that would occur in the semiconductor industry over the following ten years. In the article, he observed that the number of formerly discrete components such as transistors, diodes, and capacitors that could be integrated onto a single chip had been doubling approximately yearly and the trend was likely to continue over the subsequent ten years. This doubling formula came to be known as Moore's law. This was not a scientific law in the sense of the law of gravity. Rather, it was based on observation of historical trends, and he believed this formulation had some ability to predict the future.

Moore's law turned out to be impressively accurate over those ten years. In 1975, he revised the predicted growth rate for the following ten years to doubling the number of components per integrated circuit every two years rather than yearly. This pace continued for decades, up until about 2010. In more recent years, the growth rate has appeared to decline slightly. In 2015, Brian Krzanich, Intel CEO, stated that the company's growth rate had slowed to doubling about every two and a half years.

Despite the fact that the time to double integrated circuit density is increasing, the current pace represents a phenomenal rate of growth that can be expected to continue into the future, just not quite as rapidly as it once progressed.

Moore's law has proven to be a reliable tool for evaluating the performance of semiconductor companies over the decades. Companies have used it to set goals for the performance of their products and to plan their investments. By comparing the integrated circuit density increases for a company's products against prior performance, and against other companies, it is possible for semiconductor executives and industry analysts to evaluate and score company performance. The results of these analyses have fed directly into decisions to build enormous new fabrication plants and to push the boundaries of ever-smaller integrated circuit feature sizes.

The decades since the introduction of the IBM PC have seen tremendous growth in the capability of single-chip microprocessors. Current processor generations are hundreds of times faster, operate on 32-bit and 64-bit data natively, have far more integrated memory resources, and unleash vastly more functionality, all packed into a single integrated circuit.

The increasing density of semiconductor features, as predicted by Moore's law, has enabled all of these improvements. Smaller transistors run at higher clock speeds due to the shorter connection paths between circuit elements. Smaller transistors also, obviously, allow more functionality to be packed into a given amount of die area. Being smaller and closer to neighboring components allows the transistors to consume less power and generate less heat.

There was nothing magical about Moore's law. It was an observation of the trends in progress at the time. One trend was the steadily increasing size of semiconductor dies. This was the result of improving production processes that reduced the density of defects, hence allowing acceptable production yield with larger integrated circuit dies. Another trend was the ongoing reduction in the size of the smallest components that could be reliably produced in a circuit. The final trend was what Moore referred to as the "cleverness" of circuit designers in making increasingly efficient and effective use of the growing number of circuit elements placed on a chip.

Traditional semiconductor manufacturing processes have begun to approach physical limits that will eventually put the brakes on growth under Moore's law. The smallest features on current commercially available integrated circuits are around 10 **nanometers** (**nm**). For comparison, a typical human hair is about 50,000 nm thick and a water molecule (one of the smallest molecules) is 0.28 nm across. There is a point beyond which it is simply not possible for circuit elements to become smaller as the sizes approach atomic scale.

In addition to the challenge of building reliable circuit components from a small number of molecules, other physical effects with names such as *Abbe diffraction limit* become significant impediments to single-digit nanometer-scale circuit production. We won't get into the details of these phenomena; it's sufficient to know the steady increase in integrated circuit component density that has proceeded for decades under Moore's law is going to become a lot harder to continue over the next few years.

This does not mean we will be stuck with processors essentially the same as those that are now commercially available. Even as the rate of growth in transistor density slows, semiconductor manufacturers are pursuing several alternative methods to continue growing the power of computing devices. One approach is specialization, in which circuits are designed to perform a specific category of tasks extremely well rather than performing a wide variety of tasks merely adequately.

Graphical Processing Units (GPUs) are an excellent example of specialization. Original GPUs focused exclusively on improving the speed at which three-dimensional graphics scenes could be rendered, mostly for use in video gaming. The calculations involved in generating a three-dimensional scene are well defined and must be applied to thousands of pixels to create a single frame. The process must be repeated for each subsequent frame, and frames may need to be redrawn at a 60 Hz or higher rate to provide a satisfactory user experience. The computationally demanding and repetitive nature of this task is ideally suited for acceleration via hardware parallelism. Multiple computing units within a GPU simultaneously perform essentially the same calculations on different input data to produce separate outputs. Those outputs are combined to generate the final scene. Modern GPU designs have been enhanced to support other domains, such as training neural networks on massive amounts of data. GPUs will be covered in detail in *Chapter 6, Specialized Computing Domains*.

As Moore's law shows signs of beginning to fade over the coming years, what advances might take its place to kick off the next round of innovations in computer architectures? We don't know for sure today, but some tantalizing options are currently under intense study. Quantum computing is one example of these technologies. We will cover that technology in *Chapter 14, Future Directions in Computer Architectures*.

Quantum computing takes advantage of the properties of subatomic particles to perform computations in a manner that traditional computers cannot. A basic element of quantum computing is the **qubit**, or quantum bit. A qubit is similar to a regular binary bit, but in addition to representing the states 0 and 1, qubits can attain a state that is a superposition of the 0 and 1 states. When measured, the qubit output will always be 0 or 1, but the probability of producing either output is a function of the qubit's quantum state prior to being read. Specialized algorithms are required to take advantage of the unique features of quantum computing.

Another possibility is that the next great technological breakthrough in computing devices will be something that we either haven't thought of, or if we did think about it, we may have dismissed the idea out of hand as unrealistic. The iPhone, discussed in the preceding section, is an example of a category-creating product that revolutionized personal communication and enabled use of the Internet in new ways. The next major advance may be a new type of product, a surprising new technology, or some combination of product and technology. Right now, we don't know what it will be or when it will happen, but we can say with confidence that such changes are coming.

Computer architecture

The descriptions of a small number of key architectures from the history of computing mentioned in the previous section included some terms that may or may not be familiar to you. This section will provide an introduction to the building blocks used to construct modern-day processors and related computer subsystems.

One ubiquitous feature of modern computers is the use of voltage levels to indicate data values. In general, only two voltage levels are recognized: a low level and a high level. The low level is often assigned the value zero and the high level assigned the value one. The voltage at any point in a circuit (digital or otherwise) is analog in nature and can take on any voltage within its operating range. When changing from the low level to the high level, or vice versa, the voltage must pass through all voltages in between. In the context of digital circuitry, the transitions between low and high levels happen quickly and the circuitry is designed to not react to voltages between the high and low levels.

Binary and hexadecimal numbers

The circuitry within a processor does not work directly with numbers, in any sense. Processor circuit elements obey the laws of electricity and electronics and simply react to the inputs provided to them. The inputs that drive these actions result from the code developed by programmers and from the data provided as input to the program. The interpretation of the output of a program as, say, numbers in a spreadsheet, or characters in a word processing program, is a purely human interpretation that assigns meaning to the result of the electronic interactions within the processor. The decision to assign zero to the low voltage and one to the high voltage is the first step in the interpretation process.

The smallest unit of information in a digital computer is a binary digit, called a **bit**, which represents a discrete data element containing the value zero or one. A number of bits can be placed together to enable representation of a greater range of values. A **byte** is composed of eight bits placed together to form a single value. The byte is the smallest unit of information that can be read from or written to memory by most modern processors.

A single bit can take on two values: 0 and 1. Two bits placed together can take on four values: 00, 01, 10, and 11. Three bits can take on eight values: 000, 001, 010, 011, 100, 101, 110, and 111. In fact, any number of bits, n, can take on 2^n values, where 2^n indicates multiplying n copies of two together. An 8-bit byte, therefore, can take on 2^8 or 256 different values.

The binary number format is not most people's first choice when it comes to performing arithmetic, and working with numbers such as 11101010 can be confusing and error prone, especially when dealing with 32- and 64-bit values. To make working with these numbers somewhat easier, **hexadecimal** numbers are often used instead. The term hexadecimal is often shortened to *hex*. In the hexadecimal number system, binary numbers are separated into groups of four bits. Since there are four bits in the group, the number of possible values is 2^4, or 16. The first ten of these 16 numbers are assigned the digits 0-9. The last six are assigned the letters A-F. *Table 1.1* shows the first 16 binary values starting at zero along with the corresponding hexadecimal digit and the decimal equivalent to the binary and hex values.

Table 1.1: Binary, hexadecimal, and decimal numbers

Binary	Hexadecimal	Decimal
0000	0	0
0001	1	1
0010	2	2
0011	3	3
0100	4	4
0101	5	5
0110	6	6
0111	7	7
1000	8	8
1001	9	9
1010	A	10
1011	B	11
1100	C	12
1101	D	13
1110	E	14
1111	F	15

The binary number 11101010 can be represented more compactly by breaking it into two 4-bit groups (1110 and 1010) and writing them as the hex digits EA. Because binary digits can take on only two values, binary is a base-2 number system. Hex digits can take on 16 values, so hexadecimal is base-16. Decimal digits can have ten values, therefore decimal is base-10.

When working with these different number bases, it is possible for things to become confusing. Is the number written as 100 a binary, hexadecimal, or decimal value? Without additional information, you can't tell. Various programming languages and textbooks have taken different approaches to remove this ambiguity. In most cases, decimal numbers are unadorned, so the number 100 is usually decimal. In programming languages such as C and C++, hexadecimal numbers are prefixed by *0x* so the number 0x100 is 100 hex. In assembly languages, either the prefix character *$*, or the suffix *h* might be used to indicate hexadecimal numbers. The use of binary values in programming is less common, mostly because hexadecimal is preferred due to its compactness. Some compilers support the use of *0b* as a prefix for binary numbers.

> **Hexadecimal number representation**
>
> This book uses either the prefix *$* or the suffix *h* to represent hexadecimal numbers, depending on the context. The suffix *b* will represent binary numbers, and the absence of a prefix or suffix indicates decimal numbers.

Bits are numbered individually within a binary number, with bit zero as the rightmost, least significant bit. Bit numbers increase in magnitude leftward. Some examples should make this clear: In *Table 1.1*, the binary value 0001b (1 decimal) has bit number zero set and the remaining three bits are cleared. In 0010b (2 decimal), bit 1 is set and the other bits are cleared. In 0100b (4 decimal), bit 2 is set and the other bits are cleared.

> **Set versus cleared**
>
> A bit that is *set* has the value 1. A bit that is *cleared* has the value 0.

An 8-bit byte can take on values from $00h to $FF, equivalent to the decimal range 0-255. When performing addition at the byte level, it is possible for the result to exceed 8 bits. For example, adding $01 to $FF results in the value $100. When using 8-bit registers, this represents a carry, which must be handled appropriately.

In unsigned arithmetic, subtracting $01 from $00 results in a value of $FF. This constitutes a wraparound to $FF. Depending on the computation being performed, this may or may not be the desired result.

When desired, negative values can be represented using binary numbers. The most common signed number format in modern processors is **two's complement**. In two's complement, 8-bit signed numbers span the range from -128 to 127. The most significant bit of a two's complement data value is the sign bit: a 0 in this bit represents a positive value and a 1 represents a negative value. A two's complement number can be negated (multiplied by -1) by inverting all of the bits, adding 1, and ignoring any carry. Inverting a bit means changing a 0 bit to 1 and a 1 bit to 0.

Table 1.2: Negation operation examples

Decimal value	Binary value	Invert the bits	Add one	Negated result
0	00000000b	11111111b	00000000b	0
1	00000001b	11111110b	11111111b	-1
-1	11111111b	00000000b	00000001b	1
127	01111111b	10000000b	10000001b	-127
-127	10000001b	01111110b	01111111b	127

Note that negating zero returns a result of zero, as you would expect mathematically.

Two's complement arithmetic

Two's complement arithmetic is identical to unsigned arithmetic at the bit level. The manipulations involved in addition and subtraction are the same whether the input values are intended to be signed or unsigned. The interpretation of the result as signed or unsigned depends entirely on the intent of the user.

Table 1.3: Signed and unsigned 8-bit numbers

Binary	Signed Decimal	Unsigned Decimal
00000000b	0	0
00000001b	1	1
00000010b	2	2
⋮	⋮	⋮
01111110b	126	126
01111111b	127	127
10000000b	-128	128
10000001b	-127	129
10000010b	-126	130
⋮	⋮	⋮
11111101b	-3	253
11111110b	-2	254
11111111b	-1	255

Signed and unsigned representations of binary numbers extend to larger integer data types. 16-bit values can represent unsigned integers from 0 to 65,535 and signed integers in the range -32,768 to 32,767. 32-bit, 64-bit, and even larger integer data types are commonly available in modern programming languages.

The 6502 microprocessor

This section will introduce the architecture of a processor with a relatively simple design compared to more powerful modern processors. The intent here is to provide a whirlwind introduction to some basic concepts shared by processors spanning the spectrum from the very low end to sophisticated modern processors.

The 6502 processor was introduced by MOS Technology in 1975. The 6502 found widespread use in its early years in video game consoles from Atari and Nintendo and in computers marketed by Commodore and Apple. The 6502 continues in widespread use today in embedded systems, with estimates of between five and ten billion (yes, *billion*) units produced as of 2018. In popular culture, both Bender the robot in *Futurama* and the T-800 robot in *The Terminator* appear to have employed the 6502, based on onscreen evidence.

Many early microprocessors, like the 6502, were powered by a constant voltage of 5 volts (5V). In these circuits, a low signal level is any voltage between 0 and 0.8V. A high signal level is any voltage between 2 and 5V. The low signal level is defined as logical 0 and the high signal level is defined as logical 1. *Chapter 2, Digital Logic*, will delve further into digital electronics.

The **word length** of a processor defines the size of the fundamental data element the processor operates upon. The 6502 has a word length of 8 bits. This means the 6502 reads and writes memory 8 bits at a time and stores data internally in 8-bit wide registers.

Program memory and data memory share the same address space and the 6502 accesses its memory over a single bus. As was the case with the Intel 8088, the 6502 implements the von Neumann architecture. The 6502 has a 16-bit address bus, enabling access to 64 KB of memory.

One **kilobyte** (abbreviated KB) is defined as 2^{10}, or 1,024 bytes. The number of unique binary combinations of the 16 address lines is 2^{16}, equal to 64 multiplied by 1,024, or 65,536 locations. Note that just because a device can address 64 KB, it does not mean there must be memory at all of those locations. The Commodore VIC-20, based on the 6502, contained just 5 KB of **Random Access Memory (RAM)** and 20 KB of **Read-Only Memory (ROM)**.

The 6502 contains internal storage areas called registers. A **register** is a location in a logical device in which a word of information can be stored and acted upon during computation. A typical processor contains a small number of registers for temporarily storing data values and performing operations such as addition or address computation.

The following figure 1.1 shows the 6502 register structure. The processor contains five 8-bit registers (A, X, Y, P, and S) and one 16-bit register (PC). The numbers above each register indicate the bit numbers at each end of the register:

Figure 1.1: 6502 register set

Each of the A, X, and Y registers can serve as a general-purpose storage location. Program instructions can load a value into one of those registers and, some instructions later, use the saved value for some purpose, as long as the intervening instructions did not modify the register contents. The A register is the only register capable of performing arithmetic operations. The X and Y registers, but not the A register, can be used as index registers in calculating memory addresses.

The P register contains processor flags. Each bit in this register has a unique purpose, except for the bit labeled 1. The 1 bit is unused and can be ignored. Each of the remaining bits in this register is called a **flag** and indicates a specific condition that has occurred or represents a configuration setting. The 6502 flags are as follows:

- **N**: Negative sign flag: This flag is set when the result of an arithmetic operation sets bit 7 in the result. This flag is used in signed arithmetic.

- **V**: Overflow flag: This flag is set when a signed addition or subtraction results in overflow or underflow outside the range -128 to 127.

- **B**: Break flag: This flag indicates a Break (BRK) instruction has executed. This bit is not present in the P register itself. The B flag value is only relevant when examining the P register contents as stored onto the stack by a BRK instruction or by an interrupt. The B flag is set to distinguish a software interrupt resulting from a BRK instruction from a hardware interrupt during interrupt processing.

- **D**: Decimal mode flag: This flag indicates processor arithmetic will operate in **Binary-Coded Decimal (BCD)** mode. BCD mode is rarely used and won't be discussed here, other than to note that this base-10 computation mode evokes the architectures of the Analytical Engine and ENIAC.

- **I**: Interrupt disable flag: This flag indicates that interrupt inputs (other than the non-maskable interrupt) will not be processed.

- **Z**: Zero flag: This flag is set when an operation produces a result of zero.

- **C**: Carry flag: This flag is set when an arithmetic operation produces a carry.

The N, V, Z, and C flags are the most important flags in the context of general computing involving loops, counting, and arithmetic.

The S register is the **stack pointer**. In the 6502, the stack is the region of memory from addresses $100 to $1FF. This 256-byte range is used for temporary storage of parameters within subroutines and holds the return address when a subroutine is called. At system startup, the S register is initialized to point to the top of this range. Values are "pushed" onto the stack using instructions such as PHA, which pushes the contents of the A register onto the stack. When a value is pushed onto the stack, the 6502 stores the value at the address indicated by the S register, after adding the fixed $100 offset, then decrements the S register. Additional values can be placed on the stack by executing more push instructions. As additional values are pushed, the stack grows downward in memory. Programs must take care not to exceed the fixed 256-byte size of the stack when pushing data onto it.

Data stored on the stack must be retrieved in the reverse of the order from which it was pushed onto the stack. The stack is a **Last-In, First-Out (LIFO)** data structure, meaning when you "pop" a value from the stack, it is the byte most recently pushed onto it. The PLA instruction increments the S register by one, then copies the value at the address indicated by the S register (plus the $100 offset) into the A register.

The PC register is the program counter. This register contains the memory address of the next instruction to be executed. Unlike the other registers, the PC is 16 bits long, allowing access to the entire 6502 address space. Each instruction consists of a 1-byte operation code, called **opcode** for short, and may be followed by zero to two operand bytes, depending on the instruction. After each instruction executes, the PC updates to point to the next instruction following the one that just completed. In addition to these automatic updates during sequential instruction execution, the PC can be modified by jump instructions, branch instructions, and subroutine call and return instructions.

The 6502 instruction set

Each of the 6502 instructions has a three-character mnemonic. In assembly language source files, each line of code contains an instruction mnemonic followed by any operands associated with the instruction. The combination of the mnemonic and the operands defines the **addressing mode**. The 6502 supports several addressing modes providing a great deal of flexibility in accessing data in registers and memory. For this introduction, we'll only work with the **immediate** addressing mode, in which the operand itself contains a value rather than indicating a register or memory location containing the value. An immediate value is preceded by a # character.

In 6502 assembly, decimal numbers have no adornment (48 means 48 decimal) while hexadecimal values are preceded by a $ character ($30 means 30 hexadecimal, equivalent to 00110000b and to 48 decimal). An immediate decimal value looks like #48 and an immediate hexadecimal value looks like #$30.

Some assembly code examples will demonstrate the 6502 arithmetic capabilities. Five 6502 instructions are used in the following examples:

- LDA loads register A with a value.

- ADC performs addition using the Carry (C flag) as an additional input and output.

- SBC performs subtraction using the Carry flag as an additional input and output.

- SEC sets the Carry flag directly.

- CLC clears the Carry flag directly.

Since the Carry flag is an input to the addition and subtraction instructions, it is important to ensure it has the correct value prior to executing the ADC or SBC instructions. Before initiating an addition operation, the C flag must be clear to indicate there is no carry from a prior addition. When performing multi-byte additions (say, with 16-bit, 32-bit, or 64-bit numbers), the carry, if any, will propagate from the sum of one byte pair to the next as you add the more significant bytes to each other. If the C flag is set when the ADC instruction executes, the effect is to add one to the result. After the ADC completes, the C flag serves as the ninth bit of the result: a C flag result of 0 means there was no carry, and a 1 indicates there was a carry from the 8-bit register.

Subtraction using the SBC instruction tends to be a bit more confusing to novice 6502 assembly language programmers. Schoolchildren learning subtraction use the technique of borrowing when subtracting a larger digit from a smaller digit. In the 6502, the C flag represents the opposite of Borrow. If C is 1, then Borrow is 0, and if C is 0, Borrow is 1. Performing a simple subtraction with no incoming Borrow requires setting the C flag before executing the SBC command.

The examples in the following employ the 6502 as a calculator using inputs defined directly in the code and with the result stored in the A register. The **Results** columns show the final value of the A register and the N, V, Z, and C flags.

Table 1.4: 6502 arithmetic instruction sequences

Instruction Sequence	Description	Results				
		A	N	V	Z	C
CLC LDA #1 ADC #1	8-bit addition with no Carry input: Clear the Carry flag, then load an immediate value of 1 into the A register and add 1 to it.	$02	0	0	0	0
SEC LDA #1 ADC #1	8-bit addition with a Carry input: Set the Carry flag, then load an immediate value of 1 into the A register and add 1 to it.	$03	0	0	0	0
SEC LDA #1 SBC #1	8-bit subtraction with no Borrow input: Set the Carry flag, then load an immediate value of 1 into the A register and subtract 1 from it. C = 1 indicates no borrow occurred.	$00	0	0	1	1
CLC LDA #1 SBC #1	8-bit subtraction with a Borrow input: Clear the Carry flag, then load an immediate value of 1 into the A register and subtract 1 from it. C = 0 indicates a borrow occurred.	$FF	1	0	0	0
CLC LDA #$FF ADC #1	Unsigned overflow: Add 1 to $FF. C = 1 indicates a carry occurred.	$00	0	0	1	1
SEC LDA #0 SBC #1	Unsigned underflow: Subtract 1 from 0. C = 0 indicates a borrow occurred.	$FF	1	0	0	0
CLC LDA #$7F ADC #1	Signed overflow: Add 1 to $7F. V = 1 indicates signed overflow occurred.	$80	1	1	0	0
SEC LDA #$80 SBC #1	Signed underflow: Subtract 1 from $80. V = 1 indicates signed underflow occurred.	$7F	0	1	0	1

If you don't happen to have a 6502-based computer with an assembler and debugger handy, there are several free 6502 emulators available online that you can run in your web browser. One excellent emulator is at `https://skilldrick.github.io/easy6502/`. Visit the website and scroll down until you find a default code listing with buttons for assembling and running 6502 code. Replace the default code listing with a group of three instructions from *Table 1.4*, then assemble the code. To examine the effect of each instruction in the sequence, use the debugger controls to single-step through the instructions and observe the result of each instruction on the processor registers.

This section has provided a very brief introduction to the 6502 processor and a small subset of its capabilities. One point of this analysis was to illustrate the challenge of dealing simply with the issue of carries when performing addition and borrows when doing subtraction. From Charles Babbage to the designers of the 6502, computer architects have developed solutions to the problems of computation and implemented them using the best technology available to them.

Summary

This chapter began with a brief history of automated computing devices and described significant technological advances that drove leaps in computational capability. A discussion of Moore's law was followed with an assessment of its applicability over previous decades and implications for the future. The basic concepts of computer architecture were introduced through a discussion of the 6502 microprocessor. The history of computer architecture is fascinating, and I encourage you to explore it further.

The next chapter will introduce digital logic, beginning with the properties of basic electrical circuits and proceeding through the design of digital subsystems used in modern processors. You will learn about logic gates, flip-flops, and digital circuits including multiplexers, shift registers, and adders. It includes an introduction to hardware description languages, which are specialized computer languages used in the design of complex digital devices such as computer processors.

Exercises

1. Using your favorite programming language, develop a simulation of a single-digit decimal adder that operates in the same manner as in Babbage's Analytical Engine. First, prompt the user for two digits in the range 0-9: the addend and the accumulator. Display the addend, the accumulator, and the carry, which is initially zero. Perform a series of cycles as follows:

    a. If the addend is zero, display the values of the addend, accumulator, and carry and terminate the program.

    b. Decrement the addend by one and increment the accumulator by one.

    c. If the accumulator incremented from nine to zero, increment the carry.

    d. Go back to step a.

    Test your code with these sums: 0+0, 0+1, 1+0, 1+2, 5+5, 9+1, and 9+9.

2. Create arrays of 40 decimal digits each for the addend, accumulator, and carry. Prompt the user for two decimal integers of up to 40 digits each. Perform the addition digit by digit using the cycles described in *Exercise 1*, and collect the carry output from each digit position in the carry array. After the cycles are complete, insert carries, and, where necessary, ripple them across digits to complete the addition operation. Display the results after each cycle and at the end. Test with the same sums as in *Exercise 1* and test 99+1, 999999+1, 49+50, and 50+50.

3. Modify the program of *Exercise 2* to implement subtraction of 40-digit decimal values. Perform borrowing as required. Test with 0-0, 1-0, 1000000-1, and 0-1. What is the result for 0-1?

4. 6502 assembly language references data in memory locations using an operand value containing the address (without the # character that indicates an immediate value). For example, the LDA $00 instruction loads the byte at memory address $00 into A. STA $01 stores the byte in A into address $01. Addresses can be any value in the range 0 to $FFFF, assuming memory exists at the address and the address is not already in use for some other purpose. Using your preferred 6502 emulator, write 6502 assembly code to store a 16-bit value into addresses $00-$01, store a second value into addresses $02-$03, then add the two values and store the result in $04-$05. Be sure to propagate any carry between the two bytes. Ignore any carry from the 16-bit result. Test with $0000+$0001, $00FF+$0001, and $1234+$5678.

5. Write 6502 assembly code to subtract two 16-bit values in a manner similar to *Exercise 4*. Test with $0001-$0000, $0001-$0001, $0100-$00FF, and $0000-$0001. What is the result for $0000-$0001?

6. Write 6502 assembly code to store two 32-bit integers to addresses $00-03 and $04-$07, then add them, storing the results in $08-$0B. Use a looping construct, including a label and a branch instruction, to iterate over the bytes of the two values to be added. Search the Internet for the details of the 6502 decrement and branch instructions and the use of labels in assembly language. Hint: The 6502 zero-page indexed addressing mode works well in this application.

2
Digital Logic

This chapter builds upon the introductory topics presented in *Chapter 1, Introducing Computer Architecture* and provides a firm understanding of the digital building blocks used in the design of modern processors. We begin with a discussion of the properties of electrical circuits, before introducing transistors and examining their use as switching elements in logic gates. We then construct latches, flip-flops, and ring counters from the basic logic gates. More complex components, including registers and adders, are developed by combining the devices introduced earlier. The concept of sequential logic, meaning logic that contains state information that varies over time, is developed. The chapter ends with an introduction to hardware description languages, which are the preferred design method for complex digital devices.

The following topics will be covered in this chapter:

- Electrical circuits

- The transistor

- Logic gates

- Latches

- Flip-flops

- Registers

- Adders

- Clocking

- Sequential logic

- Hardware description languages

Electrical circuits

We begin this chapter with a brief review of the properties of electrical circuits.

Conductive materials, such as copper, exhibit the ability to easily produce an electric current in the presence of an electric field. Nonconductive materials, for example, glass, rubber, and **polyvinyl chloride (PVC)**, inhibit the flow of electricity so thoroughly that they are used as insulators to protect electrical conductors against short circuits. In metals, electrical current consists of electrons in motion. Materials that permit some electrical current to flow, while predictably restricting the amount allowed to flow, are used in the construction of resistors.

The relationship between electrical current, voltage, and resistance in a circuit is analogous to the relation between flow rate, pressure, and flow restriction in a hydraulic system. Consider a kitchen water tap: pressure in the pipe leading to the tap forces water to flow when the valve is opened. If the valve is opened just a tiny bit, the flow from the faucet is a trickle. If the valve is opened further, the flow rate increases. Increasing the valve opening is equivalent to reducing the resistance to water flow through the faucet.

In an electrical circuit, voltage corresponds to the pressure in the water pipe. Electrical current, measured in **amperes** (often shortened to **amps**), corresponds to the rate of water flow through the pipe and faucet. Electrical resistance corresponds to the flow restriction resulting from a partially opened valve.

The quantities voltage, current, and resistance are related by the formula $V = IR$, where V is the voltage (in volts), I is the current (in amperes), and R is the resistance (in ohms). In words, the voltage across a resistive circuit element equals the product of the current through the element and its resistance. This is Ohm's Law, named in honor of Georg Ohm, who first published the relationship in 1827.

Figure 2.1 shows a simple circuit representation of this relationship. The stacked horizontal lines to the left indicate a voltage source, such as a battery or a computer power supply. The zig-zag shape to the right represents a resistor. The lines connecting the components are wires, which are assumed to be perfect conductors. The current, denoted by the letter I, flows around the circuit clockwise, out the positive side of the battery, through the resistor, and back into the negative side of the battery. The negative side of the battery is defined in this circuit as the voltage reference point, with a voltage of zero volts:

Figure 2.1: Simple resistive circuit

In the water pipe analogy, the wire at zero volts represents a pool of water. A "pump" (the battery in the diagram) draws in water from the pool and pushes it out of the "pump" at the top of the battery symbol into a pipe at a higher pressure. The water flows as current I to the faucet, represented by resistor R to the right. After passing through the flow-restricted faucet, the water ends up in the pool where it is available to be drawn into the pump again.

If we assume that the battery voltage, or pressure rise across the water pump, is constant, then any increase in resistance R will reduce the current I by an inversely proportional amount. Doubling the resistance cuts the current in half, for example. Doubling the voltage, perhaps by placing two batteries in series as is common in flashlights, will double the current through the resistor.

In the next section, we will introduce the transistor, which serves as the basis for all modern digital electronic devices.

The transistor

A **transistor** is a semiconductor device that, for the purpose of this discussion, functions as a digital switch. This switching operation is electrically equivalent to changing between very high and very low resistance based on the state of an input signal. One important feature of switching transistors is that the switching input does not need to be very strong. This means that a very small current at the switching input can turn on and turn off a much larger current passing through the transistor. A single transistor's output current can drive many other transistor inputs. This characteristic is vital to the development of complex digital circuits.

Figure 2.2 shows the schematic diagram of the NPN transistor. NPN refers to the construction of the interconnected silicon regions that make up the transistor. An *N* region of silicon has material added to it (using a process called **doping**) that increases the number of electrons present, making it somewhat negatively charged. A *P* region is doped to have a reduced number of electrons, making it somewhat positively charged. An NPN transistor contains two *N* sections, with a *P* section sandwiched between them. The three terminals of the device are connected to each of these regions:

Figure 2.2: NPN transistor schematic symbol

The collector, labeled C in Figure 2.2, is connected to one of the *N* regions, and the emitter, *E*, is connected to the other *N* region. The base, *B*, connects to the *P* region between the two *N* regions. The collector "collects" current and the emitter "emits" current, as indicated by the arrow. The base terminal is the control input. By changing the voltage applied to the base terminal, and thus altering the amount of current flowing into the base, current entering via the collector and exiting via the emitter can be turned on and off.

Figure 2.3 is a schematic diagram of a transistor NOT gate. This circuit is powered by a 5 V supply. The input signal might come from a pushbutton circuit that produces 0V when the button is not pressed and 5 V when it is pressed. R1 limits the current flowing from the input terminal to the transistor base terminal when the input is high (near 5 V). In a typical circuit, R1 has a value of about 1,000 ohms. R2 might have a value of 5,000 ohms. R2 limits the current flowing from the collector to the emitter when the transistor is switched on:

Figure 2.3: Transistor NOT gate

The input terminal accepts voltage inputs over the range 0 to 5 V, but since we are interested in digital circuit operation, we are only interested in signals that are either near 0 V (low) or near 5 V (high). All voltage levels between the low and high states are assumed to be transient during near-instantaneous transitions between the low and high states.

A typical NPN transistor has a switching voltage of about 0.7 V. When the input terminal is held at a low voltage, 0.2 V for example, the transistor is switched off and has a very large resistance between the collector and emitter. This allows R2, connected to the 5 V power supply, to pull the output signal to a high state near 5 V.

When the input signal goes above 0.7 V and into the range 2 V to 5 V, the transistor switches on and the resistance between the collector and the emitter becomes very small. This, in effect, connects the output terminal to 0 V through a resistance that is much smaller than R2. As a result, the output terminal is pulled to a low voltage, typically around 0.2 V.

To summarize the behavior of this circuit, when the input terminal is high, the output terminal is low. When the input terminal is low, the output terminal is high. This function describes a NOT gate, in which the output is the inverse of the input. Assigning the low signal level the binary value 0 and the high signal level the value 1, the behavior of this gate can be summarized in the truth table shown in Table 2.1.

Table 2.1: NOT gate truth table

Input	Output
0	1
1	0

A **truth table** is a tabular representation of the output of a logical expression as a function of all possible combinations of inputs. Each column represents one input or output, with the output(s) shown on the right-hand side of the table. Each row presents one set of input values as well as the output of the expression given those inputs.

Logic gates

Circuits such as the NOT gate in *Figure 2.3* are so common in digital electronics that they are assigned schematic symbols to enable construction of higher-level diagrams representing more complex logic functions.

The symbol for a NOT gate is a triangle with a small circle at the output, shown in Figure 2.4:

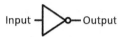

Figure 2.4: NOT gate schematic symbol

The triangle represents an amplifier, meaning this is a device that turns a weaker input signal into a stronger output signal. The circle represents the inversion operator.

More complex logical operations can be developed by building upon the design of the NOT gate.

The circuit in Figure 2.5 uses two transistors to perform an AND operation on the inputs *Input₁* and *Input₂*. An AND operation has an *Output* of 1 when both inputs are 1, otherwise the *Output* is 0. Resistor R2 pulls the *Output* signal low unless both transistors have been switched on by the high levels of the $Input_1$ and $Input_2$ signals:

Figure 2.5: Transistor AND gate

Table 2.2 is the truth table for the AND gate circuit. In simple terms, the *Output* signal is true (at the 1 level) when both the $Input_1$ and $Input_2$ inputs are true, and false (0) otherwise.

Table 2.2: AND gate truth table

Input₁	Input₂	Output
0	0	0
1	0	0
0	1	0
1	1	1

The AND gate has its own schematic symbol, shown in Figure 2.6:

Figure 2.6: AND gate schematic symbol

An OR gate has an output of 1 when either the *A* or *B* input is 1, and also if both inputs are 1. Here is the truth table for the OR gate.

Table 2.3: OR gate truth table

A	B	Output
0	0	0
1	0	1
0	1	1
1	1	1

The OR gate schematic symbol is shown in Figure 2.7:

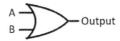

Figure 2.7: OR gate schematic symbol

The exclusive-OR, or XOR, operation produces an output of 1 when just one of the A and B inputs is 1. The output is 0 when both inputs are 0 and when both are 1. Here is the XOR truth table.

Table 2.4: XOR gate truth table

A	B	Output
0	0	0
1	0	1
0	1	1
1	1	0

The XOR gate schematic symbol is shown in Figure 2.8:

Figure 2.8: XOR gate schematic symbol

Each of the AND, OR, and XOR gates can be implemented with an inverting output. The function of the gate is exactly the same as described in the preceding section, except the output is inverted (0 is replaced with 1 in the *Output* column in *Table 2.2*, *Table 2.3*, and *Table 2.4*, and 1 is replaced with 0). The schematic symbol for an AND, OR, or XOR gate with inverted output has a small circle added on the output side of the symbol, just as on the output of the NOT gate. The names of the gates with inverted outputs are NAND, NOR, and XNOR. The letter 'N' in each of these names indicates NOT. For example, NAND means NOT AND, which is functionally equivalent to an AND gate followed by a NOT gate.

Low-level logic gates can be combined to produce more complex functions. A multiplexer is a circuit that selects one of multiple inputs to pass through to an output based on the state of a selector input. Figure 2.9 is a diagram of a two-input multiplexer:

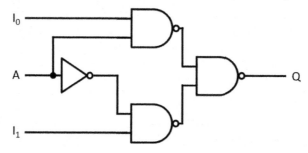

Figure 2.9: Two-input multiplexer circuit

The two single-bit data inputs are I_0 and I_1. The selector input A passes the value of I_0 through to the output Q when A is high. It passes I_1 to the output when A is low. One use of a multiplexer in processor design is to select input data from one of multiple sources when loading an internal register.

The truth table representation of the two-input multiplexer is shown in. In this table, the value X indicates "don't care", meaning it does not matter what value that signal has in determining the Q output.

Table 2.5: Two-input multiplexer truth table

A	I_0	I_1	Q
1	0	X	0
1	1	X	1
0	X	0	0
0	X	1	1

The logic gates presented in this section, and the circuits made by combining them, are referred to as **combinational logic** when the output at any moment depends only on the current state of the inputs. For the moment, we're ignoring propagation delay and assuming that the output responds immediately to changes in the inputs. In other words, the output does not depend on prior input values. Combinational logic circuits have no memory of past inputs or outputs.

Latches

Combinational logic does not directly permit the storage of data as is needed for digital functions such as processor registers. Logic gates can be used to create data storage elements through the use of feedback from a gate output to an input.

The **latch** is a single-bit memory device constructed from logic gates. Figure 2.10 shows a simple type of latch called the **Set-Reset**, or **SR**, **latch**. The feature that provides memory in this circuit is the feedback from the output of the AND gate to the input of the OR gate:

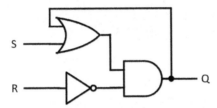

Figure 2.10: SR latch circuit

Based on the inputs S and R, the circuit can either set the output Q to high, reset Q to low, or cause the output Q to be held at its last value. In the hold state, both S and R are low, and the state of the output Q is retained. Pulsing S high (going from low to high then back to low) causes the output Q to go high and remain at that level. Pulsing R high causes Q to go low and stay low. If both S and R are set high, the R input overrides the S input and forces Q low.

The truth table for the SR latch is shown in Table 2.6. The output Q_{prev} represents the most recent value of Q selected through the actions of the S and R inputs.

Table 2.6: SR latch truth table

S	R	Action	Q
0	0	Hold	Q_{prev}
1	0	Set	1
X	1	Reset	0

One item to be aware of with this latch circuit, and with volatile memory devices in general, is that the initial state of the Q output upon power-up is not well defined. The circuit startup behavior and the resulting value of Q depend on the characteristics and timing of the individual gates as they come to life. After power-on, and prior to beginning use of this circuit for productive purposes, it is necessary to pulse the S or R input to place Q into a known state.

The **gated D latch**, where **D** stands for **data**, has many uses in digital circuits. The term **gated** refers to the use of an additional input that enables or inhibits the passage of data through the circuit. Figure 2.11 shows an implementation of the gated D latch:

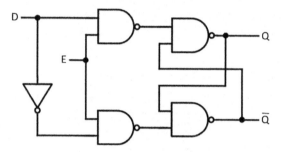

Figure 2.11: Gated D latch circuit

The D input passes through to the Q output whenever the E (Enable) input is high. When E is low, the Q output retains its previous value regardless of the state of the D input. The $\overline{Q}$ output always holds the inverse of the Q output (the horizontal bar on $\overline{Q}$ means NOT).

Table 2.7: Gated D latch truth table

D	E	Q	$\overline{Q}$
0	1	0	1
1	1	1	0
X	0	Q_{prev}	$\overline{Q}_{prev}$

It is worth taking a moment to trace the logical flow of this circuit to understand its operation. The left half of *Figure 2.11*, consisting of the D input, the NOT gate, and the two leftmost NAND gates, is a combinational logic circuit, meaning the output is always a direct function of the input.

First, consider the case when the E input is low. With E low, one of the inputs to each of the two left-hand NAND gates is low, which forces the output of both gates to 1 (refer to *Table 2.2* and the AND gate truth table, and remember that the NAND gate is equivalent to an AND gate followed by a NOT gate). In this state, the value of the D input is irrelevant, and one of Q or $\overline{Q}$ must be high and the other must be low, because of the cross-connection of the outputs of the two rightmost NAND gates feeding back to the gate inputs. This state will be retained as long as E is low.

When E is high, depending on the state of D, one of the two leftmost NAND gates will have a low output and the other will have a high output. The one with the low output will drive the connected rightmost NAND gate to a high output. This output will feed back to the input of the other right-hand side NAND gate and, with both inputs high, will produce a low output. The result is that the input D will propagate through to the output Q and the inverse of D will appear at output $\overline{Q}$.

It is important to understand that Q and $\overline{Q}$ cannot both be high or low at the same time, because this would represent a conflict between the outputs and inputs of the two rightmost NAND gates. If one of these conditions happens to arise fleetingly, such as during power-up, the circuit will self-adjust to a stable configuration, with Q and $\overline{Q}$ holding opposite states. As with the SR latch, the result of this self-adjustment is not predictable, so it is important to initialize the gated D latch to a known state before using it in any operations. Initialization is performed by setting E high, setting D to the desired initial Q output, and then setting E low.

The gated D latch described previously is a **level-sensitive device**, meaning that the output Q changes to follow the D input as long as the E input is held high. In more complex digital circuits, it becomes important to synchronize multiple circuit elements connected in series without the need to carefully account for propagation delays across the individual devices. The use of a shared clock signal as an input to multiple elements enables this type of synchronization. In a shared-clock configuration, components update their outputs based on clock signal edges (edges are the moments of transition from low to high or high to low) rather than directly based on high or low input signal levels.

Edge triggering is useful because the clock signal edges identify precise moments at which device inputs must be stable. After the clock edge has passed, the device's inputs are free to vary in preparation for the next active clock edge without the possibility of altering the outputs. The flip-flop circuit, discussed next, responds to clock edges, providing this desirable characteristic for use in complex digital designs.

Flip-flops

A device that changes its output state only when a clock signal makes a specified transition (either low-to-high or high-to-low) is referred to as an **edge-sensitive device. Flip-flops** are similar to latches, with the key difference being that the output of a flip-flop changes in response to a signal edge rather than responding to the signal level.

The **positive edge-triggered D flip-flop** is a popular digital circuit component used in a variety of applications. The D flip-flop typically includes set and reset input signals that perform the same functions as in the SR latch. This flip-flop has a D input that functions just like the D input of the gated D latch. Instead of an enable input, the D flip-flop has a clock input that triggers the transfer of the D input to the Q output and, with inversion, to the $\overline{Q}$ output on the clock's rising edge. Other than within a very narrow time window surrounding the rising edge of the clock signal, the flip-flop does not respond to the value of the D input. When active, the S and R inputs override any activity on the D and clock inputs.

Figure 2.12 shows the schematic symbol for the D flip-flop. The clock input is indicated by the small triangle on the left-hand side of the symbol:

Figure 2.12: D flip-flop schematic symbol

Consider the following table. The upward-pointing arrows in the *CLK* column indicate the rising edge of the clock signal. The Q and outputs shown in the table rows with upward-pointing arrows represent the state of the outputs following the rising clock edge.

Table 2.8: D flip-flop truth table

S	R	D	CLK	Q	$\overline{Q}$
0	0	1	↑	1	0
0	0	0	↑	0	1
0	0	X	Stable	Q_{prev}	$\overline{Q}_{prev}$
1	0	X	X	1	0
0	1	X	X	0	1

Flip-flops can be connected in series to enable the transfer of data bits from one flip-flop to the next. This is achieved by connecting the Q output of the first flip-flop to the D input of the second one, and so on for any number of stages. This structure is called a **shift register** and has many applications, two of which are serial-to-parallel conversion and parallel-to-serial conversion.

If the Q output at the end of a shift register is connected to the D input at the other end, the result is a **ring counter**. Ring counters are used for tasks such as the construction of **finite state machines**. Finite state machines implement a mathematical model that is always in one of a set of well-defined states. Transitions between states occur when inputs satisfy the requirements to transition to a different state.

The ring counter in Figure 2.13 has four positions. The counter is initialized by pulsing the *RST* input high and then low. This sets the Q output of the first (leftmost) flip-flop to 1 and the remaining flip-flop Q outputs to 0. After that, each rising edge of the *CLK* input transfers the 1 bit to the next flip-flop in the sequence. The fourth *CLK* pulse transfers the 1 back to the leftmost flip-flop. At all times, all of the flip-flops have a Q output of 0 except for one that has a 1 output. The flip-flops are edge-sensitive devices and all of them are driven by a common clock signal, making this a **synchronous circuit**:

Figure 2.13: Four-position ring counter circuit

This circuit contains four ring counter states. Adding six more flip-flops would bring the number of states to 10. As we discussed in *Chapter 1, Introducing Computer Architecture*, the ENIAC used vacuum tube-based 10-position ring counters to maintain the state of decimal digits. A 10-state ring counter based on the circuit in Figure 2.13 can perform the same function.

In the next section, we will construct registers for data storage from flip-flops.

Registers

Processor registers temporarily store data values and serve as input to and output from a variety of instruction operations, including data movement to and from memory, arithmetic, and bit manipulation. Most general-purpose processors include instructions for shifting binary values stored in registers to the left or right, and for performing rotation operations in which data bits shifted out one end of the register are inserted at the opposite end. The rotation operation is similar to the ring counter, except that the bits in a rotation can hold arbitrary values, while a ring counter typically transfers a single 1 bit through the sequence of locations. Circuits performing these functions are constructed from the low-level gates and flip-flops discussed earlier in this chapter.

Registers within a processor are usually loaded with data values and read out in parallel, meaning all the bits are written or read on separate signal lines simultaneously under the control of a common clock edge. The examples presented in this section will use four-bit registers for simplicity, but it is straightforward to extend these designs to 8, 16, 32, or 64 bits as needed.

Figure 2.14 shows a simple four-bit register with parallel input and output. This is a synchronous circuit, in which data bits provided on inputs D_0-D_3 are loaded into the flip-flops on the rising edge of the *CLK* signal. The data bits appear immediately at the Q_0-Q_3 outputs and retain their state until new data values are loaded on a subsequent rising clock edge:

Figure 2.14: Four-bit register circuit

To perform useful functions beyond simply storing data in the register, it is necessary to be able to load data from multiple sources into the register, perform operations on the register contents, and write the resulting data value to one of potentially many destinations.

In general-purpose processors, a data value can usually be loaded into a register from a memory location or an input port, or transferred from another register. Operations performed on the register contents might include incrementing, decrementing, arithmetic, shifting, rotating, and bit operations such as AND, OR, and XOR. Note that incrementing or decrementing an integer is equivalent to addition or subtraction of an operand with a second implied operand of 1. Once a register contains the result of a computation, its contents can be written to a memory location, to an output port, or to another register.

Figure 2.9 presented a circuit for a two-input multiplexer. It is straightforward to extend this circuit to support a larger number of inputs, any of which can be selected by control inputs. The single-bit multiplexer can be replicated to support parallel operation across all the bits in a processor word. Such a circuit can be used to select among a variety of sources when loading a register with data. When implemented in a processor, logic triggered by instruction opcodes sets the multiplexer control inputs to route data from the appropriate source to the specified destination register. *Chapter 3, Processor Elements*, will expand on the use of multiplexers for data routing to registers and to other units within the processor.

The next section will introduce circuits that add binary numbers.

Adders

General-purpose processors usually support the addition operation for performing calculations on data values and, separately, to manage the instruction pointer. Following the execution of each instruction, the instruction pointer increments to the next instruction location. When the processor supports multi-word instructions, the updated instruction pointer must be set to its current value plus the number of words in the just-completed instruction.

A simple adder circuit adds two data bits plus an incoming carry and produces a one-bit sum and a carry output. This circuit, shown in Figure 2.15, is called a **full adder** because it includes the incoming carry in the calculation. A **half adder** adds only the two data bits without an incoming carry:

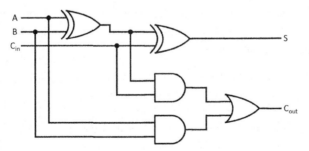

Figure 2.15: Full adder circuit

The full adder uses logic gates to produce its output as follows. The sum bit S is 1 only if the total number of 1 bits in the group A, B, C_{in} is an odd number. Otherwise, S is 0. The two XOR gates perform this logical operation. C_{out} is 1 if both A and B are 1, or if just one of A and B is 1 and C_{in} is also 1. Otherwise, C_{out} is 0.

The circuit in *Figure 2.15* can be condensed to a schematic block with three inputs and two outputs for use in higher-level diagrams. Figure 2.16 is a four-bit adder with four blocks representing copies of the full adder circuit of *Figure 2.15*. The inputs are the two words to be added, A_0-A_3 and B_0-B_3, and the incoming carry, C_{in}. The output is the sum, S_0-S_3, and the outgoing carry, C_{out}:

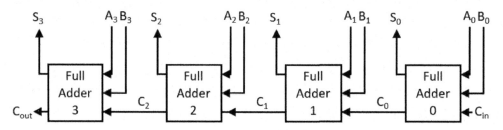

Figure 2.16: 4-bit adder circuit

It is important to note that this circuit is a combinational circuit, meaning that once the inputs have been set, the outputs will be generated directly. This includes the carry action from bit to bit, no matter how many bits are affected by carries. Because the carry flows across bit by bit, this configuration is referred to as a **ripple carry adder**. It takes some time for the carries to propagate across all the bit positions and for the outputs to stabilize at their final value.

Since we are now discussing a circuit with a signal path that passes through a significant number of devices, it is appropriate to discuss the implications of the time required for signals to travel from end to end across multiple components.

Propagation delay

When the input of a logic device changes, the output does not change instantly. There is a time delay between a change of state at the input and the final result appearing at the output called the **propagation delay**.

Placing multiple combinational circuits in series results in an overall propagation delay that is the sum of the delays of all the intermediate devices. A gate may have a different propagation delay for a low-to-high transition than for a high-to-low transition, so the larger of these two values should be used in the estimation of the worst-case delay.

From *Figure 2.15*, the longest path (in terms of the number of gates in series) from input to output for the full adder is from the A and B inputs to the C_{out} output: a total of three sequential gates. If all of the input signals in *Figure 2.16* are set simultaneously on the full adder inputs, the three-gate delay related to those inputs will take place simultaneously across all the adders. However, the C_0 output from Full Adder 0 is only guaranteed to be stable after the three-gate delay across Full Adder 0. Once C_0 is stable, there is an additional two-gate delay across Full Adder 1 (note that in *Figure 2.15*, C_{in} only passes through two sequential levels of gates).

The overall propagation delay for the circuit in *Figure 2.16* is therefore three gate delays across Full Adder 0 followed by two gate delays across each of the remaining three full adders, a total of nine gate delays. This may not seem too bad, but consider a 32-bit adder: the propagation delay for this adder is three gate delays for Full Adder 0 plus two gate delays for each of the remaining 31 adders, a total of 65 gate delays.

The path with the maximum propagation delay through a combinational circuit is called the **critical path**, and this delay places an upper limit on the clock frequency that can be used to drive the circuit.

Logic gates from the **Advanced Schottky Transistor-Transistor Logic** family, abbreviated (**AS**) **TTL**, are among the fastest individually packaged gates available today. An (AS) TTL NAND gate has a propagation delay of 2 **nanoseconds** (**ns**) under typical load conditions. For comparison, light in a vacuum travels just under two feet in 2 ns.

In the 32-bit ripple carry adder, 65 propagation delays through (AS) TTL gates result in a delay of 130 ns between setting the inputs and receiving final, stable outputs. For the purpose of forming a rough estimate, let's assume this is the worst-case propagation delay through an entire processor integrated circuit. We'll also ignore any additional time required to hold inputs stable before and after an active clock edge. This adder, then, cannot perform sequential operations on input data more often than once every 130 ns.

When performing 32-bit addition with a ripple carry adder, the processor uses a clock edge to transfer the contents of two registers (each consisting of a set of D flip-flops) plus the processor C flag to the adder inputs. The subsequent clock edge loads the results of the addition into a destination register. The C flag receives the value of C_{out} from the adder.

A clock with a period of 130 ns has a frequency of (1/130 ns), which is 7.6 MHz. This certainly does not seem very fast, especially when many low-cost processors are available today with clock speeds in excess of 4 GHz. Part of the reason for this discrepancy is the inherent speed advantage of integrated circuits containing massive numbers of tightly packed transistors, and the other part is the result of the cleverness of designers, as referenced by Gordon Moore in *Chapter 1, Introducing Computer Architecture*. To perform the adder function efficiently, many design optimizations have been developed to substantially reduce the worst-case propagation delay. *Chapter 8, Performance-Enhancing Techniques*, will discuss some of the methods processor architects use to wring higher speeds from their designs.

In addition to gate delays, there is also some delay resulting from signal travel through wires and integrated circuit conductive paths. The propagation speed through a conductive path varies depending on the material used for conduction and the insulating material surrounding the conductor. Depending on these and other factors, the propagation speed in digital circuits is typically 50-90% of the speed of light in a vacuum.

The next section discusses the generation and use of clocking signals in digital circuits.

Clocking

The clock signal serving as the heartbeat of a processor is usually a square wave signal operating at a fixed frequency. A square wave is a digital signal that oscillates between high and low states, spending equal lengths of time at the high and low levels on each cycle. Figure 2.17 shows an example of a square wave over time:

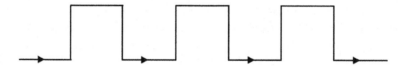

Figure 2.17: Square wave signal

The clock signal in a computer system is usually generated with a crystal oscillator providing a base frequency of a few **megahertz (MHz)**. 1 MHz is 1 million cycles per second. A crystal oscillator relies on the resonant vibration of a physical crystal, usually made of quartz, to generate a cyclic electrical signal using the piezoelectric effect. Quartz crystals resonate at precise frequencies, which leads to their use as timing elements in computers, wristwatches, and other digital devices.

Although crystal oscillators are more accurate time references than alternative timing references that may be used in low-cost devices, crystals exhibit errors in frequency that accumulate over periods of days and weeks to gradually drift by seconds and then minutes away from the correct time. To avoid this problem, most Internet-connected computers access a time server periodically to reset their internal clocks to the current time as defined by a precise atomic reference clock.

Phase-locked loop (PLL) frequency multiplier circuits are used to generate the high-frequency clock signals needed by multi-GHz processors. A PLL frequency multiplier generates a square wave output frequency at an integer multiple of the input frequency provided to it from the crystal oscillator. The ratio of the PLL clock output frequency to the input frequency it receives is called the **clock multiplier**.

A PLL frequency multiplier operates by continuously adjusting the frequency of its internal oscillator to maintain the correct clock multiplier ratio relative to the PLL input frequency. Modern processors usually have a crystal oscillator clock signal input and contain several PLL frequency multipliers producing different frequencies. Different clock multiplier values are used to drive core processor operations at the highest possible speed while simultaneously interacting with devices that require lower clock frequencies, such as system memory.

Sequential logic

Digital circuitry that generates outputs based on a combination of current inputs and past inputs is called **sequential logic**. This is in contrast to combinational logic, in which outputs depend only on the current state of the inputs. When a sequential logic circuit composed of several components operates those components under the control of a shared clock signal, the circuit implements **synchronous logic**.

The steps involved in the execution of processor instructions take place as a series of discrete operations that consume input in the form of instruction opcodes and data values received from various sources. This activity takes place under the coordination of a master clock signal. The processor maintains internal state information from one clock step to the next, and from one instruction to the next.

Modern complex digital devices, including processors, are almost always implemented as synchronous sequential logic devices. Low-level internal components, such as the gates, multiplexers, registers, and adders discussed previously, are usually combinational logic circuits. These lower-level components, in turn, are provided inputs under the control of synchronous logic. After allowing sufficient time for propagation across the combinational components, the shared clock signal transfers the outputs of those components into other portions of the architecture under the control of processor instructions and the logic circuits that carry out those instructions.

Chapter 3, Processor Elements, will introduce the higher-level processor components that implement more complex functionality, including instruction decoding, instruction execution, and arithmetic operations.

The next section introduces the concept of designing digital hardware using computer programming languages.

Hardware description languages

It is straightforward to represent simple digital circuits using logic diagrams similar to the ones presented earlier in this chapter. When designing digital devices that are substantially more complex, however, the use of logic diagrams quickly becomes unwieldy. As an alternative to the logic diagram, a number of **hardware description languages** have been developed over the years. This evolution has been encouraged by Moore's Law, which drives digital system designers to continually find new ways to quickly make the most effective use of the constantly growing number of transistors available in integrated circuits.

Hardware description languages are not the exclusive province of digital designers at semiconductor companies; even hobbyists can acquire and use these powerful tools at an affordable cost, even for free in many cases.

A **gate array** is a logic device containing a large number of logic elements such as NAND gates and D flip-flops that can be connected to form arbitrary circuits. A category of gate arrays called **field programmable gate arrays (FPGAs)** enables end users to implement their own designs into gate array chips using just a computer, a small development board, and an appropriate software package.

A developer can define a complex digital circuit using a hardware description language and program it into a chip directly, resulting in a fully functional, high-performance custom digital device. Current-generation low-cost FPGAs contain a sufficient number of gates to implement complex modern processor designs. As one example, an FPGA-programmable design of the RISC-V processor (discussed in detail in *Chapter 11, The RISC-V Architecture and Instruction Set*) is available in the form of open source hardware description language code.

VHDL

VHDL is one of the leading hardware description languages in use today. Development of the VHDL language began in 1983 under the guidance of the U.S. Department of Defense. The syntax and some of the semantics of VHDL are based on the Ada programming language, which, incidentally, is named after Ada Lovelace, the programmer of Charles Babbage's Analytical Engine, discussed in *Chapter 1, Introducing Computer Architecture*. Verilog is another popular hardware design language with capabilities similar to VHDL. This book will use VHDL exclusively, but the examples could be implemented just as easily in Verilog.

VHDL is a multilevel acronym where the V stands for VHSIC, which means Very High-Speed Integrated Circuit, and **VHDL** stands for **VHSIC Hardware Description Language**. The following code presents a VHDL implementation of the full adder circuit shown in *Figure 2.15*:

```vhdl
-- Load the standard libraries

library IEEE;
  use IEEE.STD_LOGIC_1164.ALL;

-- Define the full adder inputs and outputs

entity FULL_ADDER is
  port (
    A     : in    std_logic;
    B     : in    std_logic;
    C_IN  : in    std_logic;
    S     : out   std_logic;
    C_OUT : out   std_logic
  );
end entity FULL_ADDER;

-- Define the behavior of the full adder

architecture BEHAVIORAL of FULL_ADDER is
```

```
begin

   S       <= (A XOR B) XOR C_IN;
   C_OUT <= (A AND B) OR ((A XOR B) AND C_IN);

end architecture BEHAVIORAL;
```

This code is a fairly straightforward textual description of the full adder in *Figure 2.15*. Here, the section introduced with `entity FULL_ADDER is` defines the inputs and outputs of the full adder component. The `architecture` section toward the end of the code describes how the circuit logic operates to produce the outputs *S* and *C_OUT* given the inputs *A*, *B*, and *C_IN*. The term `std_logic` refers to a single-bit binary data type. The `<=` characters represent wire-like connections, driving the output on the left-hand side with the value computed on the right-hand side.

The following code references the FULL_ADDER VHDL as a component in the implementation of the four-bit adder design presented in *Figure 2.16*:

```
-- Load the standard libraries

library IEEE;
   use IEEE.STD_LOGIC_1164.ALL;

-- Define the 4-bit adder inputs and outputs

entity ADDER4 is
   port (
      A4        : in    std_logic_vector(3 downto 0);
      B4        : in    std_logic_vector(3 downto 0);
      SUM4      : out   std_logic_vector(3 downto 0);
      C_OUT4    : out   std_logic
   );
end entity ADDER4;

-- Define the behavior of the 4-bit adder

architecture BEHAVIORAL of ADDER4 is
```

```vhdl
-- Reference the previous definition of the full adder

component FULL_ADDER is
  port (
    A               : in      std_logic;
    B               : in      std_logic;
    C_IN            : in      std_logic;
    S               : out     std_logic;
    C_OUT           : out     std_logic
  );
end component;

-- Define the signals used internally in the 4-bit adder
signal c0, c1, c2 : std_logic;

begin

-- The carry input to the first adder is set to 0
FULL_ADDER0 : FULL_ADDER
  port map (
    A               => A4(0),
    B               => B4(0),
    C_IN            => '0',
    S               => SUM4(0),
    C_OUT           => c0
  );

FULL_ADDER1 : FULL_ADDER
  port map (
    A               => A4(1),
    B               => B4(1),
    C_IN            => c0,
    S               => SUM4(1),
    C_OUT           => c1
  );
```

```
FULL_ADDER2 : FULL_ADDER
   port map (
      A              => A4(2),
      B              => B4(2),
      C_IN           => c1,
      S              => SUM4(2),
      C_OUT          => c2
   );


FULL_ADDER3 : FULL_ADDER
   port map (
      A              => A4(3),
      B              => B4(3),
      C_IN           => c2,
      S              => SUM4(3),
      C_OUT          => C_OUT4
   );


end architecture BEHAVIORAL;
```

This code is a textual description of the four-bit adder in *Figure 2.16*. Here, the section introduced with entity ADDER4 is defines the inputs and outputs of the four-bit adder component. The phrase std_logic_vector(3 downto 0) represents a four-bit data type with bit number 3 in the left-hand (most significant) position and bit number 0 on the right-hand side.

The FULL_ADDER component is defined in a separate file, referenced here by the section beginning component FULL_ADDER is. The statement signal c0, c1, c2 : std_logic; defines the internal carry values between the full adders. The four port map sections define the connections between the four-bit adder signals and the inputs and outputs of each of the single-bit full adders. To reference a bit in a multi-bit value, the bit number follows the parameter name in parentheses. For example, *A4(0)* refers to the least significant of the four bits in *A4*.

Note the use of hierarchy in this design. A simple component, the single-bit full adder, was first defined as a discrete, self-contained block of code. This block was then used to construct a more complex circuit, the four-bit adder. This hierarchical approach can be extended through many levels to define an extremely complex digital device constructed from less complex components, each of which, in turn, is constructed from even simpler parts. This general approach is used routinely in the development of modern processors containing hundreds of millions of transistors, while managing complexity in a manner that keeps the design understandable by humans at each level of the architectural hierarchy.

The code in this section provides all the circuit information that a logic synthesis software tool suite requires to implement the four-bit adder as a component in an FPGA device. Of course, additional circuitry is required to present meaningful inputs to the adder circuit and then to process the results of an addition operation after allowing for propagation delay.

This has been a very brief introduction to VHDL. The intent here has been to make you aware that hardware description languages such as VHDL are the current state of the art in complex digital circuit design. In addition, you should know that some very low-cost options are available for FPGA development tools and devices. The exercises at the end of this chapter will introduce you to some highly capable FPGA development tools at no cost. You are encouraged to search the Internet and learn more about VHDL and other hardware description languages and try your hand at developing some simple (and not-so-simple) circuit designs.

Summary

This chapter began with an introduction to the properties of electrical circuits and showed how components such as voltage sources, resistors, and wires are represented in circuit diagrams. The transistor was introduced, with a focus on its use as a switching element in digital circuits. The NOT gate and the AND gate were constructed from transistors and resistors. Additional types of logic gates were defined and truth tables were presented for each one. Logic gates were used to construct more complex digital circuits, including latches, flip-flops, registers, and adders. The concept of sequential logic was introduced, and its applicability to processor design was discussed. Finally, hardware description languages were introduced, and a four-bit adder example was presented in VHDL.

You should now have an understanding of the basic digital circuit concepts and design tools used in the development of modern processors. The next chapter will expand upon these building blocks to explore the functional components of modern processors, leading to a discussion of how those components coordinate to implement the primary processor operational cycle of instruction loading, decoding, and execution.

Exercises

1. Rearrange the circuit in *Figure 2.5* to convert the AND gate to a NAND gate. Hint: there is no need to add or remove components.

2. Create a circuit implementation of an OR gate by modifying the circuit in *Figure 2.5*. Wires, transistors, and resistors can be added as needed.

3. Search the Internet for free VHDL development software suites that include a simulator. Get one of these suites, set it up, and build any simple demo projects that come with the suite to ensure it is working properly.

4. Using your VHDL tool set, implement the four-bit adder using the code listings presented in this chapter.

5. Add test driver code (search the Internet to learn how) to your four-bit adder to drive it through a limited set of input sets and verify that the outputs are correct.

6. Expand the test driver code and verify that the four-bit adder produces correct results for all possible combinations of inputs.

3
Processor Elements

This chapter begins our development of a comprehensive understanding of modern processor architectures. Building upon the basic digital circuits introduced in *Chapter 2, Digital Logic,* we discuss the functional units of a simple, generic computer processor. Concepts related to the instruction set and register set are introduced, followed by a discussion of the steps involved in instruction loading, decoding, execution, and sequencing. Addressing modes and instruction categories are discussed in the context of the 6502 architecture. The need for processor interrupt handling is introduced, using the example of 6502 interrupt processing. The standard approaches modern processors employ for **input/output (I/O)** operations are introduced, including direct memory access.

After completing this chapter, you will understand the basic parts of a processor and the structure of processor instruction sets. You will have learned the types of processor instructions, why interrupt processing is necessary, and will understand I/O operations.

The following topics will be covered in this chapter:

- A simple processor
- The instruction set
- Addressing modes
- Instruction categories
- Interrupt processing
- Input/output operations

A simple processor

The 6502 processor architecture and a small subset of its instructions were introduced in *Chapter 1, Introducing Computer Architecture*. In this section, we will build upon that introduction to present the generic functional components universally employed in processor architectures, from the tiniest embedded controllers to the most powerful server CPUs.

The integrated circuit at the core of a computer system goes by a few different names: the **Central Processing Unit (CPU)**, microprocessor, or, simply, processor. A microprocessor is a single integrated circuit that implements the functions of a processor. This book will refer to all categories of CPUs and microprocessors as processors.

A typical processor contains three logically distinct functional units:

- The **control unit**, which manages the overall operation of the device: This management activity includes fetching the next instruction from memory, decoding the instruction to determine the operation to perform, and distributing the execution of the instruction to appropriate elements within the processor.

- The **Arithmetic Logic Unit (ALU)**: This is a combinational circuit that executes arithmetic and bit manipulation operations.

- The **register set**: This provides temporary storage as well as source and destination locations for instruction inputs and outputs.

The following diagram shows the flow of control and data among the control unit, the registers, the ALU, system memory, and input/output devices:

Figure 3.1: Interactions between processor functional units

The control unit directs overall processor operations to carry out each instruction. The registers, ALU, memory, and input/output devices respond to commands initiated by the control unit.

Control unit

The control unit of a modern processor is a synchronous sequential digital circuit. Its function is to interpret processor instructions and manage the execution of those instructions by interacting with the other functional units within the processor and with external components, including memory and input/output devices. The control unit is a key part of the von Neumann architecture.

For the purposes of this chapter, the term *memory* refers to system **Random Access Memory (RAM)** external to the processor's execution units. Cache memory will be covered in later chapters.

Some examples of I/O devices are the computer keyboard, mouse, disk storage, and graphical video displays. Other common I/O devices include network interfaces, Wi-Fi and Bluetooth® wireless interfaces, sound output to speakers, and microphone input.

When a computer system is powered on, the processor undergoes a reset process to initialize its internal components to defined values. During the reset process, it loads the **Program Counter (PC)** register with the memory location of the first instruction to be executed. Software developers who construct the lowest-level system software components must configure their development tools to produce a code memory image that begins execution at the address required by the processor architecture.

The PC is a central component of the control unit. The PC register contains the memory address of the next instruction to be executed. At the beginning of the instruction execution cycle, the control unit reads the data word at the memory address indicated by the PC and loads it into an internal register for decoding and execution. The first word of an instruction contains an **opcode**. Based on the opcode bit pattern, the control unit may read additional memory locations following the opcode to retrieve data needed by the instruction, such as a memory address or data operand.

As the control unit completes the reset process and begins executing instructions, it performs the repetitive cycle shown in Figure 3.2:

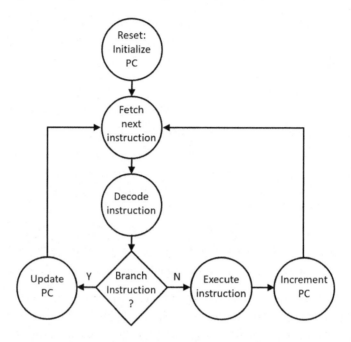

Figure 3.2: Instruction execution cycle

Once the reset has completed, the PC register contains the initial instruction location. The control unit fetches the first instruction from memory and decodes it. Decoding is the process the control unit performs to determine the actions required by the instruction.

As part of the decoding process, the control unit identifies the category of instruction. The two basic instruction categories represented in Figure 3.2 are branching instructions and all other instructions. Branching instructions are implemented directly by the control unit. These instructions cause the contents of the PC to be replaced with the memory address of the branch destination. Examples of instructions that perform branching are conditional branch instructions (when the branch is taken), subroutine calls, subroutine returns, and unconditional branching (also called *jump*) instructions.

Instructions that do not involve branching are carried out by processor circuitry under the direction of the control unit. In a sense, the control unit manages the execution of the non-branching instructions in a manner similar to the Analytical Engine's mill (see *Chapter 1, Introducing Computer Architecture*), except instead of using the presence of studs on a rotating barrel to engage portions of the mill machinery, the control unit uses the decoded bits of the instruction opcode to activate particular sections of digital circuitry. The selected circuit components perform the tasks required by the instruction.

The steps in executing an instruction include tasks such as reading or writing a register, reading or writing a memory location, directing the ALU to perform a mathematical operation, or other miscellaneous activities. In most processors, the execution of a single instruction takes place over multiple processor clock cycles. The instruction clock cycle count can vary significantly from simple instructions that require only a small number of clock cycles to complex operations that take many cycles to complete. The control unit orchestrates all of this activity.

The circuits managed by the control unit are constructed from the simple logic gates discussed in *Chapter 2, Digital Logic* and are often composed of higher-level constructs such as multiplexers, latches, and flip-flops. Multiplexers, in particular, are commonly used in control unit logic to selectively route data to a destination.

Executing an instruction – a simple example

Consider a simplified example of two 6502 instructions, TXA and TYA. TXA copies the contents of register X to register A, and TYA does the same thing using the Y register as the source. If we consider these two instructions in isolation, the execution of both instructions can be implemented as shown in Figure 3.3:

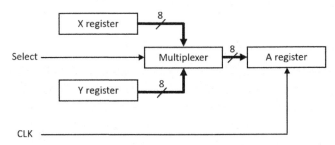

Figure 3.3: 6502 TXA and TYA instructions

The circuit in Figure 3.3 assumes the X and Y registers are D flip-flop registers (as in *Figure 2.14*), except in the 6502, they are 8-bit registers rather than holding just 4 bits. The multiplexer is implemented as eight copies of the two-input, single-bit multiplexer of *Figure 2.9*, all controlled by a single selector input. In Figure 3.3, thicker lines represent 8-bit data buses and thinner lines are individual logic signals. The short lines crossing the thick lines with the numeral 8 above them indicate the number of bits in the bus.

To execute the TXA instruction, these steps are performed:

1. The control unit first sets the **Select** input to direct the X register data bits through to the output of the multiplexer. This presents the data from X at the inputs to the A register.

2. After the **Select** input to the multiplexer has been set, the control unit must pause for the propagation of the data bits to the multiplexer outputs.

3. After the multiplexer outputs have stabilized, the control unit generates a rising edge on the **CLK** signal to load the X register data bits into register A.

To execute the TYA instruction, the control unit performs the same sequence of steps, except it initially sets the **Select** input to feed the Y register to the multiplexer output.

This is a very simple example of control unit instruction execution, but it emphasizes the points that any individual instruction may require multiple steps and may involve only a small portion of the circuitry present in the processor. Most of the processor circuitry is not used in the execution of any individual instruction. Unused components within the processor must be managed by the control unit to ensure they remain idle when not required by an executing instruction.

Arithmetic logic unit

The ALU performs arithmetic and bit-oriented operations under the direction of the control unit. To perform an operation, the ALU requires data input values, called **operands**, and a code indicating the operation to be performed. The ALU output is the result of the operation. ALU operations may use one or more processor flags, such as the carry flag, as input and set the states of processor flags as outputs. In the 6502, ALU operations update the carry, negative, zero, and overflow flags.

An ALU is a combinational circuit, implying the outputs update asynchronously in response to changes at the inputs and that it retains no memory of previous operations. To execute an instruction involving the ALU, the control unit applies inputs to the ALU, pauses for the propagation delay across the ALU, then transfers the ALU output to the destination specified by the instruction.

The ALU contains an adder circuit to perform addition and subtraction operations. In a processor with two's complement arithmetic, subtraction can be implemented by first performing a two's complement negation of the right operand and adding that result to the left operand. Mathematically, when performing subtraction in this manner, the expression *A-B* is transformed into *A+(-B)*.

As you'll recall, the two's complement negation of a signed number is achieved by inverting all of the bits in the operand and adding 1 to the result. Incorporating this operation, subtraction represented as *A+(-B)* becomes *A+(NOT(B)+1)*. Looking at subtraction in this form should make the use of the 6502 carry flag in conjunction with the SBC instruction clear. The C flag provides the "+1" in subtraction when there is no borrow. If there is a borrow, the sum must be reduced by 1, which is accomplished by setting the C flag to 0.

To summarize, in the 6502, subtraction logic is identical to addition logic with the single difference that the *B* operand in *A-B* is routed through a set of NOT gates to invert all eight of the bits prior to feeding *NOT(B)* to the adder input.

Figure 3.4 is a functional representation of the addition and subtraction operations in the 6502:

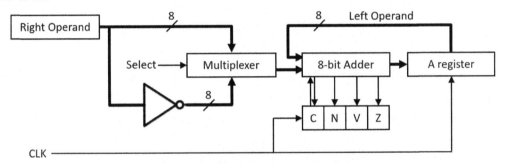

Figure 3.4: 6502 addition and subtraction operations

Similar to *Figure 3.3*, Figure 3.4 is a highly simplified representation of the 6502 processor depicting only the components involved in the ADC and SBC instructions. The **Select** input in Figure 3.4 chooses whether the operation is addition or subtraction. Addition requires selecting the upper multiplexer input, while the lower multiplexer input selects subtraction. In the 6502 architecture, the A register is always the left operand for subtraction.

The inputs to the adder are the left and right operands and the C flag. When executing an ADC or SBC instruction, the control unit presents the right operand to the multiplexer data inputs and sets the multiplexer select input to the appropriate state for the given instruction. After pausing for propagation through the NOT gate, the multiplexer, and the adder, the control unit generates a clock edge that latches the adder outputs into the A register and the processor flags register.

The processor flags are set as shown in the following execution of an ADC or
SBC instruction:

- **C** indicates whether an addition generated in a carry (C = 1) or whether a
  subtraction produced a borrow (C = 0).

- **N** contains the value of bit 7 of the result.

- **V** indicates whether a signed overflow occurred (V = 1 if overflow occurred).

- **Z** is 1 if the result is zero. Z is 0 otherwise.

An ALU supports a variety of operations in addition to adding and subtracting two
numbers. In the 6502, operations with two operands generally use the A register as the
left operand. The right operand is either read from a memory location or provided as an
immediate value in the next memory location after the opcode. All 6502 ALU operands
and results are 8-bit values. The 6502 ALU operations are as follows:

- ADC, SBC: Add or subtract two operands with carry input.

- DEC, DEX, DEY: Decrement a memory location or register by one.

- INC, INX, INY: Increment a memory location or register by one.

- AND: Perform a bitwise logical AND operation on two operands

- ORA: Perform a bitwise logical OR operation on two operands.

- EOR: Perform a bitwise logical XOR operation on two operands.

- ASL, LSR: Shift the A register or memory location left or right by one bit position
  and insert 0 into the vacated bit position.

- ROL, ROR: Rotate the A register or memory location left or right by one bit position
  and insert the C flag value into the vacated bit position.

- CMP, CPX, CPY: Subtract two operands and discard the result, setting the N, Z, and
  C flags based on the result of the subtraction.

- BIT: Perform a bitwise logical AND between two operands and use the Z flag to
  indicate whether the result is 0. In addition, copy bits 7 and 6 of the left operand
  to the N and V flags.

The 6502 has limited ALU capabilities in comparison to more complex modern processors
such as the x86 family. For example, the 6502 can perform addition and subtraction,
but multiplication and division must be implemented in code as repetitive addition
and subtraction operations. The 6502 can shift or rotate a value by just one bit position
per instruction. The x86 processors instruction set, however, directly implements
multiplication and division instructions, and the shift and rotate instructions include
a parameter indicating the number of bit positions to shift in a single instruction.

An ALU is a necessarily complex logic device, making it an ideal candidate for design with a hardware design language. The following listing is a VHDL implementation of a portion of a 6502-like ALU:

```vhdl
-- Load the standard libraries

library IEEE;
    use IEEE.STD_LOGIC_1164.ALL;
    use IEEE.NUMERIC_STD.ALL;


-- Define the 8-bit ALU inputs and outputs

entity ALU is
    port (
        -- Left operand
        LEFT        : in     std_logic_vector(7 downto 0);
        -- Right operand
        RIGHT       : in     std_logic_vector(7 downto 0);
        -- ALU operation
        OPCODE      : in     std_logic_vector(3 downto 0);
        -- Carry input
        C_IN        : in     std_logic;
        -- ALU output
        RESULT      : out    std_logic_vector(7 downto 0);
        -- Carry output
        C_OUT       : out    std_logic;
        -- Negative flag output
        N_OUT       : out    std_logic;
        -- Overflow flag output
        V_OUT       : out    std_logic;
        -- Zero flag output
        Z_OUT       : out    std_logic
    );
end entity ALU;


-- Define the behavior of the 8-bit ALU

```

```vhdl
architecture BEHAVIORAL of ALU is

begin

  P_ALU : process (LEFT, RIGHT, OPCODE, C_IN) is

    variable result8  : unsigned(7 downto 0);
    variable result9  : unsigned(8 downto 0);
    variable right_op : unsigned(7 downto 0);

  begin

    case OPCODE is

      when "0000" | "0001" => -- Addition or subtraction

        if (OPCODE = "0000") then
          right_op := unsigned(RIGHT);      -- Addition
        else
          right_op := unsigned(not RIGHT); -- Subtraction
        end if;

        result9 := ('0' & unsigned(LEFT)) +
                   unsigned(right_op) +
                   unsigned(std_logic_vector'(""& C_IN));
        result8 := result9(7 downto 0);

        C_OUT <= result9(8);                -- C flag

        -- V flag
        if (((LEFT(7) XOR result8(7)) = '1') AND
           ((right_op(7) XOR result8(7)) = '1')) then
          V_OUT <= '1';
        else
          V_OUT <= '0';
        end if;
```

```vhdl
        when "0010" =>                          -- Increment
            result8 := unsigned(LEFT) + 1;
        when "0011" =>                          -- Decrement
            result8 := unsigned(LEFT) - 1;
        when "0101" =>                          -- Bitwise AND
            result8 := unsigned(LEFT and RIGHT);
        when "0110" =>                          -- Bitwise OR
            result8 := unsigned(LEFT or RIGHT);
        when "0111" =>                          -- Bitwise XOR
            result8 := unsigned(LEFT xor RIGHT);
        when others =>
            result8 := (others => 'X');

    end case;


    RESULT <= std_logic_vector(result8);


    N_OUT <= result8(7);                        -- N flag


    if (result8 = 0) then                       -- Z flag
      Z_OUT <= '1';
    else
      Z_OUT <= '0';
    end if;


  end process P_ALU;


end architecture BEHAVIORAL;
```

Registers

Processor registers are internal storage locations that serve as sources and destinations for instruction operations. Registers provide the quickest data access in a processor, but are limited to a very small number of locations. The width of a register in bits is generally the same as the processor word size.

The 6502, as we have seen, has only three 8-bit registers: A, X, and Y. The x86 has six 32-bit registers suitable for temporary data storage: EAX, EBX, ECX, EDX, ESI, and EDI. In many processor architectures, specific registers are assigned to support functions performed by certain instructions. For example, in the x86 architecture, a single REP MOVSD instruction moves a block of data with a length (in words) provided in ECX beginning at a source address in ESI to a destination address in EDI.

When designing a new processor architecture, it is critical to evaluate the tradeoff between the number of registers and the number and complexity of instructions available to the processor. For a given integrated circuit die size and fabrication process (which together define the number of transistors available for the processor), adding more registers to the architecture reduces the number of transistors available for executing instructions and other functions. In contrast, adding instructions with complex capabilities may limit the die space available for registers. This tension between instruction set complexity and the number of registers is expressed in the categorization of an architecture as CISC or RISC.

CISC (Complex Instruction Set Computer) processors are characterized as having a rich instruction set providing a variety of features, such as the ability to load operands from memory, perform an operation, and store the result to memory, all in one instruction. In a CISC processor, an instruction may take many clock cycles to execute as the processor performs all of the required subtasks. The REP MOVSD instruction mentioned previously is an example of a single instruction with a potentially lengthy execution time. CISC processors tend to have a smaller number of registers due, in part, to the die space required for the circuitry occupied by the instruction set logic. The x86 is a classic example of CISC architecture.

RISC (Reduced Instruction Set Computer) processors, on the other hand, have a smaller number of instructions that each perform simpler tasks in comparison to CISC instructions. Performing an operation on data values stored in memory might require a pair of load instructions to load two operands from memory into registers, another instruction to perform the operation, and a final instruction to store the result back to memory. The key difference between CISC and RISC is that RISC architectures are optimized to execute individual instructions at very high speed. Even though reading memory, performing the operation, and writing the result back to memory require several more instructions in a RISC processor than in a CISC processor, the overall start-to-finish time may be comparable or even faster for the RISC processor. Examples of RISC architectures are ARM, discussed in *Chapter 10, Modern Processor Architectures and Instruction Sets*, and RISC-V, discussed in *Chapter 11, The RISC-V Architecture and Instruction Set*.

The reduction in instruction set complexity in RISC processors leaves more die space available for registers, which generally results in a larger number of registers in RISC processors compared to CISC. The ARM architecture has 13 general-purpose registers, while the RISC-V base 32-bit architecture has 31 general-purpose registers. The larger number of registers in RISC architectures reduces the need to access system memory because more registers are available for storage of intermediate results. This helps with performance because accessing system memory is significantly more time consuming than accessing data located in processor registers.

You can think of a processor register as a set of D flip-flops in which each flip-flop contains one bit of the register's data. All of the flip-flops in the register are loaded with data by a common clock signal. Input to a register may arrive at the flip-flop inputs after passing through a multiplexer that selects one of potentially many data sources under the control of the executing instruction.

As an alternative to using a multiplexer to select a register's input, an instruction may load a register from a data bus internal to the processor. In this configuration, the control unit manages the internal bus to ensure that only the desired data source is driving the data bus lines during the clock edge that loads the register, while all other data sources on the bus are inhibited from placing data on the bus.

This leads us to the next section, which introduces the full range of instructions in a processor instruction set and the addressing modes they use.

The instruction set

The following sections introduce the full range of instruction categories implemented by the 6502 processor. Similar instructions are implemented within most general-purpose architectures, though more sophisticated processors augment their capabilities with additional types of instructions. The more advanced instructions available in modern processor architectures will be introduced in later chapters.

CISC processors generally support multiple addressing modes. Addressing modes are designed to enable efficient access to sequential memory locations for software algorithms running on the processor. The next section describes the instruction addressing modes implemented by the 6502 processor. The section following that will introduce the categories of instructions implemented by the 6502, most of which are represented in some way in modern processor architectures. Specialized instructions for interrupt processing and input/output operations will then be covered, including an explanation of special processor features that enable high-performance input and output operations.

Addressing modes

CISC processors support multiple addressing modes for instructions that require transferring data between memory and registers. RISC processors have a more limited number of addressing modes. Each processor architecture defines its collection of addressing modes based on an analysis of the anticipated memory access patterns that software will use on that architecture.

To introduce the 6502 addressing modes, this section will employ a simple example of 6502 code that adds together four data bytes. To avoid extraneous details, the example will ignore any carry from the 8-bit sum.

Immediate addressing mode

For the first example, assume we are given the values of the four bytes to sum and asked to write a 6502 program to perform that task. This allows us to enter the byte values directly into our code. The bytes in this example are $01 through $04. We'll be adding the bytes together in reverse order ($04 down to $01) in anticipation of the use of a looping construct later in this section. This code uses **immediate addressing mode** to add the four bytes together:

```
; Add four bytes together using immediate addressing mode
LDA #$04
CLC
ADC #$03
ADC #$02
ADC #$01
```

Note that assembly language comments begin with a semicolon character. When these instructions complete execution, the A register will hold the value $0A, the sum of the four bytes.

Recall from *Chapter 1, Introducing Computer Architecture*, that in 6502 assembly language, an immediate value is preceded by a # character and the $ character indicates the value is hexadecimal. An immediately addressed operand is read from the memory address following the instruction opcode. Immediate addressing is handy because there is no need to reserve the memory location from which to read the operand. However, immediate addressing mode is only useful when the data value is known at the time the program is written.

Absolute addressing mode

Absolute addressing mode specifies the memory location containing the value to be read or written by the instruction. The 6502 has 16 address bits, so an address field that supports accessing all available memory is two bytes long. A complete instruction to access data at an arbitrary 6502 memory location consists of three bytes: the first byte is the opcode followed by two bytes for the address to be read or written. The two address bytes must be stored with the lower-order byte first, followed by the higher-order byte.

The convention of storing the lower-order byte of a two-byte address at the lower memory address makes the 6502 a **little-endian** processor. The x86 and RISC-V are also little-endian. The ARM architecture allows selection of big- or little-endian mode under software control (this is called **bi-endianness**), but most operating systems running on the ARM architecture select little-endian mode.

For the absolute addressing mode example, we begin with some setup code to store the four bytes to be added together into addresses $200 through $203. The instructions to add the four bytes follow the setup code. This example uses absolute addressing mode to sum the four bytes:

```
; Initialize the data in memory
LDA #$04
STA $0203
LDA #$03
STA $0202
LDA #$02
STA $0201
LDA #$01
STA $0200


; Add four bytes together using absolute addressing mode
LDA $0203
CLC
ADC $0202
ADC $0201
ADC $0200
```

Unlike immediate addressing mode, absolute addressing permits summing four values that are not known until the time of program execution: the code will add together whatever values have been stored in locations $200-$203. A limitation of this addressing mode is that the addresses of the bytes to be added must be specified when the program is written. This code cannot sum bytes located at an arbitrary location in memory.

Our simple example has the downside of unnecessarily stringing together a sequence of nearly identical instructions. To avoid this, it is usually desirable to place repetitive sequence of code into a loop construct. The next two examples use a 6502 addressing mode that facilitates looping operations, though we won't implement a loop until the second example.

Absolute indexed addressing mode

Absolute indexed addressing mode computes a memory address by adding a base address provided in the instruction to a value contained in the X or Y register. The following example adds the bytes at addresses $0200 through $0203 using absolute indexed addressing. The X register provides an offset from the base of the byte array at address $0200:

```
; Initialize the data in memory
LDA #$04
STA $0203
LDA #$03
STA $0202
LDA #$02
STA $0201
LDA #$01
STA $0200


; Add four bytes together using absolute indexed addressing
mode
LDX #$03
CLC
LDA $0200, X
DEX
ADC $0200, X
```

```
DEX
ADC $0200, X
DEX
ADC $0200, X
```

The DEX instruction decrements (subtracts 1 from) the X register. Although this code makes things worse in terms of increasing the number of instructions it takes to add the four bytes together, note that the instruction sequence, DEX, followed by ADC $0200, X now repeats three times.

By using conditional branching, we can perform the same addition sequence in a loop:

```
; Initialize the data in memory
LDA #$04
STA $0203
LDA #$03
STA $0202
LDA #$02
STA $0201
LDA #$01
STA $0200


; Add four bytes together using absolute indexed addressing
mode
LDX #$03
LDA $0200, X
DEX
CLC
ADD_LOOP:
ADC $0200, X
DEX
BPL ADD_LOOP
```

The BPL instructions means "branch on plus," which conditionally transfers control to the instruction preceded by the ADD_LOOP label. BPL executes the branch only when the processor N flag is clear. If the N flag is set, BPL continues with the next instruction in memory.

The code in this example might not seem to have been worth the effort involved in constructing a loop just to add up four bytes. However, note that this version can be modified to add together 100 sequential bytes by simply changing the operand of the LDX instruction. Extending the previous example to add 100 bytes together in the same manner would require quite a bit more work, and the instructions would consume far more memory.

This example has the same limitation as the absolute address mode example, both of which set the start of the byte array at a memory location defined at the time the program was written. The next addressing mode will remove this limitation and sum an array of bytes starting at any address in memory.

Indirect indexed addressing mode

Indirect indexed addressing mode uses a two-byte address stored in the memory address range $00-$FF as the base address and adds the contents of the Y register to that base to produce the memory address used by the instruction. In the following example, the base address of the byte array ($0200) is first stored in little-endian order at addresses $0010 and $0011. The code uses indirect indexed addressing in a loop to add the bytes together:

```
; Initialize the data in memory
LDA #$04
STA $0203
LDA #$03
STA $0202
LDA #$02
STA $0201
LDA #$01
STA $0200


; Initialize the pointer to the byte array
LDA #$00
STA $10
LDA #$02
STA $11


; Add four bytes together using indirect indexed addressing
mode
```

```
LDY #$03
LDA ($10), Y
DEY
CLC
ADD_LOOP:
ADC ($10), Y
DEY
BPL ADD_LOOP
```

With indirect indexed addressing, any memory address can be stored at addresses $10-$11 before the summing code executes. Note that indirect indexed addressing must use the Y register as the address offset. The X register is not available in this addressing mode.

The 6502 has some other addressing modes available: **zero-page addressing mode** provides instructions that are smaller (one byte less in length) and faster to execute for absolute and absolute indexed addressing by working only with memory addresses in the range $00-$FF. The term *zero-page* refers to the high byte of the 16-bit address, which is zero for addresses in this range. Other than exhibiting improved performance in terms of faster execution speed and reduced code memory usage, the zero-page addressing modes behave the same as the corresponding addressing modes described earlier.

Another mode is called **indexed indirect addressing mode,** which is similar to indirect indexed addressing, except the X register is used instead of Y and the offset contained in X is added to the address provided in the instruction to determine the address of the pointer to the data. For example, assume X contains the value 8. The LDA ($10, X) instruction will add the contents of X to $10, producing the result $18. The instruction then uses the 16-bit memory address read from addresses $18-$19 as the target memory address to load into the A register.

Indexed indirect addressing is not relevant to our example summing a sequence of bytes. One example application of this mode is selecting a value from a sequential list of pointers, where each pointer contains the address of a character string. The X register can reference one of the strings as an offset from the beginning of the pointer list. An instruction similar to LDA ($10, X) will load the address of the selected string into A.

The addressing modes available in CISC processor architectures and, to a more limited degree, in RISC processors are intended to support efficient methods for accessing various types of data structures in system memory.

The next section will discuss the categories of instructions implemented in the 6502 architecture and how each instruction makes use of the available addressing modes.

Instruction categories

This section lists the categories of instructions available in the 6502 processor. The purpose of discussing the 6502 here is to introduce the concepts associated with the instruction set of a processor architecture that is much simpler than the modern 32- and 64-bit processors we will examine in later chapters. By the time we get to those processors, the underlying instruction set concepts should be quite familiar to you.

Memory load and store instructions

The 6502 uses load and store instructions to read data values from system memory into processor registers and to write registers out to system memory. In the 6502 architecture, the LDA, LDX, and LDY instructions load the register identified in the instruction with an 8-bit word from system memory. LDA supports all addressing modes available in the 6502, while LDX and LDY each support a more limited subset of addressing modes: immediate, absolute, and absolute indexed.

After each of these instructions finishes executing, the N and Z flags indicate whether the value that was loaded is negative (that is, bit 7 equals 1) and whether the value is zero.

STA, STX, and STY store the register identified in the instruction to memory. Each store instruction supports the same addressing modes as the load instruction for that register, except the store instructions do not support immediate addressing mode. These instructions update the N and Z flags to reflect the value stored.

Register-to-register data transfer instructions

These instructions copy an 8-bit word from one of the A, X, and Y registers to another register. These instructions use **implied addressing mode**, which means the source and destination of each instruction are indicated directly by the instruction opcode.

TAX copies the A register contents to the X register. TAY, TXA, and TYA perform similar operations between the register pairs indicated by the instruction mnemonic. These instructions update the N and Z flags.

Stack instructions

The TXS instruction copies the X register to the stack pointer (S) register. This instruction must be used to initialize the S register during system startup. TSX copies the S register to the X register. TSX updates the N and Z flags. TXS does not affect any flags.

PHA pushes the A register contents onto the stack. PHP pushes the processor flags onto the stack as an 8-bit word. These instructions do not affect the processor flags. Pushing a value onto the stack consists of writing the register to the memory address computed by adding $100 to the S register, then decrementing the S register.

PLA and PLP pop the A register and the flags register from the stack respectively. Popping a value first increments the S register then transfers the value at the location computed by adding $100 to the S register to the target register location.

PLA updates the N and Z flags. PLP sets or clears six of the seven processor flags based on the value popped from the stack. The B (break) flag is only meaningful in a copy of the processor flags register that has been pushed onto the stack by an interrupt or by the PHP instruction. This distinguishes a BRK instruction from a hardware interrupt request. Both the PHP and BRK instructions push the flags register with the B bit (bit 4) set. Hardware interrupts generated via the processor **IRQ (Interrupt Request)** and **NMI (Non-Maskable Interrupt)** pins push the processor flags register with the B bit cleared.

Arithmetic instructions

As we've already discussed, addition and subtraction are performed by the ADC and SBC instructions. The left operand to each instruction is the A register, which is also the destination for the result of the operation. All addressing modes are available for designating the right operand. The Z, C, N, and V flags are updated to reflect the result of the operation.

INC and DEC, respectively, increment or decrement the specified memory location by adding 1 to, or subtracting 1 from, the value at that location. The result is stored at the same memory location. Absolute and absolute indexed addressing modes are supported. These instructions update the N and Z flags based on the result of the operation.

The INX, DEX, INY, and DEY instructions increment or decrement the X or Y register, as indicated by the mnemonic. These instructions update the N and Z flags.

The CMP instruction performs a comparison by subtracting the operand value from the A register. The behavior of CMP is very similar to the instruction sequence SEC followed by SBC. The N, Z, and C flags are set to reflect the result of the subtraction. The differences between CMP and SBC are as follows:

- CMP discards the result of the subtraction (the value in A is unaffected by the CMP instruction).
- CMP does not use decimal mode if the D flag is set.
- CMP does not affect the value of the V flag.
- CMP supports all addressing modes.

The CPX and CPY instructions are similar to CMP except the X or Y register is used as the left operand as indicated in the mnemonic and only absolute and absolute indexed addressing modes are supported for the right operand.

Logical instructions

The AND, EOR, and ORA instructions perform bitwise AND, XOR, and OR operations respectively between the A register and the operand. The result is stored in the A register. The Z and N flags are updated to reflect the result of the operation. All addressing modes are supported.

The ASL instruction shifts the operand one bit left, inserting a zero as the least significant bit. The most significant bit is shifted into the C flag. This is equivalent to multiplying the A register by two and placing the most significant bit of the 9-bit result in C.

Similar to ASL, LSR shifts the operand one bit right, inserting a zero as the most significant bit. The least significant bit is shifted into the C flag. This is equivalent to division by two of an unsigned operand, with the remainder placed in C.

The ROL and ROR instructions shift the A register one bit to the left or right, respectively. The previous value of the C flag is shifted into the bit location vacated by the shift operation. The bit shifted out of A is stored in the C flag.

ASL, LSR , ROL, and ROR support **accumulator addressing mode,** which uses the A register as the operand. This mode is specified by using the special operand value "A," as in ASL A. These four instructions also support absolute and absolute indexed addressing modes.

The BIT instruction performs a bitwise AND between the operand and the A register, and the result is discarded. The Z flag is updated based on the result of this operation. Bits 7 and 6 from the memory location are copied to the N and V flags, respectively. Only absolute addressing mode is supported.

Branching instructions

The JMP instruction loads the operand into the PC register and continues execution from the instruction at that location. The destination is a two-byte absolute address and can be anywhere in the 6502's 16-bit address space.

The BCC and BCS instructions perform conditional branching if the C flag is clear or set, respectively.

The BNE and BEQ instructions perform conditional branching if the Z flag is clear or set, respectively.

The BPL and BMI instructions perform conditional branching if the N flag is clear or set, respectively.

The BVC and BVS instructions perform conditional branching if the V flag is clear or set, respectively.

The conditional branch instructions use **relative addressing mode**, which is a signed 8-bit offset (in the range -128 to +127 bytes) from the address of the instruction following the branch instruction.

Subroutine call and return instructions

The JSR instruction pushes the address of the instruction following the JSR instruction (minus one) onto the stack, then loads the address specified as the 16-bit operand into the PC and continues execution from the instruction at that location.

RTS is used to end a subroutine. The return PC value (minus one) is pulled from the stack and loaded into the PC register. The RTS instruction increments the PC register after pulling it from the stack, before it is used as the address of the next instruction to execute.

Processor flag instructions

The SEC and CLC instructions set and clear the C flag, respectively.

The SED and CLD instructions set and clear the D flag, respectively.

The CLV instruction clears the V flag. There is no instruction that simply sets the V flag.

Interrupt-related instructions

The SEI and CLI instructions set and clear the I flag, respectively. When the I flag is set, maskable interrupts are disabled.

The BRK instruction triggers a non-maskable interrupt. The memory address two bytes after the BRK instruction is pushed onto the stack, followed by the processor flags register. The PC register is loaded with the interrupt service routine address, which is read from memory addresses $FFFE-$FFFF. The interrupt service routine then begins to execute.

The BRK instruction does not alter any register contents (other than the stack pointer) or processor flags. The flags register pushed onto the stack has the B bit set to indicate the interrupt is the result of a BRK instruction.

RTI returns from an interrupt service routine. This instruction restores the processor flags from the stack and restores the PC register. After the processor flags are restored, the B flag is not meaningful and should be ignored.

Interrupt processing and the use of the BRK instruction will be discussed further in the *Interrupt processing* section later.

No operation instruction

The NOP instruction (often referred to as no-op) does nothing except advance the PC register to the following instruction.

NOP instructions are sometimes used as a debugging tool during program development. For example, one or more instructions can be effectively "commented out" by filling the memory addresses for those instructions with $EA bytes. $EA is the hexadecimal value of the 6502 NOP opcode.

Interrupt processing

Processors generally support some form of interrupt handling for responding to service requests from external devices. Conceptually, interrupt handling is similar to a scenario in which you are busy working on a task and your phone rings. After answering the call and perhaps jotting a note for later action ("buy bread"), you resume the task that was interrupted. We humans employ several similar mechanisms, such as doorbells and alarm clocks, which enable us to interrupt lower priority activities and respond to more immediate needs.

IRQ processing

The 6502 integrated circuit has two input signals that allow external components to notify the processor of a need for attention. The first is the interrupt request input, IRQ. IRQ is an active low (that's what the bar over the IRQ characters means) input that generates a processor interrupt when pulled low. Think of this signal as similar to a telephone ringer notifying the processor that a call is coming in.

The 6502 cannot respond instantly to a low signal level on the IRQ input. Before the 6502 can begin to process the interrupt, it must first complete the instruction already in progress. Next, it pushes the return address (the address of the next instruction that would have been executed after the instruction in progress) onto the stack, followed by the processor flags register. Since this interrupt was generated by the IRQ input, the B flag in the processor flags on the stack will be 0.

Unlike the JSR instruction, the return address pushed in response to the IRQ input is the actual address of the next instruction to be executed, rather than the instruction address minus 1. The interrupt return address will not be incremented to generate the return address as occurs during RTS instruction execution.

In the next stage of interrupt processing, the processor loads the address of the IRQ handler routine from memory addresses $FFFE-$FFFF into the PC register. The 6502 then begins executing the interrupt handler code at that address.

When the interrupt handler is finished, it executes the RTI instruction. RTI pops the processor flags and the PC register values from the stack and resumes execution at the instruction following the instruction that was in progress when the IRQ input was driven low.

The IRQ input is a **maskable interrupt**, meaning it is possible to perform the equivalent of putting the telephone ringer on mute. When IRQ processing begins, the 6502 automatically sets the I flag, which masks (disables) the IRQ input until the I flag is cleared.

The I flag will be cleared by the RTI instruction because the I flag could not have been set when the processor began responding to the IRQ. The I flag can also be cleared by the CLI instruction, which means it is possible to enable IRQ interrupts while processing an IRQ interrupt. An interrupt handled while processing another interrupt is referred to as a **nested interrupt**.

The IRQ input is level-sensitive, which means any time the IRQ input is low and the I flag is cleared, the processor will initiate the interrupt processing sequence. The consequence of this is that, at the completion of processing an interrupt, the 6502's interactions with the interrupt source must ensure the IRQ input is no longer low. If IRQ remains low when the RTI instruction is executed, the 6502 will immediately begin the interrupt handling process all over again.

Interrupts initiated via the IRQ input handle most routine interactions between the 6502 and peripheral devices. For example, the keyboard is an interrupt source in most computers. Each keypress generates an IRQ interrupt. During keyboard interrupt processing, the 6502 reads the identification of the key from the keyboard interface and stores it into a queue for later processing by the currently active application. The IRQ handler code does not need to know anything about what the key press information will be used for; it just saves the data for later use.

NMI processing

The second interrupt input to the 6502 is the **non-maskable interrupt**, NMI. As its name implies, the NMI input is not masked by the I flag. NMI is an edge-sensitive input that triggers on the falling edge of the signal.

The processing of $\overline{\text{NMI}}$ interrupts is similar to the processing of $\overline{\text{IRQ}}$ interrupts, except the address of the interrupt handler routine is loaded from memory addresses $FFFA-$FFFB and the I flag has no effect on this type of interrupt.

Because $\overline{\text{NMI}}$ is non-maskable, it can be triggered at any time, including when the 6502 is in the middle of handling an $\overline{\text{IRQ}}$ interrupt, or even while handling an earlier $\overline{\text{NMI}}$ interrupt.

The $\overline{\text{NMI}}$ input is normally reserved for very high priority conditions that cannot be delayed or missed. One possible use of $\overline{\text{NMI}}$ interrupts is to trigger the incrementing of a real-time clock at regular intervals.

This $\overline{\text{NMI}}$ handler code increments a 32-bit clock counter located at addresses $10-$13 each time the interrupt occurs:

```
; Increment a 32-bit clock counter at each /NMI interrupt
NMI_HANDLER:
INC $10
BNE NMI_DONE
INC $11
BNE NMI_DONE
INC $12
BNE NMI_DONE
INC $13
NMI_DONE:
RTI
```

Notice that when referring to hardware signals in program source code, a leading forward slash can be used to indicate active low. $\overline{\text{NMI}}$ is represented as /NMI in the preceding code comment.

BRK instruction processing

The BRK instruction triggers processing similar to an $\overline{\text{IRQ}}$ interrupt. Because BRK is an instruction, there is no need to wait for the completion of an instruction in progress before initiating interrupt processing. During BRK execution, the return address (the address of the BRK instruction plus 2) and the processor flags are pushed onto the stack, similar to the response to a low level on the $\overline{\text{IRQ}}$ input. Note that by adding 2 to the BRK instruction address, the return address is not pointed to the byte after BRK, but to the second byte after it.

The BRK instruction is non-maskable: the state of the I flag does not affect the execution of the BRK instruction.

The BRK handler address is the same as the $\overline{\text{IRQ}}$ handler, which is located at memory addresses $FFFE-$FFFF. Since the BRK instruction and $\overline{\text{IRQ}}$ share the same handler, the B flag must be consulted to identify the interrupt source during processing. The B flag in the processor flags pushed onto the stack (note that this is *not* the B flag in the processor flags (P) register) will be set in response to a BRK instruction and it will be clear during the processing of an $\overline{\text{IRQ}}$ interrupt.

The BRK instruction finds little use in most 6502 applications. A traditional usage for this instruction is to set breakpoints when debugging a program. By temporarily replacing the opcode byte at the desired break location with a BRK instruction, it is possible for the debugging program (often called a **monitor** in smaller computer systems) to gain control and allow the user to display and modify register contents and memory contents and then resume execution.

This code example implements a minimal $\overline{\text{IRQ}}$ handler that differentiates between $\overline{\text{IRQ}}$ interrupts and BRK instructions. It uses memory address $14 as a temporary storage location dedicated for use by this routine:

```
; Handle /IRQ interrupts and BRK instructions
IRQ_BRK_HANDLER:
; Save the A register
STA $14

; Retrieve the processor flags from the stack into A
PLA
PHA

; Check if the B bit is set in the flags on the stack
AND $10 ; $10 selects the B bit

; If the result is nonzero, B was set: Handle the BRK
BNE BRK_INSTR

; B was not set: Handle the /IRQ here
; ...

JMP IRQ_DONE
```

```
BRK_INSTR:
; Handle the BRK instruction here
; ...

IRQ_DONE:
; Restore the A register and return
LDA $14
RTI
```

This example showed how to differentiate between interrupts initiated by the processor IRQ input and those resulting from the BRK instruction in the 6502 architecture. In more sophisticated processors, including those we will discuss in later chapters, the architectures generally implement unique interrupt vectors (interrupt service routine starting addresses) for each interrupt source. These architectures contain extensive support for debugging actions such as setting breakpoints at specified instruction locations.

This section introduced the categories of instructions in the 6502 architecture and provided a brief description of each instruction within those categories. Although the 6502 is much simpler than modern 32- and 64-bit processors, this discussion introduced the most common categories of instructions and addressing modes used in even the most sophisticated modern processors, including instructions supporting the universal concept of interrupt processing.

The next section will present the fundamentals of I/O processing, which performs data transfer between the processor and peripheral devices.

Input/output operations

The goal of the I/O portion of a processor architecture is to efficiently transfer data between external peripheral devices and system memory. Input operations transfer data from the external world into memory and output operations send data from memory to an outside destination.

The format of the data on the external side of the I/O interface varies widely. Here are some examples of the external representations of computer I/O data:

- Signals on a video cable connected to a monitor
- Voltage fluctuations on the wires in an Ethernet cable
- Magnetic patterns on the surface of a disk
- Sound waves produced by computer speakers

Regardless of the form the data takes when it is outside the computer, the connection of any I/O device with the processor must comply with the processor's I/O architecture, and the I/O device must be compatible with any other I/O devices that happen to be present in the computer system.

The processor uses the instruction categories, addressing modes, and interrupt processing methods described earlier in this chapter for interactions with I/O devices. The difference here is that instead of reading and writing system memory, the instructions read from and write to locations that communicate with an I/O device.

Memory-mapped I/O and **port-mapped I/O** are the two main approaches employed in modern processors to access I/O devices. Memory-mapped I/O dedicates portions of the system address space to I/O devices. The processor accesses peripheral devices at predefined addresses using the same instructions and addressing modes it uses to read and write system memory. The 6502 uses memory-mapped I/O to communicate with its peripherals.

Processors using port-mapped I/O implement a separate category of instructions for performing I/O operations. Port-mapped I/O devices have a dedicated address space independent of system memory. I/O devices are assigned **port numbers** as addresses. The x86 architecture employs port-mapped I/O.

One drawback of memory-mapped I/O is the need to dedicate part of the system address space to I/O devices, which reduces the maximum amount of memory that can be installed in the computer system. A drawback of port-mapped I/O is the requirement for the processor to implement additional instructions to perform the I/O operations.

Some implementations of port-mapped I/O provide additional hardware signals to indicate when an I/O device is being addressed as opposed to system memory. Using this signal as a selector (essentially another address bit), the same address lines can then be used for accessing memory and I/O devices. Alternatively, some higher-end processors implement a completely separate bus for performing port-mapped I/O operations. This architecture allows I/O and memory access operations to proceed simultaneously.

In the simplest approach to I/O, the processor handles all steps in an I/O operation itself, using instructions to transfer data between memory and the I/O device. More complex processor architectures provide hardware features to accelerate repetitive I/O operations. We will now discuss three methods of performing I/O with varying degrees of processor involvement: programmed I/O, interrupt-driven I/O, and direct memory access.

Programmed I/O

Programmed I/O simply means the processor performs every step of the I/O data transfer operation itself using program instructions. Consider a keyboard that presents itself to the processor as two memory-mapped one-byte addresses in the processor's I/O address region. One of these bytes contains status information, specifically a bit indicating when a key has been pressed. The second byte contains the value of the key that was pressed.

Each time a key is pressed, the *key available* status bit is set. When using programmed I/O, the processor must periodically read the keyboard status register to see whether a key has been pressed. If the status bit indicates a key has been pressed, the processor reads the keyboard data register, which turns off the key available status bit until the next keypress occurs.

If the keyboard data register can only hold one key at a time, this keyboard status checking operation must occur frequently enough that no key presses get lost, even when a very fast typist is at the keyboard. As a result, the processor must spend a significant amount of its time checking to see whether a key has been pressed. Most of these checks will turn out to be fruitless whenever fast typing is not taking place.

It should be clear that programmed I/O is not a very efficient method for general use. It is similar in concept to checking your phone every few seconds to see whether someone is calling you.

The use of programmed I/O makes sense in some situations. For example, the one-time configuration of a peripheral device during system startup is a reasonable use of this technique.

Interrupt-driven I/O

An I/O device can use interrupts to notify the processor when action is needed. In the case of the simple keyboard interface, instead of merely setting a bit in a status register, the peripheral could pull the 6502's $\overline{\text{IRQ}}$ line low to initiate an interrupt each time a key is pressed. This allows the processor to go about its business without checking for keypresses. The processor will only focus attention on the keyboard interface when there is work to be done, as indicated by the interrupt. Using interrupts to trigger I/O operations is analogous to adding a ringer to the phone that we had to check for incoming calls every few seconds when using programmed I/O.

The 6502 has a single maskable interrupt input signal ($\overline{\text{IRQ}}$) available for I/O operations. Computer systems usually contain multiple sources of I/O interrupts. This makes the task of servicing interrupts a bit more complicated in the 6502 because the processor must first identify which peripheral initiated the interrupt before it can begin transferring data. The interrupt service routine must poll each interrupt-capable device to locate the interrupt source. In the case of the keyboard interface, this polling operation consists of reading the keyboard status register to determine whether the bit is set, indicating a keypress occurred. Once the processor has identified the device responsible for the interrupt, it branches to code that interacts with the device to complete the requested I/O task. In the case of the keyboard interface, this processing performs the steps of reading the keyboard data register and clearing the key available status bit, which deactivates the $\overline{\text{IRQ}}$ input signal.

Interrupts from external devices are asynchronous events, meaning they can occur at any time. Computer system design must include careful consideration of the possibility that interrupts may be generated at potentially unexpected times such as during system startup or while processing other interrupts. Interrupts from multiple devices may occur simultaneously, or nearly simultaneously, and in random order. Interrupt handling hardware circuitry and interrupt servicing code must ensure that all interrupts are detected and processed regardless of any timing peculiarities.

Interrupt-driven I/O eliminates the processor's need to periodically check I/O devices to see whether action is needed. However, handling an interrupt may consume significant processor time if it involves transferring a large block of data, such as when reading from or writing to a disk drive. The next I/O method we will discuss removes the need for the processor to perform the work of transferring large blocks of data.

Direct memory access

Direct Memory Access (DMA) permits peripheral device I/O operations to access system memory independent of the processor. When using DMA to transfer a block of data, the processor sets up the operation by configuring a DMA controller with the starting address of the data block to be transferred, the block length, and the destination address. After initiating the DMA, the processor is free to continue other work. At the completion of the operation, the DMA controller generates an interrupt to inform the processor the transfer is complete.

Within a computer system, a DMA controller may be implemented as a separate integrated circuit managed by the processor, or a processor architecture may contain one or more integrated DMA controllers.

I/O devices that move substantial amounts of data, such as disk drives, sound cards, graphics cards, and network interfaces, generally rely on DMA to efficiently transfer data into and out of system memory. DMA is also useful for transferring blocks of data within system memory.

The 6502 architecture does not support DMA operations, but the original IBM PC included a DMA controller, and almost every 32- bit and 64-bit processor architecture provides extensive support for DMA operations.

DMA is one of many techniques that improve computer system performance by accelerating repetitive operations. DMA will be discussed further in later chapters.

Summary

This chapter described the primary functional units of a simple processor, consisting of the control unit, the ALU, and the registers. An overview of processor instructions and addressing modes followed. The instruction categories implemented by the 6502 processor were introduced with the intent of demonstrating the variety and utility of instructions available in a simple processor architecture.

The concepts involved in interrupt processing were introduced and demonstrated in the context of the 6502 architecture. This chapter concluded with an overview of the most common architectural approaches to input/output operations (memory-mapped I/O and port-mapped I/O) and the basic modes of performing I/O in a computer system (programmed I/O, interrupt-driven I/O, and DMA).

Having completed this chapter, you should now possess a conceptual understanding of processor functional units, instruction processing, interrupt handling, and input/output operations. This information forms the basis for the next chapter, which covers architecture at the computer system level.

Exercises

1. Consider the addition of two signed 8-bit numbers (that is, numbers in the range -128 to +127) where one operand is positive and the other is negative. Is there any pair of 8-bit numbers of different signs that, when added together, will exceed the range -128 to +127? This would constitute a signed overflow. Note: We're only looking at addition here because, as we've seen, subtraction in the 6502 architecture is the same as addition with the right operand's bits inverted.

2. If the answer to *Exercise 1* is "no," this implies the only way to create a signed overflow is to add two numbers of the same sign. If an overflow occurs, what can you say about the result of performing XOR between the most significant bit of each operand with the most significant bit of the result? In other words, what will be the result of the expressions, left(7) XOR result(7) and right(7) XOR result(7)? In these expressions, (7) indicates bit 7, the most significant bit.

3. Review the VHDL listing in the *Arithmetic logic unit* section in this chapter and determine whether the logic for setting or clearing the V flag is correct for addition and subtraction operations. Check the results of adding 126+1, 127+1, -127+(-1), and -128+(-1).

4. When transferring blocks of data over an error-prone transmission medium, it is common to use a **checksum** to determine whether any data bits were lost or corrupted during transmission. The checksum is typically appended to the transferred data record. One checksum algorithm uses these steps:

    a. Add all of the bytes in the data record together, retaining only the lowest 8 bits of the sum.

    b. The checksum is the two's complement of the 8-bit sum.

    c. Append the checksum byte to the data record.

    After receiving a data block with the appended checksum, the processor can determine whether the checksum is valid by simply adding all of the bytes in the record, including the checksum, together. The checksum is valid if the lowest 8 bits of the sum are zero. Implement this checksum algorithm using 6502 assembly language. The data bytes begin at the memory location stored in addresses $10-$11 and the number of bytes (including the checksum byte) is provided as an input in the X register. Set the A register to 1 if the checksum is valid, and to 0 if it is invalid.

5. Make the checksum validation code from *Exercise 4* into a labeled subroutine that can be called with a JSR instruction and that ends with an RTS instruction.

6. Write and execute a set of tests to verify the correct operation of the checksum testing subroutine you implemented in *Exercises 4-5*. What is the shortest block of data your code can perform checksum validation upon? What is the longest block?

4

Computer System Components

This chapter begins with an introduction to the **metal-oxide-semiconductor (MOS)** transistor, used extensively in memory circuits and in most other modern digital devices. We then examine the design of computer memory circuits based on MOS transistors and their interface to the processor. We'll look at modern computer input/output interfaces, with a focus on the use of high-speed serial communication within the computer's case, as well as over cable connections to external peripherals. The functional requirements of system I/O devices including the graphics display, network interface, keyboard, and mouse will be discussed. The chapter ends with a descriptive example of the specifications for a modern computer motherboard.

After completing this chapter, you will have a solid understanding of the hardware components of modern computer systems, from the technical specifications down to the circuit level. You will have learned how system memory is implemented, including the basics of caching. You will understand the mechanisms of efficient I/O operations, and how USB is used to connect the keyboard, mouse, and other I/O devices. You will understand the computer's network interface and will have become familiar with several examples of modern computer system architectures.

The following topics will be covered in this chapter:

- Memory subsystem

- Introducing the MOSFET

- Constructing DRAM circuits with MOSFETs

- Input/output subsystem

- Graphics display interfaces

- Network interface

- Keyboard and mouse

- Modern computer system specifications

Technical requirements

Files for this chapter, including answers to the exercises, are available at https://github.com/PacktPublishing/Modern-Computer-Architecture-and-Organization.

Memory subsystem

The Babbage Analytical Engine's design employed a collection of axes, each holding 40 decimal digit wheels, as the mechanism for storing data during computations. Reading data from an axis was a destructive operation, resulting in zeros on all of an axis's wheels after the read had completed.

From the 1950s to the 1970s, the preferred technology for digital computer memory was the magnetic core. One bit of core memory is stored in a small toroidal (donut-shaped) ceramic magnet. The cores making up a memory array are arranged in a rectangular grid with horizontal and vertical connecting wires. Writing to a bit location involves producing enough current in the wires connected to the bit location to flip the polarity of the core's magnetic field. A 0 bit might be defined as clockwise magnetic flux circulation within the core and a 1 bit as counterclockwise flux circulation.

Reading a bit from core memory consists of attempting to set the bit to the 0 polarity and observing the response. If the selected core already contains a 0 bit, there will be no response. If the core holds a 1, a detectable voltage pulse occurs as the polarity changes. As in the Analytical Engine, a core memory read operation is destructive. After reading a word of memory, an immediate write must be performed to restore the state of the bits.

Magnetic core memory is non-volatile: the contents continue to be retained indefinitely without power. It also has characteristics that make it valuable in applications such as spacecraft where radiation tolerance is important. The Space Shuttle computers employed core memory into the late 1980s.

Modern consumer and business computer systems use MOSFET-based DRAM circuits almost exclusively for main system memory. The next section describes the features of the MOSFET.

Introducing the MOSFET

Chapter 2, Digital Logic, introduced the NPN transistor, a type of **bipolar junction transistor (BJT)**. The NPN transistor is called bipolar because it relies on both positive and negative charge carriers to function.

In semiconductors, electrons serve as the negative charge carriers. There are no physical particles with positive charge involved in a semiconductor operation; rather, the absence of a normally present electron in an atom exhibits the same properties as a positively charged particle. These missing electrons are referred to as **holes**. Holes function as the positive charge carriers in bipolar junction transistors.

The concept of holes is so fundamental to semiconductor operation that William Shockley, one of the inventors of the transistor, wrote a book entitled *Electrons and Holes in Semiconductors*, published in 1950. We'll next examine the behavior of positive and negative charge carriers in unipolar transistors.

As an alternative to the BJT transistor structure, the **unipolar transistor** relies on only one of the two types of charge carriers. The **metal-oxide-semiconductor field-effect transistor (MOSFET)** is a unipolar transistor suitable for use as a digital switching element. Like the NPN transistor, the MOSFET is a three-terminal device employing a control input that turns the flow of current across the other two terminals on and off. The following figure is the schematic representation of an n-channel enhancement mode MOSFET:

Figure 4.1: N-channel enhancement mode MOSFET

For our purposes, the n-channel enhancement mode MOSFET functions as a switch: When the gate terminal voltage is low (below a threshold voltage), there is very high resistance between the drain and source terminals. When the gate terminal voltage is high (above a threshold voltage), there is very low resistance between those terminals. The "n" in n-channel refers to a channel in the silicon doped to produce an increased number of electrons (negative charge carriers).

This behavior is similar to the operation of the NPN transistor discussed in *Chapter 2, Digital Logic*. There is, however, a key difference: the MOSFET is a voltage-controlled device, while the NPN transistor is a current-controlled device. The base terminal of the NPN transistor requires a small but steady current to activate the device as a switch, allowing current to flow between the emitter and collector terminals. The MOSFET, on the other hand, requires only a voltage level above a threshold on the gate terminal to switch the current flow on between the drain and source terminals. The gate input requires almost no current flow to keep the switch open. Because of this, a MOSFET consumes significantly less power than an NPN transistor performing the equivalent digital function.

Mohamed Atalla and Dawon Kahng invented the MOSFET at Bell Telephone Laboratories in 1959. It was not until the early 1970s that production processes had matured sufficiently to support the reliable production of MOS integrated circuits. Since then, the MOSFET has been by far the most common type of transistor used in integrated circuits. As of 2018, it is estimated that 13 sextillion (a **sextillion** is one followed by 21 zeros) transistors had been manufactured, 99.9 percent of which were MOS transistors. The MOSFET is the most frequently manufactured device in human history.

The p-channel enhancement mode MOSFET is similar to the n-channel enhancement mode MOSFET, except it exhibits the opposite response to the gate terminal: a low voltage on the gate allows current to flow between the drain and source, while a high voltage on the gate inhibits current between the drain and source. The "p" in p-channel refers to channel doping that increases the number of holes (positive charge carriers). The following figure is the schematic diagram of a p-channel enhancement mode MOSFET:

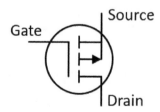

Figure 4.2: P-channel enhancement mode MOSFET

In the schematic representations of both the n-channel and p-channel MOSFETs, the source terminal is connected to the center of the three internal connections. The directional arrow on this connection points toward the gate for an n-channel MOSFET and away from the gate for a p-channel MOSFET.

MOS transistors are most commonly employed in n-channel and p-channel pairs to perform logic functions. A device built from these pairs of MOS transistors is called a **complementary MOS (CMOS)** integrated circuit. Except when switching is taking place, CMOS circuits consume almost no power because the gate input requires essentially no current. Chih-Tang Sah and Frank Wanlass of Fairchild Semiconductor developed the CMOS configuration in 1963.

The following diagram presents a NOT gate circuit with the NPN transistor replaced by a complementary pair of MOSFETs:

Figure 4.3: CMOS NOT gate circuit

When the *Input* signal is low (near 0V), the lower n-channel MOSFET is switched off and the upper p-channel MOSFET is switched on. This connects the *Output* to the positive side of the voltage source, raising the *Output* signal to nearly 5V. When *Input* is high, the upper MOSFET is switched off and the lower MOSFET is switched on, pulling the *Output* to nearly 0V. The *Output* signal is always the inverse of the *Input* signal, which is the definition of NOT gate behavior.

Today, virtually all high-density digital integrated circuits are based on CMOS technology. In addition to performing logic functions, the MOSFET is a key component of modern random-access memory circuit designs. The next section discusses the use of the MOSFET in memory circuits.

Constructing DRAM circuits with MOSFETs

A single bit in a standard **dynamic random-access memory (DRAM)** integrated circuit is composed of two circuit elements: a MOSFET and a capacitor. The following section provides a brief introduction to the electrical characteristics of capacitors.

The capacitor

A **capacitor** is a two-terminal passive circuit element capable of storing energy. Energy enters and leaves a capacitor as electrical current. The voltage across the capacitor terminals is proportional to the quantity of electrical energy contained in the capacitor.

To continue the hydraulic system analogy introduced in *Chapter 2, Digital Logic,* think of a capacitor as a balloon attached to the side of the pipe leading to a water tap. Water pressure in the pipe causes the balloon to inflate, filling it with some of the water from the pipe. Let's assume this is a strong balloon, and that as it inflates, the balloon stretches, increasing the pressure inside the balloon. The balloon inflates until the pressure in the balloon equals the pressure in the pipe, and then stops filling.

If you open the tap at the end of the pipe all the way, the release of water causes the pressure in the pipe to decrease. Some of the water in the balloon will flow back into the pipe, until the balloon pressure again equals the pipe pressure.

Hydraulic devices called **water hammer arrestors** function in exactly this manner to solve the problem of pipes that make banging noises when water taps are turned on and off. A water hammer arrestor uses balloon-stretching-like behavior to smooth out the abrupt changes in water pressure that result from taps opening and closing.

The quantity of electrical energy contained in a capacitor is analogous to the amount of water in the balloon. The voltage across the capacitor is analogous to the pressure inside the balloon exerted by stretching.

An electrical capacitor can be constructed from two parallel metal plates separated by an insulating material, such as air. One terminal is connected to each of the plates. The ratio of the quantity of stored electrical energy to the voltage across the capacitor is called **capacitance**, and it depends on the size of the parallel plates, the distance separating them, and the type of material used as the insulator between them. The capacitance of a capacitor is analogous to the size of the balloon in the hydraulic example. A capacitor with a larger capacitance corresponds to a larger balloon. A large balloon requires more water to fill to a given pressure than a smaller balloon. The schematic symbol for a capacitor is shown here:

Figure 4.4: Capacitor schematic symbol

The two horizontal lines with space between them represent the metal plate capacitor architecture described in the preceding section. The unit of capacitance is the **farad**, named after the English scientist Michael Faraday.

The DRAM bit cell

A DRAM bit cell is a readable and writeable storage location for a single bit of data. The DRAM modules used in modern computers contain billions of these bit cells. A single bit in a DRAM circuit consists of a MOSFET and a capacitor, arranged as follows:

Figure 4.5: DRAM bit cell circuit

In this figure, the symbol with three horizontal lines at the bottom right is the ground symbol, which is an alternative to the 0V designation used in earlier figures such as *Figure 4.3*.

This single-bit cell must be replicated in a rectangular grid to form a complete DRAM memory bank. The following figure shows the configuration of a 16-bit DRAM bank consisting of 4 words with 4 bits in each word:

Figure 4.6: DRAM memory bank organization

Of course, real DRAM banks contain a much larger number of bits than the simple circuit in this diagram. Typical DRAM devices have a word size of 8 bits (rather than the four bits labeled B0-B3 in the figure). This means each DRAM chip can store or retrieve 8 bits in parallel.

The number of instances of bit cells along a wordline in an actual DRAM bank array is an integer multiple of the device word size. The large DRAM modules used in personal computers contain many words along each wordline. A DRAM chip implemented with 8-bit words and 1,024 words per row contains 8,192 bits per row, with all of the MOSFET gate terminals along the row controlled by a single wordline signal. These devices include additional multiplexer logic to select the specific word the processor is requesting from the numerous words in the row selected by the active wordline.

The vertical dimension of the DRAM bank consists of replicated copies of cell rows with one wordline controlling each row. The wordline connects all the bit cells horizontally while the bitline signals connect the cells in all of the rows vertically.

The state of each memory bit is stored in the cell's capacitor. A low voltage on the capacitor represents a 0 bit while a high voltage represents a 1 bit. In the context of real-world DRAM devices, low voltage is near 0V and high is typically near 1.2V.

The wordline for each row is held low most of the time. This keeps the MOSFET turned off, maintaining the capacitor state. When it is time to read a word (actually, an entire row) of DRAM memory, addressing circuitry selects the appropriate wordline and drives it high while keeping all the other wordlines in the bank low. This turns on the MOSFET in each bit cell along the active wordline, allowing the cell capacitors to drive their voltages onto the connected bitlines. Bitlines for cells at the 1 (high) voltage level will have higher voltages than cells at the 0 (low) voltage level. The bitline voltages are sensed by circuitry in the DRAM device and latched into the chip's output register.

Writing to a DRAM word begins by setting the selected wordline high in the same manner as reading a word. Instead of sensing the voltage on the bitlines, the DRAM device drives each bitline with the voltage to be written to each cell, either 0V or 1.2V, depending on whether the data bit is a 0 or a 1. As with filling or emptying a balloon, it takes a bit of time for each capacitor to charge or discharge to the voltage presented on its bitline. After this delay has transpired, the wordline is driven low to turn the MOSFETs off and lock the capacitors at their new charge levels.

DRAM circuit technology is complicated by the fact that capacitors leak. After charging a capacitor to a non-zero voltage, the charge will bleed off over time, reducing the quantity of stored charge and the voltage across the capacitor. Because of this, the contents of each cell must be refreshed periodically.

A refresh operation consists of reading each cell value and writing it back to the cell. This recharges the capacitor to its "full" voltage level, if it is a 1, or drives it to near 0V if it is a 0. A typical refresh interval for modern DRAM devices is 64 ms. DRAM refresh proceeds continuously, row by row, in the background during system operation and synchronizes with processor access to memory to avoid conflicts.

While the need for periodic refreshing significantly complicates the design of systems using DRAM devices, the benefit of storing a bit with just one transistor and one capacitor is so immense that DRAM has supplanted all alternatives as the preferred technology for main memory in consumer and business computer systems.

DDR4 SDRAM

Intel produced the first commercial DRAM integrated circuit in 1970. The Intel 1103 held 1,024 bits of data with a word size of 1 bit. The 1103 had to be refreshed every 2 ms. By the early 1970s, MOS semiconductor DRAM overtook magnetic core memory as the preferred memory technology in computer systems. DRAM is volatile, meaning when power is removed, the charge in the bit cell capacitors dissipates and the data content is lost. The current generation of DRAM technology in widespread use is DDR4 SDRAM.

Modern personal computers and personal devices such as smartphones generally contain multiple **gigabytes (GB)** of RAM. One GB is 2^{30} bytes, equivalent to 1,073,741,824 (just over one billion) bytes. As the name implies, random access memory allows the processor to read or write any memory location within the RAM address space in a single operation. As of 2019, a high-end memory module available for use in laptop computers contains 32 GB of DRAM distributed across 16 integrated circuits. Each DRAM chip in this module contains 2 gigawords, with a word length of 8 bits.

As of 2019, the leading memory module standard is DDR4 SDRAM, an evolutionary optimization of DRAM interface technologies built upon the DDR1, DDR2, and DDR3 generations. A DDR4 memory module is packaged as a **dual inline memory module (DIMM)**. A DIMM has electrical contacts on both sides of the circuit board edge (hence the term *dual* in the name), providing connectivity to the DIMM socket in the motherboard. A standard DDR4 DIMM has 268 pins. A smaller module format called the **small outline DIMM (SODIMM)** is available for systems such as laptops where space is at a premium. A DDR4 SODIMM has 260 pins. Because of the reduced number of pins, SODIMM modules lack features that some DIMMs support, such as the ability to detect and correct bit errors in data retrieved from the device.

The term **double data rate DDR** refers to the transfer timing characteristics between a memory module and the processor memory controller. The original **single data rate (SDR)** DRAM performed one data transfer per memory clock cycle. DDR memory devices perform two transfers per clock cycle: one on the clock rising edge and one on the falling edge. The number following "DDR" identifies the generation of DDR technology. DDR4, therefore, is the fourth generation of the DDR standard. The term **synchronous DRAM (SDRAM)** indicates the DRAM circuitry is synchronized with the processor memory controller through a shared clock signal.

DDR4 memory modules are nominally powered by 1.2V and use a 2.5V auxiliary voltage input to provide a "boost" for the wordline signal. As a representative example, a particular DDR4 module can perform up to 3.2 billion data transfers per second, double the memory clock speed of 1600 MHz. At 8 bytes per transfer, this DDR4 device can move 25.6 GB per second. DDR4 modules are available in a variety of clock speeds, memory sizes, and price points.

Although real-world DRAM modules implement rectangular banks of single-bit cells as described in the previous section, the internal architecture of a DDR4 device is somewhat more complex. A DRAM integrated circuit generally contains multiple banks. The addressing logic selects the bank containing the desired memory location before performing a read or write operation. In DDR4 modules, banks are further arranged into **bank groups**, necessitating additional addressing logic to choose the correct group. A DDR4 device contains four bank groups, each with four banks. The reason for partitioning the DDR4 memory module architecture into multiple bank groups is to maximize data transfer speed by enabling multiple simultaneous, overlapped memory access operations to proceed in parallel. This allows data transfer between processor and RAM to flow at peak speed while minimizing the need to wait for each internal DRAM bank access operation to complete.

In addition to specifying the correct address location within a DDR4 memory module, the system must provide a command via interface signals to indicate the action to be taken, specifically, whether to read from, write to, or refresh the selected row.

The DDR4 SDRAM standard, available for purchase from the Joint Electron Device Engineering Council (JEDEC) at `https://www.jedec.org/standards-documents/docs/jesd79-4a`, provides the detailed definition of the DDR4 memory interface to host computer systems. This standard contains all the information needed to design memory modules compatible with any computer system supporting DDR4.

Historically, each numerical generation of the DDR SDRAM standards has been incompatible with previous generations. A motherboard built for DDR4 memory modules will only work with DDR4 modules. The slot for each DDR generation is constructed in such a way that it is not possible to insert an incorrect module. For example, a DDR3 DRAM module will not fit into a DDR4 slot.

As memory technologies evolve, the primary improvements in each new generation are increased data transfer rate and greater memory density. To assist in achieving these goals, power supply voltages have decreased in later generations, reducing system power consumption and enabling denser memory circuitry without excessive heating.

Most modern processors view system memory as a linear array of sequential addresses. In less sophisticated processor architectures, such as the 6502, the processor directly addresses RAM chips using addresses provided in instructions. Because of the complexity of the control signals and bank management logic in DDR4 SDRAM devices, modern computer systems must provide a memory controller to translate each linear processor address into command and addressing signals selecting the appropriate DDR4 module (in a system with multiple memory modules), bank group, bank, and row/column location within the selected bank. The memory controller is a sequential logic device that manages the details of communication between the processor and DRAM memory modules. To achieve peak system performance, the memory controller must intelligently exploit the capability for overlapped operations provided by DDR4 memory modules.

Sophisticated modern processors generally integrate the memory controller function into the processor integrated circuit itself. It is also possible to design a system with a separate memory controller that sits between the processor and RAM.

A memory controller interface may contain multiple channels, where each channel is a separate communication path between the processor and one or more memory modules. The benefit of providing multiple channels in a memory architecture is that it is possible to perform memory accesses over each channel in parallel.

A system containing multiple memory channels does not achieve an automatic increase in memory access speed, however. System software must actively manage the assignment of memory regions to each application or system process to balance memory usage access across channels. If the operating system were to simply assign processes to physical memory regions sequentially, filling one memory module first then moving to the next, there would be no benefit from multi-channel memory when all processes are forced to use the same memory channel.

> **DDR5**
>
> The next-generation DDR5 standard is in development and is scheduled for release in 2020. DDR5 is planned to double the bandwidth of DDR4 while further reducing power consumption by operating at 1.1V.

Graphics DDR

Graphics DDR (GDDR) is a DDR memory technology optimized for use as video RAM in graphics cards. GDDR has a wider memory bus to support the high-throughput requirements of video display. Standard DDR memory, on the other hand, is optimized to provide minimum latency access to data. Note that the generation numbers for GDDR and DDR are not aligned. As of 2019, GDDR5 modules have been available for several years, while the DDR5 standard remains in development.

Prefetching

One DRAM performance attribute that improves very little from one generation to the next is the speed of reading from or writing to an individual bit location in DRAM. To achieve an increase in the average data transfer rate into and out of DRAM modules, the devices must employ other techniques to improve performance. One technique for achieving faster average data transfer speeds is prefetching.

The idea behind **prefetching** is to exploit the fact that whenever a particular memory location is being accessed by a processor, it is likely that access will soon be needed to a location close to the first location. Prefetching consists of reading a larger block of memory than the single location a processor instruction references and passing the entire block from the DRAM device to the processor. In the context of a DDR4 memory module, the block size is normally 64 bytes.

The DDR4 module can read 64 bytes quickly because it accesses all 512 bits of those 64 bytes simultaneously. In other words, the DDR4 module reads an integer multiple of 512 bitlines from the cells selected by a wordline. The bits of the selected row are read simultaneously, then pass through a multiplexer to select the desired 512 bits from the perhaps 8,192 bits in the entire row, which are then latched into an output register. The latched bits transfer from the DRAM module to the processor using DDR clocking. With the effective use of multiple bank groups, multiple reads of memory and transfers of the resulting data can overlap in time and ensure the data moves between the memory module and the processor at the highest rate the interface can support.

Upon receiving the 64-byte block, the processor stores the data in internal cache memory and selects the specific data element (perhaps as small as one byte) from the block requested by the executing instruction. If a subsequent instruction accesses different data contained in the same block, the processor only needs to consult its local cache, resulting in much faster execution than the instruction that originally retrieved the data block from DRAM.

In addition to interacting with main memory, the processor must communicate with the outside world through input and output devices. The next section discusses the implementation of I/O interfaces in modern computer systems.

I/O subsystem

Chapter 3, Processor Elements, introduced two broad categories of I/O architecture: memory-mapped I/O and port-mapped I/O. The pros and cons of each of these approaches were significant in the early days of PCs when the number of physical address lines limited the total processor memory space to a 1 MB range. Modern processor architectures are capable of addressing a far larger memory range, typically in the tens of gigabytes. A consequence of this address space expansion is the ready availability of address regions for use in I/O interfaces. Modern 32-bit and 64-bit general-purpose processors employ memory-mapped I/O for most of their interface requirements.

Sophisticated modern processors usually implement a memory controller within the processor chip, interfacing directly with DDR memory modules. Most other I/O performed by these processors is offloaded to one or more external integrated circuits, typically referred to as a **chipset**. The term chipset is commonly used even when only one chip is needed to implement the I/O functions.

The chipset provides interfaces to a wide range of peripherals, such as graphics cards, disk drives, network interface, the keyboard, the mouse, and many others via USB. Most of these interfaces are implemented using one form or another of a serial bus. The following sections introduce the most common I/O technologies used in modern computers.

Parallel and serial data buses

A parallel data bus communicates multiple data bits simultaneously across separate conductors between two or more communication endpoints. Early PCs employed parallel buses for such functions as connecting a printer to the computer. Over time, several limitations of parallel buses became evident:

- Depending how many bits the bus supports, a parallel bus connection may need a lot of wires, which means cables are more expensive, and there is a greater possibility of problems when cable wires break, or connectors have dirty contacts.

- As computer system developers made efforts to increase performance (and thereby gain a competitive edge), another limitation of parallel buses became significant: even though the device transmitting a data word on the bus may output all of the parallel bits essentially simultaneously, the signals may not arrive at the destination at the same time. This could be caused by differences in the path length of the conductors in the cable or across the circuit board. Because of this, there is an upper limit on the data transfer rate a parallel bus can support.

- Another limitation of parallel buses is they can only transfer data in one direction at a time (referred to as **half-duplex**) unless a duplicate set of connections is available for simultaneously transferring data in the opposite direction. Parallel buses usually do not provide simultaneous bi-directional communication capability, referred to as **full-duplex** operation.

A serial data bus transfers data between two communication endpoints a single bit at a time using a pair of conductors. Most of the high-speed communication paths between the processor and peripheral devices in modern computers use some form of serial bus. While at first blush, switching from a parallel bus architecture to a serial bus seems to represent a substantial loss in throughput capability, serial buses exhibit several important advantages that make their use attractive in performance-critical applications.

High-speed serial buses in personal and business computer systems communicate over pairs of conductors using differential signaling. **Differential signaling** uses two conductors, carefully matched to be of the same length and to exhibit nearly identical electrical characteristics. When used in cables, these conductors are insulated wires twisted around each other to form **twisted pairs**.

The following figure represents a serial data bus using differential signaling:

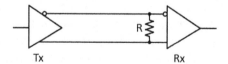

Figure 4.7: Serial bus circuit using differential signaling

The digital signal to be transmitted arrives at the transmitter (labeled Tx) via the input at the left edge of the figure. The input is transformed into a pair of voltages on the two parallel lines crossing the center of the diagram. The small circle indicates that the transmitter top signal is inverted relative to the bottom signal.

In a typical serial circuit, a high signal level at the transmitter input will generate a voltage of 1.0V on the top serial conductor and 1.4V on the bottom conductor. A low signal input produces 1.4V on the top conductor and 1.0V on the bottom conductor. The inputs to the receiver (labeled Rx) are high impedance, meaning the receiver draws a negligible amount of current from the circuit. The receiver measures the voltage across the resistor (which has a typical value of 100 Ω), with the upper resistor terminal at -0.4V relative to the lower terminal when the Tx input is high. When the Tx input is low, the upper resistor terminal is +0.4V relative to the lower terminal.

The receiver generates its output by inverting one of the inputs (the top one, with the small circle) and adding the resulting voltage to the other input. In other words, the receiver only measures the difference between the voltages on the two conductors. The primary benefit of this approach derives from the fact that most forms of corrupting interference cause voltage variations in the conductors carrying the signal. By placing the two conductors very close together, most of the noise voltage introduced on one of the conductors will also appear on the other conductor. The subtraction operation cancels out a large portion of the noise that would otherwise interfere with the accurate detection of the signal by the receiver.

A serial data bus can perform several billion bit transfers per second, far more than the old PC's parallel bus. It is possible to run several serial buses alongside each other, effectively multiplying the data transfer bandwidth by the number of buses. A crucial difference between multiple serial buses connecting two endpoints and a parallel bus making the same connection is that, for some interface standards, the serial buses are all operating somewhat independently. They do not synchronize at the level of each bit transfer as all the bits in a parallel bus must. This makes it easier to design interconnections capable of supporting very high data rates while only needing to worry about precisely matching the length and electrical characteristics within each pair of serial conductors.

The connection between a modern processor and its motherboard chipset generally consists of several serial data buses called **High-Speed Input Output (HSIO) lanes**. Each lane is a serial connection with one data path like *Figure 4.7* flowing in each direction, supporting full-duplex operation. Individual lanes can be assigned to specific types of peripheral interfaces that are also implemented as serial connections, such as PCI Express, SATA, and USB. The following sections will examine each of these interfaces.

PCI Express

The original **Peripheral Component Interconnect (PCI)** bus was a 32-bit parallel bus used in PC-compatible computers from about 1995 through 2005. The PCI slots on computer motherboards accepted a wide variety of expansion cards performing functions such as networking, video display, and audio output. By the early 2000s, the limitations of the parallel bus architecture had become apparent and development began on a serial bus replacement for PCI named PCI Express.

PCI Express, abbreviated to **PCIe**, is a bi-directional differential signaling serial bus used primarily to connect communication endpoints on computer motherboards. PCIe performance is expressed in billions of transfers per second, or GT/s. One "transfer" is a single bit propagated across the bus from transmitter to receiver. PCIe inserts additional bit periods in each communication to ensure data integrity. Different generations of PCIe have varying amounts of these overhead bits, influencing the effective data transfer rate. The following table shows the major generations of PCIe, the year each was introduced, the single-lane transfer rate in GT/S, and the effective data transfer rate in MB/s.

Table 4.1: PCI Express generations

PCIe generation	Year introduced	Transfer rate	Effective one-way data rate
1.0a	2003	2.5 GT/s	250 MB/s
2.0	2007	5 GT/s	500 MB/s
3.0	2010	8 GT/s	985 MB/s
4.0	2017	16 GT/s	1969 MB/s

The effective data rate presented here is for one-way communication, though PCIe supports full-speed data transfer in both directions simultaneously.

The PCIe standards support multi-lane connections indicated by the notations x1, x2, x4, x8, x16, and x32. Most modern motherboards implement, as a minimum, PCIe x1 and x16 slots. PCI x1 slots are compatible with a board edge connector length of 25mm while x16 slots expect a board edge connector length of 89mm. A PCIe card will operate correctly in any slot it can physically fit into. For example, a PCIe x1 card can be plugged into an x16 slot and will use just one of the 16 available lanes.

A primary application for PCIe x16 slots is the interface between the processor and the graphics card, with the goal of peak performance for graphics-intensive applications such as gaming. A PCIe 4.0 x16 interface is capable of unidirectional data transfer at 31.5 GB/s.

In modern computer architectures, the processor chip usually provides a PCIe 16-lane interface as a direct connection to a graphics board installed in a PCIe x16 slot. This avoids the need to pass the graphics card PCIe signals through the chipset integrated circuit.

Except for the graphics display and the system memory interface, most I/O in modern computer systems is managed by the chipset. The processor and chipset communicate through a collection of HSIO lanes. The chipset supports interfaces to peripheral devices such as disk drives, network interfaces, keyboard, and mouse. The interfaces to these devices commonly use SATA, M.2, and USB serial interfaces.

SATA

The **Serial AT Attachment (SATA)** is a bi-directional serial interface standard for connecting computer motherboards to storage devices. The "AT" in SATA refers to the original IBM PC AT. Similar to a single PCIe lane, SATA contains two differential signaling pairs of conductors, with one pair carrying data in each direction. Unlike PCIe, SATA is intended for operation over cables rather than using signal traces on motherboards. In addition to electrical and data format requirements, the SATA standard contains detailed specifications for compatible cables and connectors.

A SATA cable contains one bi-directional lane supporting connection between the processor and storage devices such as magnetic disk drives, optical disk drives, and solid-state drives. This table shows the major revisions of the SATA standard, the year each was introduced, and performance parameters.

Table 4.2: SATA generations

SATA generation	Year introduced	Transfer rate	Effective one-way data rate
1.0	2003	1.5 GT/s	150 MB/s
2.0	2004	3 GT/s	300 MB/s
3.0	2009	6 GT/s	600 MB/s

The data transfer rate in this table describes one-way communication, though, like PCIe, SATA supports full-duplex data transfer.

The SATA standard continues to undergo incremental improvements, but as of 2019 there has been no announcement of an upcoming SATA generation with a faster data transfer rate.

M.2

Modern **solid-state drives (SSDs)** employ flash memory to store data rather than the rotating magnetic platters in traditional hard drives. Because of the radically different technology of SSDs, the SATA drive interface that works well enough in most cases for rotating disks has proven to be a significant performance barrier for SSDs.

To access an arbitrary block of data (called a **sector**) on a magnetic disk drive, the drive head must physically move to the track containing the sector, then it must wait for the beginning of the sector to rotate to the head position before the drive can begin reading data. In contrast to these steps, an SSD can directly address any data sector in a manner very similar to the way in which a processor accesses a DRAM location.

The M.2 specification was developed to provide a small form factor and high-performance interface for flash memory storage in small, portable devices. The performance limitations of the SATA interface are removed, and it is possible to have data transfer rates to and from an SSD several times faster than SATA can support.

In addition to mass storage devices, M.2 supports other interfaces including PCIe, USB, Bluetooth, and Wi-Fi. Modern motherboards have begun to include M.2 slots, which, in addition to the higher performance, consume much less space in the computer case than traditional disks in their drive bays.

USB

The **Universal Serial Bus (USB)** interface provides a simple (from the user's viewpoint) interface for connecting a wide variety of peripheral devices to a computer system. USB cables have easily identifiable connector types and support hot-plugging (plugging devices together while powered on). USB devices are self-configuring, and, in most cases, users do not need to concern themselves with installing device drivers when attaching a new device to a computer with a USB cable.

Early USB data cables (through USB 2.0) contained a single differential signaling pair. These connections pass data in only one direction at a time. Later versions of the USB standard (USB 3.0 onward) support simultaneous bi-directional data transfer. In addition, USB 3.2 onward provides up to two lanes, doubling the data transfer rate.

The following table shows the major revisions of the USB standard, the date each was introduced, the maximum number of lanes supported, and data transfer performance.

Table 4.3: USB generations

USB generation	Year introduced	Number of lanes	Transfer rate	Effective one-way data rate
1.1	1998	1	0.012 GT/s	1.5 MB/s
2.0	2000	1	0.48 GT/s	60 MB/s
3.0	2008	1	6 GT/s	750 MB/s
3.1	2013	1	10 GT/s	1280 MB/s
3.2	2017	2	20 GT/s	2560 MB/s
4.0	2019	2	40 GT/s	5120 MB/s

In USB generations through 2.0, communication takes place entirely under the control of the host. The host initiates each communication interaction by sending packets addressed to a particular device and performs data transfers to or from the device. Beginning with USB 3.0, devices can initiate communication with the host, effectively providing an interrupt capability for connected peripherals.

Thunderbolt

Thunderbolt is a collection of high-speed serial interface standards introduced in 2011. The original Thunderbolt interface combined PCIe and DisplayPort signal transmission using two serial Thunderbolt lanes.

Thunderbolt 3 is the latest generation of the Thunderbolt standard, adding USB compatibility while supporting connectivity to PCIe devices and to multiple high-resolution displays from a single computer port. Thunderbolt 3 uses the same connector as USB 3.1 and later generations (the USB-C connector), and supports the 40 Gbit/s Thunderbolt 3 data rate while providing full compatibility with USB 3.1 at 10 Gbit/s. Any USB device should operate properly when connected to a computer's Thunderbolt 3 port. Thunderbolt 3 peripheral devices are not compatible with non-Thunderbolt 3 USB-C ports.

The next section provides an overview of the most popular graphics display interface standards.

Graphics displays

In the domains of gaming, video editing, graphic design, and animation, video processing performance is critical. Generating and displaying high-resolution graphics requires an enormous number of mathematical calculations. While general-purpose processors can perform the necessary computations, such processors lack the performance that users of these applications have come to expect.

High-performance graphics cards, called **graphics processing units (GPUs)**, are essentially miniature supercomputers, heavily optimized to perform graphical computational tasks such as 3-D scene rendering. Because the computations involved in scene rendering are highly repetitive, substantial performance gains can be achieved through the use of hardware parallelization. Graphics processors contain a large number of relatively simple computational units, each performing a small portion of the overall task.

A GPU may contain thousands of individual processing units that function in a manner similar to an ALU. While the original driving force that led to the development of high-performance GPUs was 3-D scene generation, later generations of this technology have found broad use in fields such as the analysis of "big data" and in machine learning. Any numerically intensive computational task that can be broken into a collection of parallel operations is suitable for acceleration with a GPU architecture.

Of course, not all users require extreme video performance. To accommodate users with modest graphics needs and more limited budgets, modern processors often integrate a GPU with less extreme capabilities into the processor chip. In many applications, this approach provides more than adequate graphical performance. This configuration is referred to as **integrated graphics**, meaning the GPU function is integrated into the processor die and shares system memory with the processor. Computer systems with integrated graphics are lower in cost while providing adequate graphics performance for basic computing tasks such as email, web browsing, and watching videos.

Many desktop computer systems, as well as some laptops, provide integrated graphics while offering the option of installing a high-performance graphics card. This allows users to tailor the computer system to their cost and performance needs.

Several different video standards are currently in use for connecting displays to computers. Because the output generated by a computer graphics interface must be compatible with the connected display, it is common for computers to provide more than one type of video connector. Computer monitors and high-definition televisions usually provide a selection of video connection types as well. The following sections describe some of the popular video interface standards used in computer applications, past and present.

VGA

The **Video Graphics Array (VGA)** video standard for personal computers was introduced by IBM in 1987. VGA is an analog interface that remains in widespread use today, though most modern computers do not provide a VGA connector. It is not uncommon to find older computers with VGA outputs using a converter cable to present a display on a monitor supporting DVI or HDMI video input. Modern versions of the VGA standard support display resolutions up to 1,920 pixels wide by 1,200 pixels high, refreshed at 60 Hz. Because the VGA video signal is analog, some loss of signal quality occurs during transmission to the display. This effect is most noticeable at high screen resolutions.

DVI

The **Digital Visual Interface (DVI)** video standard was developed to improve the visual quality of computer displays by transferring the video signal digitally from the computer to the monitor. To maintain backward compatibility with older computers and monitors, DVI cables are capable of carrying VGA analog signals as well.

Similar to the high-speed serial interfaces discussed earlier in this chapter, DVI uses differential serial signaling to transfer video data. A DVI connector contains four serial lanes: individual lanes carry red, green, and blue color information, and the fourth lane carries the common clock signal.

Three DVI variants are defined, depending on the combination of digital and analog video options supported:

- **DVI-A** supports only the analog video signal. This option is intended to provide backward compatibility with VGA computers and monitors. The DVI-A connector has a different pin layout than traditional VGA connectors, so an adapter cable is required to connect to legacy VGA devices.

- **DVI-D** is a digital-only interface supporting single-link and dual-link options. The dual-link option provides additional serial data lanes to increase the video bandwidth for higher-resolution displays. Dual-link does not mean the cable supports dual monitors.

- **DVI-I** is an integrated interface supporting both the analog interface of DVI-A and the digital modes of DVI-D. A DVI-I digital interface may be single- or dual-link.

DVI interfaces are used primarily in computer display applications. The effective data rate of a single-link DVI-D connection is 3.96 gigabits per second (Gbit/s). Dual-link DVI-D transfers video data at twice the single-link rate, 7.92 Gbit/s.

HDMI

The **High-Definition Media Interface** (**HDMI**) is supported by most modern computers and monitors, and by virtually all modern televisions and related video entertainment devices, such as DVD players. HDMI supports digital video only (there is no analog capability) and uses the same differential serial bus as DVI-D. In addition to video data, HDMI cables also transport multi-channel digital audio.

The HDMI standard has undergone several revisions since its introduction in 2002. Each successive revision has maintained backward compatibility while adding new capabilities. Later versions of the standard have increased video bandwidth, increased the range of supported screen resolutions, added high-definition audio capabilities, added support for Ethernet communication over the HDMI cable, and added features to support gaming. Although each HDMI version is backward compatible, newer features are only available in configurations where the signal source device, the display device, and the connecting cable are all compatible with the newer standard.

HDMI version 2.1 was released in 2017. This standard supports an effective data rate of 42.6 Gbit/s over four differential serial lanes.

DisplayPort

DisplayPort, introduced in 2006, is a digital interface standard supporting digital video, audio, and USB connections. While HDMI is targeted at consumer electronics such as televisions and home theater systems, DisplayPort is oriented more toward computer applications. DisplayPort transfers data in packets with clocking information embedded in each packet, eliminating the need for a separate clock channel.

A single computer DisplayPort output can drive multiple monitors connected in a daisy chain fashion, where one cable connects the computer to the first monitor, a second cable connects the first and second monitors, and so on. The monitors must provide support for this capability. The maximum number of displays that can be combined in this manner is limited only by the capabilities of the graphics card and the resolution and refresh rate of the displays.

DisplayPort 2.0 was released in 2019, with an effective data rate of up to 77.4 Gbit/s over four differential serial lanes.

Network interface

A computer network is a collection of digital devices interacting over a shared communication medium. A **local area network (LAN)** consists of a limited number of computers that might reside in a single physical location such as a home or office building. The connected computers, phones, and other digital devices in your home represent a LAN. Device connections within a LAN environment may use a wired interface, usually Ethernet, or wireless interface, typically Wi-Fi.

Geographically separated computers and LANs communicate using a **wide area network (WAN)**. WAN services are often provided by a telecommunication company such as a cable television provider or telephone company. Your home LAN most likely connects to the Internet via WAN services provided by your telephone or cable company. Home and business networking devices provided by WAN service providers usually provide Ethernet and Wi-Fi options for connecting local devices to the WAN. The following sections introduce the technologies of Ethernet and Wi-Fi.

Ethernet

Ethernet is a set of networking standards for connecting computers using cables in a LAN environment. The original version of Ethernet was developed by Robert Metcalfe at Xerox Palo Alto Research Center in 1974. Ethernet was released commercially in 1980 as a 10 Mbit/s communication technology for groups of computers connected with coaxial cabling. The name of the technology was derived from the historical term *luminiferous aether*, a hypothesized medium filling all of space and enabling the propagation of electromagnetic waves. The Ethernet cable serves as a conceptually similar communication medium.

The **Institute of Electrical and Electronic Engineers (IEEE)** began developing standards for LAN technologies, including Ethernet, in 1980. The IEEE 802.3 Ethernet standard was published in 1985. Since then, the standard has undergone several revisions supporting increased data rates and different network topologies. The most obvious difference in modern computers from the original Ethernet standard is the use of point-to-point twisted pair cables in place of the original shared coaxial cable.

Modern computers commonly use Gigabit Ethernet interfaces to communicate over unshielded twisted-pair cabling. Gigabit Ethernet is formally defined in the IEEE 802.3ab standard and supports 1.0 Gbit/s with an effective data transfer rate up to 99% of the raw bit rate, though the amount of overhead varies considerably depending on the communication protocol in use.

Ethernet communication is composed of variable-size data units called **frames** up to 1,518 bytes in length. The header of each frame contains addressing information identifying the source and destination Ethernet interfaces. Because modern twisted-pair connections are point-to-point, the most common structure for connecting a group of computers is to run a cable from each computer to a **switch**. A switch is a device that receives frames transmitted by the connected computers and, based on the destination address contained in each frame, immediately forwards it to the correct recipient. Ethernet cables are limited to a maximum recommended length of 100 meters, constraining the physical size of an Ethernet LAN to an area such as a single office building or home.

Modern motherboards usually contain a built-in Ethernet interface. This eliminates any need to consume a PCIe slot with an Ethernet card. An Ethernet interface, whether built into the motherboard or installed in a PCIe expansion slot, uses one HSIO lane between the processor and chipset.

Wi-Fi

The IEEE released the first version of the 802.11 wireless communication standard in 1997 with a raw data rate of 2 Mbit/s in the 2.4 GHz band. The 802.11b standard, released in 1999 with an 11 Mbit/s raw data rate, proved to be commercially popular. The technology was named **Wi-Fi** in 1999 as a reference to the term "hi-fi," referring to high-fidelity sound reproduction.

The 802.11g standard, released in 2003, has a raw bit rate of 54 Mbit/s. 802.11n, released in 2009, supports **multiple-input-multiple-output** (**MIMO**) antennas and optional operation in the 5 GHz band. The 802.11ac standard, published in 2013, supports a bit rate in the 5 GHz band of over 500 Mbit/s using enhanced MIMO antenna configurations.

Wi-Fi devices can suffer from interference produced by household appliances such as cordless phones, microwave ovens, and other Wi-Fi networks in the area. Wi-Fi signal propagation is affected by factors such as walls and other obstacles between transmitter and receiver, **multipath** (the destructive interference between a direct-path signal and a reflected copy of the signal), and is limited by the maximum amount of power a Wi-Fi transmitter is permitted to emit. The use of multiple antennas in 802.11n and 802.11ac configurations significantly mitigates multipath-related propagation issues.

Modern WAN interface devices supplied by telecommunication service providers usually contain a combination of Ethernet and Wi-Fi communication interfaces. A primary benefit of Wi-Fi in comparison to Ethernet for these applications is the reduction in the amount of cabling required. One drawback of Wi-Fi is the potential for security issues because the radio frequency signal can propagate far outside of the building containing the communicating systems. The Wi-Fi protocols provide substantial support for secure communication using protocols such as **Wi-Fi Protected Access 2 (WPA2)**, but system administrators and users must ensure the appropriate security features are enabled and that secret information such as the network password is sufficiently complex and is stored securely.

Support for Wi-Fi is ubiquitous in portable digital devices such as laptops, smartphones, and tablets, and is directly built into many motherboards.

The next section discusses the computer interfaces with the lowest bandwidth requirements: the keyboard and mouse.

Keyboard and mouse

Compared to the high-speed device interfaces discussed earlier in this chapter, the bandwidth requirements for a keyboard and mouse are quite modest. These devices are the sole input methods used by the human operator in most computer configurations, and thus are only required to operate at the speed of human actions. Even the fastest typist can only press one or two dozen keys per second.

Keyboard

A mechanical computer keyboard consists of a collection of keys, each of which operates an electrical momentary switch. A standard full-size keyboard contains 104 keys, including the arrow keys, control keys (Home, Scroll Lock, and so on), and the numeric keypad. Modern keyboards commonly provide a USB cable for connection to the computer system via cable or wirelessly. Because the bandwidth requirements for human interaction are so low, some computer motherboards provide a slower USB 2.0 port for keyboard connection while offering higher-performance USB 3.0 or better interfaces for high-speed peripherals. This results in a small cost reduction for the motherboard components.

Because the keyboard reports the press and release of each key separately, the computer is able to process combinations of keys pressed simultaneously. For example, holding the *shift* key down while pressing the *a* key produces a capital *A*.

Some computers and digital devices such as tablets and phones provide a touchscreen interface. When text input is required on these devices, the system displays a keyboard pattern on the screen and the user touches letter locations to produce keypresses.

Mechanical keyboards tend to provide more accurate input and are favored by users entering significant quantities of text. Because the surface of a touchscreen is completely flat, there is no feedback to the user's fingers indicating if the fingers are aligned with the keys. This results in more frequent input errors when using touchscreen keyboards. Of course, a touchscreen keyboard means there is no need to provide a mechanical keyboard for the device, a substantial benefit for portable devices. In addition, touchscreen keyboard input does not suffer from mechanical failures that can affect the components of mechanical keyboards, though touchscreen input is more difficult for users wearing gloves.

Mouse

A computer mouse is a hand-held device that moves a pointer horizontally and vertically across a computer screen. The user initiates actions based on the pointer location by pressing buttons on the mouse. Modern mice often provide a small wheel capable of rolling in either direction, used to perform tasks such as scrolling through a text document.

As with the keyboard, the mouse usually connects to the computer via USB over a wired or wireless connection. The mouse has low bandwidth requirements and can be supported via a USB 2.0 port.

The operation of a mouse requires a horizontal surface, typically a desktop, for the user to move the mouse upon. Modern mice usually use optical emitters and sensors to detect motion across the surface. Many mice have difficulty operating on highly reflective surfaces such as glass tables.

A trackball is similar in concept to a mouse, except that rather than moving a mouse across a surface, a ball is held at a fixed location but is allowed to rotate in any direction using hand motion. By rolling the ball forward, backward, left, and right, the user is able to move the pointer on the computer display.

A trackball does not require the quantity of surface space a mouse needs, and the trackball can be fixed at a stationary location. The ability to firmly attach a trackball to a surface makes the trackball the preferred pointing device for computer stations installed in ground vehicles, ships, and aircraft.

As with the keyboard, the computer detects the press and release of each mouse button as separate events. Users can exploit this capability to perform operations such as dragging an icon across the screen by following these steps:

1. Place the pointer over the icon.
2. Press and hold the left mouse button.
3. Move the pointer (with the icon now attached) to the new location.
4. Release the mouse button.

Together, the keyboard and mouse provide all of the input capability most computer users need to perform their interactive tasks.

The next section brings together the interface descriptions provided in this chapter to examine the specifications of a modern computer motherboard.

Modern computer system specifications

Having absorbed the information provided up to this point, you should be able to interpret most of the specifications of a modern computer motherboard, processor, and chipset. This section provides an example of the specifications for a current (2019) motherboard with some explanation of the individual features.

The designers of a computer motherboard must make a number of decisions such as the number of PCIe expansion ports, number of DIMM slots, number of USB ports, and the number of SATA ports to be provided in a particular motherboard model. These decisions are guided by the target customer demographic, whether it be gamers, business users, or cost-conscious home users.

The following example motherboard presented is the Gigabyte Z390 Designare, a higher-performance board intended for gaming applications that supports gaming-related technical capabilities such as overclocking. **Overclocking** involves increasing the clock frequencies for the processor and other system components with the goal of improving performance.

Overclocking introduces the possibility of increased heat generation and unstable performance if a component is driven at an excessive frequency.

Table 4.4: Example motherboard specifications

Feature	Specification	Notes
Processor	LGA 1151 socket-compatible with Intel 8th and 9th generation i3, i5, i7, or i9 processors	The **land grid array (LGA)** 1151 socket contains 1,151 contacts. The processor interfaces directly to an optional GPU over PCIe 3.0 x16. It also interfaces directly to DDR4 system memory.
Chipset	Intel Z390 24 x PCIe 3.0 lanes	The processor-to-chipset interface is a 4-lane HSIO connection supporting a 3.93 GB/s transfer rate. The 24 chipset PCIe lanes are in addition to the 16 lanes the processor provides for graphics.
Video output	1 x HDMI 2 x Thunderbolt 3	The Thunderbolt 3 video output supports multiple daisy-chained displays.
Integrated graphics	Maximum screen resolution of 4096x2304@60 Hz	The use of a graphics card is optional with integrated graphics included.
Graphics card	1 x PCIe 3.0 x16 slot	Install a GPU for higher graphics performance for gaming.
Expansion slots	1 x PCIe 3.0 x16 slot 1 x PCIe 3.0 x8 (slot length is x16) 1 x PCIe 3.0 x4 (slot length is x16) 2 x PCIe 3.0 x1	The x8 slot shares lanes with the x16 slot, so a maximum of 16 lanes are available for both of them. The x8 and x4 slots provide x16-size slots, but only enable at most the listed number of PCIe lanes.
System memory	4 x Dual Channel DDR4 2666 MHz DIMM slots containing up to 128 GB total	Up to four DDR4 modules can be installed with up to 32 GB each, up to 2 modules per channel
Disk interface	2 x M.2 6 x SATA 6Gb/s	M.2 supports higher performance SSDs. SATA supports traditional disks.
Ethernet	2 x Gigabit Ethernet	The system can connect to two networks simultaneously.
USB/ Thunderbolt 3 ports	2 x USB 3.1/Thunderbolt 3 ports 13 x USB 2.0 through 3.1 ports	Use USB 2.0 for keyboard and mouse. Use USB 3.1/Thunderbolt 3 for fast peripherals such as external drives.

This example is intended to provide some perspective on the specifications of higher-end consumer-grade computer capabilities as of 2019. If you are looking to purchase a computer, use the information in this chapter to make yourself a more informed consumer.

Summary

This chapter began with an introduction to the computer memory subsystem, the MOSFET, and the capacitor. We examined the circuitry that implements the DRAM bit cell. We reviewed the architecture of DDR4 memory modules and the operation of multichannel memory controllers. Other types of I/O devices were introduced, with a focus on high-speed differential serial interfaces and their ubiquitous use in connection technologies such as PCIe, SATA, USB, and video interfaces.

Popular video standards were presented, including VGA, DVI, HDMI, and DisplayPort. We looked at the Ethernet and Wi-Fi networking technologies as well. We concluded with a discussion of standard computer peripheral interfaces including the keyboard and mouse. The chapter concluded with a description of an example modern motherboard, highlighting some of its interesting features.

With the information presented in this chapter, you should have a solid general understanding of modern computer components from the level of technical specifications down to the technologies used in implementing the circuitry.

In the next chapter, we will explore the high-level services computer systems must implement, such as disk I/O, network communications, and interactions with users. We'll examine the software layers that implement these features, starting at the level of the processor instruction set and registers. Several key aspects of operating systems will be covered including booting, multithreading, and multiprocessing.

Exercises

1. Create a circuit implementation of a NAND gate using two CMOS transistor pairs. Unlike NPN transistor gate circuits, no resistors are required for this circuit.

2. A 16-gigabit DRAM integrated circuit has two bank group selection inputs, two bank selection inputs, and 17 row address inputs. How many bits are in each row of a bank in this device?

5
Hardware-Software Interface

The vast majority of computer software is not written at the processor instruction level in assembly language. Most of the applications we work with on a daily basis are written in one high-level programming language or another, using a pre-built library of capabilities that the application programmers extended during the software development process. Practical programming environments, consisting of high-level languages and their associated libraries, offer many services, including disk **input/output (I/O)**, network communication, and interactions with users, all easily accessible from program code.

This chapter describes the software layers that implement these features, beginning at the level of processor instructions in device drivers. Several key aspects of operating systems will be covered in this chapter, including booting, multithreading, and multiprocessing.

After completing this chapter, you will understand the services provided by operating systems and the capabilities provided in **Basic Input/Output System (BIOS)** and **Unified Extensible Firmware Interface (UEFI)** firmware. You will have learned how execution threads function at the processor level and how multiple processors coordinate within a single computer system. You will also have a broad understanding of the process of booting into an operating system, beginning with the first instruction executed.

We will cover the following topics:

- Device drivers
- BIOS and UEFI
- The boot process
- Operating systems
- Processes and threads
- Multiprocessing

Device drivers

A device driver provides a standardized interface for software applications to interact with a category of peripheral devices. This avoids the need for the developer of each application to understand and implement all of the technical details required for the proper operation of each type of device. Most device drivers allow multiple simultaneously executing applications to interact with multiple instances of associated peripherals in a secure and efficient manner.

At the lowest level of interaction, device driver code provides software instructions that manage communication interactions with the peripheral, including handling interrupts generated by device service requests. A device driver controls the operation of hardware resources provided by the processor, the peripheral device, and by other system components such as the processor chipset.

In computer systems supporting privileged execution modes, device drivers usually operate at an elevated privilege level, which grants access to peripheral interfaces that are inaccessible to less privileged code. This ensures that only trusted code is permitted to interact with these interfaces directly. If unprivileged application code were able to access a peripheral's hardware interface, a programming error that caused the device to behave improperly would immediately affect all applications that attempt to use the device. The steps involved in transitioning the flow of instruction execution and data between unprivileged user code and privileged driver code will be introduced in *Chapter 9, Specialized Processor Extensions.*

As we learned in *Chapter 3, Processor Elements*, the two principal methods for accessing I/O devices are port-mapped I/O and memory-mapped I/O. Although memory-mapped I/O is predominant in modern computers, some architectures—such as x86—continue to support and use port-mapped I/O. In an x86 system, many modern peripheral devices provide an interface that combines port-mapped I/O and memory-mapped I/O.

Programming tools for modern operating systems, such as those available for Linux and Windows, provide resources for developing device drivers capable of interacting with peripheral devices using port- and memory-mapped I/O techniques. Installing a device driver in these operating systems requires elevated privilege, but users of the driver do not require any special privileges.

Although device drivers for sophisticated peripheral devices can be quite complex and difficult to understand for those not intimately familiar with the device's hardware and internal firmware, some legacy devices are fairly simple. One example is the parallel printer port introduced on early PCs, and a standard component of personal computers for many years. Even though modern computers rarely include these interfaces, inexpensive parallel port expansion cards remain readily available, and modern operating systems provide driver support for these interfaces. Electronics hobbyists frequently use a parallel port as a simple interface for interacting with external circuits using **Transistor-Transistor Logic (TTL)** 5V digital signals on PCs running Windows or Linux.

The next section will examine some of the device driver-level details of the parallel port interface.

The parallel port

The programming interface for the PC parallel printer port consists of three 8-bit registers, originally located at sequential I/O port numbers beginning at 0x378. This collection of I/O ports provides the interface for printer 1, identified as LPT1 in PC-compatible computers running MS-DOS and Windows. Modern PCs may map the parallel port to a different range of I/O ports during **Peripheral Component Interconnect (PCI)** device initialization, but operation of the interface is otherwise unchanged from early PCs.

Device drivers for the parallel port in modern computers perform the same functions using the same instructions as in early PCs. In this section, we'll assume that the printer port is mapped to the legacy I/O port range.

To interact with parallel port hardware, the x86 processor executes in and out instructions to read from and write to I/O ports, respectively. If we assume the parallel port driver has been installed and initialized, a user application can call a driver function to read the data present on the parallel port input lines. The following pair of instructions within the driver code reads the digital voltage levels present on the eight data lines of the parallel port and stores the resulting 8-bit value in the processor's al register:

```
mov    edx,0x378
in     al,dx
```

In x86 assembly language, instructions containing two operands are written in the form opcode destination, source. This example uses the al, edx, and dx processor registers. The al register is the lowest 8 bits of the 32-bit eax register. dx is the lowest 16 bits of the 32-bit edx register. This sequence of instructions loads the immediate value 0x378 into the edx register, and then reads the 8-bit data value from the port number contained in dx into al.

The C language source code that generated the preceding assembly instructions is as follows:

```
char input_byte;
input_byte = inb(0x378);
```

The inb function is provided by the Linux operating system to perform 8-bit input from an I/O port. This code will only function properly if it is running at the elevated privilege level of the operating system. An application running with a user privilege will fail if it attempts to execute these instructions, because such code is not authorized to perform port I/O directly.

Drivers that execute at this elevated level are referred to as **kernel-mode drivers**. The **kernel** is the central core of the operating system, serving as the interface between computer hardware and higher-level operating system functions such as the scheduler.

The instructions for writing a byte to the parallel port data register, and thus setting the state of the eight digital output signals, are shown in the following code block:

```
mov     edx,0x378
movzx   eax,BYTE PTR [rsp+0x7]
out     dx,al
```

These instructions set the edx register to the port number, and then load eax from a variable on the stack. rsp is the 64-bit stack pointer. rsp is 64 bits because this driver is running on a 64-bit version of Linux. movzx stands for "move with zero extension", which means move the 8-bit data value (designated by BYTE PTR) at the address given as rsp+0x7 into the lower 8 bits of the 32-bit eax register, and fill the 24 remaining bits in eax with zeros. The final instruction writes the byte in al to the port number in dx.

The C source code that produces these instructions is as follows:

```
char output_byte = 0xA5;
outb(output_byte,0x378);
```

Similar to `inb`, the `outb` function is provided by Linux to enable device drivers to write an 8-bit value to the given I/O port.

This example demonstrates how interaction between software executing on the processor and peripheral device hardware registers happens at the lowest level of device driver operation. Drivers for more complex devices on x86 systems usually combine port-mapped I/O (as shown in the preceding examples) with memory-mapped I/O, which accesses a device interface using reads and writes that are, in terms of processor instructions, identical to memory accesses.

These examples presented hardware access methods used by drivers on the original parallel PCI bus architecture. The next section discusses features that allow legacy PCI drivers to continue to operate properly on modern **PCI Express (PCIe)**-based computers, taking full advantage of PCIe's high-speed serial communication technology.

PCIe device drivers

As we saw in the previous chapter, PCIe uses high-speed serial connections for communication between the processor and PCIe peripheral devices. You may be wondering about the steps a device driver must perform to interact with this fancy hardware. The simple answer is that drivers do not need to do anything special to take full advantage of the high-performance capabilities of PCIe. PCIe was expressly designed to be software-compatible with the parallel PCI bus used in PCs of the 1990s. Device drivers written for PCI continue to work properly in computers using the serial PCIe bus. The task of translating between processor I/O instructions such as `in` and `out` and the sequential serial data transfers necessary to communicate with PCIe devices is handled transparently by the PCIe bus controllers in the processor, chipset, and PCIe devices.

PCI and PCIe devices perform an automated configuration operation during system startup and when a device is hot plugged in a running system. **Hot plugging** is the installation of hardware in a system that is powered on.

Once configuration is complete, the device interface is known to the operating system. The interface between a PCI or PCIe peripheral and the processor may include any combination of the following communication paths:

- One or more I/O port ranges
- One or more memory regions supporting memory-mapped I/O
- Connection to a processor interrupt handler

The interface configuration procedure applies to both PCI and PCIe drivers, enabling legacy PCI drivers to work properly in PCIe systems. Of course, the physical card interface differs greatly between parallel PCI and serial PCIe devices, so the cards themselves are not interchangeable across bus technologies. The bus slots for PCIe are intentionally different from PCI slots to prevent the accidental insertion of PCI devices into PCIe slots, and vice versa.

Bulk data transfer to and from peripheral devices generally relies on **Direct Memory Access (DMA)** in both PCI and PCIe systems. In PCIe systems, DMA operations take full advantage of the high data rates possible with multi-lane serial connections, blasting data across the interface at close to the theoretical maximum speed each single- or multi-lane link can support. The technological evolution that supplanted legacy parallel bus PCI technology with the vastly higher-performing multi-lane serial technology of PCIe, while retaining seamless device driver compatibility, has been quite remarkable.

Device driver structure

A device driver is a software module that implements a set of predefined functions, enabling the operating system to associate the driver with compatible peripheral devices and perform controlled access to those devices. This allows system processes and user applications to perform I/O operations on shared devices.

This section provides a brief overview of some of the most commonly used functions a Linux device driver must implement for use by application developers. This example will prefix the function names with the fictitious device name mydevice and is written in the C programming language.

The following functions perform tasks related to initialization and termination of the driver itself:

```
int mydevice_init(void);
void mydevice_exit(void);
```

The operating system calls mydevice_init to initialize the device at system startup or at a later time if the device is connected by hot plugging. The mydevice_init function returns an integer code, indicating if the initialization was successful or, if unsuccessful, the error that occurred. Successful driver initialization is indicated by a return code of zero.

When the driver is no longer needed, such as during system shutdown or when the device is removed while the system is running, mydevice_exit is called to release any system resources allocated by the driver.

The next pair of functions, shown here, allows system processes and user applications to initiate and terminate communication sessions with the device:

```
int mydevice_open(struct inode *inode, struct file *filp);
int mydevice_release(struct inode *inode, struct file *filp);
```

mydevice_open attempts to initiate access to the device and reports any errors that may occur in the process. The inode parameter is a pointer to a data structure containing information required to access a specific file or other device. The filp parameter is a pointer to a data structure containing information about the open file. In Linux, all types of devices are consistently represented as files, even if the device itself is not inherently file-based. The name filp is short for *file pointer*. All functions operating on the file receive a pointer to this structure as an input. Among other details, the filp structure indicates whether the file is opened for reading, writing, or both.

The mydevice_release function closes the device or file and deallocates any resources allocated in the call to mydevice_open.

Following a successful call to mydevice_open, application code can begin to read from and write to the device. The functions performing these operations are as follows:

```
ssize_t mydevice_read(struct file *filp, char *buf,
                      size_t count, loff_t *f_pos);
ssize_t mydevice_write(struct file *filp, const char *buf,
                       size_t count, loff_t *f_pos);
```

The mydevice_read function reads from the device or file and transfers the resulting data to a buffer in application memory space. The count parameter indicates the requested amount of data, and f_pos indicates the offset from the start of the file at which to begin reading. The buf parameter is the address of the destination for the data. The number of bytes actually read (which may be less than the number requested) is provided as the function return value, with a data type of ssize_t.

The mydevice_write function has most of the same parameters as mydevice_read, except that the buf parameter is declared const (constant) because mydevice_write reads from the memory address indicated by buf and writes that data to the file or device.

One point of interest in the implementation of these functions is that the privileged driver code cannot (or at least should not, if the system permits it) access user memory directly. This is to prevent driver code from accidentally or intentionally reading from or writing to inappropriate memory locations, such as kernel space.

To avoid this potential problem, special functions named `copy_to_user` and `copy_from_user` are provided by the operating system for use by drivers to access user memory. These functions take the necessary steps to validate the user-space addresses provided in the function call before copying data.

This section provided a brief introduction to the hardware-level operations performed by device drivers and introduced the top-level structure of a device driver.

During system power-up, before the operating system can boot and initialize its drivers, firmware must execute to perform low-level self-testing and system configuration. The next section presents an introduction to the code that first executes when the computer receives power: the BIOS.

BIOS

A computer's BIOS contains the code that first executes at system startup. In the early days of personal computers, the BIOS provided a set of programming interfaces that abstracted the details of peripheral interfaces such as keyboards and video displays.

In modern PCs, the BIOS performs system testing and peripheral device configuration during startup. After that process has completed, the processor interacts with peripheral devices directly without further use of the BIOS.

Early PCs stored the BIOS code in a **read-only memory** (**ROM**) chip on the motherboard. This code was permanently programmed and could not be altered. Modern motherboards generally store the motherboard BIOS in a reprogrammable flash memory device. This allows BIOS updates to be installed to add new features or to fix problems found in earlier firmware versions. The process of updating the BIOS is commonly known as *flashing the BIOS*.

One downside of BIOS reprogrammability is that this capability makes it possible for malicious code to be introduced into a system by writing to the BIOS flash memory. When this type of attack is successful, it enables the malicious code to execute every time the computer starts up. Fortunately, successful BIOS firmware attacks have proven to be quite rare.

As the BIOS takes control during system startup, one of the first things it does is run a **Power-On Self-Test (POST)** of key system components. During this testing, the BIOS attempts to interact with system components including the keyboard, video display, and boot device, typically a disk drive. Although the computer may contain a high-performance graphics processor, the video interface used by the BIOS during startup is normally a primitive video mode, supporting text display only.

The BIOS uses the video and keyboard interfaces to display any errors detected during system testing and allows the user to enter configuration mode and change stored settings. The keyboard and video interfaces provided by the BIOS enable the initial setup and configuration of a computer that does not yet contain a boot device.

When the video display is not working properly, the BIOS will be unable to present information related to the error. In this situation, the BIOS attempts to use the PC speaker to indicate the error, using a pattern of beeps. Motherboard documentation provides information about the type of error indicated by each beep pattern.

Depending on the system configuration, either the BIOS or the operating system manages the initialization of PCI devices during system startup. At the completion of a successful configuration process, all PCI devices have been assigned compatible I/O port ranges, memory-mapped I/O ranges, and interrupt numbers.

As startup proceeds, the operating system identifies the appropriate driver to associate with each peripheral based on manufacturer and device identification information provided through PCI/PCIe. Following successful association, the driver interacts directly with each peripheral to perform I/O operations upon request. System processes and user applications call a set of standardized driver functions to initiate access to the device, perform read and write operations, and close the device.

One common BIOS-related procedure is to select the boot order among the available storage devices. For example, this feature lets you configure the system to first attempt to boot from an optical disk containing a valid operating system image, if such a disk is in the drive. If no bootable optical disk is found, the system might then attempt to boot from the main disk drive. Several mass storage devices can be configured in priority order in this manner.

BIOS configuration mode is accessed by pressing a specific key, such as *Esc* or the *F2* function key, during the early stage of the boot process. The appropriate key to press is usually indicated on screen during boot-up. Upon entering BIOS configuration mode, settings are displayed on screen in a menu format. You can select among different screens to modify parameters associated with features such as boot priority order. After making parameter changes, an option is provided to save the changes to **nonvolatile memory** (**NVM**) and resume the boot process. Be careful when doing this, because making inappropriate changes to the BIOS settings can leave the computer unbootable.

The capabilities of BIOS implementations have grown substantially over the years since the introduction of the IBM PC. As PC architectures grew to support 32-bit and then 64-bit operating systems, the legacy BIOS architecture, however, failed to keep pace with the needs of the newer, more capable systems. Major industry participants undertook an initiative to define a system firmware architecture that left behind the limitations of the BIOS. The result of this effort was the UEFI standard, which replaced the traditional BIOS capabilities in modern motherboards.

UEFI

UEFI is a 2007 standard defining an architecture for firmware that implements the functions provided by the legacy BIOS and adds several significant enhancements. As with BIOS, UEFI contains code executed immediately upon system startup.

UEFI supports a number of design goals, including enabling support for larger boot disk devices (specifically, disk sizes greater than 2 **terabytes** (**TB**), faster start up times, and improved security during the boot process. UEFI provides several features that, when enabled and used properly, substantially reduce the possibility of accidental or malicious corruption of firmware stored in UEFI flash memory.

In addition to the capabilities provided by legacy BIOS implementations described previously, the UEFI supports these features:

- **UEFI applications** are executable code modules stored in UEFI flash memory. UEFI applications provide extensions of capabilities available in the motherboard pre-boot environment and, in some cases, provide services for use by operating systems during runtime. One example of a UEFI application is the UEFI shell, which presents a **command-line interface** (**CLI**) for interacting with the processor and peripheral devices. The UEFI shell supports device data queries and permits modification of nonvolatile configuration parameters. The GNU **GRand Unified Bootloader** (**GRUB**) is another example of a UEFI application. GRUB supports *multi-boot* configurations by presenting a menu from which the user selects one of multiple available operating system images to boot during system startup.

- **Architecture-independent device drivers** provide processor-independent implementations of device drivers for use by UEFI. This enables a single implementation of UEFI firmware to be used on architectures as diverse as x86 and **Advanced RISC Machine** (**ARM**) processors. Architecture-independent UEFI drivers are stored in a byte-code format that is interpreted by processor-specific firmware. These drivers enable UEFI interaction with peripherals such as graphics cards and network interfaces during the boot process.

- **Secure Boot** employs cryptographic certificates to ensure that only legitimate device drivers and operating system loaders are executed during system startup. This feature validates the digital signature of each firmware component before allowing it to execute. This validation process protects against many classes of malicious firmware-based attacks.

- **Faster booting** is achieved by performing operations in parallel that took place sequentially under the BIOS. In fact, booting is so much faster that many UEFI implementations do not offer the user an option to press a key during boot because waiting for a response would delay system startup. Instead, operating systems such as Windows enable entry to UEFI settings by allowing the user to request access while the operating system is running, followed by a reboot to enter the UEFI configuration screen.

The UEFI does not simply replace the functions of the old BIOS. It is a miniature operating system that supports advanced capabilities, such as allowing a remotely located technician to use a network connection to troubleshoot a PC that refuses to boot.

Following POST and the low-level configuration of system devices, and having identified the appropriate boot device based on boot priority order, the system begins the operating system boot process.

The boot process

The procedure for booting a system image varies, depending on the partition style of the mass storage device containing the image. Beginning in the early 1980s, the standard disk partition format was called the **master boot record** (**MBR**). An MBR partition has a boot sector located at the logical beginning of its storage space. The MBR boot sector contains information describing the device's logical partitions. Each partition contains a filesystem organized as a tree structure of directories and the files within them.

Due to the fixed format of MBR data structures, an MBR storage device can contain a maximum of four logical partitions and can be no larger than 2 TB in size, equal to 2^{32} 512-byte data sectors. These limits have become increasingly constraining as commercially available disk sizes grew beyond 2 TB. To resolve these issues, and in tandem with the development of UEFI, a new partition format called **GUID partition table** (**GPT**) (where **GUID** stands for **globally unique identifier**) was developed to eliminate restrictions on disk size and the number of partitions, while providing some additional enhancements.

A GPT-formatted disk has a maximum size of 2^{64} 512-byte sectors, accommodating over 8 billion TB of data. As normally configured, GPT supports up to 128 partitions per drive. The type of each partition is indicated by a 128-bit GUID, allowing an effectively unlimited number of new partition types to be defined in the future. Most users do not need very many partitions on a single disk, so the most obvious user benefit of GPT is its support for larger drives.

The boot process takes place with some differences between BIOS and UEFI motherboards, as described in the following sections.

BIOS boot

Following POST and device configuration, BIOS begins the boot process. BIOS attempts to boot from the first device in the configured priority sequence. If a valid device is present, the firmware reads a small piece of executable code called the *boot loader* from the MBR boot sector and transfers control to it. At that point, the BIOS firmware has completed execution and is no longer active for the duration of system operation. The boot loader initiates the process of loading and starting the operating system.

If a *boot manager* is used with a BIOS motherboard, the MBR boot sector code must start the manager rather than loading an operating system directly. A boot manager (such as GRUB) presents a list from which the user selects the desired operating system image. The BIOS firmware itself has no knowledge of multi-booting, and the boot manager operating system selection process takes place without BIOS involvement.

> **Multi-booting versus boot priority order**
> Multi-booting allows the user to select the desired operating system from a menu of available choices. This differs from the boot priority list maintained by the BIOS, which empowers the BIOS itself to select the first available operating system image.

UEFI boot

After the POST and device configuration stages have completed (in a manner very similar to the corresponding BIOS steps), UEFI begins the boot process. In a UEFI motherboard, a boot manager may be displayed as part of the UEFI start up procedure. A UEFI boot manager, which is part of the UEFI firmware, presents a menu from which the user can select the desired operating system image.

If the user does not select an operating system from the boot manager within a few seconds (or if no boot manager menu is displayed), the UEFI attempts to boot from the first device in the configured priority sequence.

The UEFI firmware reads the boot manager executable code (which is separate from the UEFI boot manager) and boot loader files from configured locations on the system disk and executes these files during the start up process.

The following screenshot shows portions of the system **boot configuration data** (**BCD**) information stored on a Windows 10 system. To display this information on your computer, you must run the bcdedit command from a command prompt with Administrator privilege:

```
C:\>bcdedit


Windows Boot Manager
--------------------
identifier              {bootmgr}
device                  partition=\Device\HarddiskVolume1
path                    \EFI\MICROSOFT\BOOT\BOOTMGFW.EFI
...


Windows Boot Loader
--------------------
identifier              {current}
device                  partition=C:
path                    \WINDOWS\system32\winload.efi
...
```

In this example, the **Windows Boot Manager** is located at \EFI\MICROSOFT\BOOT\ BOOTMGFW.EFI. This file is normally stored on a hidden disk partition and is not readily available for display in directory listings.

The **Windows boot loader** is identified as \WINDOWS\system32\winload.efi and is located at C:\Windows\System32\winload.efi.

Unlike personal computers, most embedded devices use a much simpler boot process that does not involve BIOS or UEFI. The next section discussions the boot process in embedded devices.

Embedded devices

Most embedded systems, such as smartphones, do not generally have separate boot firmware such as the BIOS or UEFI in a PC. As we saw with the 6502, these devices perform a processor hardware reset when power is turned on and begin code execution at a specified address. All code in these devices is typically located in a nonvolatile storage region such as flash memory.

During startup, embedded devices perform a sequence of events similar to the PC boot process. Peripheral devices are tested for proper operation and initialized prior to first use. The boot loader in such devices may need to select among multiple memory partitions to identify an appropriate system image. As with UEFI, embedded devices often incorporate security features during the boot process to ensure that the boot loader and operating system image are authentic before allowing the boot process to proceed.

In both PC and embedded systems, startup of the boot loader is the first step in bringing up the operating system, which is the subject of the next section.

Operating systems

An operating system is a multilayer suite of software, providing an environment in which applications perform useful functions such as word processing, placing telephone calls, or managing the operation of a car engine. Applications running within the operating system execute algorithms implemented as processor instruction sequences and perform I/O interactions with peripheral devices as required to complete their tasks.

The operating system provides standardized programming interfaces that application developers use to access system resources such as processor execution threads, disk files, input from a keyboard or other peripherals, and output to devices such as a computer screen or instruments on a dashboard.

Operating systems can be broadly categorized into real-time and non-real-time systems.

A **real-time operating system** (**RTOS**) provides features to ensure that responses to inputs occur within a defined time limit. Processors performing tasks such as managing the operation of a car engine or a kitchen appliance typically run an RTOS to ensure that the electrical and mechanical components they control receive responses to any change in inputs within a bounded time.

Non-real-time operating systems do not attempt to ensure that responses are generated within any particular time limit. Instead, these systems attempt to perform the processing as quickly as possible, even if it sometimes takes a long time.

> **Real-time versus non-real-time operating systems**
>
> RTOSes are not necessarily faster than non-real-time operating systems. A non-real-time operating system may be faster on average compared to an RTOS, but the non-real-time system may occasionally exceed the time limit specified for the RTOS. The goal of the RTOS is to never exceed the response time limit.

For the most part, general-purpose operating systems such as Windows and Linux are non-real-time operating systems. They try to get assigned tasks—such as reading a file into a word processor or computing a spreadsheet—finished as quickly as possible, though the time to complete an operation may vary widely, depending on what other tasks the system is performing.

Some aspects of general-purpose operating systems, particularly audio and video output, have specific real-time requirements. We've all seen poor video replay at one time or another, in which the video stutters and appears jerky. This behavior is the result of failing to meet the real-time performance demands of video display. Cell phones have similar real-time requirements for supporting two-way audio during voice telephone calls.

For both real-time and non-real-time operating systems, in standard PCs as well as in embedded devices, operating system startup tends to follow a similar sequence of steps. The boot loader either loads the operating system kernel into memory or simply jumps to an address in NVM to begin executing operating system code.

The operating system kernel performs the following steps, not necessarily in this order:

- The processor and other system devices are configured. This includes setting up any required registers internal to the processor and any associated I/O management devices, such as a chipset.
- In systems using paged virtual memory (introduced in *Chapter 7, Processor and Memory Architectures*), the kernel configures the memory management unit.
- Base-level system processes, including the **scheduler** and the **idle process**, are started. The scheduler manages the sequence of execution for process threads. The idle process contains the code that executes when there are no other threads ready for the scheduler to run.
- Device drivers are enumerated and associated with each peripheral in the system. Initialization code is executed for each driver, as discussed earlier in this chapter.
- Interrupts are configured and enabled. Once interrupts have been enabled, the system begins to perform I/O interactions with peripheral devices.
- System services are started. These processes support non-operating system activities (such as networking) and persistent installed capabilities (such as a web server).

- For PC-type computers, a user interface process is started, which presents a login screen. This screen allows the user to initiate an interactive session with the computer. In embedded devices, the real-time application begins execution. The basic operational sequence for a simple embedded application is to read inputs from I/O devices, execute a computation algorithm to generate outputs, and write the outputs to I/O devices, repeating this procedure at fixed time intervals.

This section uses the term *process* to indicate a program running on a processor. The term *thread* indicates a flow of execution within a process, of which there may be more than one. The next section examines these topics in more detail.

Processes and threads

Many, but not all, operating systems support the concept of multiple threads of execution. A **thread** is a sequence of program instructions that logically executes in isolation from other threads. An operating system running on a single-core processor creates the illusion of multiple simultaneously running threads with **time-slicing**.

When performing time-slicing, an operating system scheduler grants each ready-to-run thread a period of time in which to execute. As a thread's execution interval ends, the scheduler interrupts the running thread and continues executing the next thread in its queue. In this manner, the scheduler gives each thread a bit of time to run before going back to the beginning of the list and starting over again.

In operating systems capable of supporting multiple runnable programs simultaneously, the term *process* refers to a running instance of a computer program. The system allocates resources such as memory and membership in the scheduler's queue of runnable threads to each process.

When a process first begins execution, it contains a single thread. The process may create more threads as it executes. Programmers create multithread applications for various reasons, including the following:

- One thread can perform I/O while a separate thread executes the main algorithm of the program. For example, a primary thread can periodically update a user display with received information while a separate thread waits in a blocked state for user input from the keyboard.

- Applications with substantial computational requirements can take advantage of multiprocessor and multi-core computer architectures by splitting large computational jobs into groups of smaller tasks capable of execution in parallel. By running each of these smaller tasks as a separate thread, programs enable the scheduler to assign threads to execute on multiple cores simultaneously.

A process passes through a series of states during its life cycle. Some process states assigned by operating systems are as follows:

- **Initializing**: When a process is first started, perhaps as the result of a user double-clicking an icon on the desktop, the operating system begins loading the program code into memory and assigning system resources for its use.

- **Waiting**: After process initialization has completed, it is ready to run. At this point, its thread is assigned to the scheduler's queue of runnable threads. The process remains in the Waiting state until the scheduler permits it to start running.

- **Running**: The thread executes the program instructions contained in its code section.

- **Blocked**: The thread enters this state when it requests I/O from a device that causes execution to pause. For example, reading data from a file normally causes blocking. In this state, the thread waits in the Blocked state for the device driver to finish processing the request. As soon as a running thread becomes blocked, the scheduler is free to switch to another runnable thread while the first thread's I/O operation is in progress. When the operation completes, the blocked thread returns to the Waiting state in the scheduler queue and eventually returns to the Running state, where it processes the results of the I/O operation.

Ready-to-run processes rely on the system scheduler to receive execution time. The scheduler process is responsible for granting execution time to all system and user threads.

The scheduler is an interrupt-driven routine that executes at periodic time intervals, as well as in response to actions taken by threads such as the initiation of an I/O operation. During operating system initialization, a periodic timer is attached to the scheduler interrupt handler, and the scheduler timer is started.

While each process is in the Initializing state, the kernel adds a data structure called a **process control block** (**PCB**) to its list of running processes. The PCB contains information that the system requires to maintain and interact with the process over its lifetime, including memory allocations and details regarding the file containing its executable code. A process is usually identified by an integer that remains unique during its lifetime. In Windows, the **Resource Monitor** tool (you can start this tool by typing `Resource Monitor` into the Windows search box and clicking on the result identified as **Resource Monitor**) displays running processes, including the **process identifier** (**PID**) associated with each process. In Linux, the `top` command displays the processes consuming the most system resources, identifying each by its PID.

The scheduler maintains information associated with each thread in a **thread control block (TCB)**. Each process has a list of associated TCBs, with a minimum of one entry in the list. The TCB contains information related to the thread, including processor context. The **processor context** is the collection of information the kernel uses to resume execution of a blocked thread, consisting of these items:

- The saved processor registers
- The stack pointer
- The flags register
- The instruction pointer

Similar to the PID, each thread has an integer thread identifier that remains unique during its lifetime.

The scheduler uses one or more scheduling algorithms to ensure that execution time is allocated equitably among system and user processes. Two main categories of thread scheduling algorithms have been widely used since the early days of computing—non-preemptive and preemptive, described here:

- **Non-preemptive scheduling** grants a thread complete execution control, allowing it to run until it terminates, or voluntarily releases control to the scheduler so that other threads have a chance to run.

- In **preemptive scheduling**, the scheduler has the authority to stop a running thread and hand execution control over to another thread without requesting approval from the first thread. When a preemptive scheduler switches execution from one thread to another, it performs the following steps:

1. Either a timer interrupt occurs that causes the scheduler to begin execution, or a running thread performs an action that causes blocking, such as initiating an I/O operation.

2. The scheduler consults its list of runnable threads and determines which thread to place in the Running state.

3. The scheduler copies the departing thread's processor registers into the context fields of the thread's TCB.

4. The scheduler loads the context of the incoming thread into the processor registers.

5. The scheduler resumes execution of the incoming thread by jumping to the instruction pointed to by the thread's program counter.

Thread scheduling occurs at a high frequency, which implies the code involved in scheduler activity must be as efficient as possible. In particular, storing and retrieving processor context takes some time, so operating system designers make every effort to optimize the performance of the scheduler's context switching code.

Because there may be numerous processes competing for execution time at a given moment, the scheduler must ensure that critical system processes are able to execute at required intervals. At the same time, from the user's point of view, applications must remain responsive to user inputs while providing an acceptable level of performance during lengthy computations.

Various algorithms have been developed over the years to efficiently manage these competing demands. A key feature of most thread scheduling algorithms is the use of process priorities. The next section introduces several priority-based thread scheduling algorithms.

Scheduling algorithms and process priority

Operating systems supporting multiple processes generally provide a prioritization mechanism to ensure that the most important system functions receive adequate processing time, even when the system is under heavy load, while continuing to provide adequate time for the execution of lower-priority user processes. Several algorithms have been developed to meet various performance goals for different types of operating systems. Some algorithms that have been popular over the years, beginning with the simplest, are as follows:

- **First come, first served (FCFS)**: This non-preemptive approach was common in legacy batch processing operating systems. In an FCFS scheduling algorithm, each process is granted execution control and retains control until execution is completed. There is no prioritization of processes, and the time to complete any process is dependent on the execution time of processes preceding it in the input queue.

- **Cooperative multithreading**: Early versions of Windows and macOS used a non-preemptive multithreading architecture that relied on each thread to voluntarily relinquish control to the operating system at frequent intervals. This required significant effort by application developers to ensure a single application did not starve other applications of opportunities to execute by failing to release control at appropriate intervals. Each time the operating system received control, it selected the next thread to execute from a prioritized list of runnable threads.

- **Round-robin scheduling**: A preemptive round-robin scheduler maintains a list of runnable threads and grants each of them an execution interval in turn, starting over at the beginning of the list upon reaching the end. This approach effectively sets all process priorities equally, giving each a chance to execute for defined periods of time, at time intervals dependent on the number of processes in the scheduler's list.

- **Fixed-priority preemptive scheduling**: In this algorithm, each thread is assigned a fixed priority value indicating the importance of its receiving execution control when it is in the Waiting state. When a thread enters the Waiting state, if it has a higher priority than the currently running thread, the scheduler immediately stops the running thread and turns control over to the incoming thread. The scheduler maintains the list of Waiting processes in priority order, with the highest priority threads at the head of the line. This algorithm can result in the failure of lower-priority threads to get any execution time at all if higher-priority threads monopolize the available execution time.

- **Rate-monotonic scheduling (RMS)** is a fixed-priority preemptive scheduling algorithm commonly used in real-time systems with hard deadlines (a hard deadline is one that cannot be missed). Under RMS, threads that execute more frequently are assigned higher priorities. As long as a few criteria are satisfied (the thread execution interval equals the deadline; there can be no delay-inducing interactions between threads; and context switch time is negligible), if the maximum possible execution time of each thread is below a mathematically derived limit, deadlines are guaranteed to be met.

- **Fair scheduling**: Fair scheduling attempts to maximize the utilization of processor time while ensuring that each user is granted an equal amount of execution time. Rather than assigning numeric priorities to threads, the effective priority of each thread is determined by the amount of execution time it has consumed. As a thread uses more and more processor time, its priority declines, enabling other threads more opportunities to run. This approach has the benefit that, for interactive users who do not consume much execution time, the responsiveness of the system is improved. The Linux kernel uses a fair scheduling algorithm as its default scheduler.

- **Multilevel feedback queue**: This algorithm uses multiple queues, each with a different priority level. New threads are added at the tail of the highest-priority queue. At each scheduling interval, the scheduler grants execution to the thread at the head of the high-priority queue and removes the thread from the queue, which moves the remaining threads closer to execution. Eventually, the newly created thread receives an opportunity to execute. If the thread consumes all the execution time granted to it, it is preempted at the completion of its interval and added to the tail of the next lower-priority queue. The Windows Scheduler is a multilevel feedback queue.

The system idle process contains the thread that executes when there is no user- or system-assigned thread in the Waiting state. An idle process may be as simple as a single instruction that forms an infinite loop, jumping to itself. Some operating systems place the system in a power-saving mode during idle periods, rather than executing an idle loop.

The percentage of processor time consumed by running processes is computed by determining the fraction of time the system was executing a non-idle thread over a measurement period.

The following screenshot is a Windows Resource Monitor view of running processes consuming the highest average share of processor time:

Figure 5.1: Windows Resource Monitor process display

In this figure, the **PID** column displays the numeric process identifier, and the **Threads** column shows the number of threads in the process. The process state is **Running** for all of the processes visible in this display.

The following screenshot shows the result of running the `top` command on a Linux system:

```
⊗ ⊖ ⊕   jim@jim-VirtualBox: ~
top - 18:16:25 up 11:16,  1 user,  load average: 0.00, 0.21, 0.67
Tasks: 183 total,   1 running, 182 sleeping,   0 stopped,   0 zombie
%Cpu(s):  4.8 us,  1.0 sy,  0.0 ni, 94.2 id,  0.0 wa,  0.0 hi,  0.0 si,  0.0 st
KiB Mem :  4046384 total,  1135716 free,   900736 used,  2009932 buff/cache
KiB Swap:        0 total,        0 free,        0 used.  2798540 avail Mem

  PID USER      PR  NI    VIRT    RES    SHR S  %CPU %MEM     TIME+ COMMAND
 2110 jim       20   0 1224192 163008  81456 S   3.7  4.0 508:13.96 compiz
  974 root      20   0  358516  79944  36340 S   2.3  2.0  88:58.41 Xorg
 2259 jim       20   0  945448  49416  39064 S   0.7  1.2   0:11.74 nautilus
 9456 jim       20   0  665284  36824  29000 S   0.7  0.9   0:00.84 gnome-terminal-
 1808 jim       20   0  111968   2132   1780 S   0.3  0.1   0:34.57 VBoxClient
 1882 jim       20   0  344984   6452   5376 S   0.3  0.2   0:00.07 ibus-daemon
    1 root      20   0  119876   5992   3980 S   0.0  0.1   0:01.50 systemd
    2 root      20   0       0      0      0 S   0.0  0.0   0:00.00 kthreadd
    3 root      20   0       0      0      0 S   0.0  0.0   0:00.26 ksoftirqd/0
    5 root       0 -20       0      0      0 S   0.0  0.0   0:00.00 kworker/0:0H
    6 root      20   0       0      0      0 S   0.0  0.0   0:01.30 kworker/u2:0
    7 root      20   0       0      0      0 S   0.0  0.0   0:01.31 rcu_sched
    8 root      20   0       0      0      0 S   0.0  0.0   0:00.00 rcu_bh
    9 root      rt   0       0      0      0 S   0.0  0.0   0:00.00 migration/0
   10 root      rt   0       0      0      0 S   0.0  0.0   0:00.10 watchdog/0
   11 root      20   0       0      0      0 S   0.0  0.0   0:00.00 kdevtmpfs
   12 root       0 -20       0      0      0 S   0.0  0.0   0:00.00 netns
   13 root       0 -20       0      0      0 S   0.0  0.0   0:00.00 perf
   14 root      20   0       0      0      0 S   0.0  0.0   0:00.01 khungtaskd
```

Figure 5.2: Linux top command process display

The upper part of the display contains summary information, including the number of processes (referred to as `Tasks` here) in each state.

Each row in the lower part of the display presents information about one running process. As in Windows, the `PID` column indicates the PID. The state of each process is shown in the `S` column, with these possible values:

- **R**: Runnable, meaning either running or in the queue of ready-to-run threads.
- **S**: Sleeping: Paused while blocked; waiting for an event to complete.
- **T**: Stopped in response to a job control command (pressing *CTRL+Z* will do this).
- **Z**: Zombie, which occurs when a child process of another process terminates, but the child process information continues to be maintained by the system until the parent process ends.
- **PR**: The PR column displays the scheduling priority of the process. Smaller numbers represent higher priorities.

Up to this point, we have referred to the computer processor as a singular entity. In most modern PCs, the processor integrated circuit contains two or more processor cores, each implementing the features of a complete, independent processor, including a control unit, register set, and **arithmetic logic unit (ALU)**. The next section discusses the attributes of systems containing multiple processing units.

Multiprocessing

A **multiprocessing** computer contains two or more processors that simultaneously execute sequences of instructions. The processors in such a system typically share access to system resources, such as main memory and peripheral devices. The processors in a multiprocessing system may be of the same architecture, or individual processors may be of differing architectures to support unique system requirements. Systems in which all processors are treated as equal are referred to as **symmetric multiprocessing** systems. Devices that contain multiple processors within a single integrated circuit are called **multi-core processors**.

At the level of the operating system scheduler, a symmetric multiprocessing environment simply provides more processors for use in thread scheduling. In such systems, the scheduler treats additional processors as resources when assigning threads for execution.

In a well-designed symmetric multiprocessing system, throughput can approach the ideal of scaling linearly with the number of available processor cores, as long as contention for shared resources is minimal. If multiple threads on separate cores attempt to perform heavy simultaneous access to main memory, for example, there will be inevitable performance degradation as the system arbitrates access to the resource and shares it among competing threads. A multichannel interface to **dynamic random-access memory (DRAM)** can improve system performance in this scenario.

A symmetric multiprocessing system is an example of a **multiple instruction, multiple data (MIMD)** architecture. MIMD is a parallel processing configuration in which each processor core executes an independent sequence of instructions on its own set of data. A **single instruction, multiple data (SIMD)** parallel processing configuration, on the other hand, performs the same instruction operation on multiple data elements simultaneously.

Modern processors implement SIMD instructions to perform parallel processing on large datasets such as graphical images and audio data sequences. In current-generation PCs, the use of multi-core processors enables MIMD execution parallelism, while specialized instructions within the processors provide a degree of SIMD execution parallelism. SIMD processing will be discussed further in *Chapter 8, Performance-Enhancing Techniques*.

Processor clock speeds have grown from the 4.77 MHz of the original PC to over 4 GHz in modern processors, nearly a thousand-fold increase. Future speed increases are likely to be more limited as fundamental physical limits present looming obstacles. To compensate for limited future performance gains from increases in clock speed, the processor industry has turned to emphasizing various forms of execution parallelism in personal computer systems and smart devices. Future trends are likely to continue the growth in parallelism as systems integrate dozens, then hundreds, and eventually thousands of processor cores executing in parallel in PCs, smartphones, and other digital devices.

Summary

This chapter began with an overview of device drivers, including details on the instruction sequences used by driver code to read from and write to a simple I/O device, the PC parallel port. We continued with a discussion of the legacy BIOS and the newer UEFI, which provide the code that first executes on PC power-up, performs device testing and initialization, and initiates loading of the operating system.

We continued with a description of some of the fundamental elements of operating systems, including processes, threads, and the scheduler. Various scheduling algorithms used in past computers and the systems of today were introduced. We examined the output of tools available in Windows and Linux that present information about running processes.

The chapter concluded with a discussion of multiprocessing and its performance impact on the computer systems of today, as well as the implications of MIMD and SIMD parallel processing for the future of computing.

The next chapter will introduce specialized computing domains and their unique processing requirements in the areas of real-time computing, digital signal processing, and **graphics processing unit (GPU)** processing.

Exercises

1. Restart your computer and enter the BIOS or UEFI settings. Examine each of the menus available in this environment. Does your computer have BIOS or does it use UEFI? Does your motherboard support overclocking? When you are finished, be sure to select the option to quit without saving changes unless you are absolutely certain you want to make changes.

2. Run the appropriate command on your computer to display the currently running processes. What is the PID of the process you are using to run this command?

6
Specialized Computing Domains

Most computer users are, at least superficially, familiar with key performance-related attributes of personal computers and smart digital devices, such as processor speed and **random-access memory** (**RAM**) size. This chapter explores the performance requirements of computing domains that tend to be less directly visible to users, including real-time systems, digital signal processing, and **graphics processing unit** (**GPU**) processing.

We will examine the unique computing features associated with each of these domains and review some examples of modern devices implementing these concepts.

After completing this chapter, you will be able to identify application areas that require real-time computing and you will understand the uses of digital signal processing, with an emphasis on wireless communication. You will also understand the basic architecture of modern GPUs and will be familiar with some modern implementations of components in the computing domains discussed in this chapter.

This chapter covers the following topics:

- Real-time computing
- Digital signal processing
- GPU processing
- Examples of specialized architectures

Real-time computing

The previous chapter provided a brief introduction to some of the requirements of real-time-computing in terms of a system's responsiveness to changes in its inputs. These requirements are specified in the form of timing deadlines that limit how long the system can take to produce an output in response to a change in its input. This section will look at these timing specifications in more detail and will present the specific features real-time computing systems implement to ensure timing requirements are met.

Real-time computing systems can be categorized as providing soft or hard guarantees of responsiveness. A **soft real-time system** is considered to perform acceptably if it meets its desired response time most, but not necessarily all, of the time. An example of a soft real-time application is the clock display on a cell phone. When opening the clock display, some implementations momentarily present the time that was shown the last time the clock display was opened before quickly updating to the correct, current time. Of course, users would like the clock to show the correct time whenever it is displayed, but momentary glitches such as this aren't usually seen as a significant problem.

A **hard real-time system**, on the other hand, is considered to have failed if it ever misses any of its response-time deadlines. Safety-critical systems such as airbag controllers in automobiles and flight control systems for commercial aircraft have hard real-time requirements. Designers of these systems take timing requirements very seriously and devote substantial effort to ensuring the real-time processor satisfies its timing requirements under all possible operating conditions.

The control flow of a simple real-time system is shown in the following screenshot:

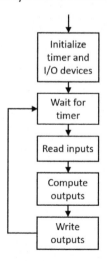

Figure 6.1: Real-time system control flow

Figure 6.1 represents a real-time computing system using a hardware interval timer to control the time sequencing of its operation. A down-counting interval timer performs a repetitive cycle of the following steps:

1. Load the counter register with a predefined numeric value.

2. Decrement the counter at a fixed clock rate.

3. When the count reaches zero, generate an event such as setting a bit in a register or triggering an interrupt.

4. Go back to Step 1.

An interval timer generates a periodic sequence of events with timing accuracy that depends on the accuracy of the system clock, which is often driven by a quartz crystal. By waiting for the timer event at the top of each loop, the system in *Figure 6.1* begins each execution pass at fixed, equal time intervals.

To satisfy the demands of hard real-time operation, the execution time of the code inside the loop (the code contained in the **Read inputs**, **Compute outputs**, and **Write outputs** blocks in *Figure 6.1*) must always be less than the timer interval. Prudent system developers ensure that no path through the code results in execution time anywhere close to the hard real-time limit. A conservative system design rule might insist the longest execution path for code inside the loop consumes no more than 50% of the timer interval.

Practical real-time systems constructed in this configuration might be based on an 8-, 16-, or 32-bit processor running at a clock frequency in the tens to hundreds of MHz. The timer employed in the main loop of such systems generates events at a developer-selected frequency, often in the range 10 to 1000 Hz.

The code represented in *Figure 6.1* runs directly on the processor hardware with no intervening software layers. This configuration contains no operating system of the type described in *Chapter 5, Hardware-Software Interface*. A sophisticated real-time application is likely to have more extensive needs than can be met by this simplistic architecture, making the use of a real-time operating system attractive.

Real-time operating systems

A **real-time operating system** (**RTOS**) contains several features superficially similar to the general-purpose operating systems discussed in *Chapter 5, Hardware-Software Interface*. An RTOS design differs significantly from general-purpose operating systems, however, in that all RTOS aspects—from kernel internals, to device drivers, to system services— are focused on meeting hard real-time requirements.

Most RTOS designs employ preemptive multithreading, often referred to as **multitasking** in RTOS literature. The terms *task* and *thread* are somewhat synonymous in the RTOS context, so for consistency we will continue to use the term *thread* to indicate an RTOS task.

RTOS designs at the lower end of the sophistication scale typically support multithreading within the context of a single application process. These simpler RTOSes support thread prioritization but often lack memory protection features.

More sophisticated RTOS architectures provide multiple thread privilege levels and operating system features such as memory protection, in addition to prioritized, preemptive multithreading. These RTOSes allow multiple processes to be in the Running state simultaneously, each potentially containing several threads. In protected memory systems, kernel memory access by application threads is prohibited and applications cannot reach into each other's memory regions. Many RTOSes support multi-core processor architectures.

RTOS environments, from lower to higher levels of sophistication, provide several data structures and communication techniques geared toward efficient data transfer between threads, and to support controlled access to shared resources. Some examples of these features are as follows:

- **Mutex**: A mutex (short for *mutual exclusion*) is a mechanism for a thread to claim access to a shared resource, without blocking the execution of other threads. In its simplest form, a mutex is a variable accessible to all threads that has the value 0 when the resource is free and 1 when the resource is in use. A thread that wants to use the resource reads the current value of the mutex variable and, if it is 0, sets it to 1 and performs the operation with the resource. After completing the operation, the thread sets the mutex back to 0. There are, however, some potential problems with mutexes:

  Thread preemption: Let's say a thread reads the mutex variable and sees that it is 0. Because the scheduler can interrupt an executing thread at any time, that thread might be interrupted before it has a chance to set the mutex to 1. A different thread then resumes execution and takes control of the same resource because it sees the mutex is still 0. When the original thread resumes, it finishes setting the mutex to 1 (even though, by now, it has already been set to 1). At this point, both threads incorrectly believe they have exclusive access to the resource, which is likely to lead to serious problems.

To prevent this scenario, many processors implement some form of a **test-and-set instruction**. A test-and-set instruction reads a value from a memory address and sets that location to 1 in a single, uninterruptable (also referred to as **atomic**) action. In the x86 architecture, the BTS (bit test and set) instruction performs this atomic operation. In processor architectures that lack a test-and-set instruction (such as the 6502), the risk of preemption can be eliminated by disabling interrupts before checking the state of the mutex variable, then re-enabling interrupts after setting the mutex to 1. This approach has the disadvantage of reducing real-time responsiveness while interrupts are disabled.

Priority inversion: Priority inversion occurs when a higher-priority thread attempts to gain access to a resource while the corresponding mutex is held by a lower-priority thread. In this situation, RTOS implementations generally place the higher-priority thread in a blocked state, allowing the lower-priority thread to complete its operation and release the mutex. The priority inversion problem occurs when a thread with a priority between the upper and lower levels of the two threads begins execution. While this mid-priority thread is running, it prevents the lower-priority thread from executing and releasing the mutex. The higher-priority thread must now wait until the mid-priority thread finishes execution, effectively disrupting the entire thread prioritization scheme. This can lead to failure of the high-priority thread to meet its deadline.

One method to prevent priority inversion is **priority inheritance**. In an RTOS implementing priority inheritance, whenever a higher-priority thread (thread2) requests a mutex held by a lower-priority thread (thread1), thread1 is temporarily raised in priority to the level of thread2. This eliminates any possibility of a mid-priority thread delaying the completion of the (originally) lower-priority thread1. When thread1 releases the mutex, the RTOS restores its original priority.

Deadlock: Deadlock can occur when multiple threads attempt to lock multiple mutexes. If thread1 and thread2 both require mutex1 and mutex2, a situation may arise in which thread1 locks mutex1 and attempts to locks mutex2, while at the same time thread2 has already locked mutex2 and attempts to lock mutex1. Neither task can proceed from this state, hence the term *deadlock*. Some RTOS implementations check the ownership of mutexes during lock attempts and report an error in a deadlock situation. In simpler RTOS designs, it is up to the system developer to ensure deadlock cannot occur.

- **Semaphore**: A semaphore is a generalization of the mutex. Semaphores can be of two types: binary and counting. A **binary semaphore** is similar to a mutex except that rather than controlling access to a resource, the binary semaphore is intended to be used by one task to send a signal to another task. If `thread1` attempts to *take* `semaphore1` while it is unavailable, `thread1` will block until another thread or interrupt service routine *gives* `semaphore1`.

  A **counting semaphore** contains a counter with an upper limit. Counting semaphores are used to control access to multiple interchangeable resources. When a thread takes the counting semaphore, the counter increments and the task proceeds. When the counter reaches its limit, a thread attempting to take the semaphore blocks until another thread gives the semaphore, decrementing the counter.

  Consider the example of a system that supports a limited number of simultaneously open files. A counting semaphore can be used to manage file open and close operations. If the system supports up to 10 open files and a thread attempts to open an 11th file, a counting semaphore with a limit of 10 will block the file open operation until another file is closed and its descriptor becomes available.

- **Queue**: A **queue** (also referred to as a **message queue**) is a unidirectional communication path between processes or threads. The sending thread places data items into the queue and the receiving thread retrieves those items in the same order they were sent. The RTOS synchronizes accesses between the sender and receiver so the receiver only retrieves complete data items. Queues are commonly implemented with a fixed-size storage buffer. The buffer will eventually fill and block further insertions if a sending thread adds data items faster than the receiving thread retrieves them.

  RTOS message queues provide a programming interface for the receiving thread to check if the queue contains data. Many queue implementations also support the use of a semaphore to signal a blocked receiving thread when data is available.

- **Critical section**: It is common for multiple threads to require access to a shared data structure. When using shared data, it is vital that read and write operations from different threads do not overlap in time. If such an overlap occurs, the reading thread may receive inconsistent information if it accesses the data structure while another thread is in the midst of an update. The mutex and semaphore mechanisms provide options for controlling access to such data structures. The use of a critical section is an alternate approach that isolates the code accessing the shared data structure and allows only one thread to execute that sequence at a time.

A simple method to implement a critical section is to disable interrupts just before entering a critical section and re-enable interrupts after completing the critical section. This prevents the scheduler from running and ensures the thread accessing the data structure has sole control until it exits the critical section. This method has the disadvantage of impairing real-time responsiveness by preventing responses to interrupts, including thread scheduling, while interrupts are disabled.

Some RTOS implementations provide a more sophisticated implementation of the critical section technique, involving the use of critical section data objects. Critical section objects typically provide options to allow a thread to either enter a blocked state until the critical section becomes available or test if the critical section is in use without blocking. The option for testing critical section availability allows the thread to perform other work while waiting for the critical section to become free.

This section provided a brief introduction to some of the communication and resource management capabilities common to RTOS implementations. There are far more real-time computing systems in operation today than there are PCs we think of as *computers*. General-purpose computers represent less than 1% of the digital processors produced each year. Devices ranging from children's toys, to digital thermometers, to televisions, to automobiles, to spacecraft contain at least one, and often contain dozens of embedded processors, each running some type of RTOS.

The next section introduces processing architectures used in the processing of digital samples of analog signals.

Digital signal processing

A **digital signal processor** (**DSP**) is optimized to perform computations on digitized representations of analog signals. Real-world signals such as audio, video, cell phone transmissions, and radar are **analog** in nature, meaning the information being processed is the response of an electrical sensor to a continuously varying voltage. Before a digital processor can begin to work with an analog signal, the signal voltage must be converted to a digital representation by an **analog-to-digital converter** (**ADC**). The following section describes the operation of ADCs and **digital-to-analog converters** (**DACs**).

ADCs and DACs

An ADC measures an analog input voltage and produces a digital output word representing the input voltage. ADCs often use a DAC internally during the conversion process. A DAC performs the reverse operation of an ADC, converting a digital word to an analog voltage.

A variety of circuit architectures are used in DAC applications, generally with the goal of achieving a combination of low cost, high speed, and high precision. One of the simplest DAC designs is the **R-2R ladder**, shown here in a 4-bit input configuration:

Figure 6.2: R-2R ladder DAC

This DAC uses a 4-bit data word on the inputs d_0-d_3 to generate an analog voltage, V_O. If we assume each bit of the 4-bit word **d** is driven at either 0 V (for a 0-bit) or 5 V (for a 1-bit), the output V_O equals $(d / 2^4) * 5\ V$, where **d** is a data value in the range 0 to 15. An input word of 0 has an output of 0 V, and an input word of 15 has an output of $(15/16)$ $* 5V = 4.6875V$. Intermediate values of **d** produce equally spaced output voltages at intervals of $(1/16) * 5V = 0.3125V$.

An ADC can use an internal DAC in this manner (though usually with a larger number of bits, with a correspondingly finer voltage resolution) to determine the digital equivalent of an analog input voltage.

Because the analog input signal can vary continuously over time, ADC circuits generally use a **sample-and-hold** circuit to maintain a constant analog voltage during the conversion process. A sample-and-hold circuit is an analog device with a digital **hold** input signal. When the hold input is inactive, the sample-and-hold output tracks the input voltage. When the hold input is active, the sample-and-hold circuit freezes its output voltage at the input voltage that was present at the moment the hold signal was activated.

With its input held constant, the ADC uses its DAC to determine the digital equivalent of the input voltage. To make this determination, the ADC uses a **comparator**, which is a circuit that compares two analog voltages and produces a digital output signal indicating which is the higher voltage. The ADC feeds the sample-and-hold output voltage into one input of the comparator and the DAC output into the other input, as shown in the following diagram, in which the DAC input word size is *n* bits:

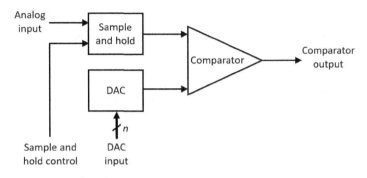

Figure 6.3: ADC architecture

The job of the ADC is to determine the DAC input word that causes the comparator to change state. A simple way to do this is to count upward from zero, writing each numeric value to the DAC inputs and observing the comparator output to see if it changed state. The DAC output that first causes the comparator to change state is the smallest DAC output voltage that is greater than the sample-and-hold output voltage. The actual sampled analog voltage is between this DAC output and the DAC output from a data word one count smaller. This ADC configuration is called a **counter type ADC**.

While simple in concept, the counter type ADC can be quite slow, especially if the word size is large. A faster method is to sequentially compare each bit in the DAC data word, beginning with the most significant bit. Starting with a data word of 1000b in our 4-bit example, the first comparator reading indicates if the analog input voltage is above or below the DAC voltage midpoint. This determines if bit $\mathbf{d}_3$ of the ADC reading is 0 or 1. Using the now-known value of $\mathbf{d}_3$, $\mathbf{d}_2$ is set to 1 to indicate which quarter of the full-scale range the input voltage lies within. This procedure is repeated to sequentially determine each of the remaining bits, ending with the least significant bit.

This ADC conversion technique is referred to as **successive approximation**. A successive approximation ADC is much faster than a counter type ADC. In our example, the maximum possible number of comparisons drops from 16 to 4. In a 12-bit successive approximation ADC, the potential number of comparisons drops from 4,096 to 12. Successive approximation ADCs are available with resolutions from 8 to 18 bits, with maximum conversion rates up to several MHz.

ADCs and DACs are characterized by resolution and maximum conversion speed. The resolution of an ADC or DAC is determined by the number of bits in its data word. The maximum conversion speed determines how quickly the ADC or DAC can produce sequential outputs.

To process real-time data, an ADC produces a sequence of measurements at periodic time intervals for use as input to further processing. Requirements for data word resolution and sample rate vary widely depending on the particular DSP application. Some examples of standard digitized analog data formats are as follows:

- Compact disk digital audio is sampled at 44.1 kHz with 16 bits per sample in two channels, corresponding to the left and right speakers.

- Video cameras measure the analog light intensity received at each pixel in a two-dimensional array and convert the reading to a digital word, usually 8 bits wide. Separate closely spaced sensors with color filters produce red, green, and blue measurements for each pixel in the image. The complete dataset for a single pixel consists of 24 bits, composed of three 8-bit color values. A single image can contain tens of millions of pixels, and video cameras typically produce 30 to 60 frames per second. Because digital video recording produces such an enormous quantity of data, compression algorithms are generally used to reduce storage and transmission requirements.

- A mobile phone contains a radio frequency transceiver that down-converts the received radio frequency signal to a frequency range suitable for input to an ADC. Typical parameters for a mobile phone ADC are 12 bits of resolution and a sample rate of 50 MHz.

- An automotive radar system samples radio frequency energy reflected from nearby obstacles with a resolution of 16 bits at a rate of 5 MHz.

DSP hardware features

DSPs are optimized to execute signal processing algorithms on digitized samples of analog information. The **dot product** is a fundamental operation used in many algorithms performed by DSPs. If A and B are two equal-length vectors (a **vector** is a one-dimensional array of numeric values), the dot product of A and B is formed by multiplying each element of A by the corresponding element of B, and summing the resulting products. Mathematically, if the length of each vector is n (indexed from 0 to n-1), the dot product of the vectors is as follows:

$$A \cdot B = \sum_{i=0}^{n-1} A_i B_i = A_0 B_0 + A_1 B_1 + A_2 B_2 + \cdots + A_{n-1} B_{n-1}$$

The repetitive nature of the dot product calculation provides a natural path for performance optimization in digital systems. The basic operation performed in the dot product computation is called **multiply-accumulate (MAC)**.

A single MAC consists of multiplying two numbers together and adding the result to an accumulator, which must be initialized to zero at the beginning of the dot product calculation. The mathematical performance of DSP chips is commonly measured in terms of MACs per second. Many DSP architectures are capable of performing one MAC per instruction clock cycle.

To perform a MAC on every clock cycle, a DSP cannot dedicate separate clock cycles to read a MAC instruction from program memory, read each of the vector elements to be multiplied from data memory, compute the product, and add it to the accumulator. All of these things must happen in one step.

The von Neumann architecture, introduced in *Chapter 1*, *Introducing Computer Architecture*, uses a single memory region for program instructions and data. This configuration results in a limitation known as the **von Neumann bottleneck**, resulting from the need to pass program instructions and data values sequentially across a single processor-to-memory interface.

This effect can be mitigated by using an architecture that separates program instructions and data storage into two separate memory regions, each with its own processor interface. This configuration, called the **Harvard architecture**, allows program instruction and data memory access to occur in parallel, enabling instructions to execute in a smaller number of clock cycles.

A DSP with a Harvard architecture must perform two data memory accesses to retrieve the elements of the *A* and *B* vectors to be multiplied in a MAC operation. This normally requires two clock cycles, failing to meet the performance goal of one MAC per clock cycle. A **modified Harvard architecture** supports the use of program memory to store data values in addition to instructions. In many DSP applications, the values of one of the vectors (let's say the *A* vector) involved in the dot product are constant values known at the time the application is compiled. In a modified Harvard architecture, the elements of the A vector can be stored in program memory and the elements of the *B* vector, representing input data read from an ADC, are stored in data memory.

To perform each MAC operation in this architecture, one element of the *A* vector is read from program memory, one element of the *B* vector is read from data memory, and the accumulated product is stored in an internal processor register. If the DSP contains cache memory for program instructions, the MAC instruction performing each step of the dot product will be read from cache once the first MAC operation reads it from program memory, avoiding further memory access cycles to retrieve the instruction. This configuration (modified Harvard architecture with program instruction caching) enables single-cycle MAC operations for all iterations of the dot product once the first MAC has completed. Since the vectors involved in real-world dot product computations commonly contain hundreds or even thousands of elements, the overall performance of the dot product operation can closely approach the ideal of one MAC per DSP clock cycle.

A DSP can be categorized as having a fixed-point or a floating-point architecture. Fixed-point DSPs use signed or unsigned integers to perform mathematical operations such as MAC. Fixed-point DSPs are generally less costly than floating-point DSPs. However, fixed-point mathematics has the potential for numeric issues such as overflow, which can manifest by exceeding the range of the dot product accumulator.

To reduce the possibility of overflow, DSPs often implement an extended range accumulator, sometimes 40 bits wide in a 32-bit architecture, to support dot products on lengthy vectors. Due to concerns regarding overflow and related numerical issues, programming fixed-point DSPs requires extra effort to ensure these effects don't result in unacceptable performance degradation.

Floating-point DSPs often use a 32-bit wide numeric format for internal calculations. Once an integer ADC reading has been received by the DSP, all further processing is performed using floating-point operations. By taking advantage of floating-point operations, the potential for issues such as overflow is drastically reduced, resulting in quicker software development cycles.

The use of floating-point also improves the fidelity of computation results, realized in terms of improved **signal-to-noise ratio** (**SNR**) in comparison to an equivalent fixed-point implementation. Fixed-point calculations quantize the result of each mathematical operation at the level of the integer's least significant bit. Floating-point operations generally maintain accurate results from each operation to a small fraction of the corresponding fixed-point least significant bit.

Signal processing algorithms

Building upon our understanding of DSP hardware and the operations it supports, we will next look at some examples of digital signal processing algorithms in real-world applications.

Convolution

Convolution is a formal mathematical operation on par with addition and multiplication. Unlike addition and multiplication, which operate on pairs of numbers, convolution operates on pairs of signals. In the DSP context, a signal is a series of digitized samples of a time-varying input measured at equally spaced time intervals. Convolution is the most fundamental operation in the field of digital signal processing.

In many practical applications, one of the two signals involved in a convolution operation is a fixed vector of numbers stored in DSP memory. The other signal is a sequence of samples originating from ADC measurements. To implement the convolution operation, as each ADC measurement is received, the DSP computes an updated output, which is simply the dot product of the fixed data vector (let's say the length of this vector is n) and the most recent n input samples received from the ADC. To compute the convolution of these vectors, the DSP must perform n MAC operations each time it receives an ADC sample.

The fixed vector used in this example, referred to as h, is called the **impulse response**. A digital impulse is defined as a theoretically infinite sequence of samples in which one sample is 1 and all the preceding and following samples are 0. Using this vector as the input to a convolution with the vector h produces an output identical to the sequence h, surrounded by preceding and following zeros. The single 1 value in the impulse sequence multiplies each element of h on successive iterations, while all other elements of h are multiplied by 0.

The particular values contained in the h vector determine the effects of the convolution operation on the input data sequence. Digital filtering is one common application of convolution.

Digital filtering

A **frequency selective filter** is a circuit or algorithm that receives an input signal and attempts to pass desired frequency ranges to the output without distortion while eliminating, or at least reducing to an acceptable level, frequency ranges outside the desired ranges.

We are all familiar with the bass and treble controls in audio entertainment systems. These are examples of frequency selective filters. The bass function implements a variable gain **lowpass filter**, meaning the audio signal is filtered to select the lower frequency portion of the audio signal, and this filtered signal is fed to an amplifier that varies its output power in response to the position of the bass control. The treble section is implemented similarly, using a **highpass filter** to select the higher frequencies in the audio signal. The outputs of these amplifiers are combined to produce the signal sent to the speakers.

Frequency selective filters can be implemented with analog technology or using digital signal processing techniques. Simple analog filters are cheap and only require a few circuit components. However, the performance of these filters leaves much to be desired.

Some key parameters of a frequency selective filter are **stopband suppression** and the width of the **transition band**. Stopband suppression indicates how good a job the filter does of eliminating undesired frequencies in its output. In general, a filter does not entirely eliminate undesired frequencies, but for practical purposes these frequencies can be reduced to a level that is so small they are irrelevant. The transition band of a filter describes the frequency span between the passband and the stopband. The **passband** is the range of frequencies to be passed through the filter, and the **stopband** is the range of frequencies to be blocked by the filter. It is not possible to have a perfectly sharp edge between the passband and stopband. Some separation between the passband and the stopband is required, and trying to make the transition from passband to stopband as narrow as possible requires a more complex filter than one with a wider transition band.

A digital frequency selective filter is implemented with a convolution operation using a carefully selected set of values for the h vector. With the proper selection of elements in h, it is possible to design highpass, lowpass, bandpass, and bandstop filters. As discussed in the preceding paragraphs, highpass and lowpass filters attempt to pass the high and low frequency ranges, respectively, while blocking other frequencies. A **bandpass filter** attempts to pass only the frequencies within a specified range and block all other frequencies outside that range. A **bandstop filter** attempts to pass all frequencies except those within a specified range.

The goals of a high-performance frequency selective filter are to impart minimal distortion of the signal in the passband, provide effective blocking of frequencies in the stopband, and have as narrow a transition band as possible. An analog filter implementing high-performance requirements may require a complex circuit design involving costly precision components.

A high-performance digital filter, on the other hand, is still just a convolution operation. A digital circuit implementing a high-performance lowpass filter with minimal passband distortion and a narrow transition band may require a lengthy h vector, possibly containing hundreds—or even thousands—of elements. The design decision to implement such a filter digitally depends on the availability of cost-effective DSP resources, capable of performing MAC operations at the rate required by the filter design.

Fast Fourier transform (FFT)

The **Fourier transform**, named after the French mathematician Jean-Baptiste Joseph Fourier, decomposes a time-domain signal into a collection of sine and cosine waves of differing frequencies and amplitudes. The original signal can be reconstructed by summing these waves together through a process called the **inverse Fourier transform**.

DSPs operate on time-domain signals sampled at fixed intervals. Because of this sampling, the DSP implementation of the Fourier transform is called the **discrete Fourier transform (DFT)**. In general, a DFT converts a sequence of n equally spaced time samples of a function into a sequence of n DFT samples, equally spaced in frequency. Each DFT sample is a complex number, composed of a real number and an imaginary number. An **imaginary number**, when squared, produces a negative result.

We won't delve into the mathematics of imaginary (also called complex) numbers here. An alternative way to view the complex number representing a DFT frequency component (called a **frequency bin**) is to consider the real part of the complex number to be a multiplier for a cosine wave at the bin frequency and the imaginary part to be a multiplier for a sine wave at the same frequency. Summing a bin's cosine and sine wave components produces the time-domain representation of that DFT frequency bin.

The simplest implementation of the DFT algorithm for a sequence of length n is a double-nested loop in which each loop iterates n times. If an increase in the length of the DFT is desired, the number of mathematical operations increases as the square of n. For example, to compute the DFT for a signal with a length of 1,000 samples, over a million operations are required.

In 1965, James Cooley of IBM and John Tukey of Princeton University published a paper describing the computer implementation of a more efficient DFT algorithm, which came to be known as the FFT. The algorithm they described was originally invented by the German mathematician Carl Friedrich Gauss around 1805.

The FFT algorithm breaks a DFT into smaller DFTs, where the lengths of the smaller DFTs can be multiplied together to form the length of the original DFT. The efficiency improvement provided by the FFT algorithm is greatest when the DFT length is a power of 2, enabling recursive decomposition through each factor of 2 in the DFT length. A 1,024-point FFT requires only a few thousand operations compared to over a million for the double-nested loop DFT implementation.

It is important to understand the FFT operates on the same input as the DFT and produces the same output as the DFT; the FFT just does it *much* faster.

The FFT is used in many practical applications in signal processing. Some examples are as follows:

- **Spectral analysis:** The output of a DFT on a time-domain signal is a set of complex numbers representing the amplitude of sine and cosine waves over a frequency range representing the signal. These amplitudes directly indicate which frequency components are present at significant levels in the signal and which frequencies contribute smaller or negligible content.

Spectral analysis is used in applications such as audio signal processing, image processing, and radar signal processing. Laboratory instruments called **spectrum analyzers** are commonly used for testing and monitoring radio frequency systems such as radio transmitters and receivers. A spectrum analyzer displays a periodically updated image representing the frequency content of its input signal, derived from an FFT of that signal.

- **Filter banks**: A filter bank is a series of individual frequency selective filters, each containing the filtered content of a separate frequency band. The complete set of filters in the bank covers the entire frequency span of the input signal. A **graphic equalizer**, used in high-fidelity audio applications, is an example of a filter bank.

An FFT-based filter bank is useful for decomposing multiple frequency-separated data channels transmitted as a single combined signal. At the receiver, the FFT separates the received signal into multiple bands, each of which contains an independent data channel. The signal contained in each of these bands is further processed to extract its data content.

The use of FFT-based filter banks is common in radio receivers for wideband digital data communication services, such as digital television and 4G mobile communications.

- **Data compression**: A signal can be compressed to reduce its data size by performing an FFT and discarding any frequency components considered unimportant. The remaining frequency components form a smaller dataset that can be further compressed using standardized coding techniques.

This approach is referred to as **lossy compression** because some of the information in the input signal is lost. Lossy compression will generally produce a greater degree of signal compression compared to **lossless compression**. Lossless compression algorithms are used in situations where any data loss is unacceptable, such as when compressing computer data files.

- **Discrete cosine transform** (**DCT**): The DCT is similar in concept to the DFT except that rather than decomposing the input signal into a set of sine and cosine functions as in the DFT, the DCT decomposes the input signal into only cosine functions, each multiplied by a real number. Computation of the DCT can be accelerated using the same technique the FFT employs to accelerate computation of the DFT.

The DCT has the valuable property that, in many data compression applications, most of the signal information is represented in a smaller number of DCT coefficients in comparison to alternative algorithms such as the DFT. This allows a larger number of the less significant frequency components to be discarded, thereby increasing data compression effectiveness.

DCT-based data compression is employed in many application areas that computer users and consumers of audio and video entertainment interact with daily, including MP3 audio, **Joint Photographic Experts Group (JPEG)** images, and **Moving Picture Experts Group (MPEG)** video.

DSPs are most commonly used in applications involving one- and two-dimensional data sources. Some examples of one-dimensional data sources are audio signals and the radio frequency signal received by a mobile phone radio transceiver. One-dimensional signal data consists of one sample value at each instant of time for each of possibly several input channels.

A photographic image is an example of two-dimensional data. A two-dimensional image is described in terms of the width and height of the image in pixels, and the number of bits representing each pixel. Each pixel in the image is separated from the surrounding pixels by horizontal and vertical spatial offsets. Every pixel in the image is sampled at the same point in time.

Motion video represents three-dimensional information. One way to define a video segment is as a sequence of two-dimensional images presented sequentially at regular time intervals. While traditional DSPs are optimized to work with the two-dimensional data of a single image, they are not necessarily ideal for processing sequential images at a high update rate. The next section introduces GPUs, which are processors optimized to handle the computing requirements of video synthesis and display.

GPU processing

A GPU is a digital processor optimized to perform the mathematical operations associated with generating and rendering graphical images for display on a computer screen. The primary applications for GPUs are playing video recordings and creating synthetic images of three-dimensional scenes. The performance of a GPU is measured in terms of screen resolution (the pixel width and height of the image) and the image update rate in frames per second. Video playback and scene generation are hard real-time processes, in which any deviation from smooth, regularly time-spaced image updates is likely to be perceived by a user as unacceptable graphical stuttering.

As with the video cameras described earlier in this chapter, GPUs generally represent each pixel as three 8-bit color values, indicating the intensities of red, green, and blue. Any color can be produced by combining appropriate values for each of these three colors. Within each color channel, the value 0 indicates the color is absent, and 255 is maximum intensity. Black is represented by the color triple (red, green, blue) = (0, 0, 0), and white is (255, 255, 255). With 24 bits of color data, over 16 million unique colors can be displayed. The granularity between adjacent 24-bit color values is, in general, finer than the human eye can distinguish.

In modern personal computers, GPU functionality is available in a variety of configurations:

- A GPU card can be installed in a **PCI Express** (**PCIe**) slot.

- A system can provide a GPU as one or more discrete integrated circuits on the main processor board.

- GPU functionality can be built into the main processor's integrated circuit.

The most powerful consumer-class GPUs are implemented as PCIe expansion cards. These high-end GPUs contain dedicated graphics memory and feature a fast communication path with the main system processor (typically PCIe x16) for receiving commands and data representing the scene to be displayed. Some GPU designs support the use of multiple identical cards in a single system to generate scenes for a single graphical display. This technology features a separate high-speed communication bus linking the GPUs to each other. The use of multiple GPUs in a system effectively increases the parallelization of graphics processing.

GPUs exploit the concept of **data parallelism** to perform identical computations simultaneously on a vector of data items, producing a corresponding vector of outputs. Modern GPUs support thousands of simultaneously executing threads, providing the capability to render complex, three-dimensional images containing millions of pixels at 60 or more frames per second.

The architecture of a typical GPU consists of one or more multi-core processors, each supporting multithreaded execution of data parallel algorithms. The interface between the GPU processors and graphics memory is optimized to provide maximum data throughput, rather than attempting to minimize access latency (which is the design goal for main system memory). GPUs can afford to sacrifice a degree of latency performance to achieve peak streaming rate between the GPU and its dedicated memory because maximizing throughput results in the highest possible frame update rate.

In computer systems with less extreme graphical performance demands, such as business applications, a lower-performance GPU integrated on the same circuit die as the main processor is a lower-cost and often perfectly acceptable configuration. Integrated GPUs are able to play streaming video and provide a more limited level of three-dimensional scene-rendering capability compared to the higher-end GPUs.

Rather than using dedicated graphics memory, these integrated GPUs use a portion of system memory for graphics rendering. Although the use of system memory rather than specialized graphics memory results in a performance hit, such systems provide sufficient graphics performance for most home and office purposes.

Smart devices such as portable phones and tablets contain GPUs as well, providing the same video playback and three-dimensional scene-rendering capabilities as larger non-portable computer systems. The constraints of small physical size and reduced power consumption necessarily limit the performance of portable device GPUs. Nevertheless, modern smartphones and tablets are fully capable of playing high-definition streaming video and rendering sophisticated gaming graphics.

GPUs as data processors

For many years, GPU architectures were designed very specifically to support the computational needs of real-time three-dimensional scene rendering. In recent years, users and GPU vendors have increasingly recognized that these devices are actually small-scale supercomputers suitable for use across a much broader range of applications. Modern GPUs provide floating-point execution speed measured in trillions of floating-point operations per second (**teraflops**). As of 2019, a high-end GPU configuration provides floating-point performance measured in the dozens of teraflops, and is capable of executing data-parallel mathematical algorithms hundreds of times faster than a standard desktop computer.

Taking advantage of the immense parallel computing power available in high-end GPUs, vendors of these devices have begun providing programming interfaces and expanded hardware capabilities to enable the implementation of more generalized algorithms. Of course, GPUs, even with enhancements to support general computing needs, are only truly effective at speeding up algorithms that exploit data parallelization.

Some application areas that have proven to be suitable for GPU acceleration are:

- **Big data**: In fields as diverse as climate modeling, genetic mapping, business analytics, and seismic data analysis, problem domains share the need to analyze enormous quantities of data, often measured in **terabytes** (**TB**) or **petabytes** (**PB**) (1 PB is 1,024 TB) in as efficient a manner as possible. In many cases, these analysis algorithms iterate over large datasets searching for trends, correlations, and more sophisticated connections among what may seem at first to be disparate, unrelated masses of samples.

  Until recently, analysis of these datasets at the appropriate level of granularity has often been perceived as infeasible due to the extensive execution time required for such an analysis. Today, however, many big data applications produce results in a reasonable length of time by combining the use of GPU processing, often on machines containing multiple interconnected GPU cards, and splitting the problem across multiple computer systems in a cloud environment. The use of multiple computers, each containing multiple GPUs, to execute highly parallel algorithms across an enormous dataset can be accomplished at a surprisingly low cost today in comparison to the historical costs of supercomputing systems.

- **Deep learning**: Deep learning is a category of **artificial intelligence** (**AI**) that uses multilayer networks of artificial neurons to model the fundamental operations of the human brain. A biological **neuron** is a type of nerve cell that processes information. Neurons are interconnected via **synapses** and use electrochemical impulses to pass information to each other. During learning, the human brain adjusts the connections among neurons to encode the information being learned for later retrieval. The human brain contains tens of billions of neurons.

  Artificial neural networks (**ANNs**) use a software model of neuron behavior to mimic the learning and retrieval processes of the human brain. Each artificial neuron receives input from potentially many other neurons and computes a single numeric output. Some neurons are driven directly by the input data to be processed, and others produce outputs that are retrieved as the result of the ANN computation. Each communication path between neurons has a weighting factor associated with it, which is simply a number that multiplies the strength of the signal traveling along that path. The numeric input to a neuron is the sum of the input signals it receives, each multiplied by the weight of the associated path.

  The neuron computes its output using a formula called the **activation function**. The activation function determines the degree to which each neuron is "triggered" by its inputs.

The following diagram represents an example of a single neuron that sums the inputs from three other neurons ($\mathbf{N_1}$-$\mathbf{N_3}$), each multiplied by a weighting factor ($\mathbf{w_1}$-$\mathbf{w_3}$). The sum passes to the activation function, $\mathbf{F(x)}$, which produces the neuron's output signal. The use of three inputs in this example is arbitrary; in actual applications, each neuron can receive input from any number of other neurons:

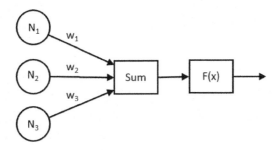

Figure 6.4: A neuron receiving inputs from three neurons

ANNs are organized in layers, where the first layer, called the **input layer**, is followed by one or more internal layers (called **hidden layers**), which are followed by an **output layer**. Some ANN configurations are arranged in a data flow sequence from input to output, called a **feedforward network**, while other configurations provide feedback from some neurons to neurons in preceding layers. This configuration is called a **recurrent network**.

The following screenshot shows an example of a simple feedforward network with three input neurons, a hidden layer consisting of four neurons, and two output neurons. This network is fully connected, meaning each neuron in the input and hidden layers connects to all neurons in the following layer. The connection weights are not shown in this diagram:

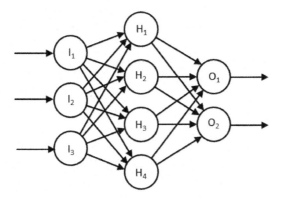

Figure 6.5: A three-layer feedforward network

Training an ANN consists of adjusting the weighted connections between neurons so that, when presented with a particular set of input data, the desired output is produced. Through the use of an appropriate learning algorithm, an ANN can be trained with a dataset composed of known correct outputs for a wide variety of inputs.

Training a large, sophisticated ANN to perform a complex task such as driving a car or playing chess requires a tremendous number of training iterations drawn from a very large dataset. During training, each iteration makes small adjustments to the weighting factors within the network, slowly driving the network to a state of convergence. Once fully converged, the network is considered trained and can be used to produce outputs when presented with novel input. In other words, the network generalizes the information it learned during training and applies that knowledge to new situations.

The feature that makes ANNs particularly suitable for GPU processing is their parallel nature. The human brain is effectively a massively parallel computer with billions of independent processing units. This form of parallelism is exploited during the ANN training phase to accelerate network convergence by performing the computations associated with multiple artificial neurons in parallel.

The next section will present some examples of computer system types based on the architectural concepts presented in this chapter.

Examples of specialized architectures

This section examines some application-focused computing system configurations and highlights the specialized requirements addressed in the design of each. The configurations we will look at are as follows:

- **Cloud compute server**: A number of vendors offer access to computing platforms accessible to customers via the Internet. These servers allow users to load their own software applications onto the cloud server and perform any type of computation they desire. In general, these services bill their customers based on the type and quantity of computing resources being used and the length of time they are in use. The advantage for the customer is that these services cost nothing unless they are actually in use.

At the higher end of performance, servers containing multiple interconnected GPU cards can be harnessed to perform large-scale, floating-point intensive computations on huge datasets. In the cloud context, it is straightforward and often cost-effective to break a computation into smaller parts suitable for parallel execution across multiple GPU-enabled servers. In this manner, it is feasible for organizations—and even individuals with limited funding—to harness computing capabilities that, until just a few years ago, were the exclusive province of government, big business, and research universities possessing the wherewithal to implement supercomputing facilities.

- **Business desktop computer**: Business information technology managers strive to provide employees with the computing capability they need to do their jobs at the lowest cost. Most office workers do not require exceptional graphics or computing performance, though their computer systems need to support modest video presentation requirements for such purposes as displaying employee training videos.

  For business users, the GPU integrated into modern processors is usually more than adequate. For a reasonable price, business buyers can purchase computer systems containing processors in the midrange of performance with integrated graphics. These systems provide full support for modern operating systems and standard office applications such as word processors, email, and spreadsheets. Should the need arise to expand a system's capabilities with higher-performance graphics, the installation of a GPU in an expansion slot is a straightforward upgrade.

- **High-performance gaming computer**: Computer gaming enthusiasts running the latest 3D games demand an extreme level of GPU performance to generate detailed, high-resolution scenes at the highest achievable frame rate. These users are willing to invest in a powerful, power-hungry, and fairly costly GPU (or even multiple GPUs) to achieve the best possible graphics performance.

  Almost as important as the graphics performance, a high-performance gaming computer must have a fast system processor. The processor and GPU work together over the high-speed interface connecting them (typically PCIe x16) to determine the position and viewing direction of the scene observer, as well as the number, type, location, and orientation of all objects in the scene. The system processor passes this geometric information to the GPU, which performs the mathematical operations necessary to render a lifelike image for display. This process must repeat at a rate sufficient to deliver a smooth presentation of complex, rapidly changing scenes.

- **High-end smartphone**: Today's smartphones combine high-performance computational and graphic display capabilities with strict limits on power consumption and heat generation. Users insist on fast, smooth, vibrant graphics for gaming and video display, but they will not tolerate this performance at the expense of unacceptably short battery life or a device that becomes hot to the touch.

  Modern phone displays contain millions of full-color pixels, up to 12 GB of RAM, and support up to 1 TB of flash storage. These phones generally come with two high-resolution cameras (one on the front and one on the back), capable of capturing still images and recording video. High-end phones typically contain a 64-bit multi-core processor with an integrated GPU, as well as a variety of features intended to achieve an optimal combination of energy efficiency and high performance.

Smartphone architectures contain DSPs to perform tasks such as encoding and decoding voice audio during telephone calls and processing the received and transmitted radio frequency signals flowing through the phone's various radio transceivers. A typical phone includes support for digital cellular service, Wi-Fi, Bluetooth, and **near-field communication** (**NFC**). Modern smartphones are powerful, well-connected computing platforms optimized for operation under battery power.

This section discussed computer system architectures representing just a tiny slice of current and future applications of computing technology. Whether a computer system sits on an office desk, is in a smartphone, or is flying a passenger aircraft, a common set of general architectural principles applies during the process of system design and implementation.

Summary

This chapter examined several specialized domains of computing, including real-time systems, digital signal processing, and GPU processing. Having completed this chapter, you should have greater familiarity with the features of modern computers related to real-time operation, the processing of analog signals, and graphics processing in applications including gaming, voice communication, video display, and the supercomputer-like applications of GPUs. These capabilities are important extensions to the core computing tasks performed by the central processor, whether in a cloud server, a desktop computer, or a smartphone.

The next chapter will take a deeper look at modern processor architectures, specifically the von Neumann, Harvard, and modified Harvard variants. The chapter will also cover the use of paged virtual memory (PVM) and the features and functions of a generalized memory management unit.

Exercises

1. **Rate monotonic scheduling (RMS)** is an algorithm for assigning thread priorities in preemptive, hard, real-time applications in which threads execute periodically. RMS assigns the highest priority to the thread with the shortest execution period, the next-highest priority to the thread with the next-shortest execution period, and so on. An RMS system is schedulable, meaning all tasks are guaranteed to meet their deadlines (assuming no inter-thread interactions or other activities such as interrupts cause processing delays) if the following condition is met:

$$\sum_{k=1}^{n} \frac{C_i}{T_i} \le n\left(2^{1/n} - 1\right)$$

This formula represents the maximum fraction of available processing time that can be consumed by n threads. In this formula, C_i is the maximum execution time required for thread i, and T_i is the execution period of thread i.

Is the following system composed of three threads schedulable?

Thread	Execution time (Ci), ms	Execution period (Ti), ms
Thread 1	50	100
Thread 2	100	500
Thread 3	120	1000

2. A commonly used form of the one-dimensional discrete cosine transform is as follows:

$$X_k = \sum_{n=0}^{N-1} x_n \cos\left[\frac{\pi}{N}\left(n + \frac{1}{2}\right)k\right]$$

In this formula, k, the index of the DCT coefficient, runs from 0 to N-1.

Write a program to compute the DCT of the following sequence:

$$x = \{0.5, 0.2, 0.7, -0.6, 0.4, -0.2, 1.0, -0.3\}$$

The cosine terms in the formula depend only on the indexes n and k, and do not depend on the input data sequence x. This means the cosine terms can be computed once and stored as constants for later use. Using this as a preparatory step, the computation of each DCT coefficient reduces to a sequence of MAC operations.

This formula represents the unoptimized form of the DCT computation, requiring N^2 iterations of the MAC operation to compute all N DCT coefficients.

3. The hyperbolic tangent is often used as an activation function in ANNs. The hyperbolic tangent function is defined as follows:

$$\tanh(x) = \frac{e^x - e^{-x}}{e^x + e^{-x}}$$

Given a neuron with inputs from three preceding neurons as depicted in *Figure 6.4*, compute the neuron's output with the hyperbolic tangent as the activation function F(x) using the following preceding neuron outputs and path weights:

Neuron	Neuron output	Weight
N_1	0.6	0.4
N_2	-0.3	0.8
N_3	0.5	-0.2

Section 2: Processor Architectures and Instruction Sets

In this section, we will examine the architectures of modern computer processors and their instruction sets. We will take a detailed look at the cutting-edge RISC -V instruction set architecture.

This section comprises the following chapters:

- *Chapter 7, Processor and Memory Architectures*
- *Chapter 8, Performance-Enhancing Techniques*
- *Chapter 9, Specialized Processor Extensions*
- *Chapter 10, Modern Processor Architectures and Instruction Sets*
- *Chapter 11, The RISC-V Architecture and Instruction Set*

7
Processor and Memory Architectures

This chapter takes a deeper look at modern processor architectures, specifically the von Neumann, Harvard, and modified Harvard variants, and the computing domains in which each architecture tends to be applied. The concepts and benefits of paged virtual memory, used extensively in consumer and business computing and in portable smart devices, are also introduced. We will examine the practical details of memory management in the real-world context of Windows NT and later Windows versions. The chapter concludes with a discussion of the features and functions of a memory management unit.

After completing this chapter, you will have learned the key features of modern processor architectures and the use of physical and virtual memory. You will understand the benefits of memory paging and the functions of the memory management unit.

This chapter covers the following topics:

- The von Neumann, Harvard, and modified Harvard architectures
- Physical and virtual memory
- Paged virtual memory
- The memory management unit

Technical Requirements

Answers to the Exercises can be found at: `https://github.com/PacktPublishing/Modern-Computer-Architecture-and-Organization`

The von Neumann, Harvard, and modified Harvard architectures

In earlier chapters, we touched briefly on the history and modern applications of the von Neumann, Harvard, and modified Harvard processor architectures. In this section, we'll examine each of these configurations in greater detail and look at the types of computing applications where each of these architectures tends to be applied.

The von Neumann architecture

The von Neumann architecture was introduced by John von Neumann in 1945. This processor configuration consists of a control unit, an arithmetic logic unit, a register set, and a memory region containing program instructions and data. The key feature distinguishing the von Neumann architecture from the Harvard architecture is the use of a single area of memory for program instructions and the data acted upon by those instructions. It is conceptually straightforward for programmers, and relatively easier for circuit designers, to locate all of the code and data a program requires in a single memory region.

This diagram shows the elements of the von Neumann architecture:

Figure 7.1: The von Neumann architecture

Although the single-memory architectural approach simplified the design and construction of early generations of processors and computers, the use of shared program and data memory has presented some significant challenges related to system performance and, in recent years, security. Some of the more significant issues were as follows:

- **The von Neumann bottleneck**: Using a single interface between the processor and the main memory for instruction and data access frequently requires multiple memory cycles to retrieve a single instruction and to access the data it requires. In the case of an immediate value stored next to its instruction opcode, there might be little or no bottleneck penalty because, at least in some cases, the immediate value is loaded along with the opcode in a single memory access. Most programs, however, spend much of their time working with data stored in memory allocated separately from the program instructions. In this situation, multiple memory access operations are required to retrieve the opcode and any required data items.

  The use of cache memories for program instructions and data, discussed in detail in *Chapter 8*, *Performance-Enhancing Techniques*, can significantly mitigate this limitation. However, when working with code sequences and data objects that exceed the size of cache memory, the benefit of caching is reduced, possibly by a substantial amount. There is no avoiding the fact that placing code and data in the same memory region with a shared communication path to the processor will, at times, act as a limitation on system performance.

- **von Neumann security considerations**: The use of a single memory area for code and data opens possibilities for creative programmers to store sequences of instructions in memory as "data," and direct the processor to execute those instructions. Programs that write code into memory and execute it are implementing **self-modifying code**. Besides being difficult to troubleshoot and debug (because many software debugging tools expect the program in memory to contain the instructions that were originally compiled into it), this capability has been exploited for years by hackers with more sinister motives.

  Buffer overflow is a distressingly common flaw in widely used software tools such as operating systems, web servers, and databases. Buffer overflow occurs when a program requests input and stores that input in a fixed-length data buffer. If the code is not careful to check the length of the input provided by the user, it is possible for the user to enter an input sequence longer than the available storage space. When this happens, the additional data overwrites memory intended for other purposes.

If the buffer being overwritten is stored on the program's stack, it is possible for a creative user to provide a lengthy input sequence that overwrites the return address of the currently executing function, which happens to be stored on the same stack. By carefully crafting the contents of the input data sequence, the attacker can seize control of the executing application and direct it to execute any desired sequence of instructions. To do this, the hacker must prepare an input sequence that overflows the input buffer, overwrites the function's return address with a different, carefully chosen address, and writes a sequence of instructions into memory that begins execution at this address. The sequence of instructions inserted by the attacker begins execution when the function that originally requested user input returns, transferring control to the hacker's code. This allows the hacker to "own" the computer.

Various attempts to resolve the buffer overflow problem have occupied an enormous amount of computer security researchers' time over the years since the first widespread occurrence of this type of attack in 1988. Processor vendors and operating system developers have implemented a variety of features to combat buffer overflow attacks, such as **data execution prevention (DEP)** and **address space layout randomization (ASLR)**. While these fixes have been effective to some degree, the fundamental processor feature that enables this type of exploitation is the use of the same memory region for program instructions and data in the von Neumann architecture.

The Harvard architecture

The Harvard architecture was originally implemented in the Harvard Mark I computer in 1944. A strict Harvard architecture uses one address space and memory bus for program instructions and a separate address space and memory bus for data. This configuration has the immediate benefit of enabling simultaneous access to instructions and data, thereby implementing a form of parallelism. Of course, this enhancement comes at the expense of essentially duplicating the number of address lines, data lines, and control signals that must be implemented by the processor to access both of the memory regions.

The following diagram shows the layout of a processor implementing the Harvard architecture:

Figure 7.2: Harvard architecture

The Harvard architecture potentially provides a higher performance level by parallelizing accesses to instructions and data. This architecture also removes the entire class of security issues associated with maliciously executing data as program instructions, as long as the instruction memory cannot be modified by program instructions. This assumes that the program memory is loaded with instructions in a trustworthy manner.

In hindsight, with knowledge of the proliferation of von Neumann architecture-enabled security threats, there is reason to wonder whether the entire information technology industry would not have been vastly better off had there been early agreement to embrace the Harvard architecture and its complete separation of code and data memory regions, despite the costs involved.

In practice, a strict Harvard architecture is rarely used in modern computers. Several variants of the Harvard architecture are commonly employed, under the name modified Harvard architecture.

The modified Harvard architecture

Computers designed with a **modified Harvard architecture** have, in general, some degree of separation between program instructions and data. This separation is rarely absolute. While systems with modified Harvard architectures contain separate program instruction and data memory regions, such systems typically support some means of storing data in program memory and, in some cases, storing instructions in data memory.

The following diagram shows a typical modified Harvard architecture representing a variety of real-world computer systems:

Figure 7.3: Modified Harvard architecture

As we saw in the previous chapter, digital signal processors (DSPs) achieve substantial benefits from the use of a Harvard-like architecture. By storing one numeric vector in instruction memory and a second vector in data memory, a DSP can execute one multiply-accumulate (MAC) operation per processor clock cycle. In these systems, instruction memory and the data elements it contains are typically read-only memory devices. This is indicated by the unidirectional arrow connecting the instruction memory to the processor in Figure 7.3. Consequently, only constant data values are suitable for storage in the instruction memory region.

Besides DSPs, most modern general-purpose processors contain separate instruction and data caches, thereby implementing significant aspects of the Harvard architecture. Processor architectures such as x86 and ARM support parallel, independent access to instructions and data when the requested items happen to reside in the first level of cache memory. When on-chip cache lookups are unsuccessful, the processor must access the main memory over the von Neumann-style shared bus, which takes significantly longer.

As a practical matter, the implementation details of a particular processor in terms of von Neumann-versus-Harvard architectural features seldom matter to software developers, other than in terms of performance considerations. Programmers generally develop programs in their high-level language of choice and the compiler or interpreter handles the details related to allocating data and instructions to the appropriate memory regions.

Physical and virtual memory

Memory devices in computers can be categorized as **random-access memory (RAM)**, which can be read from and written to at will, and **read-only memory (ROM)**, which, as the name indicates, can be read but not written. Some types of memory devices, such as flash memory and **electrically erasable programmable read-only memory (EEPROM)**, inhabit a middle ground, where the data content of the devices can be changed, just not as easily, or as quickly, or updated such a large number of times, as standard RAM.

Memory devices within a computer must be configured to ensure that each device occupies a unique span of the system address space, enabling the processor to access each of possibly several RAM and ROM devices by setting its address lines appropriately. Modern computer systems generally perform this address space allocation automatically, based on the slot a memory device occupies.

Software running on early computer systems, and on the less-sophisticated computers and embedded processors of today (such as 6502-based systems), uses the addresses of RAM and ROM devices in program instructions to perform reads and writes.

For example, a 6502 instruction such as JMP $1000 instructs the processor to load its instruction pointer with the hexadecimal value $1000 and execute the instruction at that memory location. In executing this instruction, the 6502 control unit places the value $1000 on the 6502's 16 address lines and reads the byte from that memory address. This byte is interpreted as the opcode of the next instruction to be executed. Similarly, loading a byte from memory with an instruction such as LDA $0200 results in placing the value $0200 on the address lines and copying the byte at that address into the A register.

In systems using physical addressing, the memory addresses in instructions are the actual addresses of the referenced instruction or data item. This means the memory address contained in an instruction is the same address used to electrically access the appropriate location in a memory device.

This architectural approach is conceptually straightforward to implement in processor designs, but in any application scenario involving multiple simultaneously executing programs (referred to as **multiprogramming**), the burden of software development can become excessive. If each one of multiple programs is developed in isolation from the others (in a scenario with multiple independent developers, for example), there must be some way to allocate the available RAM and ROM address spaces to individual programs so that multiple programs can be in the running state simultaneously (perhaps in the context of an RTOS) without interfering with each other's use of memory.

One well-known early effort to support the execution of multiple programs in a single address space is the MS-DOS **terminate and stay resident** (**TSR**) program concept. TSR programs allocate memory and load their code into it, and then return control to the operating system. Users can continue to work with the system normally, loading and using other applications (one at a time, of course), but they can also access the TSR as needed, typically by typing a special key combination. It is possible to load multiple TSR programs in memory simultaneously, each accessible via its own key combination. After activating a TSR program, the user interacts with it as needed, and then executes a TSR command to return to the currently running main application.

While limited in many ways (including consuming a portion of the maximum of 640 KB of RAM available in those early PCs), TSR programs effectively enabled the execution of multiple programs in a single RAM address space.

Developing TSR applications was a challenging task, and the more advanced TSR programs available in the 1980s and 1990s took advantage of undocumented MS-DOS features in order to provide maximum utility to their users. As a result of this complexity, TSR programs developed a reputation for causing system instability. A different approach for supporting multiprogramming was clearly needed.

The use of virtual memory overcomes the biggest challenges that prohibited the widespread use of multiprogramming in the original PC design. **Virtual memory** is a method of memory management that enables each application to operate in its own memory space, seemingly independent of any other applications that may be in the running state simultaneously on the same system. In a computer with virtual memory management, the operating system is responsible for the allocation of physical memory to system processes and to user applications. The memory management hardware and software translate memory requests originating in the application's virtual memory context to physical memory addresses.

Apart from easing the process of developing and running concurrent applications, virtual memory also enables the allocation of a larger amount of physical memory than actually exists in the computer. This is possible through the use of secondary storage (typically a disk file) to temporarily hold copies of sections of memory removed from physical memory to allow a different program (or a different part of the same program) to run in the now-free memory.

In modern general-purpose computers, memory sections are usually allocated and moved in multiples of a fixed-size chunk, called a **page**. Memory pages are typically 4 KB or larger. Moving memory pages to and from secondary storage in virtual memory systems is called **page swapping**. The file containing the swapped-out pages is the **swap file**.

In a virtual memory system, neither application developers nor the code itself need to be concerned about how many other applications are running on the system or how full the physical memory may be getting. As the application allocates memory for data arrays and calls library routines (which requires the code for those routines to be loaded into memory), the operating system manages the use of physical memory and takes the steps necessary to ensure that each application receives memory upon request. Only in the unusual case of completely filling the available physical memory while also filling the swap file to its limit is the system forced to return a failure code in response to a memory allocation request.

Virtual memory provides several notable benefits besides making things easier for programmers:

- Not only are applications able to ignore each other's presence, they are prevented from interfering with each other, accidentally or intentionally. The virtual memory management hardware is responsible for ensuring that each application can only access memory pages that have been assigned to it. Attempts to access another process's memory, or any other address outside its assigned memory space, result in an **access violation** exception.

- Each memory page has a collection of attributes that restrict the types of operations supported within it. A page may be marked read-only, causing any attempts to write data to the page to fail. A page may be marked executable, meaning it contains code that can be executed as processor instructions. A page may be marked read-write, indicating the application is free to modify the page at will. By setting these attributes appropriately, operating systems can improve stability by ensuring that instructions can't be modified and that the execution of data as instructions cannot occur, whether such an attempt is the result of an accident or malicious intent.

- Memory pages can be marked with a minimum required privilege level, allowing pages to be restricted for access only by code running with kernel privilege. This restriction ensures that the operating system continues operating properly even in the presence of misbehaving applications. This allows system memory to be mapped into each process's address space while prohibiting application code from interacting directly with that memory. Applications can only access system memory indirectly, via a programming interface consisting of system function calls.

- Memory pages can be marked as shareable among applications, meaning a page can be explicitly authorized as accessible from more than one process. This enables efficient interprocess communication.

Early versions of Microsoft Windows implemented some features of memory virtualization using 80286 and 80386 processor memory segmentation capabilities. In the Windows context, the use of virtual memory came into its own with the introduction of Windows NT 3.1 in 1993. The Windows NT system architecture was based on the Digital Equipment Corporation **Virtual Address Extension** (**VAX**) architecture, developed in the 1970s. The VAX architecture implemented a 32-bit virtual memory environment with a 4 GB virtual address space available to each of potentially many applications running in a multiprogramming context. One of the key architects of the VAX operating system, **Virtual Memory System** (**VMS**), was David Cutler, who later led the development of Microsoft Windows NT.

Windows NT has a flat 32-bit memory organization, meaning any address in the entire 32-bit space is accessible using a 32-bit address. No additional programmer effort is required to manipulate segment registers. By default, the Windows NT virtual address space is divided into two equal-sized chunks: a 2 GB user address space in the lower half of the range, and a 2 GB kernel space in the upper half.

The next section delves into the implementation of paged virtual memory in 32-bit Windows NT on Intel processors in some detail. While Windows NT is not entirely representative of virtual memory implementations in other operating systems, similar general principles apply even if other environments differ in the details. This introduction will provide background on the concepts of virtual memory, while holding off on additional details related to more modern architectures, such as 64-bit processors and operating systems, until later chapters.

Paged virtual memory

In 32-bit Windows NT on Intel processors, memory pages are 4 KB in size. This implies that addressing a location within a particular page requires 12 address bits (2^{12}=4096). The remaining 20 bits of a 32-bit virtual address are used in the virtual-to-physical translation process.

In Windows NT, all memory addresses in a program (both in the source code and in compiled executable code) are virtual addresses. They are not associated with physical addresses until the program runs under the control of the memory management unit.

A contiguous 4 KB section of Windows NT physical memory is called a **page frame**. The page frame is the smallest unit of memory managed by the Windows virtual memory system. Each page frame starts on a 4 KB boundary, meaning the lower 12 address bits are all zero at the base of any page frame. The system tracks information related to page frames in page tables.

A Windows NT **page table** is sized to occupy a single 4 KB page. Each 4-byte entry in a page table enables the translation of a 32-bit address from the virtual address space used by program instructions to a physical address required to access a location in RAM or ROM. A 4 KB page table contains 1,024 page address translations. A single page table manages access to 4 MB of address space: each page table contains 1,024 page frames multiplied by 4 KB per page. A process may have several associated page tables, all of which are managed by a page table directory.

A **page table directory** is a 4 KB page containing a series of 4-byte references to page tables. A page table directory can contain 1,024 page table references. A single page table directory covers the entire 4 GB address space (4 MB per page table multiplied by 1,024 page table references) of 32-bit Windows NT.

Each Windows NT process has its own page table directory, set of page tables, and collection of page frames allocated for its use. The process page tables apply to all threads within the process because all of a process's threads share the same address space and memory allocations. When the system scheduler switches from one process to another, the virtual memory context of the incoming process replaces the context of the outgoing process.

Intel x86 processors maintain the address of the current process page table directory in the CR3 register, also known as the **Page Directory Base Register (PDBR)**. This single entry point to the page table directory, and indirectly to the page tables, enables the processor to translate any valid virtual address to the corresponding physical address.

In accessing an arbitrary valid location in memory, and assuming information to expedite the access is not already stored in cache memory, the processor first looks up the physical address of the relevant page table in the page table directory using the upper 10 bits of the virtual address. It then accesses the page table and uses the next most significant 10 address bits to select the physical page containing the requested data. The lower 12 bits of the address then specify the memory location in the page frame requested by the executing instruction.

> **Page frames do not represent actual divisions in physical memory**
>
> Physical memory is not actually divided into page frames. The page structure is merely a method that the system uses to keep track of the information required to translate virtual addresses to physical memory locations.

To meet users' performance needs, memory access must be as fast as possible. At least one virtual-to-physical translation must take place during the execution of every instruction to fetch instruction opcodes and data. Due to the high-frequency repetition of this process, processor designers expend an extraordinary amount of effort ensuring that the process of virtual address translation takes place as efficiently as possible.

In modern processors, cache memory retains the results of recent virtual memory translation lookups. When implemented effectively, this approach enables a very high percentage of virtual memory translations to occur internally in the processor, without any of the clock cycles that would be required if the processor needed to look up a page table address in the page table directory and then access the page table to determine the requested physical address.

The data structures used in virtual-to-physical address translations are not accessible to applications running at user privilege level. All of the activity related to address translation takes place in processor hardware and in kernel mode software processes.

To help clarify the use of virtual memory, the following diagram presents an example of how Windows translates a 32-bit virtual address to a physical address:

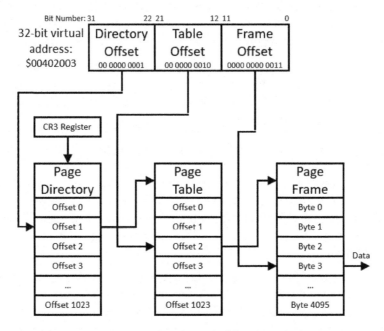

Figure 7.4: Virtual to physical address translation

We'll go through the translation process in Figure 7.4 step by step. Assume the processor is requesting the 8-bit data value stored at virtual address $00402003 with an instruction such as mov al, [ebx], where ebx has previously been loaded with the value $00402003. We will assume the translation for this address is not already stored in the processor cache, and we'll also assume that the page is resident in the main memory. The following procedure describes the translation process:

1. The processor attempts to execute the mov al, [ebx] instruction, but it cannot complete it because it does not have immediate access to the information needed to perform the translation of the virtual address in ebx to the corresponding physical address. This generates a **page fault**, which transfers control to the operating system so that it can resolve the address translation. The use of the term *fault* here does not imply that some kind of error occurred. Page faults are a routine part of application execution.

2. The requested virtual address is shifted right by 22 bit positions, leaving the 10-bit directory offset, which has the value 1 in this example.

3. The directory offset is shifted left by 2 bit positions (because each entry in the page directory is 4 bytes) and is added to the content of processor register CR3 (the PDBR). The result is the address of the page table directory entry containing the address of the relevant page table.

4. The requested virtual address is shifted right by 12 bit positions, and masked to leave only the 10-bit table offset, which has the value 2 in this example.

5. The table offset is shifted left by 2 bit positions (because each entry in this table is also 4 bytes) and added to the page table address identified in Step 3. The 32-bit address read from this location is the physical address of the page frame containing the requested data.

6. The processor stores the translation, which is a conversion from the upper 20 bits of a virtual address to the corresponding upper 20 bits of a page frame address, in its translation cache.

7. The processor restarts the `mov al, [ebx]` instruction, which will now succeed in moving the requested data byte into the `al` register using the cached virtual-to-physical translation. The lower 12 bits of the virtual address (the frame offset), which contain the value 3 in this example, are added to the page frame address computed in Step 5 to access the requested byte.

Once these steps are complete, the translation for the requested page frame remains available in the processor cache memory. Subsequent requests for the same virtual address or for other locations in the same page frame will execute without delay until the cache entry for this page frame is overwritten by code executing at a later time.

The page fault procedure described in the preceding steps is a **soft fault**, which sets up the virtual-to-physical translation for a page that is already accessible by the processor but that is not in the translation cache.

A **hard fault** occurs when accessing a page that has been swapped to secondary storage. Processing a hard fault requires several additional steps, including allocating a page frame to receive the requested frame, requesting the page from secondary storage, and updating the page table with the physical address of the page. Because hard faults involve a disk transfer, this type of fault has a much greater impact on application performance than a soft fault.

The translation process converts the upper 20 bits of a virtual address to the corresponding 20 bits of the physical address. This leaves 12 bits in each page table entry available to contain status and configuration information for the page frame. The use of these bits is described in the following section.

Page status bits

The following table describes each of the 12 status bits in a 32-bit Windows NT page table entry.

Table 7.1: Page status bits

Bit	Name	Description
0	Valid	1 indicates that this page table entry is usable for translation. If this bit is 0, the remaining bits may have different meanings, as defined by the operating system. The following bit descriptions assume that the valid bit is 1.
1	Write	1 indicates that the page is writeable. 0 means that the page is read-only.
2	Owner	1 indicates that the page is user mode. 0 indicates that the page is kernel mode.
3	Write through	1 indicates that changes to the page are to be flushed to disk immediately. 0 indicates that page changes will be maintained in RAM.
4	Cache disabled	1 indicates that caching is disabled for the page. 0 means that caching is enabled.
5	Accessed	1 indicates that the page has been read or written. 0 indicates the page has not been accessed in any way.
6	Dirty	1 indicates that the page has been written. 0 indicates that no writes have occurred.
7	Reserved	Unused.
8	Global	1 indicates that this translation applies to all processes. 0 means that this entry applies to only one process.
9	Reserved	Unused.
10	Reserved	Unused.
11	Reserved	Unused.

The processor uses the page status bits to maintain status information and to control access to each page by system and user processes. The `Owner` bit identifies a page as owned by the kernel or by a user. User processes cannot read or write any pages owned by the kernel. Any attempt to write to a page marked read-only (where the page's `Write` bit is 0) results in an access violation exception.

The system uses the page status bits to manage memory as efficiently as possible. If the `Accessed` bit is clear, the page has been allocated but never used. When the system needs to free physical memory, pages that have never been accessed are prime candidates for removal because there is no need to save their contents when removing them from memory. Similarly, if a page's `Dirty` bit is clear, the page has not had its contents modified since it was brought into memory. The memory manager can release pages that do not have the `Dirty` bit set with the knowledge that when the page is needed again, it can be reloaded from its source location (typically a disk file) to restore it accurately.

Pages that have the `Dirty` bit set require storage in the swap file when they are removed from memory. When a page is moved to the swap file, the page table entry is updated in a different format from Table 7.1 to indicate that it is not valid for translation (the `Valid` bit is clear) and to store its location within the swap file.

The format for valid page table entries is defined by the processor architecture, in this case, the Intel x86 family. The processor hardware directly accesses the page table entries to perform virtual-to-physical address translation and enforce page protections as the processor runs at full speed.

In addition to managing the memory used by each process, the system must keep track of all of the RAM and ROM page frames in the computer, whether in use by a process or not. The system maintains this information in lists called memory pools, described next.

Memory pools

Windows NT categorizes memory pools into two types: non-paged and paged.

- **Non-paged pool**: The non-paged pool contains all page frames that are guaranteed to remain resident in memory at all times. Code for interrupt service routines, device drivers, and the memory manager itself must always remain directly accessible by the processor for system performance reasons and, in the case of the memory manager itself, for the system to function at all. Non-paged virtual addresses reside in the system portion of a process's virtual address space.

- **Paged pool**: The paged pool contains virtual memory pages that can be temporarily swapped out of physical memory as needed.

The system tracks the status of every page frame in physical memory in a structure called the **page frame number (PFN)** database. The PFN is the upper 20 bits of the physical base address of a page frame. Each page frame can be in one of several states depending on its current and previous usage. These are some of the key page frame states:

- **Active**: The page frame is part of a system or user process working set. A **working set** is the portion of a process's virtual address space currently present in physical memory.

- **Standby**: Standby pages have been removed from process working sets and have not been modified.

- **Modified**: Modified pages have been removed from process working sets and have been modified. These pages must be written to disk before their page frames are reused.

- **Free**: Free pages are unused but still contain data from their last membership in a working set. For security reasons, these pages cannot be made available to a user process until their data content has been overwritten with zeros.

- **Zeroed**: Zeroed pages are free and have been overwritten with zeros. These pages are available for allocation by user processes.

- **Bad**: Bad pages have generated hardware errors during processor accesses. Bad pages are tracked in the PFN database and are not used by the operating system.

As system services and applications start up, run, and shut down, page frames transition between states under system control. In Windows NT, a system task runs during idle periods and converts free pages to zeroed pages by overwriting those pages with zeros.

This discussion has focused on the implementation of virtual memory in the x86 processor architecture under Windows NT. Other processor architectures and operating systems implement virtual memory using similar concepts.

The processor component that controls the memory allocation, address translation, and protection functions is called a memory management unit. The next section examines the memory management unit as a generalized computer system component.

Memory management unit

Processor architectures supporting paged virtual memory either implement the **memory management unit (MMU)** functionality within the processor itself or, sometimes, particularly in the case of older designs, as a separate integrated circuit. Within the MMU, the processor's virtual address space is divided into page-sized allocation units.

Pages may be of a fixed size, as in the Windows NT example, or an MMU may support multiple sizes. Modern processors, including later generation x86 processors, often support two page sizes, one small and one large. Small pages are typically a few KB while a large page may be a few MB. Large page support avoids the inefficiencies associated with allocating numerous smaller pages when working with large data objects.

As discussed, the MMU generally contains a cache to improve the speed of memory access by avoiding the need to traverse the page table directory and perform a page table lookup during each memory access. Although the use of caching for performance enhancement is a topic of *Chapter 8, Performance-Enhancing Techniques,* we'll introduce the virtual-to-physical address translation cache here because this capability is a core feature of most MMU designs.

The caching component within the MMU that stores previously used virtual-to-physical translations is called a **translation lookaside buffer (TLB)**. In order to avoid looking up a page table in the page table directory, and then looking up the page frame in the referenced page table on every memory access, the TLB stores translations between virtual addresses and page frames resulting from those lookups in a hardware structure called an **associative memory**.

Each time the processor needs to access physical memory, which may occur multiple times during the execution of a single instruction, it first checks the TLB's associative memory to determine whether the translation information is resident in the TLB. If it is, the instruction immediately uses the information stored in the TLB to access physical memory. If the TLB does not contain the requested translation, a page fault occurs and the processor must traverse the page table directory and a page table to determine the translated address, assuming the referenced page is resident in memory.

The following diagram represents the operation of the TLB:

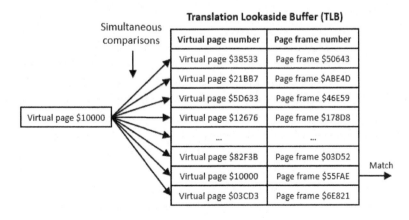

Figure 7.5: Translation lookaside buffer operation

On each memory access, the processor extracts the upper 20 bits of the virtual address to identify the virtual page number. This page number, `$10000` in this example, is used to search the TLB for a matching entry. The TLB hardware simultaneously compares the requested virtual page number with all of the virtual page numbers resident in the TLB. If a match is found, the corresponding page frame number is immediately provided for use in accessing physical memory.

The TLB contains a limited number of entries, typically 64 or fewer. The processor must manage which TLB entries are retained and which are discarded as address requests for disparate memory locations are processed. When the TLB is full, the MMU decides which of the existing TLB entries to overwrite with the new information. The MMU may choose a TLB entry at random to replace, or a more sophisticated implementation may use age information to replace the TLB entry that has gone the longest without being used.

In addition to performing virtual-to-physical address translation, MMUs generally perform the following functions:

- **Separation of virtual memory into kernel space and user space**: Kernel memory is reserved for use by the operating system and related components such as device drivers. User space is available for use by applications and for other actions initiated by users, such as processing commands typed into a command prompt window. User-level code cannot access system memory directly. Instead, user code must call system functions to request services such as the allocation of memory.

- **Isolation of process memory**: Each process has its own address space, which is the only memory it is allowed to access. Unless a system-authorized memory sharing region is set up between processes, each process is prohibited from accessing memory in use by another process. One process cannot erroneously or intentionally modify memory that is private to another process.

- **Page-level access restrictions**: In addition to protecting system pages from user access and protecting process-private pages from access by other processes, a process can set protections on individual pages that it owns. Pages can be marked read-only, which prohibits the modification of the contents. Pages marked no-execute cannot be used to provide instructions for processor execution. In some architectures, pages can be marked no-access, which prohibits both reading and writing. Pages containing executable code may be marked read-only to prevent the accidental or intentional modification of instructions in memory.

- **Detection of software problems**: In some programming languages, particularly the C language, it is unfortunately common to attempt to use a pointer (a **pointer** is a variable that contains the address of another variable) containing an invalid address. The most common invalid address encountered in this situation is 0, because variables are often initialized to zero. This problem is so common that the system's response to it has its own name: the **null pointer exception**. When a C program attempts to access a memory location that is not in the program's valid virtual address range, such as the address $00000000, the MMU triggers an exception, which, unless handled by the program, typically results in a program crash with an error message printed to the console window. In systems without virtual memory, accesses to erroneous locations may simply read or write the memory at the referenced address without any indication of an error, leading to the incorrect operation of the application or the entire system. Such bugs in systems without an MMU can be extremely difficult to fix if the problem does not become apparent immediately.

Modern processors running Linux, Windows, and most smart device operating systems generally require their host systems to use virtual memory management and provide the page protection mechanisms described in this chapter.

Real-time embedded processors performing safety-critical tasks such as operating aircraft flight controls or managing automotive airbag operation may or may not support the full feature set of an MMU. One drawback related to the use of virtual memory in hard real-time systems is the variable time delay resulting from the need to process soft faults and, if page swapping is implemented, hard faults. Because execution timing must be strictly controlled in many real-time systems, their designers often avoid the use of virtual memory. Such systems do not contain an MMU, but they normally implement many of the other features an MMU provides, such as hardware protection of system memory and access control for RAM regions.

Summary

This chapter examined the principal modern processor architectural categories, including the von Neumann, Harvard, and modified Harvard variants, and their use in different computing domains. The concepts of paged virtual memory were examined, including some details pertaining to the implementation of paged virtual memory in Windows NT on the x86 processor.

The general structure of memory management units was discussed, with emphasis on the use of the TLB as a virtual-to-physical translation performance optimization technique.

The next chapter will expand beyond the performance enhancement provided by the TLB to look in depth at widely used processor acceleration methods including caching, instruction pipelining, and instruction parallelism.

Exercises

1. A 16-bit embedded processor has separate memory regions for code and data. Code is stored in flash memory and modifiable data is stored in RAM. Some data values, such as constants and initial values for RAM data items, are stored in the same flash memory region as the program instructions. RAM and ROM reside in the same address space. Which of the processor architectures discussed in this chapter best describes this processor?

2. The processor described in Exercise 1 has memory security features that prevent executing code from modifying program instruction memory. The processor uses physical addresses to access instructions and data. Does this processor contain an MMU?

3. The order of accessing sequential elements in a large data structure can have a measurable impact on processing speed due to factors such as the reuse of TLB entries. Accessing distant array elements in sequence (that is, elements that are not in the same page frame as previously accessed elements) requires frequent soft faults as new TLB entries are loaded and old TLB entries are discarded.

    Write a program that creates a two-dimensional array of numbers with a large size such as 10,000 rows by 10,000 columns. Iterate through the array in column-major order, assigning each element the sum of the row and column indices. Column-major means the column index increments fastest. In other words, the column index increments in the inner loop. Measure precisely how long this procedure takes. Note, you may need to take steps to ensure your programming language does not optimize away the entire calculation if the results from the array are not used later. If may suffice to print one of the array values after the timing is complete, or you may need to do something like sum all the array elements and print that result.

Repeat the process, including the timing, exactly as explained before, except change the inner loop to iterate over the row index and the outer loop to iterate over the column index, making the access sequence row-major.

Since general-purpose computers perform many other tasks while running your code, you may need to perform both procedures a number of times to get a statistically valid result. You might start by running the experiment 10 times and averaging the times for column-major and row-major array access.

Are you able to determine a consistently superior array access method? Which order is fastest on your system using the language you selected? Note that the difference between the column-major and row-major access order may not be dramatic – it might be just a few percent.

8
Performance-Enhancing Techniques

The fundamental aspects of processor and memory architectures discussed in previous chapters enable the design of a complete and functional computer system. However, the performance of such a system would be poor compared to most modern processors without the addition of features to increase the speed of instruction execution.

Several performance-enhancing techniques are employed routinely in processor and system designs to achieve peak execution speed in real-world computer systems. These techniques do not alter what the processor does in terms of program execution and data processing; they just help get it done faster.

After completing this chapter, you will understand the value of multilevel cache memory in computer architectures and the benefits and challenges associated with instruction pipelining. You'll also understand the performance improvement resulting from simultaneous multithreading and the purpose and applications of single instruction, multiple data processing.

The following topics will be covered in this chapter:

- Cache memory

- Instruction pipelining

- Simultaneous multithreading

- SIMD processing

Cache memory

A **cache memory** is a memory region that stores program instructions or data, usually instructions or data that have been accessed recently, for future use. The primary purpose of cache memory is to increase the speed of repeatedly accessing the same memory location or nearby memory locations. To be effective, accessing the cached data must be significantly faster than accessing the original source of the data, referred to as the **backing store**.

When caching is in use, each attempt to access a memory location begins with a search of the cache. If the data is present, the processor retrieves and uses it immediately. This is called a **cache hit**. If the cache search is unsuccessful (a **cache miss**), the data must be retrieved from the backing store. In the process of retrieving the requested data, a copy is added to the cache for anticipated future use.

Cache memory is used for a variety of purposes in computer systems. Some examples of cache memory applications are:

- **Translation lookaside buffer (TLB):** The TLB, as we saw in in *Chapter 7, Processor and Memory Architectures*, is a form of cache memory used in processors supporting paged virtual memory. The TLB contains a collection of virtual-to-physical address translations that speed access to page frames in physical memory. As instructions execute, each main memory access requires a virtual-to-physical translation. Successful searches of the TLB result in much faster instruction execution compared to the page table lookup process following a TLB miss. The TLB is part of the MMU, and is not directly related to the varieties of processor cache memory discussed later in this section.

- **Disk drive caches:** Reading and writing the magnetized platters of rotating disk drives is orders of magnitude slower than accessing DRAM devices. Disk drives generally implement cache memory to store the output of read operations and to temporarily hold data in preparation for writing. Drive controllers often read more data than the amount originally requested in internal cache memory in the expectation that future reads will request data adjacent to the initial request. If this turns out to be a correct assumption, which it often is, the drive will satisfy the second request immediately from cache without the delay associated with accessing the disk platters.

- **Web browser caches:** Web browsers generally store copies of recently accessed web pages in memory in the expectation that the user will sometimes click the "Back" button to return to a previously viewed page. When this happens, the browser can retrieve some or all of the page content from its local cache and immediately redisplay the page without the need to access the remote web server and retrieve the same information again.

- **Processor instruction and data caches:** The following sections examine processor cache structures in detail. The purpose of these caches is to improve the speed of access to instructions and data in comparison to the latency incurred when accessing DRAM modules.

Cache memory improves computer performance because many algorithms executed by operating systems and applications exhibit locality of reference. **Locality of reference** refers to the reuse of data that has been accessed recently (this is referred to as **temporal locality**) and to the access of data in physical proximity to data that has been accessed previously (called **spatial locality**).

Using the structure of the TLB as an example, temporal locality is exploited by storing a virtual-to-physical translation in the TLB for some period of time following initial access to a particular page frame. Any additional references to the same page frame in subsequent instructions will enjoy speedy access to the translation until it is eventually replaced in the cache by a different translation.

The TLB exploits spatial locality by referencing an entire page frame with a single TLB entry. Any subsequent accesses to different addresses on the same page will benefit from the presence of the TLB entry resulting from the first reference to the page.

As a general rule, cache memory regions are small in comparison to the backing store. Cache memory devices are designed for maximum speed, which generally means they are more complex and costly per bit than the data storage technology used in the backing store. As a consequence of their limited size, cache memory devices tend to fill quickly. When a cache does not have an available location to store a new entry, an older entry must be discarded. The cache controller uses a **cache replacement policy** to select which cache entry will be overwritten by the new entry.

The goal of processor cache memory is to maximize the percentage of cache hits over time, thus providing the highest sustained rate of instruction execution. To achieve this objective, the caching logic must determine which instructions and data will be placed into the cache and retained for future use.

In general, a processor's caching logic does not have any assurance that a cached data item will ever be used again once it has been inserted into the cache. The logic relies on the likelihood that, due to temporal and spatial locality, there is a very good chance the cached data will be accessed in the near future. In practical implementations on modern processors, cache hits typically occur on 95 to 97 percent of memory accesses. Because the latency of cache memory is a small fraction of the latency of DRAM, a high cache hit rate leads to a substantial performance improvement in comparison to a cache-less design.

The following sections discuss the multilevel caching technologies of modern processors and some of the cache replacement policies commonly used in their implementations.

Multilevel processor caches

In the years since the introduction of personal computers, processors have undergone dramatic increases in the speed of instruction processing. The internal clocks of modern Intel and AMD processors are close to 1,000 times faster than the 8088 processor used in the first IBM PC. The speed of DRAM technology, in comparison, has increased at a much slower rate over time. Given these two trends, if a modern processor were to access DRAM directly for all of its instructions and data, it would spend the vast majority of its time simply waiting for the DRAM to respond to each request.

To attach some approximate numbers to this topic, consider a modern processor capable of accessing a 32-bit data value from a processor register in 1 ns. Accessing the same value from DRAM might take 100 ns. Oversimplifying things somewhat, if each instruction requires a single access to a memory location, and the execution time for each instruction is dominated by the memory access time, we can expect a processing loop that accesses the data it requires from processor registers to run 100 times faster than the same algorithm accessing main memory on each instruction.

Now, assume a cache memory is added to the system with an access time of 4 ns. By taking advantage of cache memory, the algorithm that accesses DRAM on each instruction will suffer the 100 ns performance penalty the first time a particular address is referenced, but subsequent accesses to the same and nearby addresses will occur at the cache speed of 4 ns. Although accessing the cache is four times slower than accessing registers, it is 25 times faster than accessing DRAM. This example represents the degree of execution speedup achievable through the effective use of cache memory in modern processors.

High-performance processors generally employ multiple cache levels with the goal of achieving peak instruction execution rate. Processor cache hardware is constrained in terms of size and performance by the economics of semiconductor technology. Selecting an optimally performing mix of processor cache types and sizes while achieving a price point acceptable to end users is a key goal of processor designers.

The two types of RAM circuits in common use as main memory and for processor internal storage are dynamic RAM (DRAM) and static RAM. DRAM is inexpensive, but has a comparatively slow access time, due largely to the time required to charge and discharge the bit cell capacitors during read and write operations. Static RAM is much faster than DRAM, but is much more costly, resulting in its use in smaller quantities in applications where performance is critical. DRAM designs are optimized for density, resulting in the largest possible number of bits stored on a single DRAM integrated circuit. Static RAM designs are optimized for speed, minimizing the time to read or write a location. Processor cache memory is generally implemented using SRAM.

Static RAM

Static RAM (SRAM) boasts a substantially faster access time than DRAM, albeit at the expense of significantly more complex circuitry. SRAM bit cells take up much more space on the integrated circuit die than the cells of a DRAM device capable of storing an equivalent quantity of data. As you will recall from *Chapter 4, Computer System Components*, a single DRAM bit cell consists of just one MOSFET transistor and one capacitor.

The standard circuit for a single bit of SRAM contains six MOSFET transistors. Four of these transistors are used to form two NOT gates. These gates are based on the CMOS circuit shown in *Figure 4.3* in *Chapter 4, Computer System Components* in the *Digital switching circuits based on the MOSFET*section. These gates are labeled **G**₁ and **G**₂ in the following diagram:

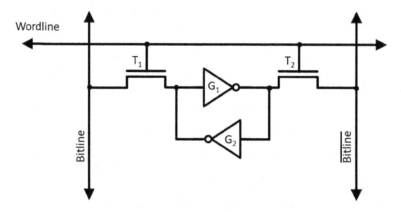

Figure 8.1: SRAM circuit diagram

The output of each of the NOT gates is connected to the input of the other, forming a flip-flop. Most of the time, the wordline is low, which turns off transistor switches T_1 and T_2, isolating the pair of gates. While the wordline is low, as long as power is applied, the gates will persist on one of two states:

- The stored bit is 0: The input of G_1 is low and its output is high.
- The stored bit is 1: The input of G_1 is high and its output is low.

The access transistors (T_1 and T_2) function as switches that connect the bitlines to the cell for reading and writing. As with DRAM, driving the wordline high enables access to the bit cell by reducing the resistance across each access transistor to a very small value. To read the cell contents, the readout circuitry measures the voltage between the bitline pair labeled Bitline and $\overline{\text{Bitline}}$ where the overbar represents the NOT operation). The two bitline signals always have opposing senses, forming a differential pair. Measuring the sign of the voltage difference between the two signals determines whether the cell contains a 0 or a 1.

To write the bit cell, the wordline is driven high, and the and signals are driven to opposite voltage levels representing the desired value (0 or 1) to be written. The transistors writing the data to the bitlines must have substantially greater drive capability than the bit cell NOT gate transistors. This allows the desired value to be written to the cell, even if the flip-flop state must be overpowered to switch it to the state being written.

An SRAM bank is arranged in a rectangular grid of rows and columns in the same manner as DRAM. The wordline enables access to all SRAM bit cells along a single row. The bitlines connect to all columns of the grid of bit cells.

Note that, unlike DRAM, SRAM does not require periodic refreshes to retain its data content. This is why it is referred to as *static* RAM.

Level 1 cache

In a multilevel cache architecture, the cache levels are numbered, beginning with 1. A level 1 cache (also referred to as an **L1 cache**) is the first cache the processor searches when requesting an instruction or data item from memory. Because it is the first stop in the cache search, an L1 cache is generally constructed using the fastest SRAM technology available and is physically located as close to the processor's logic circuitry as possible. The emphasis on speed makes an L1 cache costly and power-hungry, which means it must be relatively small in size, particularly in cost-sensitive applications. Even when it is quite small, a fast level 1 cache can provide a substantial performance boost in comparison to an equivalent processor that does not employ caching.

The processor (or the MMU, if present) transfers data between DRAM and cache in fixed-size data blocks called **cache lines**. Computers using DDR DRAM modules generally use a cache line size of 64 bytes. The same cache line size is commonly used in all cache levels.

Modern processors often divide the L1 cache into two sections of equal size, one for instructions and one for data. This configuration is referred to as a **split cache**. In a split cache, the level 1 instruction cache is referred to as the **L1 I-cache** and the level 1 data cache is referred to as the **L1 D-cache**. The processor uses separate buses to access each of the two caches, thereby implementing a significant aspect of the Harvard architecture. This arrangement speeds instruction execution by enabling access to instructions and data in parallel, assuming L1 cache hits for both.

Modern processors employ a variety of strategies to organize cache memory and control its operation. The simplest cache configuration is direct mapping, introduced in the next section.

Direct-mapped cache

A **direct-mapped cache** is a block of memory organized as a one-dimensional array of cache sets, where each address in the main memory maps to a single set in the cache. Each **cache set** consists of the following items:

- A cache line, containing a block of data read from main memory
- A tag value, indicating the location in main memory corresponding to the cached data
- A valid bit, indicating whether the cache set contains data

There are times when the cache contains no data, such as immediately following processor power-on. The valid bit for each cache set is initially clear to indicate the absence of data in the set. When the valid bit is clear, use of the set for lookups is inhibited. Once data has been loaded into a cache set, the hardware sets the valid bit.

We will use a small L1 I-cache size of 512 bytes as an example. Because this is a read-only instruction cache, it need not support the ability to write to memory. The cache line size is 64 bytes. Dividing 512 bytes by 64 bytes per set results in 8 cache sets. The 64 bytes in each set equals 2^6 bytes, which means the least significant 6 bits in the address select a location within the cache line. Three additional bits of an address are required to select one of the eight sets in the cache.

From this information, the following diagram shows the division of a 32-bit physical memory address into tag, set number, and cache line byte offset components:

Figure 8.2: Components of a 32-bit physical memory address

Each time the processor reads an instruction from DRAM (which is necessary any time the instruction is not already present in the cache), the MMU reads the 64-byte block containing the addressed location, and stores it in the L1 I-cache set selected by the three **Set** bits of Figure 8.2. The upper 23 bits of the address are stored in the **Tag** field of the cache set, and the **Valid** bit is set, if it was not already set.

As the processor fetches each subsequent instruction, the control unit uses the three **Set** bits in the instruction's address to select a cache set for comparison. The hardware compares the upper 23 bits of the executing instruction's address with the **Tag** value stored in the selected cache set. If the values match, a cache hit has occurred, and the processor reads the instruction from the cache line. If a cache miss occurs, the MMU reads the line from DRAM into cache and provides the instruction to the control unit for execution.

The following diagram represents the organization of the entire 512-byte cache and its relation to the three fields in a 32-bit instruction address:

Figure 8.3: Relation of a 32-bit physical address to cache memory

To demonstrate why a direct-mapped cache can produce a high hit rate, assume we're running a program containing a loop starting at physical memory address 8000h (we're ignoring the upper 16 bits of the 32-bit address here for simplicity) and containing 256 bytes of code. The loop executes instructions sequentially from the beginning to the end of the 256 bytes, and then branches back to the top of the loop for the next iteration.

Address 8000h contains 000b in its **Set** field, so this address maps to the first cache set, as shown in Figure 8.3. On the first pass through the loop, the MMU retrieves the 64-byte Set 000b cache line from DRAM and stores it in the first set of the cache. As the remaining instructions stored in the same 64-byte block execute, each will be retrieved directly from cache. As execution flows into the second 64 bytes, another read from DRAM is required. By the time the end of the loop is reached, Sets 000b through 011b have been populated with the loop's 256 bytes of code. For the remaining passes through the loop, assuming the thread runs without interruption, the processor will achieve a 100 percent cache hit rate, and will achieve maximum instruction execution speed.

Alternatively, if the instructions in the loop happen to consume significantly more memory, the advantage of caching will be reduced. Assume the loop's instructions occupy 1,024 bytes, twice the cache size. The loop performs the same sequential execution flow from top to bottom. When the instruction addresses reach the midpoint of the loop, the cache has been completely filled with the first 512 bytes of instructions. At the beginning of the next cache line beyond the midpoint, the address will be 8000h plus 512, which is 8200h. 8200h has the same **Set** bits as 8000h, which causes the cache line for address 8000h to be overwritten by the cache line for address 8200h. Each subsequent cache line will be overwritten as the second half of the loop's code executes.

Even though all of the cached memory regions are overwritten on each pass through the loop, the caching structure continues to provide a substantial benefit because, once read from DRAM, each 64-byte line remains in the cache and is available for use as its instructions are executed. The downside in this example is the increased frequency of cache misses. This represents a substantial penalty because, as we've seen, accessing an instruction from DRAM may be 25 (or more) times slower than accessing the same instruction from the L1 I-cache.

> **Virtual and physical address tags in caching**
>
> The example in this section assumes that cache memory uses physical memory addresses to tag cache entries. This implies that the addresses used in cache searches are the output of the virtual-to-physical address translation process in systems using paged virtual memory. It is up to the processor designer to select whether to use virtual or physical addresses for caching purposes.
>
> In modern processor caches, it is not uncommon to use virtual address tags in one or more cache levels and physical address tags in the remaining levels. One advantage of using virtual address tagging is speed, due to the fact that no virtual-to-physical translation is required during cache accesses. As we've seen, virtual-to-physical translation requires a TLB lookup and potentially a page table search in the event of a TLB miss. However, virtual address tagging introduces other issues such as **aliasing**, which occurs when the same virtual address refers to different physical addresses. As with many other aspects of processor performance optimization, this is a trade-off to be considered during cache system design.

This example was simplified by assuming instruction execution flows linearly from the top to the bottom of the loop without any detours. In real-world code, there are frequent calls to functions in different areas of the application memory space and to system-provided libraries. In addition to those factors, other system activities such as interrupt processing and thread context switching frequently overwrite information in the cache, leading to a higher cache miss frequency. Application performance is affected because the main-line code must perform additional DRAM accesses to reload the cache following each detour that causes a cache entry to be overwritten.

One way to reduce the effects of deviations from straight-line code execution is to set up two caches operating in parallel. This configuration is called a two-way set associative cache, discussed next.

Set associative cache

In a two-way set associative cache, the memory is divided into two equal-sized caches. Each of these has half the number of entries of a direct-mapped cache of the same total size. The hardware consults both of these caches in parallel on each memory access and a hit may occur in either one. The following diagram illustrates the simultaneous comparison of a 32-bit address tag against the tags contained in two L1 I-caches:

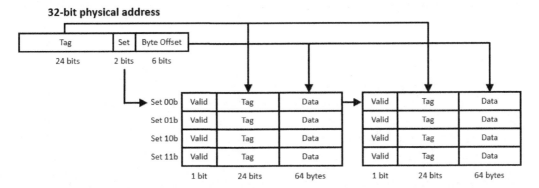

Figure 8.4: Set associative cache operation

The cache configuration shown here contains the same cache line size (64 bytes) as the cache in *Figure 8.3*, but only half as many sets per cache. The overall size of cache memory is the same as the previous example: 64 bytes per line times 4 rows times 2 caches equals 512 bytes. Because there are now four sets, the **Set** field in the physical address reduces to two bits and the **Tag** field increases to 24 bits. Each set consists of two cache lines, one in each of the two caches.

When a cache miss occurs, the memory management logic must select which of the two cache tables to use as the destination for the data being loaded from DRAM. A common method is to track which of the relevant sets in the two tables has gone the longest without being accessed, and overwrite that entry. This replacement policy, called **least-recently used** (**LRU**), requires hardware support to keep track of which cache line has been idle the longest. The LRU policy relies on the temporal locality heuristic stating that data that has not been accessed for an extended period of time is less likely to be accessed again in the near future.

Another method for selecting between the two tables is to simply alternate between them on successive cache insertions. The hardware to implement this replacement policy is simpler than the LRU policy, but there may be a performance impact due to the arbitrary selection of the line being invalidated. Cache replacement policy selection represents another area of trade-off between increased hardware complexity and incremental performance improvements.

In a two-way set associative cache, two cache lines from different physical locations with matching **Set** fields are present in cache simultaneously, assuming both cache lines are valid. At the same time, in comparison to a direct-mapped cache of the same total size, each of the two-way set associative caches is half the size. This represents yet another design tradeoff.

The number of unique **Set** values that can be stored in a two-way set associative cache is reduced compared to direct mapping, but multiple cache lines with identical **Set** fields can be cached simultaneously. The cache configuration that provides the best overall system performance will depend on the memory access patterns associated with the types of processing activity performed on the system.

Set associative caches can contain more than the two caches of this example. Modern processors often have four, eight, or 16 parallel caches, referred to as 4-way, 8-way, and 16-way set associative caches, respectively. These caches are referred to as **set associative** because an address **Tag** field associates with all of the cache lines in the set simultaneously. A direct-mapped cache implements a one-way set associative cache.

The advantage of multi-way set associative caches over direct-mapped caches is that they tend to have higher hit rates, thereby providing better system performance than direct-mapped caches in most practical applications. If multi-way set associative caches provide better performance than one-way direct mapping, why not increase the level of associativity even further? Taken to the limit, this progression ends with fully associative caching.

Fully associative cache

Assuming the number of lines in the cache is a power of two, repetitively dividing the overall cache memory into a larger number of smaller parallel caches, until each cache contains only one line, results in a **fully associative cache**. In our example of a 512 byte cache with 64 bytes per cache line, this process would result in eight parallel caches, each with only one set.

In this architecture, every memory access leads to a parallel comparison with the **Tag** values stored in all of the cache lines. A fully associative cache using an effective replacement policy such as LRU can provide a very high hit rate, though at a substantial cost in circuit complexity and a corresponding consumption of integrated circuit die area. In power-sensitive applications such as battery-powered mobile devices, the additional circuit complexity of a fully associative cache leads to increased battery drain. In desktop computers and cloud servers, excessive processor power consumption must be minimized to avoid the need for extraordinary cooling requirements and to minimize the electric utility bill for cloud providers operating thousands of servers. Because of these costs, fully associative caches are rarely used as instruction and data caches in modern processors.

The concept behind the fully associative cache may sound familiar because it is the same concept employed in the TLB presented in *Chapter 7, Processor and Memory Architectures*. The TLB is typically a fully associative cache containing virtual-to-physical address translations. Although the use of fully associative caching in the TLB results in the drawbacks of circuit complexity, die area consumption, and power consumption described in the preceding paragraph, the performance benefit provided by the TLB is so substantial that full associativity is used in virtually all high-performance processors that implement paged virtual memory.

Our discussion to this point has focused on instruction caching, which is normally a read-only process. The functional requirements for the data cache are similar to those of the instruction cache, with one significant extension: in addition to reading from data memory, the processor must be free to write to data memory.

Processor cache write policies

In processors with split caches, the L1 D-cache is similar in structure to the L1 I-cache, except that the circuitry must permit the processor to write to memory as well as read from it. Each time the processor writes a data value to memory, it must update the L1 D-cache line containing the data item, and, at some point, it must also update the DRAM location in physical memory containing the cache line. As with reading DRAM, writing to DRAM is a slow process compared to the speed of writing to the L1 D-cache.

The most common cache write policies in modern processors are as follows:

- **Write-through**: This policy updates DRAM immediately every time the processor writes data to memory.

- **Write-back**: This policy holds the modified data in the cache until the line is about to be evicted from cache. A write-back cache must provide an additional status bit associated with each cache line indicating whether the data has been modified since it was read from DRAM. This is called the **dirty bit**. If set, the dirty bit indicates that the data in that line is modified and the system must write the data to DRAM before its cache line can be freed for reuse.

The write-back policy generally results in better system performance because it allows the processor to perform multiple writes to the same cache line without the need to access main memory on each write. In systems with multiple cores or multiple processors, the use of write-back caching introduces complexity, because the L1 D-cache belonging to a core that writes to a memory location will contain data that differs from the corresponding DRAM location, and from any copies in the caches of the other processors or cores. This memory content disagreement will persist until the cache line has been written to DRAM and refreshed in any processor caches it occupies.

It is generally unacceptable to have different processor cores retrieve different values when accessing the same memory location, so a solution must be provided to ensure that all processors see the same data in memory at all times. The challenge of maintaining identical views of memory contents across multiple processors is called the **cache coherence** problem.

A multi-core processor can resolve this issue by sharing the same L1 D-cache among all the cores, but modern multi-core processors usually implement a separate L1 D-cache for each core to maximize access speed. In multiprocessor systems with shared main memory, where the processors are on separate integrated circuits, and in multi-core processors that do not share L1 cache, the problem is more complex.

Some multiprocessor designs perform **snooping** to maintain cache coherence. Each processor snoops by monitoring memory write operations performed by the other processors. When a write occurs to a memory location present in the snooping processor's cache, the snooper takes one of two actions: it can invalidate its cache line by setting the **Valid** bit to `false`, or it can update its cache line with the data written by the other processor. If the cache line is invalidated, the next access to the line's physical memory location will result in a DRAM access, which picks up the data modified by the other processor.

Snooping can be effective in systems with a limited number of processors, but it does not scale well to systems containing dozens or hundreds of processors, because each processor must monitor the write behavior of all the other processors at all times. Other, more sophisticated, cache coherence protocols must be implemented in systems with large numbers of processors.

Level 2 and level 3 processor caches

The discussion to this point has focused on L1 instruction and data caches. These caches are designed to be as fast as possible, but the focus on speed limits their size because of cache circuit complexity and power requirements. Because of the great disparity in the latency performance of L1 cache and DRAM, it is reasonable to wonder whether providing an additional level of cache between L1 and DRAM could improve performance beyond that of a processor containing just an L1 cache. The answer is, yes: adding an L2 cache provides a substantial performance enhancement.

Modern high-performance processors generally contain a substantial bank of L2 cache on-chip. Unlike an L1 cache, an L2 cache typically combines instruction and data memory in a single memory region, representing the von Neumann architecture more than the Harvard architectural characteristic of the split L1 cache structure. An L2 cache is generally slower than an L1 cache, but still much faster than direct accesses to DRAM. Although an L2 cache uses SRAM bit cells with the same basic circuit configuration shown in Figure 8.1, the L2 circuit design emphasizes a reduction in the per-bit die area and power consumption relative to L1. These modifications permit an L2 cache to be much larger than an L1 cache, but they also make it slower.

A typical L2 cache might be four or eight times as large as the combined L1 I- and D-caches, with an access time 2-3 times as long as L1. The L2 cache may or may not be inclusive of the L1 cache, depending on the processor design. An **inclusive L2 cache** always contains the cache lines contained in the L1 cache, plus others.

As we have seen, each time the processor accesses memory, it first consults the L1 cache. If an L1 miss occurs, the next place to check is the L2 cache. Because L2 is larger than L1, there is a significant chance the data will be found there. If the cache line is not in L2, a DRAM access is required. Processors generally perform some of these steps in parallel to ensure that a cache miss does not result in a lengthy sequential search for the needed data.

Each miss of both an L1 and L2 cache results in a DRAM read that populates the corresponding cache lines in L1 and L2, assuming L2 is inclusive. Each time the processor writes to data memory, both L1 and L2 must be updated eventually. An L1 D-cache implements a cache write policy (typically write-through or write-back) to determine when it must update the L2 cache. L2, similarly, implements its own write policy to determine when to write dirty cache lines to DRAM.

If using two cache levels helps with performance, why stop there? In fact, most modern high-performance processors implement three (or more!) levels of cache on-chip. As with the transition from L1 to L2, the transition from L2 to L3 involves a larger block of memory with slower access speed. Similar to L2, an L3 cache usually combines instructions and data in a single memory region. On a consumer-grade PC processor, an L3 cache typically consists of a few megabytes of SRAM with an access time 3-4 times slower than an L2 cache.

> **The programmer's view of cache memory**
>
> Although software developers do not need to take any steps to take advantage of cache memory, an understanding of the execution environment in which their software operates can help improve the performance of code running on processors containing multilevel cache. Where flexibility permits, sizing data structures and code inner loops to fit within the confines of anticipated L1, L2, and L3 cache sizes can result in a significant increase in execution speed.
>
> Since the performance of any piece of code is affected by many factors related to the processor architecture and system software behavior, the best way to determine the optimal algorithm among multiple viable alternatives is to carefully benchmark the performance of each one.

The multilevel cache hierarchy in modern processors results in a dramatic performance improvement in comparison to an equivalent system that does not use cache memory. Caching allows the speediest processors to run with minimal DRAM access delay. Although cache memory adds substantial complexity to processor designs and consumes a great deal of valuable die area and power, processor vendors have determined that the use of a multilevel cache memory architecture is well worth the cost.

Cache memory speeds the execution of instructions by reducing memory access latency when retrieving instructions and the data referenced by those instructions. The next area of performance enhancement that we'll look at is optimization opportunities within the processor to increase the rate of instruction execution. The primary method modern processors use to achieve this performance boost is pipelining.

Instruction pipelining

Before we introduce pipelining, we will first break down the execution of a single processor instruction into a sequence of discrete steps:

- **Fetch**: The processor control unit accesses the memory address of the next instruction to execute, as determined by the previous instruction, or from the predefined reset value of the program counter immediately after power-on, or in response to an interrupt. Reading from this address, the control unit loads the instruction opcode into the processor's internal instruction register.

- **Decode**: The control unit determines the actions to be taken during instruction execution. This may involve the ALU and may require read or write access to registers or memory locations.

- **Execute**: The control unit executes the requested operation, invoking an ALU operation if required.

- **Writeback**: The control unit writes the results of instruction execution to register or memory locations, and the program counter is updated to the address of the next instruction to be executed.

The processor performs this fetch-decode-execute-writeback cycle repetitively from the time of power application until the computer is turned off. In a relatively simple processor such as the 6502, the processor executes each of these steps as essentially isolated, sequential operations. From the programmer's viewpoint, each instruction completes all of these steps before the next instruction begins. All of the results and side effects of each instruction are available in registers, memory, and processor flags for immediate use by the following instruction. This is a straightforward execution model, and assembly language programs can safely assume that all the effects of previous instructions are completed when the next instruction begins execution.

The following diagram is an example of instruction execution in a processor that requires one clock cycle for each of the fetch-decode-execute-writeback steps. Note that each step in this diagram is indicated by its initial: F, D, E or W:

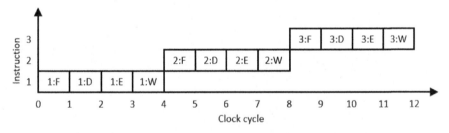

Figure 8.5: Sequential instruction execution

Each instruction requires four clock cycles to complete. At the hardware level, the processor represented in Figure 8.5 consists of four execution subsystems, each of which becomes active during one of the four instruction clock cycles. The processing logic associated with each of these steps reads input information from memory and from processor registers, and stores intermediate results in latches for use in later execution stages. After each instruction finishes, the next instruction begins execution immediately.

The number of completed **instructions per clock** (**IPC**) provides a performance metric indicating how quickly a processor executes instructions relative to the processor clock speed. The processor in the example of Figure 8.5 requires four clock cycles per instruction, leading to an IPC of 0.25.

The potential for improved performance in this example arises from the fact that the circuitry involved in each of the four steps is idle while the three remaining steps execute. Suppose that instead, as soon as the fetch hardware finishes fetching one instruction, it immediately begins fetching the next instruction. The following diagram shows the execution process when the hardware involved in each of the four instruction execution steps shifts from processing one instruction to the next instruction on each clock cycle:

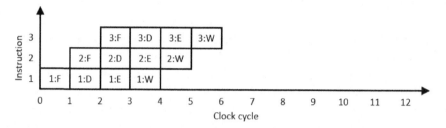

Figure 8.6: Pipelined instruction execution

This execution procedure is referred to as a **pipeline** because instructions enter and move through the execution stages from beginning to completion, like fluid moving through a physical pipeline. The processor pipeline contains multiple instructions at various stages of execution simultaneously. The reason for going to this trouble is evident in the preceding example: the processor is now completing one instruction per clock cycle, an IPC of 1.0, a four-fold speedup from the non-pipelined execution model of Figure 8.5. Similar levels of performance improvement are achieved in real-world processing using pipelining techniques.

In addition to overlapping the execution of sequential instructions via pipelining, there may be other opportunities to make productive use of processor subsystems that may otherwise be idle. Processor instructions fall into a few different categories that require different portions of the processor circuitry for their execution. Some examples include the following:

- **Branching instructions**: Conditional and unconditional branch instructions manipulate the program counter to set the address of the next instruction to be executed.

- **Integer instructions**: Instructions involving integer arithmetic and bit manipulation access the integer portion of the ALU.

- **Floating-point instructions**: Floating-point operations, on processors that provide hardware support for these operations, generally use separate circuitry from the integer ALU.

By increasing the sophistication of the processor's instruction scheduling logic, it may be possible to initiate the execution of two instructions on the same clock cycle if they happen to use independent processing resources. For example, it has long been common for processors to dispatch instructions to the **floating-point unit (FPU)** for execution in parallel with non-floating-point instructions executing on the main processor core.

In fact, many modern processors contain multiple copies of subsystems such as integer ALUs to support the execution of multiple instructions simultaneously. In this architecture, the processor initiates the execution of multiple instructions at the same time, referred to as **multiple-issue** processing. The following diagram depicts multiple-issue processing in which two instructions are initiated on each processor clock cycle:

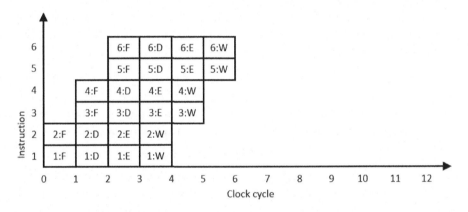

Figure 8.7: Multiple-issue pipelined instruction execution

This execution model doubles the number of instructions completed per clock cycle from the single-path pipeline of Figure 8.6, resulting in an IPC of 2.0. This is an example of a **superscalar processor**, which can issue (in other words, begin executing) more than one instruction per clock cycle. A **scalar processor**, in comparison, issues only one instruction per clock cycle. To be clear, both Figures 8.5 and 8.6 represent the behavior of a scalar processor, while Figure 8.7 represents superscalar processing. A superscalar processor implements **instruction-level parallelism (ILP)** to increase execution speed. Virtually all modern high-performance, general-purpose processors are superscalar.

Superpipelining

Looking back at the scalar, non-pipelined processing model presented in Figure 8.5, we can consider how the processor clock speed is selected. In the absence of concerns about power consumption and heat dissipation, it is generally desirable to run the processor clock at the fastest possible speed. The upper limit on the clock speed for the processor of Figure 8.5 is determined by the lengthiest path through each of the four subsystems involved in the execution stages. Different instructions may have drastically different execution time requirements. For example, an instruction to clear a processor flag requires very little execution time while a 32-bit division instruction may take much longer to produce its output.

It is inefficient to limit overall system execution speed based on the worst-case timing of a single instruction. Instead, processor designers look for opportunities to break the execution of complex instructions into a larger number of sequential steps. This approach is called **superpipelining**, and it consists of increasing the number of pipeline stages by breaking complex stages into multiple simpler stages. A superpipeline is, in essence, a processor pipeline with a large number of stages, potentially numbering in the dozens. In addition to being superscalar, modern high-performance processors are generally superpipelined.

Breaking a pipeline into a larger number of superpipeline stages allows the simplification of each stage, reducing the time required to execute each stage. With faster-executing stages, it is possible to increase the processor clock speed. As long as the rate of instruction issue can be sustained, superpipelining represents an instruction execution rate increase corresponding to the percentage increase in processor clock speed.

RISC processer instruction sets are designed to support effective pipelining. Most RISC instructions perform simple operations, such as moving data between registers and memory or adding two registers together. RISC processors usually have shorter pipelines compared to CISC processors. CISC processors, and their richer, more complex instruction sets, benefit from longer pipelines that break up long-running instructions into a series of sequential stages.

A big part of the challenge of efficiently pipelining processors based on legacy instruction sets such as x86 is that the original design of the instruction set did not fully consider the potential for later advances involving superscalar processing and superpipelining. As a result, modern x86-compatible processors devote a substantial proportion of their die area to the complex logic needed to implement these performance-enhancing features.

If breaking a pipeline into one or two dozen stages results in a substantial performance boost, why not continue by breaking the instruction pipeline into hundreds or even thousands of smaller stages to achieve even better performance? The answer: Pipeline hazards.

Pipeline hazards

Implementing pipelining in a general-purpose processor is not as straightforward as the discussion to this point might imply. If the result of an instruction relies on the outcome of the previous instruction, the current instruction will have to wait until the result of the prior instruction becomes available. Consider this x86 code:

```
inc eax
add ebx, eax
```

Let's assume these two instructions are executed on a processor operating as in Figure 8.6 (single-issue pipelining). The first instruction increments the eax register and the second adds this incremented value to the ebx register. The add instruction cannot execute the addition operation until the result of the increment operation in the previous instruction is available. If the second instruction's execute stage (labeled "2:E" in Figure 8.6) cannot execute until the first instruction's writeback stage has completed ("1:W" in the diagram), the 2:E stage has no choice but to wait for the 1:W stage to complete. Situations like this, where the pipeline cannot process the next stage of an instruction due to missing dependent information, are referred to as **pipeline hazards**.

One way in which processor pipelines deal with this issue is by implementing bypasses. After the first instruction's execute stage completes (labeled "1:E" in the diagram), the incremented value of the eax register has been computed, but it has not yet been written to the eax register. The second instruction's execute stage ("2:E" in the diagram) requires the incremented value of the eax register as an input. If the pipeline logic makes the result of the 1:E stage directly available to the 2:E stage without first writing to the eax register, the second instruction can complete execution without delay. The use of a shortcut to pass data between source and destination instructions without waiting for the completion of the source instruction is called a **bypass**. Bypasses are used extensively in modern processor designs to keep the pipeline working as efficiently as possible.

In some situations, a bypass is not possible because the necessary result simply cannot be computed before the destination instruction is ready to consume it. In this case, execution of the destination instruction must pause and await the delivery of the source instruction result. This causes the pipeline execution stage to become idle, which usually results in the propagation of the idle period through the remaining pipeline stages. This propagating delay is called a **pipeline bubble**, analogous to an air bubble passing through a fluid pipeline. The presence of bubbles in the processing sequence reduces the effectiveness of pipelining.

Bubbles are bad for performance, so pipelined processor designers undertake substantial efforts to avoid them as much as possible. One way to do this is **out-of-order instruction execution**, referred to as **OOO**. Consider the two instructions listed in the earlier example, but now followed by a third instruction:

```
inc eax
add ebx, eax
mov ecx, edx
```

The third instruction does not depend on the results of the previous instructions. Instead of using a bypass to avoid a delay, the processor can employ OOO execution to avoid a pipeline bubble. The resulting instruction sequence would look like this:

```
inc eax
mov ecx, edx
add ebx, eax
```

The outcome of executing these three instructions is the same, but the separation in time between the first and third instructions has now grown, reducing the likelihood of a pipeline bubble, or, if one still occurs, at least shortening its duration.

OOO execution requires detection of the presence of instruction dependencies and rearranges their execution order in a way that produces the same overall results, just not in the order originally coded. Some processors perform this instruction reordering in real time, during program execution. Other architectures rely on intelligent programming language compilers to rearrange instructions during the software build process to minimize pipeline bubbles. The first approach requires a substantial investment in processing logic and the associated die real estate to perform reordering on the fly, while the second approach simplifies the processor logic, but substantially complicates the job of assembly language programmers, who must now bear the burden of ensuring that pipeline bubbles do not excessively impair execution performance.

Micro-operations and register renaming

The x86 instruction set architecture has presented a particular challenge for processor designers. Although several decades old, the x86 architecture remains the mainstay of personal and business computing. As a CISC configuration with only eight registers (in 32-bit x86), the techniques of extensive instruction pipelining and exploiting a large number of registers used in RISC architectures are much less helpful in the native x86 architecture.

To gain some of the benefits of the RISC methodology, x86 processor designers have taken the step of implementing the x86 instructions as sequences of micro-operations. A micro-operation, abbreviated **µop** (and pronounced *micro-op*), is a sub-step of a processor instruction. Simpler x86 instructions decompose to 1 to 3 µops, while more complex instructions require a larger number of µops. The decomposition of instructions into µops provides a finer level of granularity for evaluating dependencies upon the results of other µops and supports an increase in execution parallelism.

In tandem with the use of µops, modern processors generally provide additional internal registers, numbering in the dozens or hundreds, for storing intermediate µop results. These registers contain partially computed results destined for assignment to the processor's physical registers after an instruction's µops have all completed. The use of these internal registers is referred to as **register renaming**. Each renamed register has an associated tag value indicating the physical processor register it will eventually occupy. By increasing the number of renamed registers available for intermediate storage, the possibilities for instruction parallelism increase.

Several µops may be in various stages of execution at any given time. The dependencies of an instruction upon the result of a previous instruction will block the execution of a µop until its input is available, typically via the bypass mechanism described in the preceding section. Once all required inputs are available, the µop is scheduled for execution. This mode of operation represents a **dataflow processing** model. Dataflow processing allows parallel operations to take place in a superscalar architecture by triggering µop execution when any data dependencies have been resolved.

High-performance processors perform the process of decoding instructions into µops after fetching each instruction. In some chip designs, the results of this decoding are stored in a Level 0 instruction cache, located between the processor and the L1-I cache. The L0-I cache provides the fastest possible access to pre-decoded µops for execution of code inner loops at the maximum possible speed. By caching the decoded µops, the processor avoids the need to re-execute the instruction decoding pipeline stages upon subsequent access of the same instruction.

In addition to the hazards related to data dependencies between instructions, a second key source of pipeline hazards is the occurrence of conditional branching, discussed in the next section.

Conditional branches

Conditional branching introduces substantial difficulty into the pipelining process. The address of the next instruction following a conditional branch instruction cannot be confirmed until the branch condition has been evaluated. There are two possibilities: if the branch condition is not satisfied, the processor will execute the instruction that follows the conditional branch instruction. If the branch condition is satisfied, the next instruction is at the address indicated in the conditional branch instruction.

Several techniques are available to deal with the challenges presented by conditional branching in pipelined processors. Some of these are as follows:

- When possible, avoid branching altogether. Software developers can design algorithms with inner loops that minimize or eliminate conditional code. Optimizing compilers attempt to rearrange and simplify the sequence of operations to reduce the negative effects of conditional branching.

- The processor may delay fetching the next instruction until the branch destination has been computed. This will typically introduce a bubble into the pipeline, degrading performance.

- The processor may perform the computation of the branch condition as early in the pipeline as possible. This will identify the correct branch more quickly, allowing execution to proceed with minimal delay.

- Some processors attempt to guess the result of the branch condition and begin executing instructions along that path. This is called **branch prediction**. If the guess turns out to be incorrect, the processor must clear the results of the incorrect execution path from the pipeline (called **flushing the pipeline**) and start over on the correct path. Although an incorrect guess leads to a significant performance impact, correctly guessing the branch direction allows execution to proceed without delay. Some processors that perform branch prediction track the results of previous executions of branch instructions and use that information to improve the accuracy of future guesses when re-executing the same instructions.

- Upon encountering a conditional branch instruction, the processor can begin executing instructions along both branch paths using its superscalar capabilities. This is referred to as **eager execution**. Once the branch condition has been determined, the results of execution along the incorrect path are discarded. Eager execution can only proceed as long as instructions avoid making changes that cannot be discarded. Writing data to main memory or to an output device is an example of a change that can't easily be undone, so eager execution would pause if such an action occurred while executing along a speculative path.

Modern high-performance processors devote a substantial portion of their logic resources to supporting effective pipelining under a wide variety of processing conditions. The combined benefits of multicore, superscalar, and superpipelined processing provide key performance enhancements in recent generations of sophisticated processor architectures. By performing instruction pipelining and executing instructions in a superscalar context, these features introduce parallelism into code sequences not originally intended to exploit parallel execution.

It is possible to further increase processing performance by introducing parallel execution of multiple threads on a single processor core with simultaneous multithreading.

Simultaneous multithreading

As we learned in previous chapters, each executing process contains one or more threads of execution. When performing multithreading using time-slicing on a single-core processor, only one thread is in the running state at any moment in time. By rapidly switching among multiple ready-to-execute threads, the processor creates the illusion (from the user's viewpoint) that multiple programs are running simultaneously.

This chapter introduced the concept of superscalar processing, which provides a single processing core with the ability to issue more than one instruction per clock cycle. The performance enhancement resulting from superscalar processing may be limited when the executing sequence of instructions does not require a mixture of processor resources that aligns well with the capabilities of its superscalar functional units. For example, in a particular instruction sequence, integer processing units may be heavily used (resulting in pipeline bubbles), while address computation units remain mostly idle.

One way to increase the utilization of processor superscalar capabilities is to issue instructions from more than one thread on each clock cycle. This is called **simultaneous multithreading**. By simultaneously executing instructions from different threads, there is a greater likelihood that the instruction sequences will depend on disparate functional capabilities within the processor, thereby allowing increased execution parallelism.

Processors that support simultaneous multithreading must provide a separate set of registers for each simultaneously executing thread, as well as a complete set of renamed internal registers for each thread. The intention here is to provide more opportunities for utilizing the processor's superscalar capabilities.

Many modern, high-performance processors support the execution of two simultaneous threads, though some support up to eight. As with most of the other performance enhancement techniques discussed in this chapter, increasing the number of simultaneous threads supported within a processor core eventually reaches a point of diminishing returns as the simultaneous threads compete for access to shared resources.

> **Simultaneous multithreading versus multicore processors versus multiprocessing**
>
> Simultaneous multithreading refers to a processor core with the ability to support the execution of instructions from different threads in the same pipeline stage on the same clock cycle. This differs from a multicore processor, in which each of the multiple processor cores on a single silicon die executes instructions independently of the others, and only connects to the other cores through some level of cache memory.
>
> A multiprocessing computer contains multiple processor integrated circuits, each of which is usually contained in a separate package. Alternatively, a multiprocessor may be implemented as multiple processor chips assembled in a single package.

The performance optimization techniques discussed to this point attempt to enhance the performance of scalar data processing, meaning that each instruction sequence operates on a small number of data values. Even superscalar processing, implemented with or without simultaneous multithreading, attempts to accelerate the execution of instructions that typically operate on, at most, one or two register-size data items at a time.

Vector data processing involves performing the same mathematical operation on an array of data elements simultaneously. Processor architectural features that improve execution parallelism for vector processing operations are the subject of the next section.

SIMD processing

Processors that issue a single instruction, involving one or two data items, per clock cycle, are referred to as scalar processors. Processors capable of issuing multiple instructions per clock cycle, though not explicitly executing vector processing instructions, are called superscalar processors. Some algorithms benefit from explicitly vectorized execution, which means performing the same operation on multiple data items simultaneously. Processor instructions tailored to such tasks are called **single instruction, multiple data (SIMD)** instructions.

The simultaneously issued instructions in superscalar processors are generally performing different tasks on different data, representing a **multiple instruction, multiple data (MIMD)** parallel processing system. Some processing operations, such as the dot product operation used in digital signal processing described in *Chapter 6, Specialized Computing Domains*, perform the same mathematical operation on an array of values.

While the multiply-accumulate (MAC) operation described in *Chapter 6, Specialized Computing Domains* performs scalar mathematical operations on each pair of vector elements in sequence, it is also possible to implement processor hardware and instructions capable of performing similar operations on more than a single pair of numbers at one time.

In modern processors, SIMD instructions are available to perform tasks such as mathematics on numeric arrays, manipulation of graphics data, and substring searches in character strings.

The Intel implementation of **Streaming SIMD Extensions (SSE)** instructions, introduced in the Pentium III processors of 1999, provides a set of processor instructions and execution facilities for simultaneously operating on 128-bit data arrays. The data contained in the array can consist of integers or floating-point values. In the second generation of SSE **(SSE2)** instructions, the following data types can be processed in parallel:

- Two 64-bit floating-point values

- Four 32-bit floating-point values

- Two 64-bit integer values

- Four 32-bit integer values

- Eight 16-bit integer values

- Sixteen 8-bit integer values

SSE2 provides floating-point instructions for the familiar mathematical operations of addition, subtraction, multiplication, and division. Instructions are also available for computing the square root, reciprocal, reciprocal of the square root, and returning the maximum value of the array elements. SSE2 integer instructions include comparison operations, bit manipulation, data shuffling, and data type conversion.

Later generations of the SSE instruction set have increased the data width and variety of supported operations. The latest iteration of SSE-type capabilities (as of 2019) is found in the AVX-512 instructions. **AVX** stands for **Advanced Vector Extensions**, and provides register widths of 512 bits. AVX-512 includes, among other features, instructions optimized to support neural network algorithms.

One impediment to the widespread adoption of the different generations of SSE and AVX instructions is that, for end users to be able to take advantage of them, the instructions must be implemented in the processor, the operating system must support the instructions, and the compilers and other analytical tools used by the end users must take advantage of the SSE features. Historically, it has taken years, following the introduction of new processor instructions, before end users could easily take advantage of their benefits.

The SIMD instructions available in modern processors have perhaps seen their most substantial application in the area of scientific computing. For researchers running complex simulations, machine learning algorithms, or sophisticated mathematical analyses, the availability of SSE and AVX instructions provides a way to achieve a substantial performance boost in code that performs extensive mathematical operations, character manipulations, and other vector-oriented tasks.

Summary

The majority of modern 32-bit and 64-bit processors combine most, if not all, of the performance-enhancing techniques presented in this chapter. A typical consumer-grade personal computer or smartphone contains a single main processor integrated circuit containing four cores, each of which supports simultaneous multithreading of two threads. This processor is superscalar, superpipelined, and contains three levels of cache memory. The processor decodes instructions into micro-ops and performs sophisticated branch prediction.

Although the techniques presented in this chapter might seem overly complicated and arcane, in fact, each of us uses them routinely and enjoys the performance benefits that derive from their presence each time we interact with any kind of computing device. The processing logic required to implement pipelining and superscalar operation is undeniably complex, but semiconductor manufacturers go to the effort of implementing these enhancements for one simple reason: it pays off in the performance of their products and in the resulting value of those products as perceived by end users.

This chapter introduced the primary performance-enhancing techniques used in processor and computer architectures to achieve peak execution speed in real-world computing systems. These techniques do not change in any way what the processor produces as output; they just help get it done faster. We examined the most important techniques for improving system performance, including the use of cache memory, instruction pipelining, simultaneous multithreading, and SIMD processing.

The next chapter focuses on extensions commonly implemented at the processor instruction set level to provide additional system capabilities beyond generic computing requirements. The extensions discussed in *Chapter 9*, *Specialized Processor Extensions*, include privileged processor modes, floating-point mathematics, power management, and system security management.

Exercises

1. Consider a direct-mapped L1-I cache of 32 KB. Each cache line consists of 64 bytes and the system address space is 4 GB. How many bits are in the cache tag? Which bit numbers (bit 0 is the least significant bit) are they within the address word?

2. Consider an 8-way set associative L2 instruction and data cache of 256 KB, with 64 bytes in each cache line. How many sets are in this cache?

3. A processor has a 4-stage pipeline with maximum delays of 0.8, 0.4, 0.6, and 0.3 nanoseconds in stages 1-4, respectively. If the first stage is replaced with two stages that have maximum delays of 0.5 and 0.3 nanoseconds respectively, how much will the processor clock speed increase in percentage terms?

9
Specialized Processor Extensions

In the preceding chapters, we discussed the features of general-purpose computer architectures as well as some architectural specializations intended to address domain-specific requirements. This chapter will focus on extensions commonly implemented at the processor instruction set level to provide additional system capabilities beyond generic computing needs.

After reading this chapter, you will understand the purpose of privileged processor modes and how they operate in multiprocessing and multiuser contexts. You will be familiar with the concepts of floating-point processors and instruction sets, techniques for power management in battery-powered devices, and processor features intended to enhance system security.

We will discuss the following processor extensions in this chapter:

- Privileged processor modes
- Floating-point mathematics
- Power management
- System security management

Technical requirements

The files for this chapter, including solutions to the exercises, are available at `https://github.com/PacktPublishing/Modern-Computer-Architecture-and-Organization`.

Privileged processor modes

Most operating systems running on 32-bit and 64-bit processors control access to system resources using the concept of privilege levels. The primary reasons for managing access in this manner are to enhance system stability, prevent unauthorized access to system hardware, and prevent unauthorized access to data.

Privileged execution improves system stability by ensuring only trusted code is allowed to execute instructions with unrestricted access to resources such as processor configuration registers and I/O devices. The operating system kernel and related modules, including device drivers, require privileged access to perform their functions. Because any crash of a kernel process or a device driver is likely to halt the entire system immediately, these software components generally undergo a careful design process and rigorous testing before being released for general use.

Running the operating system in a privileged context prevents unauthorized applications from accessing system-managed data structures such as page tables and interrupt vector tables. Whether by accident or as a result of malicious intent, a user application may attempt to access data contained in system-owned memory or in memory belonging to a different user. The system prevents such access attempts from succeeding, and informs the misbehaving application of its transgression by initiating an exception, which commonly results in a program crash with an error message.

Chapter 3, Processor Elements, introduced the concepts associated with interrupts and how they are handled by the processor. Before getting into the details of privileged processor modes, we will first discuss interrupt and exception handling in more detail.

Handling interrupts and exceptions

Hardware interrupts, as we have seen, allow processors to respond promptly to requests for services from peripheral devices. A hardware interrupt notifies the processor of a need to take some action, usually involving data transfer to or from an external device.

Exceptions are similar to interrupts, with the key difference that exceptions generally involve responding to some condition arising internal to the processor. One example of an internally generated exception is division by zero.

It is possible for user code to intentionally generate exceptions. In fact, this is a standard method used by unprivileged code to request system services provided by privileged code in the operating system kernel and device drivers.

The distinction between the terms **interrupt** and **exception** is not precisely defined. Interrupt processing and exception processing typically rely on the same or similar processor hardware resources operating in much the same manner. In fact, in the x86 architecture, the mnemonic for the instruction that initiates a software interrupt (or exception) is `int`, short for interrupt.

Exceptions include error conditions occurring during software execution such as division by zero, as well as non-error situations such as page faults. Unless the interrupt or exception results in the drastic response of terminating the application, an interrupt service routine or exception handler processes the event and returns control to the system scheduler, which eventually resumes execution of the interrupted thread.

When an interrupt or exception occurs, the processor transfers control to the corresponding handler as follows:

- When an interrupt occurs, the processor allows the currently executing instruction to complete, then transfers control to an **interrupt service routine (ISR)** without the awareness or approval of any threads that may have been executing at the time of the interrupt.

- When responding to an exception, the processor transfers control to an exception handling routine, which is similar to an ISR. An exception may arise during the execution of an instruction, preventing completion of the instruction's operations. If the execution of an instruction is disrupted by an exception, the same instruction will be restarted after the exception handler completes and thread execution resumes. This mechanism allows page faults to occur at any point during program execution without affecting the results produced by the program (other than introducing a delay for page fault processing).

Each interrupt or exception type has a vector number referencing a row in the system interrupt vector table. The processor hardware consults the **interrupt vector table (IVT)** when an interrupt or exception occurs to determine the appropriate response. The IVT row indexed by the vector number contains the address of the handler for that vector.

When handling an interrupt or exception, the processor pushes any required context information onto the stack and transfers control to the handler. In the case of an interrupt, the handler services the device and clears its interrupt request. After processing the interrupt or exception, the handler returns control to the operating system. The following table summarizes some of the interrupt and exception types available in x86 processors running in protected mode:

Table 9.1: Example x86 IVT entries

Vector	Description	Cause
0	Divide error	A `div` or `idiv` instruction attempted an integer division by zero.
2	Non-maskable interrupt	The NMI hardware signal was asserted.
3	Breakpoint	The `int 3` instruction executed.
6	Invalid opcode	An attempt was made to execute a reserved opcode.
13	General protection	A prohibited access to memory or to a system resource was attempted.
14	Page fault	The MMU issued a request to resolve a virtual address.
32-255	User defined	These vectors are available for use by hardware interrupts or with the `int` instruction.

These are some details of interest related to the interrupts and exceptions listed in Table 9.1:

- The operation of the NMI input signal on vector 2 is similar to the $\overline{\text{NMI}}$ input of the 6502 processor, discussed in *Chapter 3, Processor Elements*.

- Although modern processors provide sophisticated, non-intrusive breakpoint capabilities, the x86 architecture retains the breakpoint facility provided by the int 3 instruction from the early days of 8086. As we saw in *Chapter 3*, *Processor Elements*, the mechanism used by 6502 software debuggers to break program execution at a specified address is to temporarily replace the opcode at the break location with the 6502 BRK opcode. When execution reaches that location, the BRK handler takes control to allow user interaction with the system. The int 3 instruction in the x86 architecture functions in the same manner. In fact, unlike the x86 int instruction used with any of the other vector numbers, the int 3 instruction is implemented as a single-byte opcode, with the value CCh. A software interrupt to a different vector, such as int 32, is a two-byte instruction. The int 3 instruction enables breakpoint insertion by replacing a single byte of code with the value CCh.

- Vector 13, the general protection exception handler, activates on any attempt by an application to access memory or a system resource not allocated for its use. In 32-bit and 64-bit operating systems, by default, the system-provided handler for this vector terminates the running application and displays an error message.

- Vector 14, the page fault handler, activates when an application attempts to access a page that is not present in physical memory. The handler attempts to locate the referenced page, which may be in a disk file or in the system swap file, loads the page into memory, updates the virtual-to-physical translation tables, and restarts the instruction that triggered the exception.

To summarize, hardware interrupts are initiated by I/O devices in need of data transfers or other types of servicing. System exceptions occur when the execution of an instruction sequence must be paused to handle a condition such as a page fault or attempted unauthorized access.

Hardware interrupts and system exceptions tend to occur at random times relative to the ongoing execution of program code, while behavior related to software-generated exceptions is generally repeatable if the same code executes again while operating on the same data.

While some exceptions, such as a general protection fault, result in the termination of the process causing the exception, most interrupts and exceptions end with the interrupted thread resuming execution after the interrupt or exception handler has completed its processing.

Programming language exceptions

Many programming languages provide a facility for performing exception handling within an application. It is important to understand that programming language exceptions are significantly different from the types of exceptions handled by the processor. Exceptions in programming languages generally relate to error conditions at a much higher level than exceptions handled by processor hardware.

For example, C++ will generate (or "throw," in C++ terminology) an exception when a memory allocation request fails. This is not the same type of exception as system exceptions handled at the processor level. Be careful not to confuse exceptions in high-level programming language with exceptions handled directly by the processor.

Protection rings

We can think of the protection strategy employed by modern processors and operating systems as similar in significant ways to the defenses implemented in the designs of medieval castles. A castle usually has a high wall surrounding the castle grounds, sometimes enhanced by the presence of a moat. This outer wall has a small number of well-defended access points, each of which is fortified against intruders by mechanisms such as drawbridges and around-the-clock guard details. Within the castle compound, the castle itself has sturdy walls and a small number of well-defended access points, further limiting access to the most sensitive areas.

The most privileged members of the castle hierarchy enjoy unrestricted access in and out of the castle and the outer wall. Less privileged members of the society may have authorization to pass inward through the outer wall but are prohibited from accessing the castle directly. The least privileged members of the local population are prohibited from entering the castle under most conditions and may have to accept limitations on what they can do on occasions when they are granted access, such as being permitted to access only specified public areas.

The protections provided by this strategy can be represented as concentric rings, with the highest privilege required to access the innermost rings, while the outer ring represents the area requiring the least privilege, as shown in this figure:

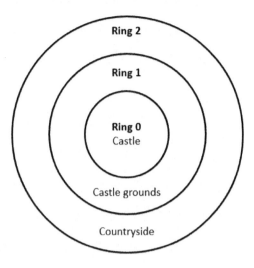

Figure 9.1: Protection ring example

This protection strategy contains three privilege levels that determine the types of access available to each individual in the system. Ring 0 requires the highest privilege level, while ring 2 requires no special privilege.

Modern processors and the operating systems that run on them use a very similar approach to prevent unauthorized access to critical resources, while granting unprivileged users access to system capabilities approved for their use.

Although, in principle, it is possible to provide multiple intermediate levels between the highest and lowest privileged rings, most modern computer architectures implement just two rings: a privileged ring, called the kernel or supervisor, and an unprivileged user ring. Some operating systems implement an intermediate ring containing device drivers, which grants access to the resources required to interact with I/O devices, but does not provide the unfettered system-wide access of the kernel ring.

One reason operating systems such as Windows and Linux support only two privilege rings is because these systems have a design goal of portability across different processor architectures. Some processors support only two privilege rings, while others support a greater number. A portable operating system cannot implement more than two privilege rings if any of the underlying processor architectures do not support the desired number of rings. The x86 architecture, for example, supports up to four rings, but only two of those (ring 0, the most privileged, and ring 3, the least privileged) are used by Windows and Linux.

The following figure represents the ring organization of most operating systems running on the x86 architecture:

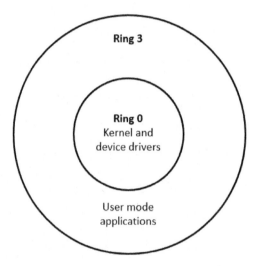

Figure 9.2: Protection rings in x86 processors

This ring-based privilege management system is the primary reason the infamous Windows "Blue Screen of Death," which was common in the 1990s, appears so rarely for users of recent versions of Windows. User applications such as web browsers, email clients, and word processors will, on occasion, experience problems that cause the programs to crash. By virtue of the privilege enforcement mechanisms provided by operating systems such as Windows, Linux, macOS, and Android, the crash of an individual application is contained by the operating system, preventing the crash from affecting the operating system itself or any other program running on the system (at least, those programs that aren't dependent upon the program that crashed for their correct operation).

Following an application crash, the operating system cleans up any resources in use by the crashed program, including allocated memory pages and open files. This allows computer systems such as web server hosts to remain operational continuously for hundreds of days, despite the occasional crashes and restarts of software applications running on them.

In addition to protecting against application crashes, ring-based privilege control provides substantial security benefits against malicious actors. One type of attack a hacker might attempt is to insert some code into a system module that runs in ring 0. This insertion could occur in an executable file on disk, or the attacker may try to modify kernel code while it is running in memory. If successful, the attacker could then use this code to access data anywhere in the system because it is running in ring 0.

While achieving success with this type of attack is by no means impossible, modern processors and operating systems have implemented an extensive array of security measures and repaired many vulnerabilities found in earlier versions of operating systems. When system administrators and users take full advantage of the ring-based security measures available in modern computer systems, there are very few feasible paths an attacker can take to access protected data. In fact, in most cases, a key element of successful hacks that make it into the news is a human-related security breakdown exploited by the attacker.

Supervisor mode and user mode

In a two-level protection ring hierarchy, the protection level of the currently executing thread is typically represented by a bit in a register. When operating in ring 0, the **supervisor mode** bit is 1, and when operating in **user mode** (ring 3 on x86) the supervisor mode bit is 0. The supervisor mode bit can only be modified by code running in supervisor mode.

The state of the supervisor mode bit determines which instructions are available for execution by the thread. Instructions that could interfere with system operation, such as the x86 `hlt` instruction, which halts processor instruction execution, are unavailable in user mode. Any attempt to execute a prohibited instruction results in a general protection fault. In user mode, access by user applications to system memory regions and the memory allocated to other users is prohibited. In supervisor mode, all instructions are available for execution and all memory regions are accessible.

In the castle analogy, the supervisor mode bit represents the identification presented to the castle guards that enables access to the castle grounds and to the castle itself. When set, the supervisor mode bit provides the keys to the kingdom.

System calls

All code belonging to the kernel and device drivers runs in ring 0, always. All user code runs in ring 3, always, even for users with enhanced operating system privileges such as system administrators. Code running in ring 3 is strictly controlled by the system and cannot directly do anything that involves allocating memory, opening a file, displaying information to the screen, or interacting with an I/O device. To access any of those system features, ring 3 user code must make a service request to the kernel.

The kernel service request must first pass through a gate (just like visitors entering our castle!) where the type of operation being requested, as well as any associated parameters, are scrutinized and validated before the execution of the operation is allowed to proceed. The code performing the requested operation runs in supervisor mode at ring 0 and, when complete, returns control to the user mode calling routine in ring 3.

In early versions of Windows (prior to Windows XP), an application used the software interrupt mechanism with vector 2eh to request system services. The system call protocol involved placing the parameters required by the requested service into processor registers and executing the int 2eh instruction, triggering a software interrupt. The handler would run in supervisor mode, resulting in a transition from ring 3 to ring 0. Upon completion of the handler, the system returned to ring 3 at the instruction following int 2eh.

One problem with the use of the int 2eh mechanism for requesting kernel services is that it is not very efficient. In fact, it takes over 1,000 processor clock cycles to get from the point at which the int 2eh instruction executes to the kernel code that actually begins to handle the exception. A busy system may request kernel services thousands of times per second.

To address this inefficiency, Intel implemented the sysenter and sysexit instructions in the x86 architecture beginning with the Pentium II processor in 1997. The purpose of these instructions is to accelerate the process of calling from ring 3 to ring 0, and later returning to ring 3. By using these instructions instead of int 2eh, entry into and exit from kernel mode speeds up by about a factor of three.

Around the time Intel began producing processors with the sysenter and sysexit instructions, AMD released the syscall and sysret instructions in their processor architectures, with the same performance objective. Unfortunately, the instructions in the Intel and AMD processor architectures are not compatible, which leads to a requirement for operating systems to differentiate between architectures when using accelerated kernel calling instructions.

Next, we will look at the data formats and operations associated with floating-point mathematical processing.

Floating-point mathematics

Modern processors usually support integer data types in widths of 8, 16, 32, and 64 bits. Some smaller embedded processors may not directly support 64-bit or even 32-bit integers, while more sophisticated devices may support 128-bit integers. Integer data types are appropriate for use in a wide range of applications, but many areas of computing, particularly in the fields of science, engineering, and navigation, require the ability to represent fractional numbers with a high degree of accuracy.

As a simple example of the limitations of integer mathematics, suppose you need to divide 5 by 3. On a computer restricted to using integers, you can perform an integer calculation of this expression as follows, in C++:

```cpp
#include <iostream>

int main(void)
{
    int a = 5;
    int b = 3;
    int c = a / b;
    std::cout << "c = " << c << std::endl;

    return 0;
}
```

This program produces the following output:

```
c = 1
```

If you punch this expression into your pocket calculator, you'll find the printed result is not very close to the actual result, which is approximately 1.6667. In computing applications where accurate calculations involving real numbers are required, the use of floating-point mathematics provides a practical solution.

Mathematically, the set of real numbers consists of all of the numbers, including all integers and fractions, along the number line from negative infinity to positive infinity. There is no limit to the number of digits in the integer and fractional parts of a real number.

Given the finite storage available in even the largest computer, it is clearly not possible to represent the entire range of real numbers in computer programs. A compromise is required if we are to represent real numbers in a useful manner. The compromise implemented nearly universally is to represent real numbers in terms of a mantissa and exponent.

In areas of study involving the mathematics of very large or very small numbers, it is common to represent such numbers in terms of a mantissa and an exponent. For example, in physics, the gravitational constant $G = 6.674 \times 10^{-11} \frac{m^3}{kg\ s^2}$. In this format, the **mantissa** represents the nonzero digits of the number after multiplication by a scaling factor that places those digits within a convenient range. The **exponent** represents the scaling factor by which the mantissa must be multiplied to produce the actual value.

In this example, the mantissa is *6.674* and the exponent is *-11*. This example uses a base-*10* mantissa, which is convenient for manual calculation because multiplication by the scale factor *10⁻¹¹* can be performed by simply moving the position of the mantissa decimal point. In this example, an exponent of -11 requires moving the decimal point 11 places to the left, resulting in the equivalent number 0.00000000006674. The use of floating-point notation avoids the error-prone use of lengthy sequences of zeros and allows both extremely large and very tiny numbers to be represented in a compact notation.

Any number along the real number line can be represented in floating-point notation. However, there can be no limit on the number of digits in the mantissa or exponent of the notation if the goal is to truly represent all real numbers.

In computer representations of floating-point numbers, both the mantissa and exponent are limited to predefined bit widths. These ranges have been chosen to fit floating-point numbers within standard data widths, typically 32 or 64 bits, while providing an adequate number of mantissa and exponent digits for a wide variety of applications.

Increasing the number of mantissa digits increases the precision of the numerical values representable in floating-point format. Increasing the number of exponent digits increases the range of numbers that can be represented. Because of the finite lengths of the mantissa and exponent, the result of a floating-point calculation often does not precisely equal the actual real-valued result. Instead, the best we can expect is that the floating-point result will be the nearest representable value to the correct result.

Modern processors commonly support 32-bit and 64-bit representations of floating-point numbers. Rather than the base-10 exponents described on the preceding page, computers work with base-2 exponents. The general format of a computer floating-point number is as follows:

$$\text{sign} \times \text{mantissa} \times 2^{exponent}$$

The sign is simply +1 or -1. In the binary representation, a positive number has a sign bit of 0 and a negative number has a sign bit of 1. Having separated the sign from the rest of the number, the remaining value is nonnegative. For any value other than zero (which is handled as a special case), this number can be scaled into the range of greater than or equal to 1 and less than 2 by multiplying it by some power of 2.

Continuing the example of the gravitational constant, because the sign is +1, the value after removing the sign is unchanged: 6.674×10^{-11}. The mantissa for this number can be scaled into the range $(1 \leq m < 2)$, where m represents the mantissa, by multiplying by 2^{34}. The result of this scaling is:

$$G = +1 \times 1.1465845 \times 2^{-34}$$

We multiplied the original number by 2^{34} to get the mantissa into the desired range, so the floating-point representation of the number must be multiplied by 2^{-34} to undo the scaling operation.

Since our computer operates on binary numbers, we must next convert the mantissa to a binary representation. The format used in floating-point processing is to represent the range between 1 and 2 with an unsigned integer.

For example, if we assume the binary mantissa is 16 bits wide, the mantissa of 1.0 is represented by 0000h and the value just below 2.0 (actually 1.99998474) is represented by FFFFh. A decimal mantissa m is converted to a 16-bit binary mantissa using the expression $1 + m \times 2^{-16}$ and rounding the result to the nearest integer. A 16-bit binary mantissa m is converted to decimal with the expression $(m - 1) \times 2^{16}$.

In our example, the decimal mantissa of 1.1465845 converts to a 16-bit binary mantissa of 0010010110000111b, or 2587h.

Using the scaling procedure described in the preceding section, floating-point numbers can be represented in binary form with any desired bit widths for the mantissa and exponent. For the purposes of compatibility, it is helpful to define a limited number of binary floating-point formats capable of supporting a wide variety of use cases and to adopt those formats industry-wide.

The IEEE 754 standard for the computer representation of floating-point numbers was adopted in 1985 for this reason. Before looking at the standard, we'll explore the design of the Intel 8087 floating-point coprocessor, which was the source of many of the concepts later enshrined in the IEEE 754 standard.

The 8087 floating-point coprocessor

Modern processors with floating-point hardware generally implement a set of instructions for floating-point computations and perform these operations in a dedicated functional unit. In a superscalar processor, the main processor core continues to execute other categories of instructions while the **floating-point unit** (**FPU**) executes floating-point calculations in parallel.

Recall from *Chapter 1, Introducting Computer Architecture*, that the original IBM PC of 1981 contained a socket for an 8087 floating-point coprocessor. The 8087 performs floating-point computations in hardware at speeds roughly 100 times faster than a functionally equivalent software implementation running on the host processor. Because installation of the 8087 was optional, most PC software applications that wished to take advantage of its capabilities first tested for the presence of the 8087 and, if it was not found, reverted to a library of much slower floating-point code.

The 8087 supports the following data types for numeric processing:

- 16-bit two's complement integer
- 32-bit two's complement integer
- 64-bit two's complement integer
- 18-digit signed packed **binary coded decimal** (**BCD**)
- 32-bit signed short real with a 24-bit mantissa and an 8-bit exponent
- 64-bit signed long real with a 53-bit mantissa and an 11-bit exponent
- 80-bit signed temporary real with a 64-bit mantissa and a 15-bit exponent

Each data type is stored as a series of bytes in memory. The formats used for the real data types are shown in the following figure:

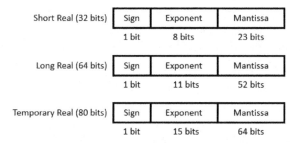

Figure 9.3: 8087 coprocessor floating-point data formats

The short and long real formats use an implied 1 bit as the most significant bit of the mantissa, and do not include this bit in their binary representations. As a special case, the value zero is represented in these formats by setting both the mantissa and exponent to zero.

The temporary real format is used internally in the 8087 to store intermediate results. This format has extended precision in comparison to the long real format to minimize the propagation of rounding errors over a series of calculations.

Each of the real number formats can be represented as $(-1)^S(2^{E-bias})(m)$, where S is the sign bit, E is the exponent, and m is the mantissa. This *bias* is 127 in the short real format, 1023 in the long real format, and 16,383 in the temporary real format. The *bias* term converts the unsigned integer stored in the exponent field to a signed value.

Our example real number, G, which has a decimal mantissa of 1.1465845 and a binary scale of 2^{-34}, is represented with a sign bit of 0, an exponent of $(-34 + 127) = 5Dh$, and a mantissa of $(1.1465845 - 1) \times 2^{23} = 12C348h$. Combining all three components, the 32-bit representation of 6.674×10^{-11} is $(\text{sign bit} = 0) \times 2^{31} + \text{biased exponent} = 5Dh\ X\ 2^{23} + (\text{mantissa} = 12C348h)$.

The 8087 adds 68 opcode mnemonics to the 8086/8088 instruction set for performing arithmetic, trigonometric, exponential, and logarithmic functions. In a PC program using the 8087, the code consists of a single stream of 8088 and 8087 instructions retrieved in the usual sequential manner by the 8088 host processor. The 8087 passively monitors the address and data buses as the host processor executes instructions and only becomes active when an 8087 opcode appears. The 8088 treats 8087 instructions as no-operation (or nop) instructions and ignores them.

When the 8087 begins executing an instruction, it is able to take control of the host bus to transfer data between its internal registers and system memory using DMA cycles. The 8087 and 8088 do not directly transfer data between themselves, and can only share data by storing it in memory for use by the other processor. 8087 instruction execution proceeds independent of the 8088, making an 8087-equipped PC a truly parallel processing system. The 8087 has a BUSY output signal for use by the 8088 host processor to determine whether the 8087 is currently processing an instruction.

When the 8088 requires the results of an 8087 operation, the 8088 must wait for the 8087 BUSY signal to de-assert, at which point the 8088 is free to access the memory locations containing the output of the 8087 instruction.

The IEEE 754 floating-point standard

The most widely used formats for representing floating-point numbers in modern computer systems are those defined in the IEEE 754 standard. **IEEE**, the **Institute of Electrical and Electronic Engineers**, publishes a wide variety of standards related to electricity, electronics, and computing. The original version of the IEEE 754 standard was adopted in 1985, based largely on the data types and mathematical operations of the Intel 8087.

The 8087 was not entirely compliant with the initial IEEE 754 standard, which was published several years after the introduction of the 8087. Later Intel floating-point coprocessors, beginning with the 80387 in 1987, were fully standard-compliant. Today's 32-bit and 64-bit processors generally implement an IEEE 754-compliant floating-point coprocessor on the same silicon die as the main processor.

The IEEE 754 standard was updated in 2008 and again in 2019. The current version is IEEE 754-2019 and contains definitions for base-2 floating-point number formats with bit widths of 16, 32, 64, 128, and 256 bits. It also contains base-10 floating-point number formats with bit widths of 32, 64, and 128 bits. The 32-bit and 64-bit base-2 floating-point formats are generally supported in programming languages that include floating-point operations. Support for the remaining IEEE 754 data types tends to be more limited and non-standardized across processors, programming languages, and operating systems.

The next section presents features that many modern processor architectures implement to manage system power consumption.

Power management

For users of portable battery-powered devices such as smartphones, tablets, and laptop computers, the ability to operate for long time periods without recharging is an important feature. Designers of portable systems place great emphasis on ensuring battery power consumption is minimized under all operating conditions. Some techniques designers use to reduce power consumption are as follows:

- Placing idle subsystems in a low-power state, or turning them off completely when they are not needed. This solution may not be possible for peripherals that must be available to respond to incoming requests, such as network interfaces.

- Reducing integrated circuit supply voltages and clock speeds during periods when execution speed is not critical.

- When possible, saving system state information and turning the processor power off completely. Users of laptop computers are familiar with two options for reducing power consumption when the system is not in use: standby and hibernate. In standby mode, system RAM continues to be powered while the rest of the system is turned off. Standby mode enables very fast startup when the user resumes using the system. This responsiveness comes at a cost: keeping RAM powered consumes a significant amount of power. In hibernate mode, the entire system state is written to disk storage and the system powers down completely. Hibernate mode requires essentially zero power, though it normally takes quite a bit longer than standby mode to resume operation.

- When periodic processing is required, such as in real-time applications, place the processor in a low-power state each time processing completes. The processor remains in that state until a timer interrupt wakes the processor for the next iteration. Many embedded processors provide a low-power idle mode in which the instruction pipeline is halted, but remains ready to instantly resume execution in response to an interrupt. Some RTOS implementations support this concept by idling the processor when all tasks are blocked waiting for an interrupt or other event.

Smartphones and other battery-powered devices make extensive use of all of these methods to drive battery usage to a minimum while remaining instantly responsive to user inputs and to external inputs such as incoming calls and social media notifications.

Modern processors in high-performance computers and in embedded devices generally support the ability to adjust processor clock speed during code execution, and in some cases provide the ability to alter the processor power supply voltage as well. This combination of power management techniques is addressed in the next section.

Dynamic voltage frequency scaling

Optimization of processor clock frequency and supply voltage to minimize power consumption is called **dynamic voltage frequency scaling (DVFS)**. When performing DVFS, a processor regularly evaluates the performance requirements of its current operating state and adjusts the processor clock frequency and power supply voltage to minimize battery usage while continuing to perform at an acceptable level.

In a CMOS chip containing a large number of transistors, a reasonable estimate of power consumption is $P = \sum_{i=1}^{N} C_i v_i^2 f_i$. In this expression, P represents the total power consumption of the chip, which contains N MOS transistors. C_i is the capacitance driven by the ith transistor, v_i is the transistor's supply voltage, and f_i is its operating frequency.

Examining this formula, we see that circuit power consumption is proportional to the square of the supply voltage, and is directly proportional to capacitance and operating frequency. Because capacitance in the circuit plays a significant role in power consumption, it is beneficial to implement the device using a fabrication process that reduces the size of circuit gates, keeping the capacitance to a minimum. This is one reason a transition to an integrated circuit fabrication process supporting smaller feature sizes results in devices with reduced power consumption.

DVFS attempts to minimize overall power consumption by reducing both the supply voltage and processor clock frequency as much as possible, at all times.

Reducing the circuit supply voltage can provide a dramatic reduction in power consumption. However, any reduction of the processor supply voltage must be carefully coordinated with adjustments to the clock frequency. When the supply voltage is reduced, CMOS transistors switch more slowly. This is because the capacitance driven by each transistor remains unchanged, but that capacitance charges and discharges at a slower rate because there is less voltage driving the charge/discharge process. As the system voltage is reduced, the clock frequency must be reduced in tandem for the circuit to function properly.

Recalling the hydraulic system analogy from *Chapter 2*, *Digital Logic*, the effect of reducing the CMOS supply voltage is equivalent to reducing the water pressure that fills the balloon attached to the side of the pipe: with reduced system pressure, the balloon fills more slowly.

Reducing the processor supply voltage also reduces the circuit's noise immunity. When this happens, it becomes easier for external interference, such as the electrical field emanating from a motor starting up in a household appliance, to disrupt the internal operation of the processor. Any processor voltage reduction must be limited to ensure continued reliable operation.

Reducing the processor clock frequency (in addition to any clock slowing required by supply voltage reduction) reduces power consumption by an approximately proportional amount. Reducing the operating frequency also increases system reliability because each gate transition has more time to propagate and reach its final state before being latched by the gates it is driving.

A complex embedded device such as a smartphone may need to transition rapidly between higher and lower power states as its various inputs stimulate it with user actions, timer-triggered events, and information arriving over wireless connections. While it is beneficial for the system to nimbly switch between lower and higher power modes as circumstances change, it is also important to limit the rate at which such transitions occur because the mere act of switching between power modes consumes some power itself.

Users expect their computers and other sophisticated digital devices to consume no more power than absolutely necessary, and they also expect those systems to be secure. The next section introduces the key aspects of system security management.

System security management

We have seen how the separation of privilege levels between kernel and user modes supports the effective separation of applications started up by one user from those of other users and from system processes. This represents security at the level of executing software. This is fine as far as it goes, but what about systems that must remain secure even when untrusted users have unrestricted physical access to them? Additional measures must be implemented at the hardware level to prevent curious or malicious users from accessing protected code, data, and hardware resources.

Before getting into the details of hardware-level security features, it is helpful to list some of the categories of information and other resources that must be protected in digital systems:

- **Personal information**: Information such as government identification numbers, passwords for accessing web accounts, contact lists, emails, and text messages must be protected even if a portable device containing that information is lost or stolen.

- **Business information**: Trade secrets, customer lists, research products, and strategic plans are some categories of confidential business data that may have great value in the hands of competitors or criminals. Businesses also collect a great deal of personal information about their customers and are required to undertake substantial efforts to keep this information secure.

- **Government information**: Government organizations maintain a great deal of personal information about their citizens and must ensure it can only be used for authorized purposes. Governments also develop a vast quantity of information related to national security that requires extensive security protocols.

Beyond the obvious physical security measures of storing sensitive information in a sturdy, access-controlled facility with effective alarm systems, a number of measures can be taken to ensure a system is secure against a wide variety of attacks.

Consider the smartphone. A technically capable individual or organization may be able to disassemble the phone's case and gain access to the circuit-level hardware. If this person is able to monitor the external electrical signals of the processor and its communication paths to other system components, what kinds of information might be gathered? The answer depends on the types and quantity of hardware security implemented in the system design.

A first step in secure system design is to avoid inserting security vulnerabilities during development. During the development of a system containing an embedded processor, it is quite useful to provide a hardware debugger interface. A **hardware debugger** enables the connection of a PC to the device using a special interface cable. Using this connection, developers can reprogram flash memory, set breakpoints in the code, display the values of registers and variables, and single-step through code. If the debugger connection remains in the circuit board in the released version of the design, it may be possible for users to connect their own debugger to the system and work with it in the same manner as the developers.

This is clearly undesirable for any system intended to operate securely. Because the ability to connect a debugger continues to be quite useful even after a product is released, developers sometimes attempt to leave the debugger signals present in the circuit but camouflage them in some manner to make their functions less obvious. While this approach may be effective to some degree, dedicated hackers have demonstrated the ability to ferret out the presence of even the most cleverly disguised debugging interfaces and leverage those interfaces to access the processor's internals. Leaving an accessible hardware debugging interface present in a released product is a serious security vulnerability.

Many processor vendors have begun implementing security features to prevent even dedicated, technically capable attackers from breaching processor protections. To be effective, system developers must enable and fully leverage these capabilities in their system designs. Some examples of security technologies include the following:

- **Password-protected hardware debugger interface**: Some processor families support the addition of a password to the standard hardware debugging interface. In these systems, an initial handshake must take place in which the connected system provides a strong password (such as a 256-bit number) before the processor enables debug functionality. This is an effective approach that retains the ability to securely troubleshoot issues that arise after the product is released.

- **Internal encryption engine with key storage**: Some processors provide encryption and decryption capabilities and store secret keys for use during operation. The keys must be stored in the processor during system manufacture and are not externally accessible after they have been stored. This combination of encryption engine and stored keys allows secure communication with authorized external devices. The use of high-speed, hardware-based encryption and decryption capabilities allows secure full-speed communication between physically separated subsystems such as those within an automobile.

- **Device memory protection**: Many processor families provide several options for the protection of memory regions. For example, a ROM bank containing code can be locked after programming to ensure it cannot be reprogrammed at a later time. Code regions can also be blocked from being read as data while still allowing access for execution. Processors that lack a full memory management unit often have a subsystem called the **memory protection unit** (**MPU**) to manage the security requirements of the various processor memory regions.

It is not sufficient to design in a standard set of security features and assume hackers will be unable to penetrate those defenses. Attackers have demonstrated extraordinary cleverness and will use any avenue to gain insight into the inner workings of a system they find interesting. Some areas to consider beyond the standard security techniques are as follows:

- **Power, timing, and emission analysis**: By using fine-grained monitoring of system power consumption, the timing of external signal activity, or even the radio frequency emissions generated during algorithm execution, it may be possible to reverse engineer the activities going on within the processor. Attacks based on these methods have been successful at extracting secret encryption keys during cryptographic algorithm execution, for example.

- **Power disruption**: Intentionally inducing power supply voltage fluctuations or dropouts during system power-up or operation has been shown to leave many systems in a vulnerable state in which some security features are inactive. A robust system design must anticipate such behavior, whether natural or intentional, and revert to a safe, secure state whenever the power supply is not performing within established parameters.

- **Physical alteration**: An attacker may replace some components in the system in an attempt to gain control. For example, replacing a boot ROM device may allow the system to operate normally while also enabling the attacker to gain unrestricted internal access using code in the replacement ROM. A growing number of processor families support the use of digital signatures to verify the authenticity of ROM code. To check the contents of the ROM device, the processor runs a **hash algorithm**, which is a complex mathematical calculation on the ROM data. The results of the hash algorithm (the signature) must match the signature preloaded in the processor before the ROM code will be executed. The hash algorithm is designed to make it essentially impossible to alter the ROM data content while still producing the expected signature. For good measure, the ROM data content can also be encrypted, which prevents the attacker from analyzing the code it contains.

This section has listed some fundamental approaches to implementing security in digital devices, and briefly examined some of the more esoteric security vulnerabilities that have been exploited by dedicated attackers. The design of a secure system must begin with a firm grounding in the basics of security, but also requires some ingenuity in considering the many ways a determined attacker may attempt to breach system security.

Summary

This chapter built upon the preceding chapters, which presented the basic aspects of computer architecture and architectural variations addressing domain-specific requirements. We focused here on extensions commonly implemented at the processor instruction set level to provide additional system capabilities beyond generic computing requirements.

You should now have a good understanding of privileged processor modes and how they are used in multiprocessing and multiuser contexts, the concepts of floating-point processors and instruction sets, techniques for power management in battery-powered devices, and processor features intended to enhance system security.

This background has prepared us for the next chapter, in which we will, the most popular processor architectures and instruction sets currently used in personal computing, business computing, and in smart portable devices. These architectures are the x86, the x64, and the 32-bit and 64-bit variants of ARM.

Exercises

1. Using a programming language that allows access to the byte representation of floating-point data types (such as C or C++), write a function that accepts a 32-bit single-precision value as input. Extract the sign, exponent, and mantissa from the bytes of the floating-point value and display them. Remove the bias term from the exponent before displaying its value and display the mantissa as a decimal number. Test the program with the values 0, -0, 1, -1, 6.674e-11, 1.0e38, 1.0e39, 1.0e-38, and 1.0e-39. The numeric values listed here containing e are using the C/C++ text representation of floating-point numbers. For example, 6.674e-11 means 6.674×10^{-11}

2. Modify the program from *Exercise 1* to also accept a double-precision floating-point value, and print the sign, exponent (with the bias removed), and mantissa from the value. Test it with the same input values as in *Exercise 1*, and also with the values 1.0e308, 1.0e309, 1.0e-308, and 1.0e-309.

3. Search the Internet for information about the NXP Semiconductors i.MX RT1060 processor family. Download the product family datasheet and answer the following questions about these processors.

4. Do the i.MX RT1060 processors support the concept of supervisor mode instruction execution? Explain your answer.

5. Do the i.MX RT1060 processors support the concept of paged virtual memory? Explain your answer.

6. Do the i.MX RT1060 processors support floating-point operations in hardware? Explain your answer.

7. What power management features do the i.MX RT1060 processors support?

8. What security features do the i.MX RT1060 processors support?

10
Modern Processor Architectures and Instruction Sets

Most modern personal computers contain a processor supporting either the Intel or AMD version of the x86 32-bit and x64 64-bit architectures. Almost all smartphones, smart watches, tablets, and many embedded systems, on the other hand, contain ARM 32-bit or 64-bit processors. This chapter takes a detailed look at the registers and instruction sets of all of these processor families.

After completing this chapter, you will understand the top-level architectures and unique attributes of the x86, x64, 32-bit ARM, and 64-bit ARM registers, instruction sets, assembly languages, and key aspects of legacy feature support in these architectures.

This chapter covers the following topics:

- x86 architecture and instruction set
- x64 architecture and instruction set
- 32-bit ARM architecture and instruction set
- 64-bit ARM architecture and instruction set

Technical requirements

The files for this chapter, including the answers to the exercises, are available at
`https://github.com/PacktPublishing/Modern-Computer-Architecture-and-Organization`.

x86 architecture and instruction set

For the purpose of this discussion, the term **x86** refers to the 16-bit and 32-bit instruction
set architecture of the series of processors that began with the Intel 8086, introduced in
1978. The 8088, released in 1979, is functionally very similar to the 8086, except it has an
8-bit data bus instead of the 16-bit bus of the 8086. The 8088 was the central processor
in the original IBM PC.

Subsequent generations of this processor series were named 80186, 80286, 80386, and
80486, leading to the term "x86" as shorthand for the family. Subsequent generations
dropped the numeric naming convention and were given the names Pentium, Core,
i Series, Celeron, and Xeon.

Advanced Micro Devices (AMD), a semiconductor manufacturing company that
competes with Intel, has been producing x86-compatible processors since 1982. Some
recent AMD x86 processor generations have been named Ryzen, Opteron, Athlon,
Turion, Phenom, and Sempron.

For the most part, compatibility is good between Intel and AMD processors. There
are some key differences between processors from the two vendors, including the chip
pin configuration and chipset compatibility. In general, Intel processors only work in
motherboards and with chipsets designed for Intel chips, and AMD processors only work
in motherboards and with chipsets designed for AMD chips. We will see some other
differences between Intel and AMD processors later in this section.

The 8086 and 8088 are 16-bit processors, despite the 8-bit data bus of the 8088. Internal
registers in these processors are 16 bits wide and the instruction set operates on 16-bit
data values. The 8088 transparently executes two bus cycles to transfer each 16-bit value
between the processor and memory.

The 8086 and 8088 do not support the more sophisticated features of modern processors,
such as paged virtual memory and protection rings. These early processors also have only
20 address lines, limiting the addressable memory to 1 MB. A 20-bit address cannot fit
in a 16-bit register, so it is necessary to use a somewhat complicated system of segment
registers and offsets to access the full 1 MB address space.

In 1985, Intel released the 80386 with enhancements to mitigate many of these limitations. The 80386 introduced these features:

- **32-bit architecture**: Addresses, registers, and the ALU are 32 bits wide and instructions operate natively on operands up to 32 bits wide.

- **Protected mode**: This mode enables the multi-level privilege mechanism, consisting of ring numbers 0 to 3. In Windows and Linux, ring 0 is kernel mode and ring 3 is user mode. Rings 1 and 2 are not used in these operating systems.

- **On-chip MMU**: The 80386 MMU supports a flat memory model, enabling any location in the 4 GB space to be accessed with a 32-bit address. Manipulation of segment registers and offsets is no longer required. The MMU supports paged virtual memory.

- **3-stage instruction pipeline**: The pipeline accelerates instruction execution, as discussed in *Chapter 8, Performance-Enhancing Techniques*.

- **Hardware debug registers**: The debug registers support setting up to four breakpoints that stop code execution at a specified virtual address when the address is accessed and a selected condition is satisfied. The available break conditions are code execution, data write, and data read or write. These registers are only available to code running in ring 0.

Modern x86 processors boot into the 16-bit operating mode of the original 8086, which is now called **real mode**. This mode retains compatibility with software written for the 8086/8088 environment, such as the MS-DOS operating system. In most modern systems running on x86 processors, a transition to protected mode occurs during system startup. Once in protected mode, the operating system generally remains in protected mode until the computer shuts down.

MS-DOS on a modern PC

Although the x86 processor in a modern PC is compatible at the instruction level with the original 8088, running an old copy of MS-DOS on a modern computer system is unlikely to be a straightforward process. This is because peripheral devices and their interfaces in modern PCs are not compatible with the corresponding interfaces in PCs from the 1980s. MS-DOS would need a driver that understands how to interact with the USB-connected keyboard of a modern motherboard, for example.

These days, the main use for 16-bit mode in x86 processors is to serve as a bootloader for a protected mode operating system. Because most developers of computerized devices and the software that runs on them are unlikely to be involved in implementing such a capability, the remainder of our x86 discussion in this chapter will address protected mode and the associated 32-bit flat memory model.

The x86 architecture supports unsigned and signed two's complement integer data types with widths of 8, 16, 32, 64, and 128 bits. The names assigned to these data types are as follows:

- **Byte**: 8 bits
- **Word**: 16 bits
- **Doubleword**: 32 bits
- **Quadword**: 64 bits
- **Double quadword**: 128 bits

In most cases, the x86 architecture does not mandate storage of these data types on natural boundaries. The **natural boundary** of a data type is any address evenly divisible by the size of the data type in bytes.

Storing any of the multi-byte types at unaligned boundaries is permitted, but is discouraged because it causes a negative performance impact: instructions operating on unaligned data require additional clock cycles. A few instructions that operate on double quadwords require naturally aligned storage and will generate a general protection fault if unaligned access is attempted.

x86 natively supports floating-point data types in widths of 16, 32, 64, and 80 bits. The 32-bit, 64-bit, and 80-bit formats are those presented in *Chapter 9*, *Specialized Processor Extensions*. The 16-bit format is called **half-precision** floating-point and has an 11-bit mantissa, an implied leading 1 bit, and a 5-bit exponent. The half-precision floating-point format is used extensively in GPU processing.

The x86 register set

In protected mode, the x86 architecture has eight 32-bit wide general-purpose registers, a flags register, and an instruction pointer. There are also six segment registers and additional processor model-specific configuration registers. The segment registers and model-specific registers are configured by system software during startup and are, in general, not relevant to the developers of applications and device drivers. For these reasons, we will not discuss the segment registers and model-specific registers further.

The 16-bit general-purpose registers in the original 8086 architecture are named AX, CX, DX, BX, SP, BP, SI, and DI. The reason for listing the first four registers in this non-alphabetic order is because this is the sequence in which these eight registers are pushed onto the stack by a pushad (push all registers) instruction.

In the transition to the 32-bit architecture of the 80386, each register grew to 32 bits. The 32-bit version of a register's name is prefixed with the letter "E" to indicate this extension.

It is possible to access portions of 32-bit registers in smaller bit widths. For example, the lower 16 bits of the 32-bit EAX register are referenced as AX. The AX register can be further accessed as individual bytes using the names AH (high-order byte) and AL (low-order byte). The following diagram shows the register names and subsets of each:

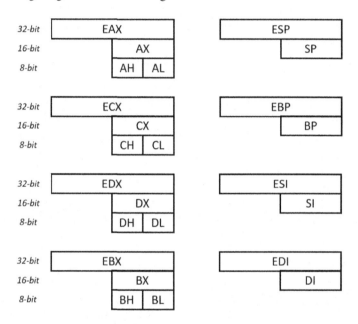

Figure 10.1: Register names and subsets

Writing to a portion of a 32-bit register, for example, register AL, affects only the bits in that portion. In the case of AL, loading an 8-bit value modifies the lowest 8 bits of EAX, leaving the other 24 bits unaffected.

In keeping with the x86's **complex instruction set computer** (**CISC**) architecture, several functions associated with various instructions are tied to specific registers. The following table provides a description of the functions associated with each of the x86 general-purpose registers:

Table 10.1: x86 general-purpose registers and associated functions

Register	Name	Function
EAX	Accumulator	Arithmetic operations
ECX	Counter	Loop counter and shift/rotate counter
EDX	Data	Arithmetic and I/O operations
EBX	Base	Pointer to data
ESP	Stack pointer	Pointer to the top of the stack
EBP	Base pointer	Pointer to the stack base within a function
ESI	Source index	Pointer to the source location in array operations
EDI	Destination index	Pointer to the destination location in array operations

These register-specific functions contrast with the architectures of many **reduced instruction set computer** (**RISC**) processors, which tend to provide a greater number of general-purpose registers. Registers within a RISC processor are, for the most part, functionally equivalent to one another.

The x86 flags register, EFLAGS, contains the processor status bits described in the following table:

Table 10.2: x86 flags register status bits

Bit	Name	Function
0	CF	Carry flag: Indicates if addition produced a carry or subtraction produced a borrow. Used as an input by addition and subtraction instructions.
2	PF	Parity flag: Set if the low 8 bits of the result contain an even number of 1 bits.
4	AF	Adjust flag: Indicates if addition produced a carry or subtraction produced a borrow from the lower 4 bits. Used in BCD arithmetic.
6	ZF	Zero flag: Set if the result of an operation is zero.
7	SF	Sign flag: Set if the result of an operation is negative.
8	TF	Trap flag: Used in single-step debugging.

Bit	Name	Function
9	IF	Interrupt enable flag: Setting this bit enables hardware interrupts.
10	DF	Direction flag: Controls the direction of string processing. When clear, the order is lowest to highest addresses. When set, the order is highest to lowest addresses.
11	OF	Overflow flag: Set if an operation resulted in a signed overflow.
12-13	IOPL	I/O privilege level: The privilege level of the currently executing thread. IOPL 0 is kernel mode and 3 is user mode.
14	NT	Nested task flag: Controls the chaining of interrupts.
16	RF	Resume flag: Used for processing exceptions during debugging.
17	VM	Virtual 8086 mode flag: If set, 8086 compatibility mode is active. This mode allows running some MS-DOS applications in the context of a protected mode operating system.
18	AC	Alignment check flag: If set, memory alignment checking is active. For example, if the AC flag is set, storing a 16-bit value to an odd address triggers an Alignment Check exception. x86 processors can perform unaligned memory accesses when this flag is not set, but the number of instruction cycles required may increase.
19	VIF	Virtual interrupt flag: Virtual version of the IF flag in virtual 8086 mode.
20	VIP	Virtual interrupt pending flag: Set when an interrupt is pending in virtual 8086 mode.
21	ID	ID flag: If this bit can be set, the cpuid instruction is supported. cpuid returns processor identification and feature information.

All bits in the EFLAGS register that are not listed in the preceding table are reserved.

The 32-bit instruction pointer, EIP, contains the address of the next instruction to execute, unless a branch is taken.

The x86 architecture is little-endian, meaning multi-byte values are stored in memory with the least significant byte at the lowest address and the most significant byte at the highest address.

x86 addressing modes

As befits a CISC architecture, x86 supports a variety of addressing modes. There are several rules associated with addressing source and destination operands that must be followed to create valid instructions. For instance, the sizes of the source and destination operands of a mov instruction must be equal. The assembler will attempt to select a suitable size for an operand of ambiguous size (for example, an immediate value of 7) to match the width of a destination location (such as the 32-bit register EAX). In cases where the size of an operand cannot be inferred, size keywords such as byte ptr must be provided.

The assembly language in these examples uses the *Intel syntax*, which places the operands in destination-source order. The Intel syntax is used primarily in the Windows and MS-DOS contexts. An alternative notation, known as the *AT&T syntax*, places operands in source-destination order. The AT&T syntax is used in Unix-based operating systems. All examples in this book will use the Intel syntax.

The x86 architecture supports a variety of addressing modes, which we will look at now.

Implied addressing

The register is implied by the instruction opcode:

```
clc ; Clear the carry flag (This is CF in the EFLAGS register)
```

Register addressing

One or both source and destination registers are encoded in the instruction:

```
mov eax, ecx ; Copy the contents of register ECX to EAX
```

Registers may be used as the first operand, the second operand, or both operands.

Immediate addressing

An immediate value is provided as an instruction operand:

```
mov eax, 7 ; Move the 32-bit value 7 into EAX
mov ax, 7 ; Move the 16-bit value 7 into AX (the lower 16 bits
of EAX)
```

When using the Intel syntax, it is not necessary to prefix immediate values with the # character.

Direct memory addressing

The address of the value is provided as an instruction operand:

```
mov eax, [078bch] ; Copy the 32-bit value at hex address 78BC
to EAX
```

In x86 assembly code, square brackets around an expression indicate the expression is an address. When performing moves or other operations on square-bracketed operands, the value being operated upon is the data at the specified address. The exception to this rule is the LEA (load effective address) instruction, which we'll look at later.

Register indirect addressing

The operand identifies a register containing the address of the data value:

```
mov eax, [esi] ; Copy the 32-bit value at the address contained
in ESI to EAX
```

This mode is equivalent to using a pointer to reference a variable in C or C++.

Indexed addressing

The operand indicates a register plus offset that calculates the address of the data value:

```
mov eax, [esi + 0bh] ; Copy the 32-bit value at the address
(ESI + 0bh) to EAX
```

This mode is useful for accessing the elements of a data structure. In this scenario, the ESI register contains the address of the structure and the added constant is the byte offset of the element from the beginning of the structure.

Based indexed addressing

The operand indicates a base register, an index register, and an offset that sum together to calculate the address of the data value:

```
mov eax, [ebx + esi + 10] ; Copy the 32-bit value starting at
the address (EBX + ESI + 10) to EAX
```

This mode is useful for accessing individual data elements within an array of structures. In this example, the EBX register contains the address of the beginning of the structure array, ESI contains the offset of the referenced structure within the array, and the constant value (10) is the offset of the desired element from the beginning of the selected structure.

Based indexed addressing with scaling

The operand is composed of a base register, an index register multiplied by a scale factor, and an offset that sum together to calculate the address of the data value:

```
mov eax, [ebx + esi*4 + 10]  ; Copy the 32-bit value starting at
  the address (EBX + ESI*4 + 10) to EAX
```

In this mode, the value in the index register can be multiplied by 1 (the default), 2, 4, or 8 before being summed with the other components of the operand address. There is no performance penalty associated with using the scaling multiplier. This feature is helpful when iterating over arrays containing elements with sizes of 2, 4, or 8 bytes.

Most of the general-purpose registers can be used as the base or index register in the based addressing modes. The following diagram shows the possible combinations of register usage and scaling in the based addressing modes:

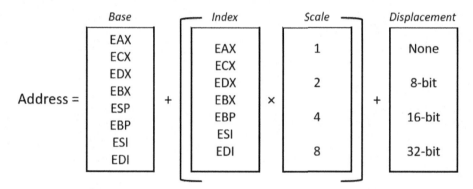

Figure 10.2: Based addressing mode

All eight general-purpose registers are available for use as the base register. Of those eight, only ESP is unavailable for use as the index register.

x86 instruction categories

The x86 instruction set was introduced with the Intel 8086 and has been extended several times over the years. Some of the most significant changes relate to the extension of the architecture from 16 to 32 bits, which added protected mode and paged virtual memory. In almost all cases, the new capabilities were added while retaining full backward compatibility.

The x86 instruction set contains several hundred instructions. We will not discuss all of them here. This section will provide brief summaries of the more important and commonly encountered instructions applicable to user mode applications and device drivers. This subset of x86 instructions can be divided into a few general categories: data movement; stack manipulation; arithmetic and logic; conversions; control flows; string and flag manipulations; input/output; and protected mode. There are also some miscellaneous instructions that do not fall into any specific category.

Data movement

Data movement instructions do not affect the processor flags. The following instructions perform data movement:

- mov: Copies the data value referenced by the second operand to the location provided as the first operand.

- cmovcc: Conditionally moves the second operand's data to the register provided as the first operand if the *cc* condition is true. The condition is determined from one or more of the processor flags: CF, ZF, SF, OF, and PF. The condition codes are e (equal), ne (not equal), g (greater), ge (greater or equal), a (above), ae (above or equal), l (less), le (less or equal), b (below), be (below or equal), o (overflow), no (no overflow), z (zero), nz (not zero), s (SF=1), ns (SF=0), cxz (register CX is zero), and ecxz (the ECX register is zero).

- movsx, movzx: Variants of the mov instruction performing sign extension and zero extension, respectively. The source operand must be a smaller size than the destination.

- lea: Computes the address provided by the second operand and stores it at the location given in the first operand. The second operand is surrounded by square brackets. Unlike the other data movement instructions, the computed address is stored in the destination rather than the data value at that address.

Stack manipulation

Stack manipulation instructions do not affect the processor flags. These instructions are as follows:

- push: Decrements ESP by 4, then places the 32-bit operand into the stack location pointed to by ESP.

- pop: Copies the 32-bit data value pointed to by ESP to the operand location (a register or memory address), then increments ESP by 4.

- `pushfd`, `popfd`: Pushes or pops the `EFLAGS` register.

- `pushad`, `popad`: Pushes or pops the `EAX`, `ECX`, `EDX`, `EBX`, `ESP`, `EBP`, `ESI`, and `EDI` registers, in that order.

Arithmetic and logic

Arithmetic and logic instructions modify the processor flags. The following instructions perform arithmetic and logic operations:

- `add`, `sub`: Performs integer addition or subtraction. When subtracting, the second operand is subtracted from the first. Both operands can be registers, or one operand can be a memory location and the other a register. One operand can be a constant.

- `adc`, `sbb`: Performs integer addition or subtraction using the `CF` flag as a carry input (for addition) or as a borrow input (for subtraction).

- `cmp`: Subtracts the two operands and discards the result while updating the `OF`, `SF`, `ZF`, `AF`, `PF`, and `CF` flags based on the result.

- `neg`: Negates the operand.

- `inc`, `dec`: Increments or decrements the operand by one.

- `mul`: Performs unsigned integer multiplication. The size of the product depends on the size of the operand. A byte operand is multiplied by `AL` and the result is placed in `AX`. A word operand is multiplied by `AX` and the result is placed in `DX:AX`, with the upper 16 bits in `DX`. A doubleword is multiplied by `EAX` and the result is placed in `EDX:EAX`.

- `imul`: Performs signed integer multiplication. The first operand must be a register and receives the result of the operation. There may be a total of two or three operands. In the two-operand form, the first operand multiplies the second operand and the result is stored in the first operand (a register). In the three-operand form, the second operand multiplies the third operand and the result is stored in the first operand register. In the three-operand form, the third operand must be an immediate value.

- `div`, `idiv`: Performs unsigned (`div`) or signed (`idiv`) division. The size of the result depends on the size of the operand. A byte operand is divided into `AX`, the quotient is placed in `AL`, and the remainder is placed in `AH`. A word operand is divided into `DX:AX`, the quotient is placed in `AX`, and the remainder is placed in `DX`. A doubleword is divided into `EDX:EAX`, the quotient is placed in `EAX`, and the remainder is placed in `EDX`.

- `and`, `or`, `xor`: Performs the corresponding logical operation on the two operands and stores the result in the destination operand location.

- not: Performs a logical NOT (bit inversion) operation on a single operand.

- sal, shl, sar, shr: Performs a logical (shl and shr) or arithmetic (sal and sar) shift of the byte, word, or doubleword argument left or right by 1 to 31 bit positions. sal and shl place the last bit shifted out into the carry flag and insert zeros into the vacated least significant bits. shr places the last bit shifted out into the carry flag and inserts zeros into the vacated most significant bits. sar differs from shr by propagating the sign bit into the vacated most significant bits.

- rol, rcl, ror, rcr: Performs a left or right rotation by 0 to 31 bits, optionally through the carry flag. rcl and rcr rotate through the carry flag while rol and ror do not.

- bts, btr, btc: Reads a specified bit number (provided as the second operand) within the bits of the first operand into the carry flag, then either sets (bts), resets (btr), or complements (btc) that bit. These instructions may be preceded by the lock keyword to make the operation atomic.

- test: Performs a logical AND of two operands and updates the SF, ZF, and PF flags based on the result.

Conversions

Conversion instructions extend a smaller data size to a larger size. These instructions are as follows:

- cbw: Converts a byte (register AL) into a word (AX).

- cwd: Converts a word (register AX) into a doubleword (DX:AX).

- cwde: Converts a word (register AX) into a doubleword (EAX).

- cdq: Converts a doubleword (register AX) into a quadword (EDX:EAX).

Control flow

Control flow instructions conditionally or unconditionally transfer execution to an address. The control flow instructions are as follows:

- jmp: Transfers control to the instruction at the address provided as the operand.

- j*cc*: Transfers control to the instruction at the address provided as the operand if the condition *cc* is true. The condition codes were described earlier, in the cmov*cc* instruction description. The condition is determined from one or more of the processor flags: CF, ZF, SF, OF, and PF.

- `call`: Pushes the current value of `EIP` onto the stack and transfers control to the instruction at the address provided as the operand.
- `ret`: Pops the top-of-stack value and stores it in `EIP`. If an operand is provided, it pops the given number of bytes from the stack to clear parameters.
- `loop`: Decrements the `loop` counter in `ECX` and, if not zero, transfers control to the instruction at the address provided as the operand.

String manipulation

String manipulation instructions may be prefixed by the `rep` keyword to repeat the operation the number of times given by the `ECX` register, incrementing or decrementing the source and destination location on each iteration, depending on the state of the `DF` flag. The operand size processed on each iteration can be a byte, word, or doubleword. The source address of each string element is given by the `ESI` register and the destination is given by the `EDI` register. These instructions are as follows:

- `mov`: Moves a string element.
- `cmps`: Compares elements at corresponding locations in two strings.
- `scas`: Compares a string element to the value in `EAX`, `AX`, or `AL`, depending on the operand size.
- `lods`: Loads the string into `EAX`, `AX`, or `AL`, depending on the operand size.
- `stos`: Stores `EAX`, `AX`, or `AL`, depending on the operand size, to the address in `EDI`.

Flag manipulation

Flag manipulation instructions modify bits in the `EFLAGS` register. The flag manipulation instructions are as follows:

- `stc`, `clc`, `cmc`: Sets, clears, or complements the carry flag, `CF`.
- `std`, `cld`: Sets or clears the direction flag, `DF`.
- `sti`, `cli`: Sets or clears the interrupt flag, `IF`.

Input/output

Input/output instructions read data from or write data to peripheral devices. The input/output instructions are as follows:

- `in`, `out`: Moves 1, 2, or 4 bytes between `EAX`, `AX`, or `AL` and an I/O port, depending on the operand size.
- `ins`, `outs`: Moves a data element between memory and an I/O port in the same manner as string instructions.

- `rep ins`, `rep outs`: Moves blocks of data between memory and an I/O port in the same manner as string instructions.

Protected mode

The following instructions access the features of the protected mode:

- `sysenter`, `sysexit`: Transfers control from ring 3 to ring 0 (`sysenter`) or from ring 0 to ring 3 (`sysexit`) in Intel processors.

- `syscall`, `sysret`: Transfers control from ring 3 to ring 0 (`syscall`) or from ring 0 to ring 3 (`sysret`) in AMD processors. In x86 (32-bit) mode, AMD processors also support `sysenter` and `sysexit`.

Miscellaneous instructions

These instructions do not fit into the categories previously listed:

- `int`: Initiates a software interrupt. The operand is the interrupt vector number.

- `nop`: No operation.

- `cpuid`: Provides information about the processor model and its capabilities.

Other instruction categories

The additional instructions listed in this section are some of the more common general-purpose instructions you will come across in x86 applications and device drivers. The x86 architecture contains a variety of instruction categories, including the following:

- **Floating-point instructions**: These instructions are executed by the x87 floating-point unit.

- **SIMD instructions**: This category includes the MMX, SSE, SSE2, SSE3, SSE4, AVX, AVX2, and AVX-512 instructions.

- **AES instructions**: These instructions support encryption and decryption using the **Advanced Encryption Standard (AES)**.

- **MPX instructions**: The **memory protection extensions (MPX)** enhance memory integrity by preventing errors such as buffer overruns.

- **SMX instructions**: The **safer mode extensions (SMX)** improve system security in the presence of user trust decisions.

- **TSX instructions**: The **transactional synchronization extensions (TSX)** enhance the performance of multithreaded execution using shared resources.

- **VMX instructions**: The **virtual machine extensions (VMX)** support the secure and efficient execution of virtualized operating systems.

Additional processor registers are provided for use by the floating-point and SIMD instructions.

There are still other categories of x86 instructions, a few of which have been retired in later generations of the architecture.

Common instruction patterns

These are examples of instruction usage patterns you will come across frequently in compiled code. The techniques used in these examples produce the desired result while minimizing code size and the number of execution cycles required:

```
xor reg, reg ; Set reg to zero
test reg, reg ; Test if reg contains zero
add reg, reg ; Shift reg left by one bit
```

x86 instruction formats

Individual x86 instructions are of variable length, and can range in size from 1 to 15 bytes. The components of a single instruction, including any optional bytes, are laid out in memory in the following sequence:

- **Prefix bytes**: One or more optional prefix bytes provide auxiliary opcode execution information. For example, the `lock` prefix performs bus locking in a multiprocessor system to enable atomic test-and-set type operations. `rep` and related prefixes enable string instructions to perform repeated operations on string elements in a single instruction. Other prefixes are available to provide hints for conditional branch instructions or to override the default size of an address or operand.

- **Opcode bytes**: An x86 opcode, consisting of 1 to 3 bytes, follows any prefix bytes. For some opcodes, an additional 3 opcode bits are encoded in a *ModR/M* byte following the opcode.

- **ModR/M byte**: Not all instructions require this byte. The *ModR/M* byte contains three information fields providing address mode and operand register information. The upper two bits of this byte (the *Mod* field) and the lower three bits (the *R/M* field) combine to form a 5-bit field with 32 possible values. Of these, 8 values identify register operands and the other 24 specify addressing modes. The remaining 3 bits (the *reg/opcode* field) either indicate a register or provide three additional opcode bits, depending on the instruction.

- **Address displacement bytes**: Either 0, 1, 2, or 4 bytes provide an address displacement used in computing the operand address.

- **Immediate value bytes**: If the instruction includes an immediate value, it is located in the last 1, 2, or 4 bytes of the instruction.

The variable-length nature of x86 instructions makes the process of instruction decoding quite complex. It is also challenging for debugging tools to disassemble a sequence of instructions in reverse order, perhaps to display the code leading up to a breakpoint. This difficulty arises because it is possible for a trailing subset of bytes within a lengthy instruction to form a complete, valid instruction. This complexity is a notable difference from the more regular instruction formats used in RISC architectures.

x86 assembly language

It is possible to develop programs of any level of complexity in assembly language. Most modern applications, however, are largely or entirely developed in high-level languages. Assembly language tends to be used in cases where the employment of specialized instructions is desirable, or a level of extreme optimization is required that is unachievable with an optimizing compiler.

Regardless of the language used in application development, all code must ultimately execute as processor instructions. To fully understand how code executes on a computer system, there is no substitute for examining the state of the system following the execution of each individual instruction. A good way to learn how to operate in this environment is to write some assembly code.

The x86 assembly language example in the following listing is a complete x86 application that runs in a Windows command console, printing a text string and then exiting:

```
.386
.model FLAT,C
.stack 400h
```

```
.code
includelib libcmt.lib
includelib legacy_stdio_definitions.lib

extern printf:near
extern exit:near

public main
main proc
    ; Print the message
    push    offset message
    call    printf

    ; Exit the program with status 0
    push    0
    call    exit
main endp

.data
message db "Hello, Computer Architect!",0

end
```

A description of the contents of the assembly language file follows:

- The .386 directive indicates that the instructions in this file should be interpreted as applying to 80386 and later-generation processors.

- The .model FLAT, C directive specifies a 32-bit flat memory model and the use of C language function calling conventions.

- The .stack 400h directive specifies a stack size of 400h (1,024) bytes.

- The .code directive indicates the start of executable code.

- The includelib and extern directives reference system-provided libraries and functions within them to be used by the program.

- The public directive indicates the function name, main, is an externally visible symbol.

- The lines between `main proc` and `main endp` are the assembly language instructions making up the `main` function.

- The `.data` directive indicates the start of data memory. The `message db` statement defines the message string as a sequence of bytes, followed by a zero byte.

- The `end` directive marks the end of the program.

This file, named `hello_x86.asm`, is assembled and linked to form the executable `hello_x86.exe` program with the following command, which runs the Microsoft Macro Assembler:

```
ml /Fl /Zi /Zd hello_x86.asm
```

The components of this command are as follows:

- `ml` runs the assembler.

- `/Fl` creates a listing file.

- `/Zi` includes symbolic debugging information in the executable file.

- `/Zd` includes line number debugging information in the executable file.

- `hello_x86.asm` is the name of the assembly language source file.

This is a portion of the `hello_x86.lst` listing file generated by the assembler:

```
                                      .386
                                      .model FLAT,C
                                      .stack 400h

 00000000                             .code
                                      includelib libcmt.lib
                                      includelib legacy_stdio_
 definitions.lib

                                      extern printf:near
                                      extern exit:near

                                      public main
 00000000                             main proc
                                      ; Print the message
 00000000  68 00000000 R              push    offset message
```

```
00000005  E8 00000000 E              call    printf

                                     ; Exit the program with
                                     status 0
0000000A  6A 00                      push    0
0000000C  E8 00000000 E              call    exit
00000011                     main endp


00000000                     .data
00000000 48 65 6C 6C 6F       message db "Hello, Computer
                                     Architect!",0
         2C 20 43 6F 6D
         70 75 74 65 72
         20 41 72 63 68
         69 74 65 63 74
         21 00
```

The preceding listing displays the address offsets from the beginning of the `main` function in the left column. On lines containing instructions, the opcode follows the address offset. Address references in the code (for example, `offset message`) are displayed as `00000000` in the listing because these values are determined during linking, and not during assembly, which is when this listing is generated.

This is the output displayed when running this program:

```
C:\>hello_x86.exe
Hello, Computer Architect!
```

Next, we will look at the extension of the 32-bit x86 architecture to the 64-bit x64 architecture.

x64 architecture and instruction set

The original specification for a processor architecture extending the x86 processor and instruction set to 64 bits, named **AMD64**, was introduced by AMD in 2000. The first AMD64 processor, the Opteron, was released in 2003. Intel found itself following AMD's lead and developed an AMD64-compatible architecture, eventually given the name **Intel 64**. The first Intel processor that implemented their 64-bit architecture was the Xeon, introduced in 2004. The name of the architecture shared by AMD and Intel came to be called **x86-64**, reflecting the evolution of x86 to 64 bits, and in popular usage, this term has been shortened to **x64**.

The first Linux version supporting the x64 architecture was released in 2001, well before the first x64 processors were even available. Windows began supporting the x64 architecture in 2005.

Processors implementing the AMD64 and Intel 64 architectures are largely compatible at the instruction level of user mode programs. There are a few differences between the architectures, the most significant of which is the difference in support of the `sysenter/sysexit` Intel instructions and the `syscall/sysret` AMD instructions we saw earlier. In general, operating systems and programming language compilers manage these differences, making them rarely an issue of concern to software and system developers. Developers of kernel software, drivers, and assembly code must take these differences into account.

The principal features of the x64 architecture are as follows:

- x64 is a mostly compatible 64-bit extension of the 32-bit x86 architecture. Most software, particularly user mode applications, written for the 32-bit environment should execute without modification in a processor running in 64-bit mode. 64-bit mode is also referred to as **long mode**.

- The eight 32-bit general-purpose registers of x86 are extended to 64 bits in x64. The register name prefix R indicates 64-bit registers. For example, in x64, the extended x86 EAX register is called RAX. The x86 register subcomponents EAX, AX, AH, and AL continue to be available in x64.

- The instruction pointer, RIP, is now 64 bits. The flags register, RFLAGS, also extends to 64 bits, though the upper 32 bits are reserved. The lower 32 bits of RFLAGS are the same as EFLAGS in the x86 architecture.

- Eight 64-bit general-purpose registers have been added, named R8 through R15.

- 64-bit integers are supported as a native data type.

- x64 processors retain the option of running in x86 compatibility mode. This mode enables the use of 32-bit operating systems and allows any application built for x86 to run on x64 processors. In 32-bit compatibility mode, the 64-bit extensions are unavailable.

Virtual addresses in the x64 architecture are 64 bits wide, supporting an address space of 16 **exabytes (EB)**, equivalent to 2^{64} bytes. Current processors from AMD and Intel, however, support only 48 bits of virtual address space. This restriction reduces processor hardware complexity while still supporting up to 256 **terabytes (TB)** of virtual address space. Current-generation processors also support a maximum of 48 bits of physical address space. This permits a processor to address 256 TB of physical RAM, though modern motherboards do not support the quantity of DRAM devices such a system would require.

The x64 register set

In the x64 architecture, the extension of x86 register lengths to 64 bits and the addition of registers R8 through R15 results in the register map shown in the following diagram:

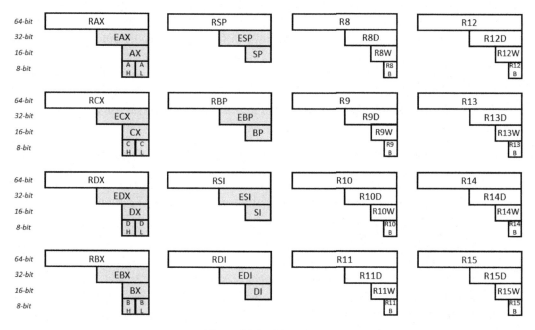

Figure 10.3: x64 registers

The x86 registers described in the preceding section, and present in x64, appear in a darker shade. The x86 registers have the same names and are the same sizes when operating in 64-bit mode. The 64-bit extended versions of the x86 registers have names starting with the letter **R**. The new 64-bit registers (R8 through R15) can be accessed in smaller widths using the appropriate suffix letter:

- Suffix **D** accesses the lower 32 bits of the register: R11D.

- Suffix **W** accesses the lower 16 bits of the register: R11W.

- Suffix **B** accesses the lower 8 bits of the register: R11B.

Unlike the x86 registers, the new registers in the x64 architecture are truly general purpose and do not perform any special functions at the processor instruction level.

x64 instruction categories and formats

The x64 architecture implements essentially the same instruction set as x86, with 64-bit extensions. When operating in 64-bit mode, the x64 architecture uses a default address size of 64 bits and a default operand size of 32 bits. A new opcode prefix byte, rex, is provided to specify the use of 64-bit operands.

The format of x64 instructions in memory matches that of the x86 architecture, with some exceptions that, for our purposes, are minor. The addition of support for the rex prefix byte is the most significant variation from the x86 instruction format. Address displacements and immediate values within some instructions can be 64 bits wide, in addition to all the bit widths supported in x86.

Although it is possible to define instructions longer than 15 bytes, the processor instruction decoder will raise a general protection fault if an attempt is made to decode an instruction longer than 15 bytes.

x64 assembly language

The x64 assembly language source file for the hello program is similar to the x86 version of this code, with some notable differences:

- There is no directive specifying a memory model because there is a single x64 memory model.

- The Windows x64 application programming interface uses a calling convention that stores the first four arguments to a called function in the RCX, RDX, R8, and R9 registers, in that order. This differs from the default x86 calling convention, which pushes parameters onto the stack. Both of the library functions this program calls (printf and exit) take a single argument, passed in RCX.

- The calling convention requires the caller of a function to allocate stack space to hold at least the number of arguments passed to the called functions, with a minimum reservation space for four arguments, even if fewer are being passed. Because the stack grows downward in memory, this requires a subtraction from the stack pointer. The sub rsp, 40 instruction performs this stack allocation. Normally, after the called function returns, it would be necessary to adjust the stack pointer to remove this allocation. Our program calls the exit function, terminating program execution, which makes this step unnecessary.

The code for the 64-bit version of the `hello` program is as follows:

```
.code
includelib libcmt.lib
includelib legacy_stdio_definitions.lib

extern printf:near
extern exit:near

public main
main proc
    ; Reserve stack space
    sub     rsp, 40

    ; Print the message
    lea     rcx, message
    call    printf

    ; Exit the program with status 0
    xor     rcx, rcx
    call    exit
main endp

.data
message db "Hello, Computer Architect!",0

end
```

This file, named `hello_x64.asm`, is assembled and linked to form the executable `hello_x64.exe` program with the following call to the Microsoft Macro Assembler (x64):

```
ml64 /Fl /Zi /Zd hello_x64.asm
```

The components of this command are:

- `ml64` runs the 64-bit assembler.
- `/Fl` creates a listing file.

- /Zi includes symbolic debugging information in the executable file.

- /Zd includes line number debugging information in the executable file.

- hello_x64.asm is the name of the assembly language source file.

This is a portion of the hello_x64.lst listing file generated by the assembler command:

```
00000000                              .code
                                      includelib libcmt.lib
                                      includelib legacy_stdio_
definitions.lib

                                      extern printf:near
                                      extern exit:near

                                      public main
00000000                              main proc
                                      ; Reserve stack space
00000000  48/ 83 EC 28                sub     rsp, 40

                                      ; Print the message
00000004  48/ 8D 0D                   lea     rcx, message
          00000000 R
0000000B  E8 00000000 E               call    printf

                                      ; Exit the program with
                                      status 0
00000010  48/ 33 C9                   xor     rcx, rcx
00000013  E8 00000000 E               call    exit
00000018                              main endp

00000000                              .data
00000000 48 65 6C 6C 6F               message db "Hello, Computer
                                      Architect!",0
         2C 20 43 6F 6D
         70 75 74 65 72
         20 41 72 63 68
         69 74 65 63 74
         21 00
```

The output of running this program is as follows:

```
C:\>hello_x64.exe
Hello, Computer Architect!
```

This completes our brief introduction to the x86 and x64 architectures. There is a great deal more to be learned, and indeed the *Intel 64 and IA-32 Architectures Software Developer's Manual, Volumes 1 through 4*, contain nearly 5,000 pages of detailed documentation on these architectures. We have clearly just scratched the surface in this chapter.

Next, we will take a similarly top-level tour of the ARM 32-bit and 64-bit architectures.

32-bit ARM architecture and instruction set

The ARM architectures define a family of RISC processors suitable for use in a wide variety of applications. Processors based on ARM architectures are preferred in designs where a combination of high performance, low power consumption, and small physical size is needed.

ARM Holdings, a British semiconductor and software company, developed the ARM architectures and licenses them to other companies who implement processors in silicon. Many applications of the ARM architectures are **system-on-chip (SoC)** designs combining a processor with specialized hardware to support functions such as cellular radio communications in smartphones.

ARM processors are used across a broad spectrum of applications, from tiny battery-powered devices to supercomputers. ARM processors serve as embedded processors in safety-critical systems, such as automotive anti-lock brakes, and as general-purpose processors in smart watches, portable phones, tablets, laptop computers, desktop computers, and servers. As of 2017, over 100 billion ARM processors have been manufactured.

ARM processors are true RISC systems, with a large set of general-purpose registers and single-cycle execution of most instructions. Standard ARM instructions have a fixed width of 32 bits, though a separate instruction set named **T32** (formerly called **Thumb**) is available for applications where memory is at a premium. The T32 instruction set consists of 16- and 32-bit wide instructions. Current-generation ARM processors support both the ARM and T32 instruction sets, and can switch between instruction sets on the fly. Most operating systems and applications prefer the use of the T32 instruction set over the ARM set because code density is improved.

ARM is a **load/store architecture**, requiring data to be loaded from memory to a register before any processing such as an ALU operation can take place upon it. A separate instruction then stores the result back to memory. While this might seem like a step back from the x86 and x64 architectures, which operate directly on operands in memory in a single instruction, in practice, the load/store approach permits several sequential operations to be performed at high speed on an operand once it has been loaded into one of the many available registers.

ARM processors are bi-endian. A configuration setting is available to select little-endian or big-endian byte order for multi-byte values. The default setting is little-endian, which is the configuration commonly used by operating systems.

The ARM architecture natively supports these data types:

- **Byte**: 8 bits
- **Halfword**: 16 bits
- **Word**: 32 bits
- **Doubleword**: 64 bits

What's in a word?

There is a confusing difference between the data type names of the ARM architecture and those of the x86 and x64 architectures: in x86 and x64, a word is 16 bits. In ARM, a word is 32 bits.

ARM processors support eight distinct execution privilege levels. These levels, and their abbreviations, are as follows:

- **User (USR)**
- **Supervisor (SVC)**
- **Fast interrupt request (FIQ)**
- **Interrupt request (IRQ)**
- **Monitor (MON)**
- **Abort (ABT)**
- **Undefined (UND)**
- **System (SYS)**

For the purposes of operating systems and user applications, the most important privilege levels are USR and SVC. The two interrupt request modes, FIQ and IRQ, are used by device drivers for processing interrupts.

In most operating systems running on ARM, including Windows and Linux, kernel mode runs in ARM SVC mode, equivalent to Ring 0 on x86/64. ARM USR mode is equivalent to Ring 3 on x86/x64. Applications running in Linux on ARM processors use software interrupts to request kernel services, which involves a transition from USR mode to SVC mode.

The ARM architecture supports system capabilities beyond those of the core processor via the concept of coprocessors. Up to 16 coprocessors can be implemented in a system, with predefined functions assigned to four of them. Coprocessor 15 implements the MMU and other system functions. If present, coprocessor 15 must support the instruction opcodes, register set, and behaviors specified for the MMU. Coprocessors 10 and 11 combine to provide floating-point functionality in processors equipped with that feature. Coprocessor 14 provides debugging functions.

The ARM architectures have evolved through several versions over the years. The architectural variant currently in common use is **ARMv8-A**. ARMv8-A supports 32-bit and 64-bit operating systems and applications. 32-bit applications can run under a 64-bit ARMv8-A operating system.

Virtually all high-end smartphones and portable electronic devices produced since 2016 are designed around processors or SoCs based on the ARMv8-A architecture. The description that follows will focus on ARMv8-A 32-bit mode. We will look at the differences in ARMv8-A 64-bit mode later in this chapter.

The ARM register set

In USR mode, the ARM architecture has 16 general-purpose 32-bit registers named R0 through R15. The first 13 registers are truly general-purpose, while the last three have the following defined functions:

- R13 is the stack pointer, also named SP in assembly code. This register points to the top of the stack.

- R14 is the link register, also named LR. This register holds the return address while in a called function. The use of a link register differs from x86/x64, which pushes the return address onto the stack. The reason for using a register to hold the return address is because it is significantly faster to resume execution at the address in LR at the end of a function than it is to pop the return address from the stack and resume execution at that address.

- R15 is the program counter, also named PC. Due to pipelining, the value contained in PC is usually two instructions ahead of the currently executing instruction. Unlike x86/x64, it is possible for user code to directly read and write the PC register. Writing an address to PC causes execution to immediately jump to the newly written address.

The **current program status register (CPSR)** contains status and mode control bits, similar to EFLAGS/RFLAGS in the x86/x64 architectures.

Table 10.3: Selected CPSR bits

Bit	Name	Function
0-3	M	Mode: The current execution privilege level (USR, SVC, and so on).
4	T	Thumb: Set if the T32 (Thumb) instruction set is active. If clear, the ARM instruction set is active. User code can set and clear this bit.
9	E	Endianness: Setting this bit enables big-endian mode. If clear, little-endian mode is active. Most code uses little-endian mode.
27	Q	Cumulative saturation flag: Set if, at some point in a series of operations, an overflow or saturation occurred.
28	V	Overflow flag: Set if an operation resulted in signed overflow.
29	C	Carry flag: Indicates if addition produced a carry or subtraction produced a borrow.
30	Z	Zero flag: Set if the result of an operation is zero.
31	N	Negative flag: Set if the result of an operation is negative.

CPSR bits not listed in the preceding table are either reserved or represent functions not discussed in this chapter.

By default, most instructions do not affect the flags. The S suffix must be used with, for example, an addition instruction (adds) to cause the result to affect the flags. Comparison instructions are the exception to this rule; they update the flags automatically.

ARM addressing modes

In true RISC fashion, the only ARM instructions that can access system memory are those that perform register loads and stores. The ldr instruction loads a register from memory, while str stores a register to memory. A separate instruction, mov, transfers the contents of one register to another or moves an immediate value into a register.

When computing the target address for a load or store operation, ARM starts with a base address provided in a register and adds an increment to arrive at the target memory address. There are three techniques for determining the increment that will be added to the base register in register load and store instructions:

- **Offset**: A signed constant is added to the base register. The offset is stored as part of the instruction. For example, ldr r0, [r1, #10] loads r0 with the word at the address r1+10. As shown in the following examples, pre- or post-indexing can optionally update the base register to the target address before or after the memory location is accessed.

- **Register**: An unsigned increment stored in a register can be added to or subtracted from the value in a base register. For example, ldr r0, [r1, r2] loads r0 with the word at the address r1+r2. Either of the registers can be thought of as the base register.

- **Scaled register**: An increment in a register is shifted left or right by a specified number of bit positions before being added to or subtracted from the base register value. For example, ldr r0, [r1, r2, lsl #3] loads r0 with the word at the address r1+(r2×8). The shift can be a logical left or right shift, lsl or lsr, inserting zero bits in the vacated bit positions, or an arithmetic right shift, asr, that replicates the sign bit in the vacated positions.

The addressing modes available for specifying source and destination operands in ARM instructions are presented in the following sections.

Immediate

An immediate value is provided as part of the instruction. The possible immediate values consist of an 8-bit value, coded in the instruction, rotated through an even number of bit positions. A full 32-bit value cannot be specified because the instruction itself is, at most, 32 bits wide. To load an arbitrary 32-bit value into a register, the ldr instruction must be used instead to load the value from memory:

```
mov r0, #10 // Load the 32-bit value 10 decimal into r0
mov r0, #0xFF000000 // Load the 32-bit value FF000000h into r0
```

The second example contains the 8-bit value FFh in the instruction opcode. During execution, it is rotated left by 24 bit positions into the most significant 8 bits of the word.

Register direct

This mode copies one register to another:

```
mov r0, r1 // Copy r1 to r0
mvn r0, r1 // Copy NOT(r1) to r0
```

Register indirect

The address of the operand is provided in a register. The register containing the address is surrounded by square brackets:

```
ldr r0, [r1] // Load the 32-bit value at the address given in
r1 to r0
str r0, [r3] // Store r0 to the address in r3
```

Unlike most instructions, str uses the first operand as the source and the second as the destination.

Register indirect with offset

The address of the operand is computed by adding an offset to the base register:

```
ldr r0, [r1, #32] // Load r0 with the value at the address
[r1+32]
str r0, [r1, #4] // Store r0 to the address [r1+4]
```

Register indirect with offset, pre-incremented

The address of the value is determined by adding an offset to the base register. The base register is updated to the computed address and this address is used to load the destination register:

```
ldr r0, [r1, #32]! // Load r0 with [r1+32] and update r1 to
(r1+32)
str r0, [r1, #4]! // Store r0 to [r1+4] and update r1 to (r1+4)
```

Register indirect with offset, post-incremented

The base address is first used to access the memory location. The base register is then updated to the computed address:

```
ldr r0, [r1], #32 // Load [r1] to r0, then update r1 to (r1+32)
str r0, [r1], #4 // Store r0 to [r1], then update r1 to (r1+4)
```

Double register indirect

The address of the operand is the sum of a base register and an increment register. The register names are surrounded by square brackets:

```
ldr r0, [r1, r2] // Load r0 with [r1+r2]
str r0, [r1, r2] // Store r0 to [r1+r2]
```

Double register indirect with scaling

The address of the operand is the sum of a base register and an increment register shifted left or right by a number of bits. The register names and the shift information are surrounded by square brackets:

```
ldr r0, [r1, r2, lsl #5] // Load r0 with [r1+(r2*32)]
str r0, [r1, r2, lsr #2] // Store r0 to [r1+(r2/4)]
```

The next section introduces the general categories of ARM instructions.

ARM instruction categories

The instructions described in this section are from the T32 instruction set.

Load/store

These instructions move data between registers and memory:

- ldr, str: Copies an 8-bit (suffix b for byte), 16-bit (suffix h for halfword), or 32-bit value between a register and a memory location. ldr copies the value from memory to a register, while str copies a register to memory. ldrb copies one byte into the lower 8 bits of a register.

- ldm, stm: Loads or stores multiple registers. Copies 1 to 16 registers to or from memory. Any subset of registers can be loaded from or stored to a contiguous region of memory.

Stack manipulation

These instructions store data to and retrieve data from the stack.

- push, pop: Pushes or pops any subset of the registers to or from the stack; for example, push {r0, r2, r3-r5}. These instructions are variants of the ldm and stm instructions.

Register movement

These instructions transfer data between registers.

- mov, mvn: Moves a register (mov), or its bit-inversion (mvn), to the destination register.

Arithmetic and logic

These instructions mostly have one destination register and two source operands. The first source operand is a register, while the second can be a register, a shifted register, or an immediate value.

Including the s suffix causes these instructions to set the condition flags. For example, adds performs addition and sets the condition flags.

- add, sub: Adds or subtracts two numbers. For example, add r0, r1, r2, lsl #3 is equivalent to the expression $r0 = r1 + (r2 \times 2^3)$. The lsl operator performs a logical shift left of the second operand, r2.
- adc, sbc: Adds or subtracts two numbers with carry or borrow.
- neg: Negates a number.
- and, orr, eor: Performs logical AND, OR, or XOR.
- orn, eon: Performs logical OR or XOR between the first operand and the bitwise-inverted second operand.
- bic: Clears selected bits in a register.
- mul: Multiplies two numbers.
- mla: Multiplies two numbers and accumulates the result. This instruction has an additional operand to specify the accumulator register.
- sdiv, udiv: Signed and unsigned division, respectively.

Comparisons

These instructions compare two values and set the condition flags based on the result of the comparison. The s suffix is not needed with these instructions to set the condition codes.

- cmp: Subtracts two numbers, discards the result, and sets the condition flags. This is equivalent to a subs instruction, except the result is discarded.
- cmn: Adds two numbers, discards the result, and sets the condition flags. This is equivalent to an adds instruction, except the result is discarded.

- tst: Performs a bitwise AND, discards the result, and sets the condition flags. This is equivalent to an ands instruction, except the result is discarded.

Control flow

These instructions transfer control conditionally or unconditionally to an address.

- b: Performs an unconditional branch to the target address.

- bcc: Branches based on one of these condition codes as *cc*: eq (equal), ne (not equal), gt (greater than), lt (less than), ge (greater or equal), le (less or equal), cs (carry set), cc (carry clear), mi (minus: N flag = 1), pl (plus: N flag = 0), vs (V flag set), vc (V flag clear), hi (higher: C flag set and Z flag clear), ls (lower or same: C flag clear and Z flag clear).

- bl: Branches to the specified address and stores the address of the next instruction in the link register (r14, also called lr). The called function returns to the calling code with the mov pc, lr instruction.

- bx: Branches and selects the instruction set. If bit 0 of the target address is 1, T32 mode is entered. If bit 0 is clear, ARM mode is entered. Bit 0 of instruction addresses must always be zero due to ARM's address alignment requirements. This frees bit 0 to select the instruction set.

- blx: Branches with link and selects the instruction set. This instruction combines the functions of the bl and bx instructions.

Supervisor mode

This instruction allows user mode code to initiate a call to supervisor mode:

- svc (**Supervisor call**): Initiates a software interrupt that causes the supervisor mode exception handler to process a system service request.

Miscellaneous

This instruction does not fit into the categories listed:

- bkpt (**Trigger a breakpoint**): This instruction takes a 16-bit operand for use by debugging software to identify the breakpoint.

Conditional execution

Many ARM instructions support conditional execution, which uses the same condition codes as the branch instructions to determine whether individual instructions are executed. If an instruction's condition evaluates false, the instruction is processed as a no-op. The condition code is appended to the instruction mnemonic. This technique is formally known as **predication**.

For example, this function converts a **nibble** (the lower 4 bits of a byte) into an ASCII character version of the nibble:

```
// Convert the low 4 bits of r0 to an ascii character in r0
nibble2ascii:
    and     r0, #0xF
    cmp     r0, #10
    addpl   r0, r0, #('A' - 10)
    addmi   r0, r0, #'0'
    mov     pc, lr
```

The cmp instruction subtracts 10 from the nibble in r0 and sets the N flag if r0 is less than 10. Otherwise, the N flag is clear, indicating the value in r0 is 10 or greater.

If N is clear, the addpl instruction executes (pl means "plus," as in "not negative"), and the addmi instruction does not execute. If N is set, the addpl instruction does not execute and the addmi instruction executes. After this sequence completes, r0 contains a character in the range '0'-'9' or 'A'-'F'.

The use of conditional instruction execution keeps the instruction pipeline flowing by avoiding branches.

Other instruction categories

ARM processors optionally support a range of SIMD and floating-point instructions. Other instructions are provided that are generally only used during system configuration.

ARM assembly language

The ARM assembly example in this section uses the syntax of the GNU Assembler, provided with the Android Studio **integrated development environment** (**IDE**). Other assemblers may use a different syntax. As with the Intel syntax for the x86 and x64 assembly languages, the operand order for most instructions is the destination-source.

The ARM assembly language source file for the `hello` program is as follows:

```
.text
.global _start


_start:
    // Print the message to file 1 (stdout) with syscall 4
    mov     r0, #1
    ldr     r1, =msg
    mov     r2, #msg_len
    mov     r7, #4
    svc     0


    // Exit the program with syscall 1, returning status 0
    mov     r0, #0
    mov     r7, #1
    svc     0


.data
msg:
    .ascii      "Hello, Computer Architect!"
msg_len = . - msg
```

This file, named `hello_arm.s`, is assembled and linked to form the executable program `hello_arm` with the following commands. These commands use the development tools provided with the **Android Studio Native Development Kit** (**NDK**). The commands assume the Windows PATH environment variable has been set to include the NDK tools directory:

```
arm-linux-androideabi-as -al=hello_arm.lst -o hello_arm.o
hello_arm.s
arm-linux-androideabi-ld -o hello_arm hello_arm.o
```

The components of these commands are as follows:

- `arm-linux-androideabi-as` runs the assembler.

- `-al=hello_arm.lst` creates a listing file named `hello_arm.lst`.

- `-o hello_arm.o` creates an object file named `hello_arm.o`.

- `hello_arm.s` is the name of the assembly language source file.

- `arm-linux-androideabi-ld` runs the linker.

- `-o hello_arm` creates an executable file named `hello_arm`.

- `hello_arm.o` is the name of the object file provided as input to the linker.

This is a portion of the `hello_arm.lst` listing file generated by the assembler command:

```
 1                              .text
 2                              .global _start
 3
 4                              _start:
 5                                  // Print the message to file 1
                                    //(stdout) with syscall 4
 6 0000 0100A0E3                    mov     r0, #1
 7 0004 14109FE5                    ldr     r1, =msg
 8 0008 1A20A0E3                    mov     r2, #msg_len
 9 000c 0470A0E3                    mov     r7, #4
10 0010 000000EF                    svc     0
11
12                                  // Exit the program with syscall 1,
                                    //returning status 0
13 0014 0000A0E3                    mov     r0, #0
14 0018 0170A0E3                    mov     r7, #1
15 001c 000000EF                    svc     0
16
17                              .data
18                              msg:
19 0000 48656C6C                    .ascii       "Hello, Computer
                                    Architect!"
19      6F2C2043
19      6F6D7075
19      74657220
19      41726368
20                              msg_len = . - msg
```

You can run this program on an Android device with **Developer options** enabled. We won't go into the procedure for enabling those options here, but you can easily learn more about it with an Internet search.

This is the output displayed when running this program on an Android ARM device connected to the host PC with a USB cable:

```
C:\>adb push hello_arm /data/local/tmp/hello_arm
C:\>adb shell chmod +x /data/local/tmp/hello_arm
C:\>adb shell /data/local/tmp/hello_arm
Hello, Computer Architect!
```

These commands use the **Android Debug Bridge** (**adb**) tool included with Android Studio. Although the hello_arm program runs on the Android device, output from the program is sent back to the PC and displayed in the command window.

The next section introduces the 64-bit ARM architecture, an extension of the 32-bit ARM architecture.

64-bit ARM architecture and instruction set

The 64-bit version of the ARM architecture, named **AArch64**, was announced in 2011. This architecture has 31 general-purpose 64-bit registers, 64-bit addressing, a 48-bit virtual address space, and a new instruction set named **A64**. The 64-bit instruction set is a superset of the 32-bit instruction set, allowing existing 32-bit code to run unmodified on 64-bit processors.

Instructions are 32 bits wide and most operands are 32 or 64 bits. The A64 register functions differ in some respects from 32-bit mode: the program counter is no longer directly accessible as a register and an additional register is provided that always returns an operand value of zero.

At the user privilege level, most A64 instructions have the same mnemonics as the corresponding 32-bit instructions. The assembler determines whether an instruction operates on 64-bit or 32-bit data based on the operands provided. The following rules determine the operand length and register size used by an instruction:

- 64-bit register names begin with the letter X; for example, x0.

- 32-bit register names begin with the letter W; for example, w1.

- 32-bit registers occupy the lower 32 bits of the corresponding 64-bit register number.

When working with 32-bit registers, the following rules apply:

- Register operations such as right shifts behave the same as in the 32-bit architecture. A 32-bit arithmetic right shift uses bit 31 as the sign bit, not bit 63.

- Condition codes for 32-bit operations are set based on the result in the lower 32 bits.

- Writes to a W register set the upper 32 bits of the corresponding X register to zero.

The A64 is a load/store architecture with the same instruction mnemonics for memory operations (`ldr` and `str`) as 32-bit mode. There are some differences and limitations in comparison to the 32-bit load and store instructions:

- The base register must be an X (64-bit) register.

- An address offset can be any of the same types as in 32-bit mode, as well as an X register. A 32-bit offset can be zero-extended or sign-extended to 64 bits.

- Indexed addressing modes can only use immediate values as an offset.

- A64 does not support the `ldm` or `stm` instructions for loading or storing multiple registers in a single instruction. Instead, A64 adds the `ldp` and `stp` instructions for loading or storing a pair of registers in a single instruction.

- A64 only supports conditional execution for a small subset of instructions.

Stack operations are significantly different in A64. Perhaps the biggest difference in this area is that the stack pointer must maintain 16-byte alignment when accessing data.

64-bit ARM assembly language

This is the 64-bit ARM assembly language source file for the `hello` program:

```
.text
.global _start

_start:
    // Print the message to file 1 (stdout) with syscall 64
    mov     x0, #1
    ldr     x1, =msg
    mov     x2, #msg_len
    mov     x8, #64
    svc     0
```

```
        // Exit the program with syscall 93, returning status 0
    mov     x0, #0
    mov     x8, #93
    svc     0

.data
msg:
    .ascii      "Hello, Computer Architect!"
msg_len = . - msg
```

This file, named hello_arm64.s, is assembled and linked to form the executable hello_arm64 program with the following commands. These commands use the 64-bit development tools provided with the Android Studio NDK. The use of these commands assumes the Windows PATH environment variable has been set to include the tools directory:

```
aarch64-linux-android-as -al=hello_arm64.lst -o hello_arm64.o
hello_arm64.s
```
```
aarch64-linux-android-ld -o hello_arm64 hello_arm64.o
```

The components of these commands are as follows:

- aarch64-linux-android-as runs the assembler.
- -al=hello_arm64.lst creates a listing file named hello_arm64.lst.
- -o hello_arm64.o creates an object file named hello_arm64.o.
- hello_arm64.s is the name of the assembly language source file.
- aarch64-linux-android-ld runs the linker.
- -o hello_arm64 creates an executable file named hello_arm64.
- hello_arm64.o is the name of the object file provided as input to the linker.

This is a portion of the hello_arm64.lst listing file generated by the assembler:

```
1                           .text
2                           .global _start
3
4                           _start:
5                               // Print the message to file 1
                              //(stdout) with syscall 64
```

6	0000	200080D2		mov	x0, #1
7	0004	E1000058		ldr	x1, =msg
8	0008	420380D2		mov	x2, #msg_len
9	000c	080880D2		mov	x8, #64
10	0010	010000D4		svc	0
11					
12				// Exit the program with syscall //93, returning status 0	
13	0014	000080D2		mov	x0, #0
14	0018	A80B80D2		mov	x8, #93
15	001c	010000D4		svc	0
16					
17			.data		
18			msg:		
19	0000	48656C6C		.ascii	"Hello, Computer Architect!"
19		6F2C2043			
19		6F6D7075			
19		74657220			
19		41726368			
20			msg_len = . - msg		

You can run this program on an Android device with **Developer options** enabled, as described earlier. This is the output displayed when running this program on an Android ARM device connected to the host PC with a USB cable:

```
C:\>adb push hello_arm64 /data/local/tmp/hello_arm64
C:\>adb shell chmod +x /data/local/tmp/hello_arm64
C:\>adb shell /data/local/tmp/hello_arm64
Hello, Computer Architect!
```

This completes our introduction to the 32-bit and 64-bit ARM architectures.

Summary

Having completed this chapter, you should have a good understanding of the top-level architectures and features of the x86, x64, 32-bit ARM, and 64-bit ARM registers, instruction sets, and assembly languages.

The x86 and x64 architectures represent a mostly CISC approach to processor design, with variable-length instructions that can take many cycles to execute, a lengthy pipeline, and (in x86) a limited number of processor registers.

The ARM architectures, on the other hand, are RISC processors with mostly single-cycle instruction execution, a large register set, and (somewhat) fixed-length instructions. Early versions of ARM had pipelines as short as three stages, though later versions have considerably more stages.

Is one of these architectures better than the other, in a general sense? It may be that each is better in some ways, and system designers must make their selection of processor architecture based on the specific needs of the system under development. Of course, there is a great deal of inertia behind the use of x86/x64 processors in personal computing, business computing, and server applications. Similarly, there is a lot of history behind the domination of ARM processors in smart personal devices and embedded systems. Many factors go into the processor selection process when designing a new computer or smart device.

In the next chapter, we'll look at the RISC-V architecture. RISC-V was developed from a clean sheet, incorporating lessons learned from the history of processor development and without any of the baggage needed to maintain support for decades-old legacy designs.

Exercises

1. Install the free Visual Studio Community edition, available at `https://visualstudio.microsoft.com/vs/community/`, on a Windows PC. After installation is complete, open the Visual Studio IDE and select **Get Tools and Features...** under the `Tools` menu. Install the **Desktop development with C++** workload.

    In the Windows search box in the Task Bar, begin typing `x86 Native Tools Command Prompt for VS 2019`. When the app appears in the search menu, select it to open a command prompt.

    Create a file named `hello_x86.asm` with the content shown in the source listing in the *x86 assembly language* section of this chapter.

Build the program using the command shown in the *x86 assembly language* section of this chapter and run it. Verify the output **Hello, Computer Architect!** appears on the screen.

2. Write an x86 assembly language program that computes the following expression and prints the result as a hexadecimal number: *[(129 – 66) × (445 + 136)] ÷ 3*. As part of this program, create a callable function to print one byte as two hex digits.

3. In the Windows search box in the Task Bar, begin typing x64 Native Tools Command Prompt for VS 2019. When the app appears in the search menu, select it to open command prompt.

    Create a file named hello_x64.asm with the content shown in the source listing in the *x64 assembly language* section of this chapter.

    Build the program using the command shown in the *x64 assembly language* section of this chapter and run it. Verify that the output **Hello, Computer Architect!** appears on the screen.

4. Write an x64 assembly language program that computes the following expression and prints the result as a hexadecimal number: *[(129 – 66) × (445 + 136)] ÷ 3*. As part of this program, create a callable function to print one byte as two hex digits.

5. Install the free Android Studio IDE, available at https://developer. android.com/studio/. After installation is complete, open the Android Studio IDE and select **SDK Manager** under the **Tools** menu. In the **Settings for New Projects** dialog, select the **SDK Tools** tab and check the **NDK** option, which may say **NDK (Side by side)**. Complete the installation of the native development kit (NDK).

    Locate the following files under the SDK installation directory (the default location is under %LOCALAPPDATA%\Android) and add their directories to your PATH environment variable: arm-linux-androideabi-as.exe and adb.exe. Hint: The following command works for one version of Android Studio (your path may vary):

    ```
    set PATH=%PATH%;%LOCALAPPDATA%\Android\Sdk\
    ndk\20.1.5948944\toolchains\arm-linux-androideabi-4.9\
    prebuilt\windows-x86_64\bin;%LOCALAPPDATA%\Android\Sdk\
    platform-tools
    ```

    Create a file named hello_arm.s with the content shown in the source listing in the The *32-bit ARM assembly language* section of this chapter.

Build the program using the commands shown in the *the 32-bit ARM assembly language* section of this chapter.

Enable **Developer Options** on an Android phone or tablet. Search the Internet for instructions on how to do this.

Connect your Android device to the computer with a USB cable.

Copy the program executable image to the phone using the commands shown in the *32-bit ARM assembly language* section of this chapter and run the program. Verify the output **Hello, Computer Architect!** appears on the host computer screen.

6. Write a 32-bit ARM assembly language program that computes the following expression and prints the result as a hexadecimal number: *[(129 – 66) × (445 + 136)] ÷ 3*. As part of this program, create a callable function to print one byte as two hex digits.

7. Locate the following files under the Android SDK installation directory (the default location is under %LOCALAPPDATA%\Android) and add their directories to your PATH environment variable: aarch64-linux-android-as.exe and adb.exe. Hint: The following command works for one version of Android Studio (your path may vary):

```
set PATH=%PATH%;%LOCALAPPDATA \Android\sdk\ndk-bundle\
toolchains\arm-linux-androideabi-4.9\prebuilt\
windows-x86_64\bin;%LOCALAPPDATA%\Android\Sdk\platform-
tools
```

Create a file named hello_arm64.s with the content shown in the source listing in the *64-bit ARM assembly language* section of this chapter.

Build the program using the commands shown in the *64-bit ARM assembly language* section of this chapter.

Enable **Developer Options** on an Android phone or tablet.

Connect your Android device to the computer with a USB cable.

Copy the program executable image to the phone using the commands shown in the *64-bit ARM assembly language* section of this chapter and run the program. Verify the output **Hello, Computer Architect!** appears on the host computer screen.

8. Write a 64-bit ARM assembly language program that computes the following expression and prints the result as a hexadecimal number: *[(129 – 66) × (445 + 136)] ÷ 3*. As part of this program, create a callable function to print one byte as two hex digits.

11
The RISC-V Architecture and Instruction Set

This chapter introduces the exciting, relatively new RISC-V (pronounced *risk five*) processor architecture and its instruction set. RISC-V is a completely open source specification for a reduced instruction set processor. A complete user-mode (non-privileged) instruction set specification has been released, and several inexpensive hardware implementations of this architecture are currently available. Work is ongoing to develop specifications for a number of instruction set extensions to support general-purpose computing, high-performance computing, and embedded applications. Commercially available processors implement many of these developmental extensions.

The following topics will be covered in this chapter:

- The RISC-V architecture and features
- The RISC-V base instruction set
- RISC-V extensions
- 64-bit RISC-V
- Standard RISC-V configurations
- RISC-V assembly language
- Implementing RISC-V in a **field-programmable gate array** (**FPGA**)

After completing this chapter, you will understand the architecture and capabilities of the RISC-V processor and its optional extensions. You will have learned the basics of the RISC-V instruction set and will understand how RISC-V can be tailored to support a variety of computer architectures, from low-end embedded systems to warehouse-scale cloud server farms. You will also have learned how to implement a RISC-V processor in a low-cost FPGA board.

Technical requirements

Files for this chapter, including answers to the exercises, are available at `https://github.com/PacktPublishing/Modern-Computer-Architecture-and-Organization`.

The RISC-V architecture and features

The RISC-V architecture, publicly announced in 2014, was developed at the University of California, Berkeley, by Yunsup Lee, Krste Asanović, David A. Patterson, and Andrew Waterman. This effort followed four previous major RISC architectural design projects at UC Berkeley, leading to the name RISC-V, where *V* represents the Roman numeral five.

The RISC-V project began as a clean sheet with these major goals:

- Design a RISC **instruction set architecture** (**ISA**) suitable for use in a wide variety of applications, spanning the spectrum from micro-power embedded devices to high-performance cloud server multiprocessors.

- Provide an ISA that is free to use by anyone, for any application. This contrasts with the ISAs of almost all other commercially available processors, which are the carefully guarded intellectual property of the company that designed them.

- Incorporate lessons learned from previous decades of processor design, avoiding wrong turns and suboptimal features that other architectures must retain in newer generations to maintain compatibility with previous, sometimes ancient in technological terms, generations.

- Provide a small but complete base ISA suitable for use in embedded devices. The base ISA is the minimal set of capabilities any RISC-V processor must implement. The base RISC-V is a 32-bit processor architecture with 31 general-purpose registers. All instructions are 32 bits long. The base ISA supports integer addition and subtraction, but does not include integer multiplication and division. This is to avoid forcing minimal processor implementations to include the fairly expensive multiplication and division hardware for applications that do not require those operations.

- Provide optional ISA extensions to support floating-point mathematics, atomic memory operations, and multiplication and division.

- Provide additional ISA extensions to support privileged execution modes, similar to the x86, x64, and ARM privileged implementations discussed in *Chapter 10, Modern Processor Architectures and Instruction Sets*.

- Support a compressed instruction set, implementing 16-bit versions of many 32-bit instructions. In processors implementing this extension, 16-bit instructions may be freely interspersed with 32-bit instructions.

- Provide optional ISA extensions to support 64-bit, and even 128-bit, processor word sizes using paged virtual memory on single- and multi-core processors, and in multiprocessing configurations.

RISC-V processors are available on the market today at competitive prices and, given the sophistication of the ISA design and the advantages of its free-to-use nature, we can expect the market share of RISC-V processors to grow rapidly in the coming years. RISC-V Linux distributions are available, which include all the software development tools needed to build and run applications on RISC-V-based computers and smart devices.

The following diagram shows the RISC-V base ISA regster set:

Figure 11.1: RISC-V base ISA register set

The registers are 32 bits wide. General-purpose registers x1 through x31 are available for use without any restrictions or special functions assigned by the processor hardware. The x0 register is hardwired to return zero when it is read, and will discard any value written to it. We will see some interesting uses of the x0 register shortly.

Each register has one or two alternate names, shown in *Figure 11.1*. These names correspond to the usage of registers in the standard RISC-V **application binary interface** (**ABI**). Because registers x1-x31 are functionally interchangeable, it is necessary for the ABI to dictate which register should serve as the stack pointer, which registers should contain arguments to functions, which should contain return values, and so forth. The meanings of the register designations are as follows:

- **ra**: Function return address.

- **sp**: Stack pointer.

- **gp**: Global data pointer.

- **tp**: Thread-local data pointer.

- **t0-t6**: Temporary storage.

- **fp**: Frame pointer for function-local stack data (this usage is optional).

- **s0-s11**: Saved registers (if the frame pointer is not in use, x8 becomes s0).

- **a0-a7**: Arguments passed to functions. Any additional arguments are passed on the stack. Function return values are passed in a0 and a1.

The pc register contains the 32-bit program counter, holding the address of the current instruction.

You may be surprised to see there is no processor flags register in the RISC-V ISA. Some operations that modify flags in other processor architectures instead store their results in a RISC-V register. For example, the signed (slt) and unsigned (sltu) RISC-V comparison instructions subtract two operands and set a destination register to 0 or 1 depending on the sign of the result. A subsequent conditional branch instruction can use the value in that register to determine which code path to take.

Some of the flags found in other processors must be computed in RISC-V. For example, there is no carry flag. To determine whether an addition resulted in a carry, it is necessary to perform a comparison between the sum and one of the operands of the addition instruction. If the sum is greater than or equal to the addend (either addend can be used for the comparison), a carry did not occur; otherwise, the addition produced a carry.

Most of the base ISA computational instructions use a three-operand format, in which the first operand is a destination register, the second operand is a source register, and the third operand is either a source register or an immediate value. The following is an example three-operand instruction:

```
add x1, x2, x3
```

This instruction adds the x2 register to the x3 register and stores the result in the x1 register.

To avoid introducing instructions that are not strictly necessary, many instructions take on extra duties that are performed by dedicated instructions in other processor architectures. For example, RISC-V contains no instruction that simply moves one register to another. Instead, a RISC-V addition instruction adds a source register and an immediate value of zero and stores the result in a destination register, producing the same result. The instruction to transfer the x2 register to the x1 register is therefore add x1, x2, 0, assigning the value (x2 + 0) to x1.

The RISC-V assembly language provides a number of pseudo-instructions using terminology that may be more familiar to implement such functions. The assembler translates the mv x1, x2 pseudo-instruction to a literal add x1, x2, 0 instruction.

The RISC-V base instruction set

The RISC-V base instruction set is composed of just 47 instructions. Eight are system instructions that perform system calls and access performance counters. The remaining 39 instructions fall into the categories of computational instructions, control flow instructions, and memory access instructions. We will examine each of these categories in the following sections.

Computational instructions

All of the computational instructions except lui and auipc use the three-operand form. The first operand is the destination register, the second is a source register, and the third operand is either a second source register or an immediate value. Instruction mnemonics using an immediate value (except for auipc) end with the letter i. This is a list of the instructions and their functions:

- add, addi, sub: Perform addition and subtraction. The immediate value in the addi instruction is a 12-bit signed value. The sub instruction subtracts the second source operand from the first. There is no subi instruction because addi can add a negative immediate value.

- sll, slli, srl, srli, sra, srai: Perform logical left and right shifts (sll and srl), and arithmetic right shifts (sra). Logical shifts insert zero bits into vacated locations. Arithmetic right shifts replicate the sign bit into vacated locations. The number of bit positions to shift is taken from the lowest 5 bits of the second source register or from the 5-bit immediate value.

- and, andi, or, ori, xor, xori: Perform the indicated bitwise operation on the two source operands. Immediate operands are 12 bits.

- slt, slti, sltu, sltui: The *set if less than* instructions set the destination register to 1 if the first source operand is less than the second source operand. This comparison is in terms of two's complement (slt) or unsigned (sltu) operands. Immediate operand values are 12 bits.

- lui: Load upper immediate. This instruction loads bits 12-31 of the destination register with a 20-bit immediate value. Setting a register to an arbitrary 32-bit immediate value requires two instructions. First, lui sets bits 12-31 to the upper 20 bits of the value. Then, addi adds in the lower 12 bits to form the complete 32-bit result. lui has two operands: the destination register and the immediate value.

- auipc: Add upper immediate to PC. This instruction adds a 20-bit immediate value to the upper 20 bits of the program counter. This instruction enables PC-relative addressing in RISC-V. To form a complete 32-bit PC-relative address, auipc forms a partial result, then an addi instruction adds in the lower 12 bits.

Control flow instructions

The conditional branching instructions perform comparisons between two registers and, based on the result, may transfer control within the range of a signed 12-bit address offset from the current PC. Two unconditional jump instructions are available, one of which (jalr) provides access to the entire 32-bit address range.

- beq, bne, blt, bltu, bge, bgeu: Branch if equal (beq), not equal (bne), less than (blt), less than unsigned (bltu), greater or equal (bge), or greater or equal, unsigned (bgeu). These instructions perform the designated comparison between two registers and, if the condition is satisfied, transfer control to the address offset provided in the 12-bit signed immediate value.

- jal: Jump and link. Transfer control to the PC-relative address provided in the 20-bit signed immediate value and store the address of the next instruction (the return address) in the destination register.

- jalr: Jump and link, register. Compute the target address as the sum of the source register and a signed 12-bit immediate value, then jump to that address and store the address of the next instruction in the destination register. When preceded by the auipc instruction, the jalr instruction can perform a PC-relative jump anywhere in the 32-bit address space.

Memory access instructions

The memory access instructions transfer data between a register and a memory location. The first operand is the register to be loaded or stored. The second operand is a register containing a memory address. A signed 12-bit immediate value is added to the address in the register to produce the final address used for the load or store.

The load instructions perform sign extension for signed values or zero extension for unsigned values. The sign or zero extension operation fills in all 32 bits in the destination register when a smaller data value (a byte or halfword) is loaded. Unsigned loads are specified by a trailing u in the mnemonic.

- lb, lbu, lh, lhu, lw: Load an 8-bit byte (lb), a 16-bit halfword (lh), or a 32-bit word (lw) into the destination register. For byte and halfword loads, the instruction will either sign-extend (lb and lh) or zero-extend (lbu and lhu) to fill the 32-bit destination register. For example, the lw x1, 16(x2) instruction loads the word at the address (x2 + 16) into register x1.

- sb, sh, sw: Store a byte (sb), halfword (sh), or word (sw) to a memory location matching the size of the data value.

- fence: Enforce memory access ordering in a multithreaded context. The purpose of this instruction is to ensure a coherent view of cached data across threads. This instruction takes two operands. The first specifies the types of memory accesses that must complete prior to the fence instruction. The second specifies the types of memory accesses controlled following the fence. The operation types ordered by this instruction are memory reads and writes (r and w) and I/O device inputs and outputs (i and o). For example, the fence rw, rw instruction will guarantee that all loads and stores involving memory addresses occurring before the fence instruction will complete before any subsequent memory loads or stores take place. This instruction ensures that any values present in processor caches are properly synchronized with memory or the I/O device.

- fence.i: This instruction ensures that any stores to instruction memory have completed before the fence.i instruction completes. This instruction is primarily useful in the context of self-modifying code.

System instructions

Of the eight system instructions, one invokes a system call, one initiates a debugger breakpoint, and the remaining six read and write system **control and status registers** (**CSRs**). The CSR manipulation instructions read the current value of the selected CSR into a register, then update the CSR by either writing a new value, clearing selected bits, or setting selected bits. The source value for the CSR modification is provided in a register or as an immediate 5-bit value. CSRs are identified by a 12-bit address. Each CSR instruction performs the read and write of the CSR as an atomic operation.

- ecall: Invoke a system call. Registers used for passing parameters into and returning from the call are defined by the ABI, not by processor hardware.

- ebreak: Initiate a debugger breakpoint.

- csrrw, csrrwi, csrrc, csrrci, csrrs, csrrsi: Read the specified CSR into a destination register and either write a source operand value to the register (csrrw), clear any 1 bit in the source operand in the register (csrrc), or set any 1 bit in the source operand in the register (csrrs). These instructions take three operands: the first is the destination register receiving the value read from the CSR, the second is the CSR address, and the third is a source register or a 5-bit immediate value (i suffix).

Six CSRs are defined in the base RISC-V architecture, all read-only. To execute any of the CSR access instructions in a read-only mode, the x0 register must be provided as the third operand. These registers define three 64-bit performance counters:

- cycle, cycleh: The lower (cycle) and upper (cycleh) 32 bits of the 64-bit count of elapsed system clock cycles since a reference time—typically, system startup. The frequency of the system clock may vary if **dynamic voltage and frequency scaling (DVFS)** is active.

- time, timeh: These are the lower (time) and upper (timeh) 32 bits of the 64-bit count of elapsed real-time clock cycles since a reference time—typically, system startup.

- instret, instreth: The lower (instret) and upper (instreth) 32 bits of the 64-bit count of processor instructions retired.

The two 32-bit halves of each performance counter cannot be read in a single atomic operation. To prevent erroneous readings, the following procedure should be used to reliably read each of the 64-bit counters:

1. Read the upper 32 bits of the counter into a register.

2. Read the lower 32 bits of the counter into another register.

3. Read the upper 32 bits into yet another register.

4. Compare the first and second reads of the upper 32 counter bits. If they differ, jump back to *Step 1*.

This procedure will read a valid count value, even though the counter continues to run between the reads. In general, execution of this sequence should require, at most, one backward jump in *Step 4*.

Pseudo-instructions

The RISC-V architecture has a truly reduced instruction set, lacking several types of instructions present in the instruction sets we have investigated in earlier chapters. The functions of many of those more familiar instructions can be performed with RISC-V instructions, though perhaps not in an immediately intuitive manner.

The RISC-V assembler supports a number of pseudo-instructions, each of which translates to one or more RISC-V instructions providing a type of functionality one might expect in a general-purpose processor instruction set. The following table presents a few of the most useful RISC-V pseudo-instructions:

Table 11.1: RISC-V pseudo-instructions

Pseudo-instruction	RISC-V instruction(s)	Function
`nop`	`addi x0, x0, 0`	No operation
`mv rd,rs`	`addi rd, rs, 0`	Copy rs to rd
`not rd, rs`	`xori rd, rs, -1`	rd = NOT rs
`neg rd, rs`	`sub rd, x0, rs`	rd = -rs
`j offset`	`jal x0, offset`	Unconditional jump
`jal offset`	`jal x1, offset`	Near function call (20-bit offset)

`call offset`	`auipc x1, offset[31:12] + offset[11]`
	
	`jalr x1, offset[11:0](x1)`
		Far function call (32-bit offset)

`ret`	`jalr x0, 0(x1)`	Return from function
`beqz rs, offset`	`beq rs, x0, offset`	Branch if equal to zero
`bgez rs, offset`	`bge rx, x0, offset`	Branch if greater than or equal to zero
`bltz rs, offset`	`blt rs, x0, offset`	Branch if less than zero
`bgt rs, rt, offset`	`blt rt, rs, offset`	Branch if greater than
`ble rs, rt, offset`	`bge rt, rs, offset`	Branch if less than or equal
`fence`	`fence iorw, iorw`	Fence all memory and I/O accesses
`csrr rd, csr`	`csrrw rd, csr, x0`	Read a CSR
`li rd, immed`	`addi rd, x0, immed`	Load 12-bit immediate

`li rd, immed`	`lui rd, immed[31:12] + immed[11]`
	
	`addi rd, x0, immed[11:0]`
		Load 32-bit immediate

`la rd, symbol`	`auipc rd, delta[31:12] + delta[11]`
	
	`addi rd, rd, delta[11:0]`
		Load the address of symbol, where delta=(symbol-pc)

Pseudo-instruction	RISC-V instruction(s)	Function
`lw rd, symbol`	`auipc rd, delta[31:12] +` `delta[11]` `lw rd, rd, delta[11:0]` `(rd)`	Load word at `symbol`, where `delta=(symbol-pc)`
`sw rd, symbol, rt`	`auipc rt, delta[31:12] +` `delta[11]` `sw rd, rd, delta[11:0]` `(rt)`	Store word at `symbol`, where `delta=(symbol-pc)`

In these instruction listings, `rd` is the destination register, `rs` is the source register, `csr` is a control and status register, `symbol` is an absolute data address, and `offset` is a PC-relative instruction address.

Instructions combining the upper 20 bits of an address or immediate value with an immediate value containing the lower 12 bits must perform a step to reverse the effect of the sign extension of bit 11 of the lower 12-bit value in the second instruction of each sequence. This is necessary because the immediate value in the `addi` instruction is always treated as signed. The most significant bit of the 12-bit immediate value will be sign-extended through bit 31 before being added to the upper 20 bits.

The following example demonstrates the problem and the solution. Assume we want to load the value `0xFFFFFFFF` into a register using `lui` and `addi` and naively add the upper and lower portions, as shown here

```
lui x1, 0xFFFFF # x1 now equals 0xFFFFF000
addi x1, x1, 0xFFF
```

The `addi` instruction sign-extends `0xFFF` to `0xFFFFFFFF` before adding it to `0xFFFFF000`. The result of the addition is then `0xFFFFEFFF`, which is not what we want. Adding bit 11 of the lower 12 bits to the upper 20 bits will fix this, as shown in the following code block:

```
lui x1, 0xFFFFF+1 # Add bit 11; x1 now equals 0x00000000
addi x1, x1, 0xFFF
```

The result is now `0xFFFFFFFF`, the correct value. This procedure will work for any other numeric value. If bit 11 happens to be zero, nothing will be added to the upper 20 bits.

One point to note regarding assembly code in this chapter is that the RISC-V assembler uses the # character to begin a comment.

Privilege levels

The RISC-V architecture defines three privilege levels at which a thread can run:

- User (U) privilege level
- Supervisor (S) privilege level
- Machine (M) privilege level

All RISC-V implementations must support M mode, the most privileged level, which is capable of accessing all system features. M mode is entered at system reset. The code in a simple embedded system can run entirely in M mode.

In a slightly more sophisticated use case, a secure boot process might run at the M privilege level, loading and starting an application that runs in U mode. This approach is appropriate for a secure embedded solution.

In addition to the mandatory M level, a RISC-V processor may implement either or both of the S and U privilege levels. A system running a general-purpose operating system uses S mode and U mode in the same manner as the kernel and user modes of the processors and operating systems discussed in previous chapters. RISC-V U-mode applications request system services with the ecall (environment call) instruction, generating an exception handled at the S level. The privilege architecture of RISC-V directly supports modern operating systems such as Linux.

Separate collections of CSRs are defined to enable configuration, control, and monitoring of the system at each of the three privilege levels. Depending on the privilege level of the running thread and the level of a CSR, the thread may have read-write, read-only, or no access to the CSR. Threads at higher privilege levels can access CSRs at lower privilege levels.

The RISC-V S privilege level supports paged virtual memory with a 32-bit address space divided into 4 KB pages. A 32-bit virtual address is separated into a 20-bit virtual page number and a 12-bit page offset. Two additional virtual memory configurations are defined for the RISC-V 64-bit environment. The first is a 39-bit address space, supporting 512 GB of virtual memory. For applications requiring even more virtual addresses, a 48-bit address space is available, supporting 256 TB of virtual memory. Although the 48-bit configuration offers far more memory than the 39-bit configuration, it also requires additional storage for page tables, and consumes more processing time during traversal of those tables.

The following instructions support privileged execution levels:

- `mret, sret, uret`: These instructions return from the exception handler initiated by an `ecall` instruction. Each of these instructions can be executed at the privilege level indicated by the first letter of the instruction or higher. Executing one of these instructions referencing a privilege level lower than that of the current thread will return from the exception initiated at the lower level.

- `wfi`: Wait for interrupt. This instruction requests the current thread to stall until an interrupt becomes available for servicing. The RISC-V specification only requires that this instruction serve as a hint, so a particular implementation may process a `wfi` instruction as a no-op rather than actually stalling the thread. Because it is possible for the processor to handle `wfi` as a no-op, the code that follows a `wfi` instruction must explicitly check for the presence of pending interrupts in need of processing. This sequence typically occurs inside a loop.

- `sfence.vma`: Flush virtual memory page table data from cache to memory. The leading `s` in the instruction mnemonic indicates this instruction is targeted for use at the supervisor privilege level.

RISC-V defines additional instructions and CSRs supporting virtualization and the hypervisor that manages the virtual environment. RISC-V virtualization will be covered in *Chapter 12, Processor Virtualization*.

RISC-V extensions

The instruction set described earlier in this chapter is named **RV32I**, which stands for the **RISC-V 32-bit integer instruction set**. Although the RV32I ISA provides a complete and useful instruction set for many purposes, it lacks several functions and features available in other processors such as x86 and ARM.

The RISC-V extensions provide a mechanism for adding capabilities to the base instruction set in an incremental and compatible manner. Implementors of RISC-V processors can selectively include extensions in a processor design to optimize tradeoffs between chip size, system capability, and performance. These flexible design options are also available to developers of low-cost FPGA-based systems. We'll see more about implementing a RISC-V processor in an FPGA later in this chapter. The major extensions we will cover now are named M, A, C, F, and D, and we'll mention some other available extensions.

The M extension

The RISC-V M extension adds integer multiplication and division functionality to the base RV32I instruction set. The following instructions are available in this extension:

- mul: Multiply two 32-bit registers and store the lower 32 bits of the result in the destination register.

- mulh. mulhu, mulhsu: Multiply two 32-bit registers and store the upper 32 bits of the result in the destination register. Treat the multiplicands as both signed (mulh), both unsigned (mulhu), or signed rs1 times unsigned rs2 (mulhsu). rs1 is the first source register in the instruction and rs2 is the second.

- div, divu: Perform division of two 32-bit registers, rounding the result toward zero, on signed (div) or unsigned (divu) operands.

- rem, remu: Return the remainder corresponding to the result of a div or divu instruction on the operands.

Division by zero does not raise an exception. To detect division by zero, code should test the divisor and branch to an appropriate handler if it is zero.

The A extension

The RISC-V A extension provides atomic read-modify-write operations to support multithreaded processing in shared memory.

The atomic load-reserved (lr.w) and store-conditional (sc.w) instructions work together to perform a memory read followed by a write to the same location as an atomic sequence. The load-reserved instruction places a reservation on the memory address during the load. If another thread writes to the same location while the reservation is in effect, the reservation is canceled.

When the store-conditional instruction executes, it returns a value indicating whether it successfully completed the atomic operation. If the reservation remains valid (in other words, no intervening write occurred to the target address), the store-conditional instruction writes the register to memory and returns zero, indicating success. If the reservation was canceled, the store-conditional instruction does not alter the memory location and returns a nonzero value indicating the store operation failed. The following instructions implement the load-reserved and store-conditional operations:

- lr.w: Load a register from a memory location and place a reservation on the address.

- `sc.w`: Store a register to a memory location conditionally. Set the destination register to zero if the operation succeeded and the memory location was written, or set the destination register to a nonzero value if the reservation was canceled. If the reservation was canceled, the memory location is not modified by this instruction.

The **atomic memory operation** (**AMO**) instructions atomically load a word from a memory location into the destination register, perform a binary operation between the value that was loaded and `rs2`, and store the result back to the memory address. The following instructions implement the AMO operations:

- `amoswap.w`: Atomically swap `rs2` into the `rs1` memory location.

- `amoadd.w`: Atomically add `rs2` into the `rs1` memory location.

- `amoand.w`, `amoor.w`, `amoxor.w`: Atomically perform AND, OR, or XOR operations with `rs2` into the `rs1` memory location.

- `amomin.w`, `amominu.w`, `amomax.w`, `amomaxu.w`: Atomically perform minimum or maximum selection of signed or unsigned (instructions with the u suffix) values with `rs2` into the `rs1` memory location.

C extension

The RISC-V C extension implements compressed instructions with the goals of minimizing the amount of memory consumed by instruction storage and reducing the amount of bus traffic required to fetch instructions.

All RV32I instructions discussed previously are 32 bits in length. The C extension provides alternate 16-bit representations of many of the most frequently used RV32I instructions. Each compressed instruction is equivalent to one full-length instruction. No mode switching is necessary, meaning programs can freely intermix 32-bit RV32I instructions and compressed 16-bit instructions. In fact, assembly language programmers do not even need to take steps to specify whether an instruction should be generated in compressed form. The assembler and linker are capable of transparently emitting compressed instructions where possible to minimize code size, with no execution performance penalty.

When working with processors and software development tool sets supporting the RISC-V C extension, the benefits of compressed instructions are immediately available to developers working in assembly language as well as to those working with higher-level languages.

The F and D extensions

The RISC-V F and D extensions provide hardware support for single-precision (F) and double-precision (D) floating-point arithmetic in accordance with the IEEE 754 standard. The F extension adds 32 floating-point registers named f0-f31 and a control and status register named fcsr to the architecture. These registers are all 32 bits. The extension includes a set of floating-point instructions that complies with the IEEE 754-2008 single-precision standard.

Most floating-point instructions operate on the floating-point registers. Data transfer instructions are provided to load floating-point registers from memory, store floating-point registers to memory, and move data between floating-point registers and integer registers.

The D extension widens f0-f31 to 64 bits. In this configuration, each f register can hold a 32-bit value or a 64-bit value. Double-precision floating-point instructions are added, in compliance with the IEEE 754-2008 double-precision standard. The D extension requires the F extension be present.

Other extensions

Several additional extensions to the RISC-V architecture, detailed in the following list, have been defined, are in development, or are at least under consideration for future development:

- **RV32E architecture**: This is not actually an extension; rather, it is a modified architecture intended to reduce processor hardware requirements below those of the RV32I instruction set for the smallest embedded systems. The only difference between RV32I and RV32E is the reduction in the number of integer registers to 15. This change is expected to reduce processor die area and power consumption by about 25% compared to an otherwise equivalent RV23I processor. x0 remains a dedicated zero register. Halving the number of registers frees up 1 bit in each register specifier in an instruction. These bits are guaranteed to remain unused in future revisions and are thus available for use in customized instruction extensions.

- **Q extension**: The Q extension supports 128-bit quad-precision floating-point mathematics, as defined in the IEEE 754-2008 standard.

- **L extension**: The L extension supports decimal floating-point arithmetic, as defined in the IEEE 754-2008 standard.

- **B extension**: The B extension supports bit manipulations such as inserting, extracting, and testing individual bits.

- **J extension**: The J extension supports dynamically translated languages such as Java and JavaScript.

- **T extension**: The T extension supports memory transactions consisting of atomic operations across multiple addresses.

- **P extension**: The P extension provides packed **Single Instruction Multiple Data (SIMD)** instructions for floating-point operations in small RISC-V systems.

- **V extension**: The V extension supports data-parallel, or vector, operations. The V extension does not specify the lengths of data vectors; that decision is left to the implementers of a RISC-V processor design. A typical implementation of the V extension might support 512-bit data vectors, though implementations with up to 4,096-bit vector lengths are currently available.

- **N extension**: The N extension provides support for handling interrupts and exceptions at the U privilege level.

- **Zicsr extension**: The Zicsr extension performs atomic read-modify-write operations on the system CSRs. These instructions are described earlier in this chapter in the *System instructions* section.

- **Zifencei extension**: The Zifencei extension defines the fence.i instruction, described in the *Memory access instructions* section.

The next section covers the extension of the base RISC-V ISA to 64 bits.

64-bit RISC-V

The RISC-V introduction to this point has discussed the 32-bit RV32I architecture and instruction set, with extensions. The RV64I instruction set extends RV32I to a 64-bit architecture. As in RV32I, instructions are 32-bits wide. In fact, the RV64I instruction set is almost entirely the same as RV32I, except for these significant differences:

- All of the integer registers are widened to 64 bits.

- Addresses are widened to 64 bits.

- Bit shift counts in instruction opcodes increase in size from 5 to 6 bits.

- Several new instructions are defined to operate on 32-bit values in a manner equivalent to RV32I. These instructions are necessary because most instructions in RV64I operate on 64-bit values, and there are many situations in which it is necessary to operate efficiently on 32-bit values. These word-oriented instructions have an opcode mnemonic suffix of W. The W-suffix instructions produce signed 32-bit results. These 32-bit values are sign-extended (even if they are unsigned values) to fill the 64-bit destination register. In other words, bit 31 of each result is copied into bits 32-63.

The following new instructions are defined in RV64I:

- addw, addiw, subw, sllw, slliw, srlw, srliw, sraw, sraiw: These instructions perform equivalently to the RV32I instruction with the same mnemonic, minus the W suffix. They work with 32-bit operands and produce 32-bit results. The result is sign-extended to 64 bits.

- ld, sd: Load and store a 64-bit **doubleword**. These are the 64-bit versions of the lw and sw instructions in the RV32I instruction set.

The remaining RV32I instructions perform the same functions in RV64I, except addresses and registers are 64 bits in length. The same opcodes, both in assembly source code and binary machine code, are used in both instruction sets.

In the next section, we will examine some standard 32-bit and 64-bit RISC-V configurations that are commercially available. Each of these consists of a base ISA plus selected extensions.

Standard RISC-V configurations

The RV32I and RV64I instruction sets provide a base set of capabilities useful mainly in smaller embedded system designs. Systems intended to support multithreading, multiple privilege levels, and general-purpose operating systems require several of the RISC-V extensions to operate correctly and efficiently.

The minimum RISC-V configuration recommended for establishing an application development target consists of a base RV32I or RV64I instruction set architecture augmented with the I, M, A, F, D, Zicsr, and Zifencei extensions. The abbreviation for this combination of features is G, as in RV32G or RV64G. Many G configurations additionally support the compressed instruction extension, with the names RV32GC and RV64GC.

In embedded applications, a common configuration is RV32IMAC, providing the base instruction set plus multiply/divide functionality, atomic operations, and compressed instruction support. Marketing materials for RISC-V processors frequently use these shorthand descriptions of processor capabilities.

The following section presents a complete program in RISC-V assembly language.

RISC-V assembly language

The following RISC-V assembly language example is a complete application that runs on a RISC-V processor:

```
.section .text
.global main


main:
    # Reserve stack space and save the return address
    addi    sp, sp, -16
    sd      ra, 0(sp)


    # Print the message using the C library puts function
1:  auipc   a0, %pcrel_hi(msg)
    addi    a0, a0, %pcrel_lo(1b)
    jal     ra, puts


    # Restore the return address and sp, and return to caller
    ld      ra, 0(sp)
    addi    sp, sp, 16
    jalr    zero, ra, 0


.section .rodata
msg:
    .asciz "Hello, Computer Architect!\n"
```

This program prints the following message in a console window and then exits:

```
Hello, Computer Architect!
```

The following are some points of interest within the assembly code:

- The `%pcrel_hi` and `%pcrel_lo` directives select the high 20 bits (`%pcrel_hi`) or low 12 bits (`%pcrel_lo`) of the PC-relative address of the label provided as an argument. The combination of the `auipc` and `addi` instructions places the address of the message string in `a0`.

- `1:` is a local label. When referencing a local label, the letter `b` is appended to reference a label earlier in the code (backward), or `f` is appended to reference a label later in the code (forward). The `%pcrel_hi` and `%pcrel_lo` directives are paired: the `1:` local label resolves the lower 12 bits of the offset to the `msg` address.

In the next section, we will run some code in a fully functional RISC-V processor implemented in an FPGA.

Implementing RISC-V in an FPGA

All of the source code, processor hardware design intellectual property, and development tools required to build and implement a complete RISC-V processor in a low-cost FPGA are freely available on the Internet. This section provides a high-level overview of the open source RISC-V design and the steps for bringing it up in an FPGA device. The total cost for the hardware to accomplish this task is less than US$200.

The RISC-V FPGA target in this example is the Digilent Arty A7-35T board, available at `https://store.digilentinc.com/arty-a7-artix-7-fpga-development-board-for-makers-and-hobbyists/`. The Arty A7-35T costs US$129 at the time of this writing.

The Arty A7-35T contains a Xilinx Artix-7 XC7A35TICSG324-1L FPGA, which can be programmed to implement a RISC-V processor. The XC7A35TICSG324-1L has the following features:

- 5,200 logic slices.

- 1,600 of the logic slices can implement a 64-bit RAM.

- 41,600 flip-flops. Each logic slice contains eight flip-flops.

- 90 DSP slices supporting high-performance DSP MAC operations.

- 400 kbits of distributed RAM.

- 1,800 kbits of total RAM.

The Artix-7 FPGA architecture uses **lookup tables** (**LUTs**) to implement combinational logic. Each of the Artix-7 LUTs has six input signals and one output signal, where each signal is one data bit. A single LUT can represent any feedback-free circuit composed of AND, OR, NOT, and XOR gates operating on the six input signals by simply storing the results of each input combination as a bit in a small ROM. With 6 input bits, the ROM contains 64 (2^6) bits of data addressed by the six input signals. If desired, each LUT can instead be configured as two 32-bit LUTs operating on five shared inputs with 2 output bits. Optionally, the LUT output can be stored in a flip-flop.

A *logic slice* contains four LUTs and eight flip-flops, plus additional multiplexer and arithmetic carry logic. Four of the eight flip-flops in a slice can be configured as latches. Each of the 1,600 slices with 64-bit RAM capability can alternatively implement a 32-bit shift register or two 16-bit shift registers.

The low-level LUTs and other facilities provided by the several thousand logic slices represent the raw materials needed to assemble a complete RISC-V processor plus peripheral devices within a single FPGA. The FPGA programming process interconnects components within the FPGA to form a complex digital device defined in a hardware definition language.

From the perspective of the system designer, it is not necessary to understand the detailed inner workings of the Xilinx FPGA. The designer works at the hardware design language level. A tool such as Vivado, introduced in the solutions to the exercises in *Chapter 2, Digital Logic*, translates the hardware design language (typically, VHDL or Verilog, though the RISC-V design is implemented in the Chisel and Scala languages) into a compiled format suitable for programming an FPGA device.

The designer's primary concerns in regard to the FPGA are that the system design is capable of fitting within the resource constraints of the FPGA device and that the resulting implementation operates with acceptable efficiency. In this example, the XC7A35TICSG324-1L FPGA provides more than enough resources to implement the RISC-V processor efficiently.

To develop and run programs on the Arty A7-35T RISC-V processor, you also need a low-cost hardware debugger. The Olimex ARM-TINY-USB-H debugger is available for US$45.67 at `https://www.digikey.com/product-detail/en/olimex-ltd/ARM-USB-TINY-H/1188-1013-ND/3471388`. You will also need some jumper wires to connect the debugger to the Arty A7-35T board. These are available for US$3.95 at `https://www.adafruit.com/product/826`. Finally, the Arty A7-35T processor requires a **Universal Serial Bus (USB)** cable to connect its USB Micro-B connector to your host computer system. Other than your host computer system, no additional hardware is required. All of the software and design data required to implement the RISC-V in Arty is available for free download from the Internet.

The processor we will implement in the Arty A7-35T is the *Freedom E310 Arty*, an open source implementation of an RV32IMAC core with support for interrupt processing. Peripheral devices include 16 **general-purpose I/O (GPIO)** signals and a serial port.

The Freedom E310 processor is provided as source code, and is therefore modifiable by users who wish to implement customized versions of the processor. The hardware design languages used in the RISC-V processor hardware code are Chisel and Scala.

Chisel is a domain-specific language targeted to the development of complex digital hardware devices such as SoCs. Chisel runs on top of **Scala**, a modern, general-purpose programming language supporting the functional and object-oriented programming paradigms. Scala is a pure object-oriented language in which every value is an object. It is also a functional language in the sense that every function is a value. Scala compiles to Java bytecode and runs on the standard Java Virtual Machine. Scala programs can directly use any of the thousands of available Java libraries.

> **RISC-V support for customized extensions**
>
> The RISC-V architecture explicitly supports customized variations in the form of custom opcodes, coprocessors, and other modifications, so long as they are compatible with the RISC-V customization rules. Starting from the open source RISC-V design, you can implement custom modifications that will be guaranteed to remain compatible with future versions of RISC-V standards and extensions.

Chisel and Scala are preferred in the design of complex digital systems today because of the higher-level nature of these languages compared to traditional hardware design languages such as VHDL and Verilog. While it's true that any circuit you might design in Chisel can also be designed in VHDL, there are some substantial benefits to using Chisel. For example, the compilation process transforms the Chisel/Scala code into a form called **Flexible Intermediate Representation for RTL (FIRRTL)**, where **RTL** stands for **register-transfer level**, which is the abstraction level used in synchronous circuit hardware design languages such as VHDL. Using freely available tools, it is possible to perform optimizations on the FIRRTL representation of a circuit that result in a better-performing FPGA implementation than a comparable design in VHDL or Verilog would be likely to provide.

One way to appreciate the difference between Chisel and VHDL/Verilog is the analogous differentiation between the Python and C programming languages. While you can implement the functional equivalent of any Python program in C, Python programs can express far more high-level functionality in a few lines of code than a similar size program in C.

We can compare Chisel code to the VHDL example we looked at in the *Hardware description languages* section of *Chapter 2, Digital Logic*. Consider the VHDL version of the single-bit full adder presented in that chapter, shown in the following code block:

```
-- Load the standard libraries

library IEEE;
  use IEEE.STD_LOGIC_1164.ALL;

-- Define the full adder inputs and outputs

entity FULL_ADDER is
  port (
    A     : in    std_logic;
    B     : in    std_logic;
    C_IN  : in    std_logic;
    S     : out   std_logic;
    C_OUT : out   std_logic
  );
end entity FULL_ADDER;
```

```
-- Define the behavior of the full adder

architecture BEHAVIORAL of FULL_ADDER is

begin

  S     <= (A XOR B) XOR C_IN;
  C_OUT <= (A AND B) OR ((A XOR B) AND C_IN);

end architecture BEHAVIORAL;
```

The Chisel equivalent of the full adder is shown in the following code block:

```
import chisel3._

class FullAdder extends Module {
  val io = IO(new Bundle {
    val a     = Input(UInt(1.W))
    val b     = Input(UInt(1.W))
    val c_in  = Input(UInt(1.W))
    val s     = Output(UInt(1.W))
    val c_out = Output(UInt(1.W))
  })

  io.s := (io.a ^ io.b) ^ io.c_in
  io.c_out := (io.a & io.b) | ((io.a ^ io.b) & io.c_in)
}
```

In this code, the IO bundle defines the module inputs and outputs. The argument to each Input and Output parameter defines the data type (Uint) and the bit width (1.W, indicating each input and output signal is 1 bit wide).

While this simple example does not demonstrate the full range of benefits of developing complex circuits in Chisel, it shows that, at the level of detailed implementation, it does not look too different from VHDL. We won't delve further into the details of Chisel here. For further information, consult the Chisel repository at https://github.com/freechipsproject/chisel3.

The process of building the RISC-V processor and programming it into the Arty A7-35T board consists of the following steps:

1. Translate the Chisel and Scala code into the FIRRTL form.

2. Translate the FIRRTL into Verilog.

3. Compile the Verilog into an FPGA image.

4. Program the FPGA image onto the Arty A7-35T board.

The detailed commands to perform each of these steps are presented in the answers to the exercises at the end of this chapter.

Once you have programmed the RISC-V image onto the Arty board, it will be possible to connect a software development suite to the board through the debugger interface. From this point, you can develop RISC-V code in assembly language or in high-level languages, compile it, and run it on the FPGA RISC-V processor in the same manner as with a hardware processor.

Summary

This chapter introduced the RISC-V processor architecture and its instruction set. The RISC-V project has defined a complete user-mode instruction set specification and a number of extensions to support general-purpose computing, high-performance computing, and embedded applications requiring minimal code size. RISC-V processors are offered commercially, and open source products are available to implement instantiations of RISC-V in FPGA devices.

Having completed this chapter, you should understand the architecture and features of the RISC-V processor and its optional extensions. You learned the basics of the RISC-V instruction set and now understand how RISC-V can be tailored to target a variety of application domains, from low-end micropower embedded systems to warehouse-scale cloud server farms. You also learned how to implement a RISC-V processor in a low-cost FPGA board.

The next chapter introduces the concept of processor virtualization, where rather than running code directly on a host processor, an entire virtual environment is implemented to run perhaps several virtual processors, each with its own operating system and applications, on a single physical processor.

Exercises

1. Visit `https://www.sifive.com/boards/` and download *Freedom Studio*. Freedom Studio is an Eclipse **integrated development environment** (**IDE**)-based development suite with a complete set of tools for building a RISC-V application and running it on a hardware RISC-V processor or in the emulation environment included with Freedom Studio. Follow the instructions in the *Freedom Studio User Manual* to complete the installation. Start Freedom Studio and create a new Freedom E SDK project. In the project creation dialog, select `qemu-sifive-u54` as the target (this is a single-core 64-bit RISC-V processor in the RV64GC configuration). Select the `hello` example program and click the **Finish** button. This will start a build of the example program and the RISC-V emulator. After the build completes, the **Edit Configuration** dialog box will appear. Click **Debug** to start the program in the emulator debug environment. Single-step through the program and verify the text `Hello, World!` appears in the console window.

2. With the project from *Exercise 1* still open, locate the `hello.c` file in the `src` folder in the `Project` window. Right-click on the file and rename it `hello.s`. Open `hello.s` in the editor and delete the entire contents. Insert the assembly language program shown in the *RISC-V assembly language* section in this chapter. Perform a clean, and then rebuild the project (press *Ctrl+ 9* to initiate the clean operation). Select **Debug** under the **Run** menu. Once the debugger starts, open windows to display the `hello.s` source file, the `Disassembly` window, and the `Registers` window. Expand the `Registers` tree to display the RISC-V processor registers. Single-step through the program and verify the text `Hello, Computer Architect!` appears in the console window.

3. Write a RISC-V assembly language program that computes the following expression and prints the result as a hexadecimal number: $[(129 - 66) \times (445 + 136)] \div 3$. As part of this program, create a callable function to print 1 byte as two hex digits.

4. Program an Arty A7-35T board with a RISC-V processor image. Build and run the `hello` assembly language program shown in the *RISC-V assembly language* section in this chapter on the RISC-V processor using the Olimex ARM-TINY-USB-H debugger, as described in the *Implementing RISC-V in an FPGA* section near the end of this chapter. Verify the program outputs the text `Hello, Computer Architect!`.

Section 3: Applications of Computer Architecture

In this section, we will learn about the issues and trade-offs involved in the development of computer architectures intended to satisfy demanding user requirements across a variety of domains.

This section comprises the following chapters:

- *Chapter 12, Processor Virtualization*
- *Chapter 13, Domain-Specific Computer Architectures*
- *Chapter 14, Future Directions in Computer Architectures*

12
Processor Virtualization

This chapter introduces the concepts underlying processor virtualization and explores the many benefits to individual users and large organizations that are achievable through the effective use of virtualization. We will discuss the principal virtualization techniques and the open source and commercial tools that implement them.

Virtualization tools enable the emulation of instruction set–accurate representations of various computer architectures and operating systems on general-purpose computers. Virtualization is used widely in the deployment of real-world software applications in cloud environments.

After completing this chapter, you will understand the technology and benefits associated with hardware virtualization and how modern processors support virtualization at the instruction set level. You will have learned the technical features of several open source and commercial tools providing virtualization capabilities and will understand how virtualization is used to build and deploy scalable applications in cloud computing environments.

The following topics will be presented in this chapter:

- Introducing virtualization
- Virtualization challenges
- Virtualizing modern processors
- Virtualization tools
- Virtualization and cloud computing

Technical requirements

The files for this chapter, including the answers to the exercises, are available at `https://github.com/PacktPublishing/Modern-Computer-Architecture-and-Organization`.

Introducing virtualization

In the domain of computer architecture, **virtualization** refers to the use of hardware and software to create an emulated version of an environment in which a piece of software runs, as opposed to the *real* environment in which the code normally expects to run.

We have already looked at one form of virtualization in some depth: virtual memory. Virtual memory uses software, with supporting hardware, to create an environment in which each running application functions as if it has exclusive access to the entire computer, including all the memory it requires at the addresses it expects. Virtual address ranges used by a program can even be the same as those in use by other currently running processes.

Systems using virtual memory create multiple sandboxed environments in which each application runs without interference from other applications, except in competition for shared system resources. In the virtualization context, a **sandbox** is an isolated environment in which code runs without interference from anything outside its boundaries, and which prevents code inside the sandbox from affecting resources external to it. This isolation between applications is rarely absolute, however. For example, even though a process in a virtual memory system cannot access another process's memory, it may do something else, such as delete a file that is needed by a second process, which may cause problems for the other process.

Our primary focus in this chapter will be on virtualization at the processor level, allowing one or more operating systems to run in a virtualized environment on a computer system, abstracted from the physical layer of the hardware. Several other types of virtualization are also widely used.

The next section will briefly describe the various categories of virtualization you are likely to encounter.

Types of virtualization

The term *virtualization* is applied in several different computing contexts, especially in larger network environments, such as businesses, universities, government organizations, and cloud service providers. The definitions that follow here will cover the most common types of virtualization you are likely to come across.

Operating system virtualization

We will cover operating system virtualization in detail later in this chapter. A virtualized operating system runs under the control of a hypervisor. A **hypervisor** is a combination of software and hardware capable of instantiating and running virtual machines. The prefix *hyper* refers to the fact that the hypervisor supervises the supervisor mode of the operating systems running in its virtual machines. Another term for hypervisor is **virtual machine monitor**.

There are two general types of hypervisor:

- A **type 1 hypervisor**, sometimes referred to as a *bare metal* hypervisor, includes software for managing virtual machines that runs directly on the hardware of a host computer.

- A **type 2 hypervisor**, also called a *hosted* hypervisor, runs as an application program that manages virtual machines under a host operating system.

> **Hypervisor versus virtual machine monitor**
>
> Technically, a virtual machine monitor is not exactly the same as a hypervisor, but for our purposes, we will treat the terms as synonymous. A virtual machine monitor is responsible for virtualizing a processor and other computer system components. A hypervisor combines a virtual machine monitor with an underlying operating system, which may be dedicated to hosting virtual machines (a type 1 hypervisor), or it may be a general-purpose operating system (a type 2 hypervisor).

The computer running the hypervisor is referred to as the **host**. Operating systems running within hypervisor-managed virtual environments on a host system are called **guests**.

Regardless of its type, a hypervisor enables guest operating systems and applications running within them to be brought up and executed in virtualized environments. A single hypervisor is capable of supporting multiple virtual machines running on a single processor simultaneously. The hypervisor is responsible for managing all requests for privileged operations initiated by guest operating systems and the applications running within them. Each of these requests requires a transition from user mode to kernel mode, and then back to user mode. All I/O requests from applications on guest operating systems involve privilege level transitions.

Since operating system virtualization in a type 2 hypervisor involves running an operating system under the hypervisor in the host operating system, a natural question is, what happens if you run another copy of the hypervisor within the operating system of the virtual machine? The answer is that this approach is supported in some, but not all, combinations of hypervisor, host OS, and guest OS. This configuration is referred to as **nested virtualization**.

The next thing you might wonder about nested virtualization is why anyone would want to do such a thing. Here is one scenario where nested virtualization is useful: assume that your business's primary web presence is implemented as a virtualized operating system image containing a variety of installed and custom software components. If your cloud service provider goes offline for some reason, you will need to bring the application up at an alternative provider quickly.

The Google Compute Engine (`https://cloud.google.com/compute`), for example, provides an execution environment implemented as a virtual machine. Compute Engine allows you to install a hypervisor in this virtual machine and bring up your application virtual machine within it, putting your web presence back online with minimal installation and configuration.

Application virtualization

Instead of creating a virtual environment to encapsulate an entire operating system, it is possible to virtualize at the level of a single application. Application virtualization abstracts the operating system from the application code and provides a degree of sandboxing.

This type of virtualization allows programs to run in an environment that differs from the intended application target environment. For example, *Wine* (`https://www.winehq.org/`) is an application compatibility layer allowing programs written for Microsoft Windows to run under POSIX-compliant operating systems, typically Linux variants. The **Portable Operating System Interface** (**POSIX**) is a set of IEEE standards providing application programming compatibility between operating systems. Wine translates Windows library and system calls to equivalent POSIX calls in an efficient manner.

Application virtualization replaces portions of the runtime environment with a virtualization layer and performs tasks such as intercepting disk I/O calls and redirecting them to a sandboxed, virtualized disk environment. Application virtualization can encapsulate a complex software installation process, consisting of hundreds of files installed in various directories, as well as numerous Windows registry modifications, in an equivalent virtualized environment contained within a single executable file. Simply copying the executable to a target system and running it brings up the application as if the entire installation process had taken place on the target.

Network virtualization

Network virtualization is the connection of software-based emulations of network components, such as switches, routers, firewalls, and telecommunication networks, in a manner that represents a physical configuration of these components. This allows operating systems and the applications running on them to interact with and communicate over the virtual network in the same manner they would on a physical implementation of the same network architecture.

A single physical network can be subdivided into multiple **virtual local area networks** (**VLANs**), each of which appears to be a complete, isolated network to all systems connected on the same VLAN.

Multiple computer systems at the same physical location can be connected to different VLANs, effectively placing them on separate networks. Conversely, computers at distant geographic separations can be placed on the same VLAN, making it appear as if they are interconnected within a small local network.

Storage virtualization

Storage virtualization is the separation of physical data storage from the logical storage structure used by operating systems and applications. A storage virtualization system manages the process of translating logical data requests to physical data transfers. Logical data requests are addressed as block locations within a disk partition. Following the logical-to-physical translation, data transfers may ultimately interact with a storage device that has an organization completely different from the logical disk partition.

The process of accessing physical data given a logical address is similar to the virtual-to-physical address translation process in virtual memory systems. The logical disk I/O request includes information such as a device identifier and a logical block number. This request must be translated to a physical device identifier and block number. The requested read or write operation then takes place on the physical disk.

Storage virtualization in data centers often includes several enhancements that increase the reliability and performance of data storage systems. Some of these improvements are as follows:

- *Centralized management* enables monitoring and control of a large collection of storage devices, possibly of different sizes, and from different vendors. Because all virtualized storage appears the same to client applications, any vendor-specific variations in storage devices are hidden from users.

- *Replication* provides transparent data backup and disaster recovery capabilities for mission-critical data. When performing real-time replication, writes to the storage array are immediately copied to one or more remote replicas.

- *Data migration* allows administrators to move data to a different physical location or switch to a replica while concurrent data I/O operations continue without interruption. Because the storage virtualization management system has full control over disk I/O, it can switch the target of any logical read or write operation to a different physical storage device at any time.

The next section will introduce some of the most common methods of processor virtualization in use today.

Categories of processor virtualization

The ideal mode of operation for a processor virtualization environment is **full virtualization**. With full virtualization, binary code in operating systems and applications runs in the virtual environment with no modifications whatsoever. Guest operating system code performing privileged operations executes under the illusion that it has complete and sole access to all machine resources and interfaces. The hypervisor manages interactions between guest operating systems and host resources, and takes any steps needed to deconflict access to I/O devices and other system resources for each virtual machine under its control.

Our focus in this chapter is processor virtualization, enabling the execution of complete operating systems and applications running on them in a virtualized environment.

Historically, there have been several different methods used for the implementation of virtualization at the processor level. We'll take a brief look at each of them, beginning with an approach first implemented on systems such as the IBM VM/370, introduced in 1972. VM/370 was the first operating system specifically designed to support the execution of virtual machines.

Trap-and-emulate virtualization

In a 1974 article entitled *Formal Requirements for Virtualizable Third Generation Architectures*, Gerald J. Popek and Robert P. Goldberg described the three properties a hypervisor must implement to efficiently and fully virtualize a computer system, including the processor, memory, storage, and peripheral devices:

- **Equivalence**: Programs (including the guest operating system) running in a hypervisor must exhibit essentially the same behavior as when they run directly on machine hardware, excluding the effects of timing.

- **Resource control:** The hypervisor must have complete control over all of the resources used by the virtual machine.

- **Efficiency**: A high percentage of instructions executed by the virtual machine must run directly on the physical processor, without hypervisor intervention.

For a hypervisor to satisfy these criteria, the hardware and operating system of the computer on which it is running must grant the hypervisor the power to fully control the virtual machines it manages.

The code within a guest operating system assumes it is running directly on the physical processor hardware and has full control of all the features accessible via system hardware. In particular, guest operating system code executing at the kernel privilege level must be able to execute privileged instructions and access regions of memory reserved for the operating system.

In a hypervisor implementing the trap-and-emulate virtualization method, portions of the hypervisor run with kernel privilege, while all guest operating systems (and, of course, the applications running within them) operate at the user privilege level. Kernel code within the guest operating systems executes normally until a privileged instruction attempts to execute or a memory-access instruction attempts to read or write memory outside the user-space address range available to the guest operating system. When the guest attempts any of these operations, a trap occurs.

Exception types: faults, traps, and aborts

The terms *fault*, *trap*, and *abort* are used to describe similar exception events. The primary differences between each of these exception types are as follows:

A fault is an exception that ends by restarting the instruction that caused the exception. For example, a page fault occurs when a program attempts to access a valid memory location that is currently inaccessible. After the page fault handler completes, the triggering instruction is restarted, and execution continues from that point.

A trap is an exception that ends by continuing the execution with the instruction following the triggering instruction. For example, execution resumes after the exception triggered by a debugger breakpoint by continuing with the next instruction.

An abort represents a serious error condition that may be unrecoverable. Problems such as errors accessing memory may cause aborts.

The fundamental trick (if you want to think of it that way) to enable trap-and-emulate virtualization is in the handling of the exceptions generated by privilege violations. While it is starting up, the hypervisor routes the host operating system exception handlers into its own code. Exception handlers within the hypervisor perform the processing of these exceptions before the host operating system has a chance to handle them.

The hypervisor exception handler examines the source of each exception to determine if it was generated by a guest operating system under the hypervisor's control. If the exception originated from a guest the hypervisor manages, the hypervisor handles the exception, emulating the requested operation, and returns execution control directly to the guest. If the exception did not come from a guest belonging to the hypervisor, the hypervisor passes the exception to the host operating system for processing in the normal manner.

For trap-and-emulate virtualization to work in a comprehensive and reliable manner, the host processor must support the criteria defined by Popek and Goldberg. The most critical of these requirements is that any guest instruction attempting to access privileged resources must generate a trap. This is absolutely necessary because the host system has only one set of privileged resources (we're assuming a single-core system here for simplicity) and the host and guest operating systems cannot share those resources.

As an example of the types of privileged information controlled by the hypervisor, consider the page tables used to manage virtual memory. The host operating system maintains a collection of page tables that oversee the entirety of the system's physical memory. Each guest operating system has its own set of page tables that it believes it is using to manage physical and virtual memory on the system it controls. These two sets of page tables contain substantially different data, even though both of them ultimately interact with the same physical memory regions. Through the trapping mechanism, the hypervisor is able to intercept all guest operating system attempts to interact with page tables and direct those interactions to a guest-specific memory region containing page tables used only by the guest operating system. The hypervisor then manages the necessary translation between addresses used by instructions executing in the guest operating system and the host system's physical memory.

The greatest barrier to the widespread use of virtualization in the late 1990s and early 2000s was the fact that the general-purpose processors in common use at the time (x86 variants) did not support the Popek and Goldberg virtualization criteria. The x86 instruction sets contained a number of instructions that allowed unprivileged code to interact with privileged data without generating a trap. Many of these instructions merely permitted unprivileged code to read selected privileged registers. While this may seem harmless, it caused a severe problem for virtualization because there is only one copy of each of those registers in the entire machine, and each guest OS may need to maintain different values in those registers.

Later versions of the x86, beginning in 2006, added hardware features (**Intel virtualization technology** (**VT-x**), and **AMD virtualization** (**AMD-V**)) enabling full virtualization under the Popek and Goldberg criteria.

The virtualization requirements defined by Popek and Goldberg assumed the use of the trap-and-emulate technique, which was widely viewed as the only practical virtualization method in the 1970s, was the only feasible method for processor virtualization. In the following sections, we will see how it is possible to perform effective and efficient virtualization on a computer system that does not fully comply with the Popek and Goldberg criteria.

Paravirtualization

Because most, if not all, of the instructions that require special handling in the virtualized environment reside in the guest operating system and its device drivers, one method for rendering the guest virtualizable is to modify the operating system and its drivers to explicitly interface with the hypervisor in a non-trapping manner. This approach can result in substantially better guest OS performance than a system running under a trap-and-emulate hypervisor because the paravirtualized hypervisor interface is composed of optimized code rather than a series of trap handler invocations. In the trap-and-emulate method, the hypervisor must process every trap in a generic handler that begins by determining whether the trap even comes from a guest OS it controls before further processing to determine the desired operation and emulate its effects.

The primary drawback of paravirtualization is the need to modify the guest operating system and its drivers to implement the hypervisor interface. There has been limited interest in fully supporting a paravirtualization interface among the maintainers of major operating system distributions.

Binary translation

One way to deal with problematic instructions within processor architectures that lack full support for virtualization is to scan the binary code prior to execution to detect the presence of nonvirtualizable instructions. Where such instructions are found, the code is translated into virtualization-friendly instructions that produce identical effects.

This has proven to be a popular approach for virtualization in the x86 architecture. The combination of trap-and-emulate with the binary translation of nonvirtualizable instructions permits reasonable guest OS performance. This technique keeps the amount of processing required to deal with nonvirtualizable instructions to a reasonable level.

Binary translation can be performed on a static or dynamic basis. Static binary translation recompiles a set of executable images into a form ready for execution in the virtual environment. This translation takes some time, but it is a one-time process providing a set of system and user images that will continue to work until new image versions are installed, necessitating a recompilation procedure for the new images.

Dynamic binary translation scans sections of code during program execution to locate problematic instructions. When such instructions are encountered, they are replaced with virtualizable instruction sequences. Dynamic binary translation avoids the recompilation step required by static binary translation, but it results in reduced performance due to the ongoing code scanning and translation process for all running code. Each code segment only needs to be scanned and translated once and is then cached—so, for example, code within a loop will not be rescanned on each iteration.

Hardware emulation

All of the virtualization techniques that we have discussed to this point have assumed the guest OS is expecting to run on a processor with the same instruction set architecture as the host processor. There are many situations in which it is desirable to run an operating system and application code on a host processor with a completely different ISA from the guest OS.

When emulating processor hardware, each instruction executing in an emulated guest system must be translated to an equivalent instruction or sequence of instructions in the host ISA. As with binary translation, this process can take place in a static or dynamic manner.

Static translation can produce an efficient executable image capable of running in the target processor ISA. There is some risk in static translation because it may not be straightforward to identify all code paths in the executable file, particularly if branch target addresses are computed in the code rather than being statically defined. This risk also applies to the static binary translation technique described in the previous section.

Dynamic translation avoids potential errors that may occur with static translation, but performance can be quite poor. This is because dynamic translation with hardware emulation involves translating every instruction from one architecture to another. This is in contrast to dynamic binary translation for the same ISA, which, although it must scan every instruction, typically only needs to perform translation for a small percentage of executed instructions.

One example of hardware emulation tools is the open source QEMU (`https://www.qemu.org/`) machine emulator and virtualizer, which supports the running of operating systems for a wide variety of processor architectures on an impressive list of differing architectures, with reasonably good performance. The Freedom Studio tool suite for the RISC-V processor includes a QEMU implementation of the RV64GC instruction set architecture. This virtualized environment was used to run the code that we worked with in the exercises for *Chapter 11, The RISC-V Architecture and Instruction Set*.

In the next section, we will discuss the challenges and benefits related to virtualization in the processor families discussed in the preceding chapters.

Virtualization challenges

In simple terms, the goal of processor virtualization is to run an operating system within a hypervisor, which itself either runs on the bare metal of a computer system or runs as an application under the control of another operating system. In this section, we will focus on the hosted (type 2) hypervisor because this mode of operation presents a few added challenges that a bare-metal hypervisor may not face because the type 1 hypervisor has been optimized to support virtualization.

In a type 2 hypervisor, the host operating system supports kernel and user modes, as does the guest operating system (in the guest's perception). As the guest operating system and the applications running within it request system services, the hypervisor must intercept each request and translate it into a suitable call to the host kernel.

In a nonvirtualized system, peripheral devices, such as the keyboard and mouse, interact directly with the host operating system. In a virtualized environment, the hypervisor must manage the interfaces to these devices whenever the user requests interaction with the guest OS.

The degree of difficulty involved in implementing these capabilities depends on the instruction set of the host computer. Even if an instruction set was not designed to facilitate virtualization, it may or may not be possible for that architecture to support virtualization in a straightforward manner. The ease of virtualization on a particular processor ISA is a function of the manner in which the processor handles unsafe instructions.

Unsafe instructions

The name of the trap-and-emulate virtualization method refers to the ability of the hypervisor to take control of processing exceptions that would normally be dealt with by kernel mode handlers in the host operating system. This allows the hypervisor to process privilege violations and system calls from guest operating systems and the applications that run within them.

Each time an application running on a guest operating system requests a system function, such as opening a file, the hypervisor intercepts the request, adjusts the parameters of the request to align with the virtual machine configuration (perhaps by redirecting the file open request from the host filesystem to the guest's virtual disk sandbox), and passes the request on to the host operating system. The process of inspecting and performing the handling of exceptions by the hypervisor is the emulation phase of the trap-and-emulate approach.

In the context of virtualization, processor instructions that either rely on or modify privileged system state information are referred to as **unsafe**. For the trap-and-emulate method to function in a comprehensively secure and reliable manner, all unsafe instructions must generate exceptions that trap to the hypervisor. If an unsafe instruction is allowed to execute without trapping, the isolation of the virtual machine is compromised and virtualization may fail.

Shadow page tables

Protected data structures used in the allocation and management of virtual and physical memory present an additional challenge to full virtualization. A guest operating system kernel presumes it has full access to the hardware and data structures associated with the system MMU. The hypervisor must translate guest operating system requests for memory allocation and deallocation in a manner that is functionally equivalent to running the guest OS on bare metal.

A particular problem arises in the x86 architecture due to the fact that virtual memory page table configuration data must be stored within the processor to properly configure the system, but that information becomes inaccessible once it has been stored. To resolve this issue, the hypervisor maintains its own copy of the page table configuration data, referred to as **shadow page tables**. Because the shadow page tables are not actual page tables managing memory for the host OS, it is necessary for the hypervisor to set access permission restrictions on shadow page table memory regions and intercept the resulting traps when the guest OS attempts to access its page tables. The hypervisor then emulates the requested operation by interacting with the physical MMU through calls to the host OS.

The use of shadow page tables incurs a significant performance penalty and has been an area of focus for the development of hardware-assisted virtualization enhancements.

Security

There is nothing inherently insecure about using a hypervisor to virtualize one or more guest applications. It is, however, important to understand the added opportunities for malicious actors to attempt to infiltrate a virtualized environment.

A guest virtual machine presents essentially the same collection of vulnerabilities to remote attackers as an identical operating system and set of applications running directly on hardware. The hypervisor provides an additional avenue that an attacker may attempt to exploit in a virtualized environment. If malicious users manage to penetrate and take control of the hypervisor, this will grant full access to all of the guest operating systems, as well as the applications and data accessible from within the guests. The guests are accessible in this scenario because they operate at a lower privilege level granting the hypervisor full control over them.

When implementing virtualization in a context that permits public access, such as web hosting, it is vital that credentials enabling login to hypervisors, and any other access methods, be strictly limited to a small number of personnel, and all reasonable protective measures must be maintained to prevent unauthorized hypervisor access.

In the next section, we will examine some key technical aspects of virtualization as implemented in modern processor families.

Virtualizing modern processors

The hardware architectures of most general-purpose processor families have matured to the point that they fully support the execution of virtualized guest operating systems, at least in their higher-end variants. The following sections briefly introduce the virtualization capabilities provided by modern general-purpose processor families.

x86 processor virtualization

The x86 architecture was not originally designed to support the execution of virtualized operating systems. As a result, x86 processors, from the earliest days through to the Pentium series, implemented instruction sets containing several unsafe but non-trapping instructions. These instructions caused problems with virtualization by, for example, allowing the guest operating system to access privileged registers that do not contain data corresponding to the state of the virtual machine.

> **x86 current privilege level and unsafe instructions**
>
> In the x86 architecture, the lower two bits of the **code segment** (**CS**) register contain the **current privilege level** (**CPL**), identifying the currently active protection ring. The CPL is generally 0 for kernel code and 3 for user applications in a nonvirtualized operating system. In most hypervisor implementations, virtual machines run at CPL 3, causing many unsafe x86 instructions to trap upon execution. Unfortunately, for the early adopters of x86 virtualization, not all unsafe x86 instructions in Pentium processors caused traps when executed at CPL 3.

For example, the `sidt` instruction permits unprivileged code to read the 6-byte **interrupt descriptor table register** (**IDTR**) and store it at a location provided as an operand. There is only one IDTR in a physical single-core x86 processor. When a guest operating system executes this instruction, the IDTR contains data associated with the host operating system, which differs from the information the guest operating system expects to retrieve. This will result in erroneous execution of the guest operating system.

Writing to the physical system's IDTR is only possible for code running at CPL 0. When a guest operating system attempts to write to the IDTR while running at CPL 3, a privilege violation occurs and the hypervisor processes the ensuing trap to emulate the write operation by writing to a shadow register instead, which is just a location in memory allocated by the hypervisor. Reads from the IDTR, however, are permitted at CPL 3. User-mode software can read the IDTR and no trap occurs. Without a trap, the hypervisor is unable to intercept the read operation and return data from the shadow register. In short, writes to the IDTR are virtualizable, while reads from the IDTR are not.

Of the hundreds of instructions in the Pentium ISA, 17 were found to be unsafe but non-trapping. In other words, these instructions are nonvirtualizable. For the Pentium x86 architecture, implementing a pure trap-and-emulate virtualization approach is therefore not possible.

The unsafe, but non-trapping, instructions are used frequently in operating systems and device drivers, but are rarely found in application code. The hypervisor must implement a mechanism to detect the presence of unsafe, non-trapping instructions in the code and handle them.

The approach settled on by several popular virtualization engines has been to combine trap-and-emulate virtualization, where possible, with the binary translation of unsafe instructions into functionally equivalent code sequences suitable for the virtualized environment.

Most guest user applications do not attempt to use unsafe instructions at all. This allows them to run at full speed, once the hypervisor has scanned the code to ensure no unsafe instructions are present. Guest kernel code, however, may contain numerous, frequently encountered unsafe instructions. To achieve reasonable performance from binary-translated code, it is necessary to cache the modified code the first time it executes and reuse the cached version on future execution passes.

x86 hardware virtualization

Between 2005 and 2006, Intel and AMD released versions of the x86 processors containing hardware extensions supporting virtualization. These extensions resolved the problems caused by the privileged but non-trapping instructions, enabling full system virtualization under the Popek and Goldberg criteria. The extensions were named AMD-V in AMD processors and VT-x in Intel processors. The virtualization extensions in modern Intel processors are referred to as VT.

The initial implementations of these hardware virtualization technologies removed the requirements for the binary translation of unsafe instructions, but overall virtual machine performance did not improve substantially following the removal of binary translation. This was because page table shadowing was still needed. Page table shadowing had been the cause of most of the performance degradation observed during virtual machine execution.

Later versions of hardware virtualization technology removed many of the performance barriers in virtual machine execution, leading to the widespread adoption of x86 virtualization across a variety of domains. Today, multiple tools and frameworks are available for implementing x86 virtualization solutions within a standalone workstation, with options available to scale up to a fully managed data center with potentially thousands of servers, each capable of running several virtual machines simultaneously.

ARM processor virtualization

The ARMv8-A architecture supports virtualization in both the 32-bit and 64-bit (AArch64) execution states. Hardware support for virtualization includes the following:

- Full trap-and-emulate virtualization
- A dedicated exception category for hypervisor use
- Additional registers supporting hypervisor exceptions and stack pointers

The ARMv8-A architecture provides hardware support for the translation of guest memory access requests to physical system addresses.

Systems running ARM processors offer a comprehensive capability for virtual machine execution using either a type 1 or type 2 hypervisor. 64-bit ARM processor performance is comparable to x64 servers with similar specifications. For many applications, such as large data center deployments, the choice between x64 and ARM as the server processor may revolve around factors unrelated to processor performance, such as system power consumption and cooling requirements.

RISC-V processor virtualization

Unlike the other ISAs discussed in this chapter, the architects of the RISC-V ISA included comprehensive virtualization support as a baseline requirement from the beginning of the ISA design. Although not yet a finalized standard, the proposal for the RISC-V hypervisor extension provides a full set of capabilities to support the efficient implementation of type 1 and type 2 hypervisors.

The RISC-V hypervisor extension fully implements the trap-and-emulate virtualization method and provides hardware support for the translation of guest operating system physical addresses to host physical addresses. RISC-V implements the concept of foreground and background control and status registers, which allows the rapid swapping of supervisor registers in and out of operation as virtual machines transition into and out of the running state.

Each hardware thread in RISC-V runs at one of three privilege levels:

- **User (U)**: This is the same as user privilege in a traditional operating system.

- **Supervisor (S)**: This is the same as supervisor or kernel mode in a traditional operating system.

- **Machine(M)**: The highest privilege level, with access to all system features.

Individual processor designs may implement all three of these modes, or they may implement the M and S mode pair, or M mode alone. Other combinations are not allowed.

In a RISC-V processor supporting the hypervisor extension, an additional configuration bit, the **V bit**, controls the virtualization mode. The V bit is set to 1 for hardware threads executing in a virtualized guest. Both the user and supervisor privilege levels can execute with the V bit set to 1. These are named the **virtual user (VU)** and **virtual supervisor (VS)** modes. In the RISC-V hypervisor context, supervisor mode with V = 0 is renamed the **hypervisor-extended supervisor mode (HS)**. This name indicates HS is the mode in which the hypervisor itself, regardless of whether it is type 1 or type 2, runs. The remaining privilege level, M mode, only functions in a non-virtualized manner (with V = 0).

In both VU and VS modes, RISC-V implements a two-level address translation scheme that converts each guest virtual address first to a guest physical address and then to a supervisor physical address. This procedure efficiently performs the translation from virtual addresses in applications running in guest operating systems to physical addresses in system memory.

The next section provides overviews of a number of popular tools that are available for processor and operating system virtualization.

Virtualization tools

In this section, we will look at several widely available open source and commercial tools that implement different forms of processor virtualization. This information may be useful as a starting point when initiating a project involving virtualization.

VirtualBox

VirtualBox is a free, open source type 2 hypervisor from Oracle Corporation. Supported host operating systems include Windows and several Linux variants. One or more guest operating systems on a single host can simultaneously run Windows and a variety of Linux distributions.

> **Guest OS licensing requirements**
>
> For organizations and individuals to remain in compliance with copyright laws, operating systems requiring licensing, such as Windows, must be properly licensed even when running as guest operating systems.

Individual virtual machines can be started, stopped, and paused under the control of the interactive VirtualBox management program or from the command line. VirtualBox has the ability to capture snapshots of executing virtual machines and save them to disk. At a later time, a snapshot can resume execution from the precise point at which it was taken.

VirtualBox requires hardware-assisted virtualization provided by platforms with the AMD-V or Intel VT extensions. A number of mechanisms are provided enabling virtual machines to communicate with the host OS and with each other. A shared clipboard supports copy-and-paste between host and guest machines or from guest to guest. An internal network can be configured within VirtualBox that allows guests to interact with each other as if they were connected on an isolated local area network.

VMware Workstation

VMware Workstation, first released in 1999, is a type 2 hypervisor that runs on 64-bit versions of Windows and Linux. VMware products are offered commercially and require the purchase of licenses by some users. A version of Workstation called VMware Workstation Player is available at no cost with the provision that it can only be used for non-commercial purposes.

VMware Workstation supports the execution of potentially multiple copies of Windows and Linux operating systems within the host Linux or Windows operating system. Like VirtualBox, Workstation can capture snapshots of the virtual machine state, save that information to disk, and later resume execution from the captured state. Workstation also supports host-to-guest and guest-to-guest communication features, such as a shared clipboard and local network emulation.

VMware ESXi

ESXi is a type 1 hypervisor intended for enterprise-class deployments in data centers and cloud server farms. As a type 1 hypervisor, ESXi runs on the bare metal of the host computer system. It has interfaces with the computer system hardware, each guest operating system, and a management interface called the service console.

From the service console, administrators can oversee and manage the operation of a large-scale data center, bringing up virtual machines and assigning them tasks (referred to as **workloads**). ESXi provides additional features necessary for large-scale deployments, such as performance monitoring and fault detection. In the event of hardware failure or to enable system maintenance, virtual machine workloads can be transitioned seamlessly to different host computers.

KVM

The **kernel-based virtual machine** (**KVM**) is an open source type 2 hypervisor initially released in 2007. KVM supports full virtualization for guest operating systems. When used with x86 or x64 hosts, the system hardware must include the AMD-V or Intel VT virtualization extensions. The KVM hypervisor kernel is included in the main Linux development line.

KVM supports the execution of one or more virtualized instances of Linux and Windows on a host system without any modification of the guest operating systems.

Although originally developed for the 32-bit x86 architecture, KVM has been ported to x64, ARM, and PowerPC. KVM supports paravirtualization for Linux and Windows guests using the VirtIO API. In this mode, paravirtualized device drivers are provided for Ethernet, disk I/O, and the graphics display.

Xen

Xen, first released in 2003, is a free and open source type 1 hypervisor. The current version of Xen runs on x86, x64, and ARM processors. Xen supports guest virtual machines running under hardware-supported virtualization (AMD-V or Intel VT) or as paravirtualized operating systems. Xen is implemented in the mainline Linux kernel.

The Xen hypervisor runs one virtual machine at the most privileged level, referred to as domain 0, or dom0. The dom0 virtual machine is typically a Linux variant and has full access to the system hardware. The dom0 machine provides the user interface for managing the hypervisor.

Some of the largest commercial cloud service providers, including Amazon EC2, IBM SoftLayer, and Rackspace Cloud, use Xen as their primary hypervisor platform.

Xen supports live migration, where a virtual machine can be migrated from one host platform to another without downtime.

QEMU

QEMU, an abbreviation for **quick emulator**, is a free and open source emulator that performs hardware virtualization. QEMU can emulate at the level of a single application or an entire computer system. At the application level, QEMU can run individual Linux or macOS applications that were built for a different ISA than the execution environment.

When performing system emulation, QEMU represents a complete computer system, including peripherals. The guest system can use an ISA that differs from the host system. QEMU supports the execution of multiple guest operating systems on a single host simultaneously. Supported ISAs include x86, MIPS, ARMv7, ARMv8, PowerPC, and RISC-V.

QEMU supports the setup and migration of KVM machines, performing hardware emulation in conjunction with the virtual machine running under KVM. Similarly, QEMU can provide hardware emulation for virtual machines running under Xen.

QEMU is unique among virtualization tools in that it is not necessary for it to run at elevated privilege because it entirely emulates the guest system in software. The downside of this approach is the performance degradation resulting from the software emulation process.

The next section will discuss the synergistic effects resulting from implementing cloud computing using virtualization.

Virtualization and cloud computing

The terms *virtualization* and *cloud computing* are often tossed about with vague, sometimes overlapping meanings. Here is an attempt to highlight the difference between them:

- Virtualization is a technology for abstracting software systems from the environment in which they operate.

- Cloud computing is a methodology for employing virtualization and other technologies to enable the deployment, monitoring, and control of large-scale data centers.

The use of virtualization in cloud computing environments enables the flexible deployment of application workloads across an array of generic computing hardware in a controlled, coherent manner. By implementing applications such as web servers within virtual machines, it is possible to dynamically scale online computing capacity to match varying load conditions.

Commercial cloud service providers generally offer the use of their systems on a pay-per-capacity-used basis. A website that normally receives a fairly small amount of traffic may spike substantially if, for instance, it receives a mention on a national news program. If the site is deployed in a scalable cloud environment, the management software will detect the increased load and bring up additional instances of the website and potentially of the backend database as well. This increased resource usage will result in a larger bill from the cloud service provider, which most businesses will happily pay if the result is a website that remains operational and responsive to user input even under a heavy traffic load.

Cloud management environments, such as VMware ESXi and Xen, provide comprehensive tools for the configuration, deployment, management, and maintenance of large-scale cloud operations. These configurations may be intended for local use by an organization, or they may offer public-facing facilities for online service providers such as Amazon Web Services.

Electrical power consumption

Electrical power consumption is a significant expense for cloud service providers. Each computer in a large-scale server farm consumes power whenever it is running, even if it is not performing any useful work. In a facility containing thousands of computers, it is important to the bottom line that servers consume power only when needed by paying customers.

Virtualization helps substantially with the effective utilization of server systems. Since a single server can potentially host several guest virtual machines, customer workloads can be allocated efficiently across server hardware in a manner that avoids low utilization of a large number of computers. Servers that are not needed at a given time can be powered off completely, thereby reducing energy consumption, which, in turn reduces costs to the cloud provider and enables more competitive pricing for end users.

This section has provided a brief introduction to the use of virtualization in the context of cloud computing. Most organizations and individuals that establish a presence on the Internet make use of virtual servers in a cloud computing environment, whether they know it or not.

Summary

This chapter presented the concepts underlying processor virtualization and explained the many benefits to individual users and large organizations achieved through the effective use of virtualization. We examined the principal virtualization techniques and the open source and commercial tools that implement them.

We also saw the benefits of virtualization in the deployment of real-world software applications in cloud environments .

You should now understand the technology and benefits associated with processor virtualization and how modern processor ISAs support virtualization at the instruction set level. We learned about several open source and commercial tools providing virtualization capabilities. You should now understand how virtualization can be used to build and deploy scalable applications in cloud computing environments.

In the next chapter, we will look at the architecture of some specific application categories, including mobile devices, personal computers, gaming systems, systems that process big data, and neural networks.

Exercises

1. Download and install the current version of VirtualBox. Download, install, and bring up Ubuntu Linux as a virtual machine within VirtualBox. Connect the guest OS to the Internet using a bridged network adapter. Configure and enable clipboard sharing and file sharing between the Ubuntu guest and your host operating system.

2. Within the Ubuntu operating system you installed in *Exercise 1*, install VirtualBox and then install and bring up a virtual machine version of FreeDOS, available from `https://www.freedos.org/download/`. Verify that DOS commands, such as `echo Hello World!` and `mem`, perform properly in the FreeDOS virtual machine. After completing this exercise, you will have implemented an instance of nested virtualization.

3. Create two separate copies of your Ubuntu guest machine in your host system's VirtualBox environment. Configure both Ubuntu guests to connect to the VirtualBox *internal* network. Set up the two machines with compatible Internet Protocol addresses. Verify each of the machines can receive a response from the other using the `ping` command. By completing this exercise, you will have configured a virtual network within your virtualized environment.

13
Domain-Specific Computer Architectures

This chapter brings together the topics discussed in previous chapters to develop an approach for architecting a computer system designed to meet unique user requirements. We will build upon this approach to gain an understanding of the user-level requirements and performance capabilities associated with several different categories of real-world computer systems.

This chapter will cover the following topics:

- Architecting computer systems to meet unique requirements
- Smartphone architecture
- Personal computer architecture
- Warehouse-scale computing architecture
- Neural networks and machine learning architectures

Technical requirements

The files for this chapter, including answers to the exercises, are available at `https://github.com/PacktPublishing/Modern-Computer-Architecture-and-Organization`.

Architecting computer systems to meet unique requirements

Every device containing a digital processor is designed to perform a particular function or collection of functions. This applies even to general-purpose devices, such as personal computers. A comprehensive list of the required and desired features and capabilities for a device provides the raw information needed to begin designing the architecture of its digital components.

The list that follows identifies some of the considerations a computer architect must weigh in the process of organizing the design of a digital system:

- **The types of processing required**: Does the device need to process audio, video, or other analog information? Is a high-resolution graphics display included in the design? Will extensive floating-point or decimal mathematics be required? Will the system support multiple, simultaneously running applications? Are special algorithms, such as neural network processing, going to be used?

- **Memory and storage requirements**: How much RAM will the operating system and anticipated user applications need to perform as intended? How much non-volatile storage will be required?

- **Hard or soft real-time processing**: Is a real-time response to inputs within a time limit mandatory? If real-time performance is not absolutely required, are there desired response times that must be met most, but not necessarily all, of the time?

- **Connectivity requirements**: What kinds of wired connections, such as Ethernet and USB, does the device need to support? How many physical ports for each type of connection are required? What types of wireless connections (cellular network, Wi-Fi, Bluetooth, NFC, GPS, and so on) are needed?

- **Power consumption**: Is the device battery-powered? If it is, what is the tolerable level of power consumption for digital system components during periods of high usage, as well as during idle periods? If the system runs on externally provided power, is it more important for it to have high processing performance or low power consumption? For both battery-powered systems and externally powered systems, what are the limits of power dissipation before overheating becomes an issue?

- **Physical constraints**: Are there tight physical constraints on the size of the digital processing components?

- **Environmental limits**: Is the device intended to operate in very hot or cold environments? What level of shock and vibration must the device be able to withstand? Does the device need to operate in extremely humid or dry atmospheric conditions?

The following sections examine the top-level architectures of several categories of digital devices and discuss the answers the architects of those systems arrived at in response to questions similar to those in the preceding list. We'll begin with mobile device architecture, looking specifically at the iPhone X.

Smartphone architecture

At the architectural level, there are three key features a smartphone must provide to gain wide acceptance: small size (except for the display), long battery life, and very high processing performance upon demand. Obviously, the requirements for long battery life and high processing power are in conflict and must be balanced to achieve an optimal design.

The requirement for small size is generally approached by starting with a screen size (in terms of height and width) large enough to render high-quality video and function as a user-input device (especially as a keyboard), yet small enough to easily be carried in a pocket or purse. To keep the overall device size small in terms of total volume, we need to make it as thin as possible.

In the quest for thinness, the mechanical design must provide sufficient structural strength to support the screen and resist damage from routine handling, drops on the floor, and other physical assaults, while simultaneously providing adequate space for batteries, digital components, and subsystems such as the cellular radio transceiver.

Because users are going to have unrestricted physical access to the external and internal features of their phones, any trade secrets or other intellectual property, such as system firmware, that the manufacturer wishes to prevent from being disclosed must be protected from all types of extraction. Yet, even with these protections in place, it must also be straightforward for end users to securely install firmware updates while preventing the installation of unauthorized firmware images.

We will examine the digital architecture of the iPhone X in the light of these requirements in the next section.

iPhone X

The iPhone X, also called the iPhone 10, was released in 2017 and discontinued in 2018. The iPhone X was Apple's flagship smartphone at the time and contained some of the most advanced technologies on the market. Since Apple releases only limited information on the design details of its products, some of the following information comes from teardowns and other types of analysis by iPhone X reviewers and should therefore be taken with a grain of salt.

The computational architecture of the iPhone X is centered on the Apple A11 Bionic SoC, an ARMv8-A six-core processor constructed with 4.3 billion CMOS transistors. Two of the cores, with an architecture code-named **Monsoon**, are optimized for high performance and support a maximum clock speed of 2.39 GHz. The remaining four cores, code-named **Mistral**, are designed for energy-efficient operation at up to 1.42 GHz. All six cores are out-of-order superscalar designs. The Monsoon cores can decode up to seven instructions simultaneously, while the Mistral cores can decode up to three instructions at a time. When executing multiple processes or multiple threads within a single process concurrently, it is possible for all six cores to run in parallel.

Of course, running all six cores simultaneously creates a significant drain on the batteries. Most of the time, especially when the user is not interacting with the device, several of the cores are placed in low-power modes to maximize battery life.

The iPhone X contains 3 GB of fourth-generation **low power double data rate RAM (LP-DDR4x)**. Each LP-DDR4x device is capable of a 4,266 Mbps data transfer rate. The enhancement indicated by the x in LP-DDR4x reduces the I/O signal voltage from the 1.112 V of the previous DDR generation (LP-DDR4) to 0.61 V in LP-DDR4x, reducing RAM power consumption in the iPhone X.

The A11 SoC integrates a three-core GPU designed by Apple. In addition to accelerating traditional GPU tasks, such as three-dimensional scene rendering, the GPU contains several enhancements supporting machine learning and other data-parallel tasks suitable for implementation on GPU hardware.

The 3D rendering process implements an algorithm tailored to resource-constrained systems (such as smartphones) called **tile-based deferred rendering (TBDR)**. TBDR attempts to identify objects within the field of view that are not visible (in other words, those that are obscured by other objects) as early in the rendering process as possible, thereby avoiding the work of completing their rendering. This rendering process divides the image into sections (the tiles) and performs TBDR on multiple tiles in parallel to achieve maximum performance.

The A11 contains a neural network processor, called the **Apple Neural Engine**, consisting of two cores capable of a total of 600 billion operations per second. This subsystem appears to be used for tasks such as identifying and tracking objects in the live video feed from the phone's cameras.

The A11 contains a motion coprocessor, which is a separate ARM processor dedicated to collecting and processing data from the phone's gyroscope, accelerometer, compass, and barometric sensors. The processed output of this data includes an estimated category of the user's current activity, such as walking, running, sleeping, or driving. Sensor data collection and processing continues at a low power level even while the remainder of the phone is in sleep mode.

The A11, fully embracing the term *system on chip*, also contains a high-performance **solid-state drive (SSD)** controller. The iPhone X contains 64 GB or, optionally, 256 GB of internal drive storage. The A11 SSD controller manages the interface to this storage, including the use of **error-correcting code (ECC)**. The combination of ECC flash memory devices and a controller that supports ECC increases the reliability of data storage in comparison to devices that do not support ECC. The interface between the A11 SoC and flash memory is PCI Express.

The following diagram displays the major components of the iPhone X:

Figure 13.1: iPhone X components

The iPhone X contains several high-performance subsystems, each described briefly in the following table:

Table 13.1: iPhone X subsystems

Subsystem	Description
Batteries	The iPhone X contains two battery cells rather than the usual one, probably because this makes it easier to arrange the internal components. Combined, the rechargeable lithium-ion batteries provide 2,716 **milliamp hours (mAh)** of energy.
Display	The display is a 5.85-inch (149 mm) diagonal flat panel with a 2,436 x 1,125 pixel resolution. The display technology is **active matrix organic light-emitting diode (AMOLED)**, where *organic* refers to the use of organic compounds in the luminescent material and *active matrix* describes the mechanism for pixel addressing. Active matrix flat panel displays use one transistor and one capacitor to store the state of each pixel, similar in concept to the DRAM bit cell circuit, discussed in *Chapter 4, Computer System Components*. The interface between the A11 SoC and the display is a four-lane **display serial interface (DSI)**. Each DSI lane is a high-speed unidirectional serial path. A separate lane provides a clock signal. The four DSI lanes transmit bits in parallel, controlled by the clock signal.
Touch sensing	Capacitive sensors are integrated into the display to detect touch interactions. These sensors detect changes in capacitance resulting from the proximity of a conductive object, such as a human finger, to the sensors in the display. After filtering and processing the raw sensor measurements, the accurate locations of multiple simultaneous touchpoints can be determined. In addition, sensors measure the pressure applied during touch interactions. This allows software to react differently to hard and soft presses on the screen. The touch-sensing system samples its input at 120 Hz.

Subsystem	Description
Dual cameras, IR projector, IR camera	The rear camera has 12 **megapixels** (**MP**), an LED flash, and a zoom lens. It is capable of recording 4K (3,840 x 2,160 pixels) video at up to 60 **frames per second** (**fps**) or 1080p (1,920 x 1,080 pixels), also up to 60 fps. The 7 MP front camera can record 1080p video at 30 fps. The front of the iPhone X contains a separate **infrared** (**IR**) camera supporting facial recognition. This feature works in conjunction with an IR projector that shines 30,000 dots to generate a three-dimensional map of the user's face. The phone uses this map to verify the user's identity and unlock the phone when a match is determined.
Wireless charging	The iPhone X supports **Qi wireless charging**, which uses electrical induction to transfer power from a charging pad to the phone at separations of up to 1.6 inches.
Cellular radio	The iPhone X contains a Qualcomm Snapdragon X16 **4th generation** (**4G**) **Long-Term Evolution** (**LTE**) cellular radio modem capable of downlink speeds of up to 1 Gbps and uplink speeds up to 150 Mbps.
Wi-Fi and Bluetooth	The iPhone X includes an integrated circuit containing a Wi-Fi interface supporting 2.4 GHz and 5 GHz bands, as well as a Bluetooth interface supporting version 5.0 of the Bluetooth standard. The interface between the A11 SoC and the Wi-Fi/Bluetooth module is PCI Express.
Audio amplifier, vibration motor	The iPhone X audio amplifier is designed for extremely low power consumption when idle and provides high efficiency and superior sound quality when in operation. Vibration is produced by a device called the **Taptic Engine**, a linear oscillator capable of generating a variety of types of interactive feedback to the user.

The iPhone X brought together the most advanced, small form factor, lightweight mobile electronic technologies available at the time of its design and assembled them into a sleek, attractive package that took the world by storm.

Next, we will look at the architecture of a high-performance personal computer.

Personal computer architecture

The next system we'll examine is a gaming PC with a processor that, at the time of writing (in late 2019), leads the pack in terms of raw performance. We will look in detail at the system processor, the GPU, and the computer's major subsystems.

Alienware Aurora Ryzen Edition gaming desktop

The Alienware Aurora Ryzen Edition desktop PC is designed to provide maximum performance for gaming applications. To achieve peak speed, the system architecture is built around the fastest main processor, GPU, memory, and disk subsystems available at prices that at least some serious gamers and other performance-focused users are willing to tolerate; however, the number of customers for this configuration is likely to be limited by its cost, which is over US $4,000.

The Aurora Ryzen Edition is available with a variety of AMD Ryzen processors at varying performance levels and price points. The current highest-performing processor for this platform is the AMD Ryzen 9 3950X. When it was introduced in mid-2019, the 3950X was promoted as the world's first 16-core processor targeted at mainstream customers.

The Ryzen 9 3950X implements the x64 ISA in a superscalar, out-of-order architecture with speculative execution, register renaming, simultaneous decoding of up to four instructions, and a 19-stage pipeline. Based on AMD-provided data, the Zen 2 microarchitecture of the 3950X has up to 15% higher **instructions per clock (IPC)** than the previous generation (Zen+) AMD microarchitecture.

The Ryzen 9 3950X processor boasts the following features:

- 16 cores
- 2 threads per processor (for a total of 32 simultaneous threads)
- Base clock speed of 3.5 GHz with a peak frequency of 4.7 GHz when overclocking
- A level 0 μ-op cache containing 4,096 entries
- A 32 KB level 1 instruction cache with 8-way associativity
- A 64-entry level 1 fully associative instruction TLB
- A 512-entry level 2 instruction TLB with 8-way associativity
- 4 KB and 2 MB virtual page sizes

- A 32 KB level 1 data cache with 8-way associativity

- A 64-entry level 1 fully associative data TLB

- A 2,048-entry level 2 data TLB with 16-way associativity

- A 64 MB L3 cache

- 16+4+4 PCIe 4.0 lanes

- Total dissipated power of 105 watts

At the time of its release, Ryzen 9 3950X was arguably the highest performing x86 processor available for the gaming and performance enthusiast market.

Ryzen 9 3950X branch prediction

The Zen 2 architecture includes a sophisticated branch prediction unit that caches information describing the branches taken and uses this data to increase the accuracy of future predictions. This analysis covers not only individual branches, but also correlates among recent branches in nearby code to further increase prediction accuracy. Increased prediction accuracy reduces the performance degradation from pipeline bubbles and minimizes the unnecessary work involved in speculative execution along branches that end up not being taken.

The branch prediction unit employs a form of machine learning called the **perceptron**. Perceptrons are simplified models of biological neurons and form the basis for many applications of artificial neural networks. Refer to the *Deep learning* section in *Chapter 6, Specialized Computing Domains*, for a brief introduction to artificial neural networks.

In the 3950X, perceptrons learn to predict the branching behavior of individual instructions based on recent branching behavior by the same instruction and by other instructions. Essentially, by tracking the behavior of recent branches (in terms of branches taken and not taken), it is possible to develop correlations involving the branch instruction under consideration that lead to increased prediction accuracy.

Nvidia GeForce RTX 2080 Ti GPU

The Aurora Ryzen Edition includes an Nvidia GeForce RTX 2080 Ti GPU. In addition to the generally high level of graphical performance you would expect from a top-end gaming GPU, this card provides substantial hardware support for ray tracing and includes dedicated cores to accelerate machine learning applications.

In traditional GPUs, visual objects are described as collections of polygons. To render a scene, the location and spatial orientation of each polygon must first be determined, and then those polygons visible in the scene are drawn at the appropriate location in the image. Ray tracing uses an alternative, more sophisticated approach. A ray-traced image is drawn by tracing the path of light emitted from one or more illumination sources in the virtual world. As the light rays encounter objects, effects such as reflection, refraction, scattering, and shadows occur. Ray-traced images generally appear much more visually realistic than traditionally rendered scenes; however, ray tracing incurs a much higher computational cost.

When the RTX 2080 Ti was introduced, there were no games on the market capable of leveraging its ray-tracing capability. Now, most popular, visually rich, highly dynamic games take advantage of ray tracing to at least some degree. For game developers, it is not an all-or-nothing decision to use ray tracing. It is possible to render portions of scenes in the traditional polygon-based mode while employing ray tracing to render the objects and surfaces in the scene that benefit the most from its advantages. For example, a scene may contain background imagery displayed as polygons, while a nearby glass window renders reflections of objects from the glass surface along with the view seen through the glass, courtesy of ray tracing.

At the time of its release, the RTX 2080 Ti was the highest-performing GPU available for running deep learning models with TensorFlow. **TensorFlow**, developed by Google's Machine Intelligence Research organization, is a popular open source software platform for machine learning applications. TensorFlow is widely used in research involving deep neural networks.

The RTX 2080 Ti leverages its machine learning capability to increase the apparent resolution of rendered images without the computational expense of actually rendering at the higher resolution. It does this by intelligently applying antialiasing and sharpening effects to the image. The technology learns image characteristics during the rendering of tens of thousands of images and uses this information to improve the quality of subsequently rendered scenes. This technology can, for example, make a scene rendered at 1080p resolution (1,920 x 1,080 pixels) appear as if it is being rendered at 1440p (1,920 x 1,440 pixels).

In addition to its ray-tracing and machine learning technologies, the RTX 2080 Ti has the following features:

- **Six graphics-processing clusters**: Each cluster contains a dedicated raster (pixel-processing) engine and six texture-processing clusters.

- **36 texture-processing clusters**: Each texture-processing cluster contains two streaming multiprocessors.

- **72 streaming multiprocessors**: Each streaming multiprocessor contains 64 CUDA cores, eight tensor cores, and one ray-tracing core. The CUDA cores provide a parallel computing platform suitable for general computational applications, such as linear algebra. The tensor cores perform the tensor and matrix operations at the center of deep learning algorithms.

- **A PCIe 3.0 x16 interface**: This interface communicates with the main processor.

- **11 GB of GDDR6 memory**: GDDR6 improves upon the prior generation of GDDR5X technology by providing an increased data transfer rate (up to 16 Gbit/sec per pin versus a maximum of 14 Gbit/sec per pin for DDR5X).

- **Nvidia Scalable Link Interface (SLI)**: The SLI links two to four identical GPUs within a system to share the processing workload. A special bridge connector must be used to interconnect the collaborating GPUs. The Alienware Aurora Ryzen Edition comes with a single GPU, though a second GPU is available as an option.

- **Three DisplayPort 1.4a video outputs**: The DisplayPort interfaces support 8K (7,680 x 4,320 pixels) resolution at 60 Hz.

- **HDMI 2.0b port**: The HDMI output supports 4K (3,840 x 2,160 pixels) resolution at 60 Hz.

- **VirtualLink USB C port**: This single-cable connection provides four lanes of DisplayPort video output and a USB 3.1 Gen2 (10 Gbps) connection for data transfer, and provides up to 27 watts of power to a connected system such as a virtual reality headset. The principal purpose of this interface is to support the use of a virtual reality headset that connects to the computer system with just one cable.

Aurora subsystems

The major subsystems of the Alienware Aurora Ryzen Edition are described briefly in the following table:

Table 13.2: Alienware Aurora Ryzen Edition subsystems

Subsystem	Description
Motherboard	The motherboard supports PCIe 4.0, doubling the bandwidth between the processor and graphics card over PCIe 3.0. Four slots are provided for DDR4 memory modules. Four PCIe slots are provided, though the double-width Nvidia GPU consumes two of them.
Chipset	The AMD B550A chipset supports processor and memory overclocking and PCIe 4.0.
Cooling	An Alienware liquid cooling system is provided to cool the processor, which is critically needed when overclocking.
Memory	The system includes 32 GB of dual-channel HyperX FURY DDR4 XMP operating at 3,200 MHz. The **Extreme Memory Profiles (XMP)** configuration capability permits simultaneously changing several memory performance-related settings by simply selecting from among different profiles. This function is usually used to select between a standard memory clocking configuration and an overclocked configuration.
Storage	The Aurora Ryzen Edition includes a 1 TB NVMe M.2 solid-state drive. **Non-volatile memory express (NVMe)** is an interface standard for connecting solid-state drives with up to four lanes of PCIe 3.0. The M.2 standard defines a small form factor for expansion cards such as SSDs.
Front panel	Three USB 3.1 ports, a USB C port, an Ethernet port, and audio input and output jacks are provided.
Rear panel	The system includes six USB 2.0 ports, four USB 3.1 ports, a USB C port, an Ethernet port, and digital and analog audio input and output jacks.

The Alienware Aurora Ryzen Edition gaming desktop integrates the most advanced technology available at the time of its introduction in terms of the raw speed of its processor, memory, GPU, and storage, as well as its use of machine learning to improve instruction execution performance.

The next section will take us from the level of the personal computer system discussed in this section and widen our view to explore the implementation challenges and design solutions employed in large-scale computing environments consisting of thousands of integrated, cooperating computer systems.

Warehouse-scale computing architecture

Providers of large-scale computing capabilities and networking services to the public and to sprawling organizations, such as governments, research universities, and major corporations, often aggregate computing capabilities in large buildings, each containing perhaps thousands of computers. To make the most effective use of these capabilities, it is not sufficient to consider the collection of computers in a **warehouse-scale computer** (**WSC**) as simply a large number of individual computers. Instead, in consideration of the immense quantity of processing, networking, and storage capability provided by a warehouse-scale computing environment, it is much more appropriate to think of the entire data center as a single, massively parallel computing system.

Early electronic computers were huge systems, occupying large rooms. Since then, computer architectures have evolved to arrive at today's fingernail-size processor chips possessing vastly more computing power than those early systems. We can imagine that today's warehouse-sized computing environments are a prelude to computer systems a few decades in the future that might be the size of a pizza box, or a smartphone, or a fingernail, packing as much processing power as today's WSCs, if not far more.

Since the Internet rose to prominence in the mid 1990s, a transition has been in progress, shifting application processing from programs installed on personal computers over to centralized server systems that perform algorithmic computing, store and retrieve massive data content, and enable direct communication among Internet users.

These server-side applications employ a thin application layer on the client side, often provided by a web browser. All of the data retrieval, computational processing, and organization of information for display takes place in the server. The client application merely receives instructions and data regarding the text, graphics, and input controls to present to the user. The browser-based application interface then awaits user input and sends the resulting requests for action back to the server.

Online services provided by Internet companies such as Google, Amazon, and Microsoft rely on the power and versatility of very large data center computing architectures to provide services to millions of users. One of these WSCs might run a small number of very large applications providing services to thousands of users simultaneously. Service providers strive to provide exceptional reliability, often promising 99.99% uptime, corresponding to approximately 1 hour of downtime per year.

The following sections introduce the hardware and software components of a typical WSC and discuss how these pieces work together to provide fast, efficient, and highly reliable Internet services to large numbers of users.

WSC hardware

Building, operating, and maintaining a WSC is an expensive proposition. While providing the necessary quality of service (in terms of metrics such as response speed, data throughput, and reliability), WSC operators strive to minimize the total cost of owning and operating these systems.

To achieve very high reliability, WSC designers might take one of two approaches in implementing the underlying computing hardware:

- **Invest in hardware that has exceptional reliability**: This approach relies on costly components with low failure rates. However, even if each individual computer system provides excellent reliability, by the time several thousand copies of the system are in operation simultaneously, occasional failures will occur at a statistically predictable frequency. This approach is very expensive and, ultimately, it doesn't solve the problem because failures will continue to occur.

- **Employ lower-cost hardware that has average reliability and design the system to tolerate individual component failures at the highest expected rates**: This approach permits much lower hardware costs compared to high-reliability components, though it requires a sophisticated software infrastructure capable of detecting hardware failures and rapidly compensating with redundant systems in a manner that maintains the promised quality of service.

Most providers of standard Internet services, such as search engines and email services, employ low-cost generic computing hardware and perform **failover** by transitioning workloads to redundant online systems when failures occur.

To make this discussion concrete, we will examine the workloads a WSC must support to function as an Internet search engine. WSC workloads supporting Internet searches must possess the following attributes:

- **Fast response to search requests**: The server-side turnaround for an Internet search request must be a small fraction of a second. If users are routinely forced to endure a noticeable delay, they are likely to switch to a competing search engine for future requests.

- **State information related to each search need not be retained at the server, even for sequential interactions with the same user**: In other words, the processing of each search request is a complete interaction. After the search completes, the server forgets all about it. A subsequent search request from the same user to the same service does not leverage any stored information from the first request.

Given these attributes, each service request can be treated as an isolated event, independent of all other requests, past, present, and future. The independence of each request means it can be processed as a thread of execution in parallel with other search requests coming from other users or even from the same user. This workload model is an ideal candidate for acceleration through hardware parallelism.

The processing of Internet searches is less a compute-intensive task than it is data intensive. As a simple example, when performing a search where the search term consists of a single word, the web service must receive the request from the user, extract the search term, and consult its index to determine the most relevant pages containing the search term.

The Internet contains, at a minimum, hundreds of billions of pages, most of which users expect to be able to locate via searches. This is an oversimplification, though, because a large share of the pages accessible via the Internet are not indexable by search engines. However, even limiting the search to the accessible pages, it is simply not possible for a single server, even one with a large number of processor cores and the maximum installable amount of local memory and disk storage, to respond to Internet searches in a reasonable time period for a large user base. There is just too much data and too many user requests. Instead, the search function must be split among many (hundreds, possibly thousands) of separate servers, each containing a subset of the entire index of web pages known to the search engine.

Each index server receives a stream of lookup requests filtered to those relevant to the portion of the index it manages. The index server generates a set of results based on matches to the search term and returns that set for higher-level processing. In more complex searches, separate searches for multiple search terms may need to be processed by different index servers. The results of those searches will be filtered and merged during higher-level processing.

As the index servers generate results based on search terms, these subsets are fed to a system that processes the information into a form to be transmitted to the user. For standard searches, users expect to receive a list of pages ranked in order of relevance to their query. For each page returned, a search engine generally provides the URL of the target page along with a section of text surrounding the search term within the page's content to provide some context.

The time required to generate these results depends more on the speed of database lookups associated with the page index and the extraction of page content from storage than it does on the raw processing power of the servers involved in the task. For this reason, many WSCs providing web search and similar services use servers containing inexpensive motherboards, processors, memory components, and disks.

Rack-based servers

WSC servers are typically assembled in racks with each server consuming one 1U slot. A 1U server slot has a front panel opening 19" wide and 1.75" high. One rack might contain as many as 40 servers, consuming 70" of vertical space.

Each server is a fairly complete computer system containing a moderately powerful processor, RAM, a local disk drive, and a 1 Gbit/sec Ethernet interface. Since the capabilities and capacities of consumer-grade processors, DRAM, and disks are continuing to grow, we won't attempt to identify the performance parameters of a specific system configuration.

Although each server contains a processor with integrated graphics and some USB ports, most servers do not have a display, keyboard, or mouse directly connected, except perhaps during their initial configuration. Rack-mounted servers generally operate in a so-called **headless** mode, in which all interaction with the system takes place over its network connection.

The following diagram shows a rack containing 16 servers:

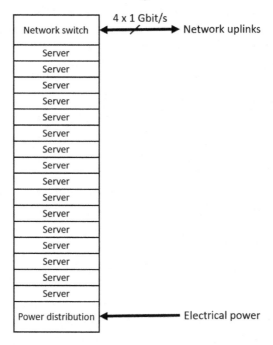

Figure 13.2: A rack containing 16 servers

Each server connects to the rack network switch with a 1 Gbit/s Ethernet cable. The rack in this example connects to the higher-level WSC network environment with four 1 Gbit/s Ethernet cables. Servers within the rack communicate with each other through the rack switch at the full 1 Gbit/s Ethernet data rate. Since there are only four 1 Gbit/s external connections leading from the rack, all 16 servers obviously cannot communicate at full speed with systems external to the rack. In this example, the rack connectivity is **oversubscribed** by a factor of 4. This means that the external network capacity is one quarter of the peak communication speed of the servers within the rack.

Racks are organized into clusters that share a second-level cluster switch. The following diagram represents a configuration in which four racks connect to each cluster-level switch that, in turn, connects to the WSC-wide network:

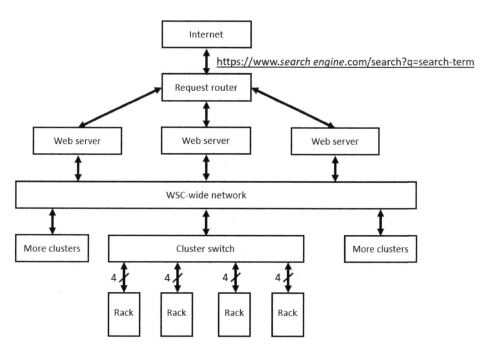

Figure 13.3: WSC internal network

In the WSC configuration of Figure 13.3, a user request arrives over the Internet to be initially processed by a routing device that directs the request to an available web server. The server receiving the request is responsible for overseeing the search process and sending the response back to the user.

Multiple web servers are online at all times to provide load sharing and redundancy in case of failure. Figure 13.3 shows three web servers, but a busy WSC may have many more servers in operation simultaneously. The web server parses the search request and forwards queries to the appropriate index servers in the rack clusters of the WSC. Based on the terms being searched, the web server directs index lookup requests to one or more index servers for processing.

To perform efficiently and reliably, the WSC must maintain multiple copies of each subset of the index database, spread across multiple clusters, to provide load sharing and redundancy in case of failures at the server, rack, or cluster level.

Index lookups are processed by the index servers, and relevant target page text is collected from document servers. The complete set of search results is assembled and passed back to the responsible web server. The web server then prepares the complete response and transmits it to the user.

The configuration of a real-world WSC will contain additional complexity beyond what is shown in *Figure 13.2* and *Figure 13.3*. Even so, these simplified representations permit us to appreciate some of the important benefits and challenges associated with a WSC implementing an Internet search engine workload.

In to responding to user search requests, the search engine must regularly update its database to remain relevant to the current state of web pages across the Internet. Search engines update their knowledge of web pages using applications called **web crawlers**. A web crawler begins with a web page address provided as its starting point, reads the targeted page, and parses its text content. The crawler stores the page text in the search engine document database and extracts any links contained within the page. For each link it finds, the crawler repeats the page reading, parsing, and link-following process. In this manner, the search engine builds and updates its indexed database of the Internet's contents.

This section summarized a conceptual WSC design configuration, which is based on racks filled with commodity computing components. The next section examines the measures the WSC must take to detect component failures and compensate for them without compromising the overall quality of service.

Hardware fault management

As we've seen, WSCs contain thousands of computer systems and we can expect that hardware failures will occur on a regular basis, even if more costly components have been selected to provide a higher, but not perfect, level of reliability. As an inherent part of the multilevel dispatch, processing, and return of results implied in *Figure 13.3*, each server sending a request to a system at a lower level of the diagram must monitor the responsiveness and correctness of the system assigned to process the request, and if the response is unacceptably delayed, or if it fails to pass validity checks, the lower-level system must be reported as unresponsive or misbehaving.

If such an error is detected, the requesting system immediately re-sends the request to a redundant server for processing. Some response failures may be due to transient events such as a momentary processing overload. If the lower-level server recovers and continues operating properly, no response is required.

If a server remains persistently unresponsive or erroneous, a maintenance request must be issued to troubleshoot and repair the offending system. When a system is identified as unavailable, WSC management (both the automated and human portions) may choose to bring up a system to replicate the failed server from a pool of backup systems and direct the replacement system to begin servicing requests.

Electrical power consumption

One of the major cost drivers of a WSC is electrical power consumption. The primary consumers of electricity in a WSC are the servers and networking devices that perform data processing for end users, as well as the air conditioning system that keeps those systems cool.

To keep the WSC electricity bill to a minimum, it is critical to only turn on computers and other power-hungry devices when there is something useful for them to do. The traffic load to a search engine varies widely over time and may spike in response to events in the news and on social media. A WSC must maintain enough servers to support the maximum traffic level it is designed to handle. When the total workload is below the maximum, any servers that do not have work to do should be powered down.

A lightly loaded server consumes a significant amount of electrical power. For best efficiency, the WSC management environment should completely turn off servers and other devices when they are not needed. When the traffic load increases, servers and associated network devices can be powered up and brought online quickly to maintain the required quality of service.

The WSC as a multilevel information cache

We examined the multilevel cache architecture employed in modern processors in *Chapter 8, Performance-Enhancing Techniques*. To achieve optimum performance, a web service such as a search engine must employ a caching strategy that, in effect, adds more levels to those that already exist within the processor.

To achieve the best response time, an index server should maintain a substantial subset of its index data in an in-memory database. By selecting content for in-memory storage based on historic usage patterns, as well as recent search trends, a high percentage of incoming searches can be satisfied without any need to access disk storage.

To make the best use of an in-memory database, the presence of a large quantity of DRAM in each server is clearly beneficial. The selection of the optimum amount of DRAM to install in each index server is dependent upon such attributes as the relative cost of additional DRAM per server in comparison to the cost of additional servers containing less memory, as well as the performance characteristics of more servers with less memory relative to fewer servers with more memory. We won't delve any further into such analysis, other than to note that such evaluations are a core element of WSC design optimization.

If we consider DRAM to be the first level of WSC-level caching, then the next level is the local disk located in each server. For misses of the in-memory database, the next place to search is the server's disk. If the result is not found in the local disk, then the next search level takes place in other servers located in the same rack. Communications between servers in the same rack can run at full network speed (1 Gbit/s in our example configuration).

The next level of search extends to racks within the same cluster. Bandwidth between racks is limited by the oversubscription of the links between racks and the cluster switch, which limits the performance of these connections. The final level of search within the WSC goes out across clusters, which will likely have further constraints on bandwidth.

A large part of the challenge of building an effective search engine infrastructure is the development of a high-performance software architecture. This architecture must satisfy a high percentage of search requests by the fastest, most localized lookups achievable by the search engine index servers and document servers. This means most search lookups must be completed via in-memory searches in the index servers.

The next section looks at the high-performance architectures employed in dedicated neural network processors.

Neural networks and machine learning architectures

We briefly reviewed the architecture of neural networks in *Chapter 6, Specialized Computing Domains*. This section examines the inner workings of a high-performance, dedicated neural net processor.

Intel Nervana neural network processor

In 2019, Intel announced the release of a pair of new processors, one optimized for the task of training sophisticated neural networks and the other for using trained networks to conduct inference, which is the process of generating neural network outputs given a set of input data.

The Nervana **neural network processor for training (NNP-T)** is essentially a miniature supercomputer tailored to the computational tasks required in the neural network training process. The NNP-T1000 is available in the following two configurations:

- The NNP-T1300 is a dual-slot PCIe card suitable for installation in a standard PC. It communicates with the host via PCIe 3.0 or 4.0 x16. It is possible to connect multiple NNP-T1300 cards within the same computer system or across computers by cable.

- The NNP-T1400 is a mezzanine card suitable for use as a processing module in an **Open Compute Project (OCP) accelerator module (OAM)**. OAM is a design specification for hardware architectures that implement artificial intelligence systems requiring high module-to-module communication bandwidth. Development of the OAM standard has been led by Facebook, Microsoft, and Baidu. Up to 1,024 NNP-T1000 modules can be combined to form a massive NNP architecture with extremely high-speed serial connections among the modules.

The NNP-T1300 fits in a standard PC, and is something an individual developer might use. A configuration of multiple NNP-T1400 processors, on the other hand, quickly becomes very costly and begins to resemble a supercomputer in terms of performance.

The primary application domains for powerful NNP architectures such as Nervana include **natural language processing (NLP)** and machine vision. NLP attempts to perform tasks such as processing sequences of words to extract the meaning behind them and generating natural language for computer interaction with humans. When you call a company's customer support line and a computer asks you to talk to it, you are interacting with an NLP system.

Machine vision is a key enabling technology for autonomous vehicles. Automotive machine vision systems process video camera feeds to identify and classify road features, road signs, and obstacles, such as vehicles and pedestrians. This processing has to produce results in real time to be useful in the process of driving a vehicle.

Building a neural network to perform a human-scale task, such as reading a body of text and interpreting its meaning or driving a car in heavy traffic, requires an extensive training process. Neural network training involves sequential steps of presenting the network with a set of inputs along with the response that the network is expected to produce given that input. This information, consisting of pairs of input datasets and known correct outputs, is called the **training set**. Each time the network sees a new input set and is given the output it is expected to produce from that input, it adjusts its internal connections and weight values slightly to improve its ability to generate correct outputs. For complex neural networks, such as those targeted by the Nervana NNP, the training set might consist of millions of input/output dataset pairs.

The processing required by NNP training algorithms boils down to mostly matrix and vector manipulations. The multiplication of large matrices is one of the most common and most compute-intensive tasks in neural network training. These matrices may contain hundreds or even thousands of rows and columns. The fundamental operation in matrix multiplication is the multiply–accumulate, or MAC, operation we learned about in *Chapter 6, Specialized Computing Domains*.

Complex neural networks contain an enormous number of weight parameters. During training, the processor must repetitively access these values to compute the signal strengths associated with each neuron in the model and perform training adjustments to the weights. To achieve maximum performance for a given amount of memory and internal communication bandwidth, it is desirable to employ the smallest usable data type to store each numeric value. In most applications of numeric processing, the 32-bit IEEE single-precision, floating-point format is the smallest data type used. When possible, it can be an improvement to use an even smaller floating-point format.

The Nervana architecture employs a specialized floating-point format for storing network signals. The **bfloat16** format is based on the IEEE-754 32-bit single-precision, floating-point format, except the mantissa is truncated from 24 bits to 8 bits. The *Floating-point mathematics* section in *Chapter 9, Specialized Processor Extensions*, discussed the IEEE-754 32-bit and 64-bit floating-point data formats in some detail.

The reasons for proposing the bfloat16 format instead of the IEEE-754 half-precision 16-bit floating-point format for neural network processing are as follows:

- The IEEE-754 16-bit format has a sign bit, 5 exponent bits, and 11 mantissa bits, one of which is implied. Compared to the IEEE-754 single-precision (32-bit), floating-point format, this half-precision format loses three bits in the exponent, reducing the range of numeric values it can represent to one-eighth the range of 32-bit floating point.

- The bfloat16 format retains all eight exponent bits of the IEEE-754 single-precision format, allowing it to cover the full numeric range of the IEEE-754 32-bit format, although with substantially reduced precision.

Based on research findings and customer feedback, Intel suggests the bfloat16 format is most appropriate for deep learning applications because the greater exponent range is more critical than the benefit of a more precise mantissa. In fact, Intel suggests the quantization effect resulting from the reduced mantissa size does not significantly affect the inference accuracy of bfloat16-based network implementations in comparison to IEEE-754 single-precision implementations.

The fundamental data type used in ANN processing is the **tensor**, which is represented as a multidimensional array. A vector is a one-dimensional tensor, and a matrix is a two-dimensional tensor. Higher-dimension tensors can be defined as well. In the Nervana architecture, a tensor is a multidimensional array of bfloat16 values. The tensor is the fundamental data type of the Nervana architecture: The NNP-T operates on tensors at the instruction set level.

The most compute-intensive operation performed by deep learning algorithms is the multiplication of tensors. Accelerating these multiplications is the primary goal of dedicated ANN processing hardware, such as the Nervana architecture. Accelerating tensor operations requires not just high-performance mathematical processing; it is also critical to transfer operand data to the core for processing in an efficient manner and move output results to their destinations just as efficiently. This requires a careful balance of numeric processing capability, memory read/write speed, and communication speed.

Processing in the NNP-T architecture takes place in **tensor processor clusters (TPCs)**, each of which contains two multiply–accumulate (MAC) processing units and 2.5 MB of high-bandwidth memory. Each MAC processing unit contains a 32 x 32 array of MAC processors operating in parallel.

An NNP-T processor contains either 22 or 24 TPCs, running in parallel, with high-speed serial interfaces interconnecting them in a fabric configuration. The Nervana devices provide high-speed serial connections to additional Nervana boards in the same system and to Nervana devices in other computers.

A single NNP-T processor is capable of performing 119 **trillion operations per second (TOPS)**. The following table shows a comparison between the two processors:

Table 13.3: Features of the two NNP T-1000 processor configurations

Feature	NNP-T1300	NNP-T1400
Device form factor	Double width card, PCIe 4.0 x16	OAM 1.0
Processor cores	22 TPCs	24 TPCs
Processor clock speed	950 MHz	1,100 MHz
Static RAM	55 MB SRAM with ECC	60 MB SRAM with ECC
High bandwidth memory	32 GB second generation **high bandwidth memory (HBM2)** with ECC	32 GB HBM2 with ECC
Memory bandwidth	2.4 Gbit/s (300 MB/s)	2.4 Gbit/s (300 MB/s)
Serial **inter-chip link (ICL)**	16 x 112 Gbit/s (448 GB/s)	16 x 112 Gbit/s (448 GB/s)

The Nervana **neural network processor for inference (NNP-I)** performs the inference phase of neural network processing. Inference consists of providing inputs to pretrained neural networks, processing those inputs, and collecting the outputs from the network. Depending on the application, the inference process may involve repetitive evaluations of a single, very large network on time-varying input data or it may involve applying many different neural network models to the same set of input data at each input update.

The NNP-I is available in two form factors:

- A PCIe card containing two NNP I-1000 devices. This card is capable of 170 TOPS and dissipates up to 75 W.

- An M.2 card containing a single NNP I-1000 device. This card is capable of 50 TOPS and dissipates only 12 W.

The Nervana architecture is an advanced, supercomputer-like processing environment optimized for training neural networks and performing inferencing on real-world data using pretrained networks.

Summary

This chapter presented several computer system architectures tailored to particular user needs, and built on the topics covered in previous chapters. We looked at application categories including smartphones, gaming-focused personal computers, warehouse-scale computing, and neural networks. These examples provided a connection between the more theoretical discussions of computer and systems architectures and components presented in earlier chapters, and the real-world implementations of modern, high-performance computing systems.

Having completed this chapter, you should understand the decision processes used in defining computer architectures to support specific user needs. You will have gained insight into the key requirements driving smart mobile device architectures, high-performance personal computing architectures, warehouse-scale cloud-computing architectures, and advanced machine learning architectures.

In the next and final chapter, we will develop a view of the road ahead for computer architectures. The chapter will review the significant advances and ongoing trends that have led to the current state of computer architectures and extrapolate those trends to identify some possible future technological directions. Potentially disruptive technologies that could alter the path of future computer architectures will be considered as well. In closing, some approaches will be proposed for the professional development of the computer architect that are likely to result in a future-tolerant skill set.

Exercises

1. Draw a block diagram of the computing architecture for a system to measure and report weather data 24 hours a day at 5-minute intervals using SMS text messages. The system is battery powered and relies on solar cells to recharge the battery during daylight hours. Assume the weather instrumentation consumes minimal average power, only requiring full power momentarily during each measurement cycle.

2. For the system of *Exercise 1*, identify a suitable commercially available processor and list the reasons that processor is a good choice for this application. Factors to consider include cost, processing speed, tolerance of harsh environments, power consumption, and integrated features, such as RAM and communication interfaces.

14

Future Directions in Computer Architectures

This chapter anticipates the road ahead for computer architecture design. We will review the significant technological advances and ongoing trends that have led us to the current state of computer architectures. We will then extrapolate from current trends and identify some of the directions that computing system designs are likely to take in the future. We will also examine some potentially disruptive technologies that may alter the evolution of future computer architectures.

This chapter offers some suggested approaches for the professional development of the computer architect. By following these recommendations, you should be able to maintain a skill set that remains relevant and tolerant of future advances, whatever they turn out to be.

After completing this chapter, you will understand the historical evolution of computer architecture that led to its current state and will be familiar with ongoing trends in computer design that are likely to indicate future technological directions. You will have a basic level of knowledge of some potentially disruptive technologies that might substantially alter future computer architectures. You will also have learned some useful techniques for maintaining an ongoing, current skill set in the field of computer architecture.

The following topics will be presented in this chapter:

- The ongoing evolution of computer architectures
- Extrapolating current trends into the future
- Potentially disruptive technologies
- Building a future-tolerant skill set

The ongoing evolution of computer architectures

Chapter 1, *Introducing Computer Architecture*, presented a brief history of automated computing devices from the mechanical design of Babbage's Analytical Engine to the advent of the x86 architecture that continues to serve as the basis for most modern personal computers. This progress has relied on several groundbreaking technological achievements, most notably the invention of the transistor and the development of integrated circuit manufacturing processes.

Through the decades since the introduction of the Intel 4004 in 1971, processors have grown dramatically in terms of the sheer number of transistors and other circuit components integrated on a single-circuit die. In concert with the growth in the number of circuit elements per chip, the clock speed of modern devices has increased by several orders of magnitude.

This increase in processor capability and instruction execution speed has unleashed the growth of software development as an enormous, worldwide industry. In the early days of digital computers, software was developed by small teams of highly trained specialists in a research setting. Today, powerful personal computers are available at a comparatively low cost, and software development tools such as programming language compilers and interpreters are widely available, often for free. As processors have increased in capability, the availability of widespread computing power has created a strong demand for software to run on those devices.

Modern processors have evolved to coalesce far more functionality into the processor's integrated circuit than early devices, such as the 6502. The 6502, in essence, contains the minimum component set required to perform useful processing: a control unit, a register set, an ALU, and an external bus for accessing instructions, data, and peripherals.

The most sophisticated modern processors targeted at business and home users incorporate basic functionally similar to the capabilities of the 6502, along with substantial added features and extensions, such as the following:

- Up to 16 processor cores, each supporting simultaneous multithreading

- Multilevel instruction and data cache memory

- A μ-op cache to avoid the processing delay associated with instruction-decode operations

- A memory-management unit supporting paged virtual memory

- Integrated multichannel high-speed serial I/O capability

- An integrated graphics processor generating digital video output

To summarize the technological evolution from the 6502 processor to the modern x64 processor, modern processors provide multiple 64-bit cores operating in parallel compared to the 6502's single 8-bit core, and they implement numerous additional features specifically designed to accelerate execution speed.

In addition to the raw computing capability of modern PC processors, the x86/x64 instruction set provides instructions to implement a wide variety of operations, ranging from simple to extremely complex. Modern RISC processors, such as ARM and RISC-V, on the other hand, implement intentionally slimmed-down instruction sets, with the goal of breaking complex operations into sequences of simpler steps, each of which executes at very high speed while working within a larger register set.

The high-level configurations of computer architectures have, arguably, not undergone drastic disruption since the days of the 6502. With each extension of the processor architecture's instruction set or the introduction of additional caching technology, these changes have incrementally expanded the functionality available to software developers or increased the speed at which algorithms execute. The expansion to multiple cores and to multithreading within a single core allows multiple independent execution threads to execute simultaneously rather than running in a time-sliced manner on a single core.

Much of the incrementalism during this evolution has been intentional, to avoid introducing changes in processor architectures that would inhibit backward compatibility with the immense universe of already-developed operating system and application software. The net result has been a series of processor generations that gradually become faster and more capable over time, but do not implement any disruptive breaks from past technology.

In the next section, we will attempt to extrapolate from the current generation of high-performance computing systems discussed in *Chapter 13, Domain-Specific Computer Architectures,* to predict the advances in computer architectures likely to occur in the next one to two decades.

Extrapolating from current trends

The capabilities of current-generation processor technology are beginning to push up against some significant physical limits that we can expect to constrain the rate of growth going forward. These limits certainly will not lead to an abrupt end of improvements in circuit density and clock speed; rather, capability improvements for future processor generations may take place in directions that differ from traditional semiconductor capability improvement patterns. To look more closely at future processor performance growth expectations, we begin by returning to Moore's law and examining its applicability to the future of semiconductor technology.

Moore's law revisited

The revised version of Moore's law, published by Gordon Moore in 1975, predicted the number of integrated circuit components per device would double roughly every two years. This law has demonstrated remarkable predictive accuracy for several decades, but as of 2015, according to Intel, the growth rate had slowed to doubling approximately every two and a half years. This indicates the rate of growth in integrated circuit density has begun to slow, but it certainly has not ended, and is not expected to end in the foreseeable future.

Integrated circuit technology will continue to improve, resulting in denser and more highly capable devices for many years to come. We can, however, expect the rate of growth in circuit density to decrease over time because of the physical limits associated with the construction of single-digit nanometer-scale circuit components.

The slower rate of increase in circuit density does not mean that the trend is near an end. As of 2020, current mass-produced integrated circuit technology is based on circuit features with dimensions as small as 10 nm. Work is in progress to develop the next generation of circuit technology with 7 nm feature sizes. A future generation with feature sizes of 5 nm is in the planning stages. Although these increased circuit densities are likely to be realized at some point, each technological advance comes with increasing cost and technical challenges that result in delays in deployment to production lines. The most advanced integrated circuit production technologies are so costly to develop and difficult to implement that only a handful of massive semiconductor companies have the financial resources and technical expertise to bring such processes online.

Given the ongoing decline in the rate of improvement in circuit density, semiconductor manufacturers have begun to focus on alternative methods for packing smaller components together on a chip. Traditionally, integrated circuits have been viewed as primarily two-dimensional entities constructed in layers, as follows:

- Different types of material are laid out in a sequence of masking operations to create doped regions of transistors, as well as other circuit components, such as capacitors and diodes

- Conductive traces serving as wires are deposited on the devices as additional layers

Communication between circuit elements within a two-dimensional device layout involves electrical interactions between components placed some distance from each other on the chip's surface. The chip is small, so the time that the electrical signal takes to propagate between components is usually not significant.

You may wonder if it is possible to organize the components of an integrated circuit in a manner other than effectively spreading them around on a flat surface. It is indeed possible to stack components on top of one another on an integrated circuit die. We will look at this design approach in the next section.

The third dimension

By developing techniques for stacking components atop one another on a single integrated circuit die, semiconductor manufacturers have taken a step toward extending Moore's law. One of the early targets for stacked-component integrated circuit configurations is the ubiquitous n-channel and p-channel MOS transistor pair in CMOS circuit designs.

Intel publicly described advances achieved by its researchers in the area of stacked CMOS transistor pairs in early 2020. Not only has the company shown an ability to stack devices on a silicon die, it has also demonstrated how to use differing fabrication technologies in each device layer to achieve maximum performance from the transistor pair.

Silicon n-channel transistors exhibit good performance characteristics, but p-channel transistors constructed on silicon have a relatively slower switching speed. P-channel transistors implemented with a germanium transistor channel instead of silicon provide increased switching speed, improving the performance of the CMOS pair. In a demonstration of Intel's mixed-technology device integration, silicon n-channel transistors were constructed on a base silicon die with germanium p-channel devices stacked on top of them. If this technique can be scaled to support integrated circuit production, it holds the promise of continued increases in device density and improved clock speeds.

Another density-increasing approach is to combine multiple separately constructed integrated circuit dies in a vertical stack, with connections between the layers for power and communication. You can think of this technique as a method of soldering integrated circuit dies on top of each other in a manner that is similar to the way surface-mounted components are soldered onto a circuit board.

Separately fabricated integrated circuits combined within a single package are referred to as **chiplets**. Chiplets can be laid out side by side on a silicon base or they can be stacked atop one another, depending on the needs of the device. This approach allows each of the chiplets in a complex device to be constructed using the most appropriate technology for that component. For example, one fabrication method may be most appropriate for a core processor, while a different process might be more suitable for a memory chiplet integrated with the processor. An integrated cellular radio interface in the same device package may be constructed using yet another process.

The use of the vertical dimension in the construction of individual integrated circuits and in the construction of complex devices composed of multiple chiplets within a single package enables a higher level of **system-on-chip (SoC)** integration and higher overall performance. As these techniques continue to be refined and rolled out into production lines, we can expect the increasing circuit complexity and functionality predicted by Moore's law to continue in future years, though perhaps at a reduced growth rate.

The next trend we will examine is the ongoing growth of the use of highly specialized processing devices in place of general-purpose processors.

Increased device specialization

In previous chapters, we explored a few specialized processing technologies targeted at application areas such as digital signal processing, three-dimensional graphical image generation, and neural network processing. It is certainly possible for all of the computations performed by these devices to be carried out by ordinary, general-purpose processors. The important difference in the processing performed by these specialized devices is the increased execution speed, with throughput that is sometimes hundreds or even thousands of times faster than an ordinary processor could achieve.

The growing importance of machine learning and autonomous technologies will continue to drive innovation in the computer architectures that underpin future digital systems. As automobiles and other complex systems gain autonomous features that either augment or replace functionality traditionally performed by human operators, the underlying processing architectures will continue to evolve to provide higher levels of performance tailored to specific tasks while minimizing power consumption.

Specialized processors will take advantage of the advances discussed earlier in this chapter while optimizing individual device designs for particular application niches. The trend toward increased specialization of processing devices will continue and may even accelerate in the coming years.

This discussion has focused on the continuation of ongoing trends into future years. The next section will examine the possibility that a technological force may arise that substantially alters the path from continued incremental improvements in computer architecture to something that is entirely different.

Potentially disruptive technologies

So far, this chapter has focused on trends currently in progress and the potential effects of their extension into the future. As with the introduction of the transistor, we saw that it is always possible that some new technology will appear that creates a drastic break with past experience and leads the future of computing technology in a new direction.

In this section, we will attempt to identify some potential sources of such technological advances in the coming years.

Quantum physics

Charles Babbage's Analytical Engine tried to take the capabilities of purely mechanical computing devices to an extreme that had not been achieved previously. His attempt, while ambitious, was ultimately unsuccessful. The development of practical automated computing devices had to wait until the introduction of vacuum tube technology provided a suitable basis for the implementation of complex digital logic.

Later, the invention of the transistor moved computing technology onto a trajectory of increasing capability and sophistication that ultimately brought us to the state of computing we enjoy today. Ever since the introduction of the Intel 4004, advances in computing technology have taken the form of incremental improvements to what is fundamentally the same underlying silicon transistor technology.

Transistor operation is based on the properties of semiconducting materials, such as silicon, and the application of those properties to implement digital switching circuits. Digital circuits constructed with semiconductors generally perform operations using discrete binary data values. These devices are designed to generate reliably repeatable results when given the same input on a subsequent execution of the same sequence of instructions.

As an alternative to this approach, numerous research efforts are underway around the world exploring the possibility of employing aspects of quantum physics in computing technology. **Quantum physics** describes the behavior of matter at the level of individual atoms and subatomic particles. The behavior of particles at the subatomic level differs in significant and surprising ways from the familiar behaviors of the macro-scale objects we interact with every day under the laws of **classical physics**. The laws of quantum physics have been discovered and described in theories since the mid-1800s.

Quantum physics is rigorously defined by a set of theories that have demonstrated remarkable predictive powers. For example, Wolfgang Pauli postulated the existence of the neutrino particle within the framework of quantum physics in 1930. Neutrinos are comparatively tiny subatomic particles that have barely any interaction with other particles, making them extremely difficult to detect. Neutrinos were not proven to exist by scientific experiments until the 1950s.

Several other types of subatomic particle have been predicted by theory and ultimately shown to exist in experiments. Quantum physics, including the strange behaviors exhibited in the subatomic world, offers a promising new direction for future computer architectures.

Physical parameters associated with human-scale objects, such as the speed of a moving vehicle, seem to vary in a continuous manner as a car accelerates or slows. The electrons within an atom, on the other hand, can only exist at specific, discrete energy levels. The energy level of an electron in an atom corresponds roughly to the speed of a particle moving in an orbit around a central body in classical physics.

There is no possibility for an electron in an atom to be between two energy levels. It is always precisely in one discrete energy level or another. These discrete energy levels lead to the use of the term **quantum** to describe such phenomena.

Spintronics

In addition to the energy level of an electron in an atom, electrons exhibit a property analogous to the spinning of an object in classical physics. As with the energy level, this spin state is quantized. Researchers have demonstrated the ability to control and measure the spin behavior of electrons in a manner that may prove suitable for use in practical digital switching circuits. The use of electron spin as a component of a digital switching circuit is referred to as **spintronics**, combining the terms *spin* and *electronics*.

This technology uses the quantum spin state of electrons to hold information in a manner similar to the charge state of capacitors in traditional electronics. The spin of an elementary atomic particle is a type of angular momentum conceptually similar to the momentum of a spinning basketball balanced on a fingertip.

There are some significant differences in the spin behavior of electrons compared to basketballs. Electrons do not actually rotate; however, their spin behavior obeys the mathematical laws of angular momentum in a quantized form. A basketball can be made to spin at an arbitrarily selected rotational speed, while electrons can only exhibit spin at one discrete, quantized level. The spin of an elementary particle is determined by its particle type, and electrons always have a spin of $\frac{1}{2}$, which represents a quantum number.

The spin of a basketball can be fully characterized by the combination of its rotational speed and the axis about which the rotation is taking place. A spinning ball balanced on a fingertip rotates about the vertical axis. The entirety of the ball's rotational motion can be described by a vector pointing along the axis of rotation (in this case, upward) with a magnitude equal to its rotational speed.

Electrons always have the same spin value of $\frac{1}{2}$, defining the angular momentum vector length, so the only way to differentiate the spin of one electron from another is the direction of the spin vector. Practical devices have been created that can enable the alignment of electron spin vectors in two different orientations, referred to as *up* and *down*.

Electron spin generates a tiny magnetic field. Materials in which most electron spins are aligned directionally produce a magnetic field with the same orientation as the aligned electrons. The effect of these aligned electrons is apparent in common devices, such as refrigerator magnets.

The magnetic field produced by electron spin cannot be explained by classical physics. Magnetism is purely an effect of quantum physics.

A switching device called a **spin valve** can be constructed from a channel with a magnetic layer at each end. The magnetic layers function as gates. If the gates are of the same spin polarity, a current consisting of spin-polarized electrons can flow through the device. If the gates have opposite polarities, the current is blocked. A spin valve can be switched on and off by reversing the polarity of one of the magnets by applying current to it with the opposite spin direction.

Switching electron spin directions can be much faster while consuming much less power than the process of charging and discharging capacitors that underlies the functioning of today's CMOS digital devices. This is the key feature providing a glimpse of the potential for spintronics to eventually augment or replace CMOS circuitry in high-performance digital devices.

Spintronics is an area of ongoing, active research. The commercialization and production of digital devices that outperform today's CMOS processors is not likely to occur for several years, if the technology turns out to be viable at all.

Spintronics relies on the laws of quantum physics to perform digital switching. Quantum computing, the subject of the next section, directly exploits quantum-mechanical phenomena to perform analog and digital processing.

Quantum computing

Quantum computing holds the promise of dramatic execution speed improvements for certain classes of problems. **Quantum computing** uses quantum-mechanical phenomena to perform processing, and can employ analog or digital approaches to solve problems.

Digital quantum computing uses quantum logic gates to perform computing operations. Quantum logic gates are based on circuits called **quantum bits**, or **qubits**. Qubits are analogous in some ways to the bits in traditional digital computers, but there are significant differences. Traditional bits can take on only the values 0 and 1. A qubit can be in the 0 or 1 quantum state; however, it can also be in a superposition of the 0 and 1 states. The principle of **quantum superposition** states that any two quantum states can be added together and the result is a valid quantum state.

Whenever the value of a qubit is read, the result returned is always either 0 or 1. This is due to the collapse of the superposition of quantum states to a single state. If, prior to the readout, the qubit held the quantum value corresponding to the binary value 0 or 1, the output of the read operation will equal the binary value. If, on the other hand, the qubit contained a superposition of states, the value returned by the read operation will be a probabilistic function of the superposition of states.

In other words, the likelihood of receiving a 0 or 1 as the result of reading the qubit depends on the characteristics of its quantum state. The value returned by the read operation will not be predictable. The reason for this unpredictability is not simply a lack of knowledge; in quantum physics, a particle simply does not have a defined state until a measurement has been taken. This is one of the counterintuitive and, frankly, mind-bending features of quantum physics.

A qubit state that is *close to* the binary value 1 will have a higher probability of returning a value of 1 when read than one that is closer to the binary value of 0. Performing a read operation on multiple qubits that all begin in identical quantum states will not always produce the same result because of the probabilistic nature of the read operation.

Qubit circuits can demonstrate and exploit the properties of quantum entanglement, a central principle of quantum physics. **Quantum entanglement** occurs when multiple particles are linked in a manner that causes the measurement of one of the particles to affect the measurement of the linked particles. The most surprising aspect of this linkage is that it remains in effect even when the particles are separated by great distances. The entanglement effect appears to propagate instantaneously, unrestricted by the speed of light. While this behavior may seem like science fiction, it has been demonstrated experimentally and has even been used in the communication technology of the NASA **Lunar Atmosphere Dust and Environment Explorer** (**LADEE**) that orbited the moon from 2013–2014.

Quantum computers are capable of exploiting entanglement in information processing. If you work through the examples at the end of this chapter, you will have an opportunity to develop a program for a quantum computer that exhibits the effects of quantum entanglement, and you will run this program on an actual quantum computer.

The somewhat unpredictable nature of the results returned by reading a qubit would seem to argue against using this technology as the basis for a digital computing system. This partial unpredictability is one reason why quantum computers are envisioned as useful for only certain classes of problems. Most customers would not appreciate a bank using a computer that calculates different account balances each time the computation is run because of quantum uncertainty.

Two key application categories currently envisioned for quantum computers are as follows:

- **Quantum cryptography**: Quantum cryptography uses digital quantum computing techniques to break modern cryptographic codes. Many cryptographic algorithms in use today are based on the assumption that it is computationally infeasible to determine the factors of a large number (containing perhaps hundreds of decimal digits) that is the product of two large prime numbers. Factoring such a number on modern computers, even with a supercomputer or relying on thousands of processors operating in parallel in a cloud environment, cannot be expected to produce a correct result in a reasonable period of time.

Shor's algorithm, developed by Peter Shor in 1994, describes the steps a quantum computer must perform to identify the prime factors of a given number. A quantum computer running Shor's algorithm can potentially factor a very large number in a much shorter time than ordinary computers, thereby rendering modern cryptographic systems based on public key cryptography vulnerable to such attacks. To date, quantum computing has only demonstrated the ability to factor relatively small numbers, such as 21, but the potential threat is recognized by organizations and governments that require high levels of communication security. The future may bring quantum computing systems capable of cracking the codes we use today for securing websites and online banking.

However, there is probably little reason to be concerned about the security of your bank account against quantum attacks. An assortment of quantum-computing-resistant public key encryption algorithms are being researched. Collectively, these algorithms are referred to as **post-quantum cryptography**. We can expect a large-scale transition to quantum-resistant cryptographic algorithms in the event that the quantum threat to current cryptography methods becomes real.

- **Adiabatic quantum computation**: This is an analog quantum computing approach that holds the promise of efficiently solving a wide variety of practical optimization problems. Imagine that you are in a rectangular region of hilly terrain surrounded by a fence. You need to find the lowest point within the fenced boundary. In this scenario, it is very foggy, and you cannot see the surrounding terrain. The only clue you have is the slope of the surface under your feet. You can follow the slope downward, but when you reach a level area, you can't be sure if you're in a local basin or have truly found the lowest point in the entire bounded region.

This is an example of a simple two-dimensional optimization problem. The goal is to find the x and y coordinates of the lowest altitude in the entire region, called the **global minimum**, without being sidetracked and getting stuck in a basin at a higher altitude, which is referred to as a **local minimum**. You don't need anything as fancy as quantum computing to find the lowest point in a hilly region, but many real-world optimization problems have a larger number of inputs, perhaps 20 to 30, that must all be adjusted in the search for the global minimum. The computational power required to solve such problems is beyond the capability of even today's fastest supercomputers.

The quantum computing approach to solving such problems begins by setting up a configuration of qubits containing the superposition of all possible solutions to the problem, then slowly reducing the superposition effect. By constraining the state of the quantum circuit configuration during this process, it is possible to ensure that the solution that remains after superposition has been removed, and all of the quantum bits are resolved to discrete 0 or 1 values, is the global minimum. The term **adiabatic** in the name of this approach refers to an analogy between the process of removing the superposition and a thermodynamic system that neither loses nor gains heat as it operates.

Adiabatic quantum optimization is an area of active research. It remains to be seen what level of capability this technology can ultimately bring to the solution of complex optimization problems.

The term **quantum supremacy** describes the transition point at which quantum computing exceeds the capability of traditional digital computing in a particular problem domain. There is spirited debate among researchers as to whether quantum supremacy has been achieved by any of the major organizations developing quantum computing technologies; when this point may be reached at a future date; or whether such a transition is ever going to occur.

A number of substantial barriers stand in the way of the widespread deployment of quantum computing in a manner similar to the ubiquitous use of CMOS-based computing devices by users around the world today. Some of the most pressing issues to be addressed are as follows:

- Increasing the number of qubits in a computer to support the solution of large, complex problems
- Providing the ability to initialize qubits to arbitrary values
- Providing mechanisms to reliably read the state of qubits
- Eliminating the effects of quantum decoherence
- The components required for quantum computers are hard to find and are very expensive

Quantum decoherence refers to the loss of phase coherence in a quantum system. For a quantum computer to function properly, phase coherence must be maintained within the system. Quantum decoherence results from interference from the outside world in the internal operation of the quantum system, or from interference generated internally within the system. A quantum system that remains perfectly isolated can maintain phase coherence indefinitely. Disturbing the system, for example by reading its state, disrupts the coherence and may lead to decoherence. The management and correction of decoherence effects is referred to as **quantum error correction**. The effective management of decoherence is one of the greatest challenges in quantum computing.

Current quantum computer designs rely on exotic materials such as Helium-3, which is produced by nuclear reactors, and they require superconducting cables. Quantum-computing systems must be cooled to temperatures near absolute zero during operation. Current quantum computers are mostly laboratory-based systems that require a dedicated staff of experts for their construction and operation. This situation is somewhat analogous to the early days of vacuum-tube-based computers. One major difference from the vacuum tube days is that today we have the Internet, which provides ordinary users with a degree of access to quantum-computing capabilities.

Current quantum-computing systems contain at most a few dozen qubits and are mainly accessible only to the commercial, academic, and government organizations that fund their development. There are, however, some unique opportunities for students and individuals to gain access to real quantum computers.

One example is the IBM Quantum Experience at `https://www.ibm.com/quantum-computing/`. With this free collection of resources, IBM provides a set of tools, including a quantum algorithm development environment called **Qisket**, available at `https://www.qiskit.org/`. Using the Qisket tools, developers can learn to code quantum algorithms and can even submit programs for execution in batch mode on a real quantum computer. The exercises at the end of this chapter suggest steps you can take to get started in this domain.

Quantum computing shows great promise for addressing particular categories of problems, though the widespread commercialization of the technology is most likely several years away.

The next technology we will examine is the carbon nanotube, which has the potential to move digital processing at least partially away from the world of silicon.

Carbon nanotubes

The **carbon nanotube field-effect transistor (CNTFET)** is a transistor that uses either a single carbon nanotube or an array of carbon nanotubes as the gate channel rather than the silicon channel of the traditional MOSFET. A carbon nanotube is a tubular structure constructed from carbon atoms with a diameter of approximately 1 nanometer.

Carbon nanotubes are exceptionally good electrical conductors, exhibit high tensile strength, and conduct heat very well. A carbon nanotube can sustain current densities over 1,000 times greater than metals such as copper. Unlike in metals, electrical current can propagate only along the axis of the nanotube.

Compared to MOSFETs, CNTFETs have the following advantages:

- Higher drive current.

- Substantially reduced power dissipation.

- Resilience to high temperatures.

- Excellent heat dissipation, allowing for high-density packing of the devices.

- The performance characteristics of n-channel and p-channel CNTFET devices match closely. In CMOS devices, on the other hand, there can be substantial variation between the performance of the n-channel and p-channel transistors. This limits overall circuit performance to the capabilities of the lower performing devices.

As with the other emerging technologies discussed in this chapter, CNTFET technology faces some substantial barriers to commercialization and widespread use:

- Production of CNTFETs is very challenging because of the need to place and manipulate the nanometer-scale tubes.

- Production of the nanotubes required for CNTFETs is also very challenging. The nanotubes can be thought of as starting from flat sheets of carbon fabric that must be rolled into tubes along a specific axis in order to produce a material with the desired semiconducting properties.

- Carbon nanotubes degrade rapidly when exposed to oxygen. Fabrication technologies must take this into account to ensure the resulting circuit is durable and reliable.

Given the challenges of mass-producing CNTFETs, it will likely be several years before commercial devices begin to make wide use of carbon nanotube-based transistors.

The preceding sections have identified some advanced technologies (spintronics, quantum computing, and carbon-nanotube-based transistors) as promising areas that may someday contribute substantially to the future of computing. None of these technologies are in wide-scale use at the time of writing, but research has shown promising results, and many government, university, and commercial laboratories are hard at work developing these technologies and finding ways to put them to use in the computing devices of the future.

In addition to technologies such as these that are widely reported and appear to be advancing along at least a semipredictable path, there is always the possibility that an organization or individual may announce an unanticipated technological breakthrough. This may occur at any time, and such an event may upend the conventional wisdom regarding the anticipated path for the future. Only time will tell.

In the context of the uncertainty of the road ahead for computer architectures, it is prudent for the architecture professional to devise a strategy to ensure ongoing relevance regardless of the twists and turns future technology takes. The next section presents some suggestions for staying up to date with technological advances.

Building a future-tolerant skill set

Given the technological transitions that kicked off the era of transistor-based digital computing, and the likelihood of similar future events, it is important for professionals in the field of computer architecture to keep up with ongoing advances and to develop some intuition as to the likely directions the technology will take in the future. This section provides some recommended practices for keeping up with state-of-the-art technology.

Continuous learning

Computer architecture professionals must be willing to embrace the idea that technology continues to evolve rapidly, and they must devote substantial ongoing efforts to monitoring advances and factoring new developments into their day-to-day work and career-planning decisions.

The prudent professional relies on a wide variety of information sources to track technological developments and assess their impact on career goals. Some sources of information, such as traditional news reports, can be skimmed quickly and fully absorbed. Other sources, such as scientific literature and websites curated by experts in particular technologies, require time to digest complex technical information. More advanced topics, such as quantum computing, may require extended study just to grasp the fundamentals and begin to appreciate potential applications of the technology.

Even with a clear understanding of a particular technology, it can be challenging, or even impossible, to accurately predict its impact on the industry and, ultimately, the ways it will be integrated into the architectures of computing systems used by governments, businesses, and the public.

A practical and easy-to-implement approach for information gathering is to develop a collection of trusted sources for both mainstream and technical news and keep up to date with the information they offer. Mainstream news organizations, including television news, newspapers, magazines, and websites, often publish articles about promising technological developments and the impacts digital devices are having on societies around the world. In addition to discussing the purely technical aspects of computing systems (to some degree), these sources provide information on the social impact of computing technologies, such as concerns about its use for government and corporate surveillance and its employment in the spread of disinformation.

Technical websites operated by research organizations, individual technology experts, and enthusiastic users offer an immense quantity of information related to advances in computer architecture. As with all information accessible on the Internet, it is advisable to consider the reliability of the source whenever you encounter surprising information. While there are many spirited debates underway regarding the efficacy of individual early-stage technologies, there are also some people who appear to disagree with published information just to hear themselves argue. It is ultimately up to you to determine how much credence you should grant any opinions expressed on a web page.

Although individuals will have their own preferences, and the landscape of technology news sources is ever-changing, the following list provides a few fairly reliable sources of news on computing technology, in no particular order:

- `https://techcrunch.com/`: TechCrunch reports on the business of the tech industry.

- `https://www.wired.com/`: Wired is a monthly magazine and website that focuses on how emerging technologies affect culture, the economy, and politics.

- `https://arstechnica.com/`: Ars Technica, founded in 1998, publishes information targeted at technologists and information technology professionals.

- `https://www.tomshardware.com/`: Tom's Hardware provides news, articles, price comparisons, and reviews of computer hardware and high-technology devices.

- `https://www.engadget.com/`: Engadget, founded in 2004, covers the intersection of gaming, technology, and entertainment.

- `https://gizmodo.com/`: Gizmodo focuses on design, technology, and science fiction. The website tagline is "We come from the future."

- `https://thenextweb.com/`: TNW was started in 2006 to bring insight and meaning to the world of technology.

This list, while by no means complete, provides some starting points for gathering information on the current state and near future of computing technology and its applications.

Information retrieved online can, when approached from a reasonably skeptical viewpoint, provide current and accurate information on the state of advances in computer architecture. Information consumed in this manner does not, however, provide an education with the rigorousness associated with formal schooling, or provide any form of public declaration that you have absorbed this information and are capable of making use of it in a professional context.

A college degree, the subject of the next section, provides a thorough grounding in a subject discipline and is generally accepted by potential employers and clients as evidence of the attainment of professional skills.

College education

If it has been a few years since you last attended college, or if you began your career without a college degree, it may be time to consider enrolling in a degree program. If even the thought of undertaking such a journey seems out of the question because of work or family responsibilities, consider that many accredited institutions offering excellent programs in areas of study directly related to computer architecture provide fully online education experiences. Online classes, combined with proctored examinations, can lead to Bachelor's and Master's degrees in technical disciplines from some of the most respected universities in the world.

For workers with a degree who have been in the workforce for several years, the technology and analytical methods learned in school may have become stale and obsolete to some degree. To restore relevance and remain fully informed about the forefront of technologies involved in the design and production of modern computer systems, the best approach may be a return to the classroom to gain a deeper understanding of technical advances that have occurred in the intervening years.

If you are not prepared to commit to a degree program, many institutions offer online courses leading to a certificate in a subject area such as computer hardware engineering or computer engineering technology. While providing a lesser credential than a Bachelor's or Master's degree, completion of a technology certificate program nevertheless demonstrates a level of educational attainment and knowledge of the subject matter.

There will be some expense for tuition and books when taking college courses, whether the learning venue is in-person or online. Some employers are willing to provide partial or complete funding for the participation of employees in accredited degree programs. This funding may be accompanied by a mandatory commitment by the student to remain with the employer for some period following completion of the coursework. Students should take care to fully understand any obligations they may incur if circumstances require them to withdraw from school or leave the employer.

Many websites are available to assist with a search for an online college degree or certificate program that meets your needs. Some examples follow:

- `https://www.usnews.com/education/online-education`: U.S. News & World Report publishes annual rankings of accredited colleges, including online programs, specifically at this URL

- `https://www.guidetoonlineschools.com/online-reviews`: The Guide to Online Schools website provides reviews from students taking online programs at hundreds of colleges

Without being too repetitive with our warnings, you should carefully scrutinize any information gleaned from the Internet regarding online colleges. Ensure any institution under consideration is appropriately accredited and that the degrees it confers are accepted and valued by employers.

Those with the necessary resources, possibly with support provided by an employer, may even consider becoming a full-time student for the duration of a degree program. Employers who pay for degree programs will typically expect the student to agree to a binding commitment to the organization following completion of such a program. This approach can provide the quickest turnaround to a college degree and, in many cases, presents opportunities for participation in cutting-edge research on some of the most advanced computing technologies under development.

While a college degree from a respected institution in a relevant field of study is the gold-standard credential sought by employers and recognized by peers, opportunities are available to keep up with the latest research findings through participation in conferences and by reading scientific literature. These learning options are explored in the next section.

Conferences and literature

For professionals interested in keeping up with the leading edge of research in technologies related to the computer architectures of the future, there may be no better forum than hearing about the latest developments from the researchers themselves. There are regular conferences at locations around the world on every advanced computing topic you can imagine. For example, a list of worldwide conferences on the subject of quantum behavior, including many focusing on aspects of quantum computing, is available at `http://quantum.info/conf/index.html`.

As with other information from the Internet, it is helpful to view any unfamiliar conference with a degree of skepticism until you have vetted it thoroughly. There is, unfortunately, a phenomenon known as **junk conferences**, in which predatory individuals or organizations arrange conferences for the purpose of revenue generation rather than for sharing scientific knowledge. Be sure that any conference you sign up for and attend is overseen by a reputable organization and contains presentations by legitimate researchers in subject areas relevant to the conference.

There is a wide variety of scientific literature related to ongoing advances in technologies related to computer architecture. Professional organizations, such as IEEE, publish numerous scholarly journals devoted to the cutting edge of current research. Journals such as these are intended to communicate directly from researcher to researcher, so the level of technical knowledge expected of readers is quite high. If you have the necessary background and the willingness to appreciate the details in the papers published in scientific journals, you can read them to establish and maintain a level of knowledge on par with that of the scientists and engineers developing the next generation of computing technology.

Summary

Let's briefly review the topics we've discussed and learned about in the chapters of this book:

- In *Chapter 1, Introducing Computer Architecture,* we began with the earliest design of an automated computing machine, Babbage's Analytical Engine, and traced the course of digital computer history from the earliest vacuum tube-based computers through to the first generations of processors. We also looked at the architecture of an early, but still prevalent, microprocessor: the 6502.

- In *Chapter 2, Digital Logic,* we learned the basics of transistor technology, digital logic, registers, and sequential logic. We also discussed the use of hardware description languages in the development of complex digital devices.

- *Chapter 3, Processor Elements,* covered the fundamental components of processors, including the control unit, the ALU, and the register set. The chapter introduced concepts related to the processor instruction set, including details on 6502 addressing modes, instruction categories, interrupt processing, and I/O operations.

- *Chapter 4, Computer System Components,* introduced the MOSFET transistor and described its use in DRAM circuit technology. The chapter covered the processing and communication subsystems of modern computers, including the I/O subsystem, graphics displays, the network interface, and interfaces for the keyboard and mouse.

- In *Chapter 5, Hardware-Software Interface,* we learned about the inner workings of drivers and how the BIOS firmware of the original PC has transitioned to UEFI in modern computers. This chapter covered the boot process and the concepts associated with processes and threads in modern operating systems.

- *Chapter 6, Specialized Computing Domains,* introduced the unique features of real-time computing, digital signal processing, and GPU processing. Examples of specialized computing architectures relying on unique processing capabilities were presented, including cloud computer servers, business desktop computers, and high-performance gaming computers.

- *Chapter 7, Processor and Memory Architectures,* addressed processor and memory architectures, including the unique features of the von Neumann, Harvard, and modified Harvard architectures. The chapter described the distinction between physical and virtual memory, and introduced the architecture of paged virtual memory, including the functions of an MMU.

- In *Chapter 8, Performance-Enhancing Techniques,* we learned about a variety of techniques used in modern processors to accelerate instruction execution speed. Topics included cache memory, instruction pipelining, superscalar processing, simultaneous multithreading, and SIMD processing.

- *Chapter 9, Specialized Processor Extensions,* addressed several auxiliary processor capabilities, including privileged execution modes, floating-point mathematics, power management, and system security management.

- *Chapter 10, Modern Processor Architectures and Instruction Sets,* delved into the details of the architectures and instruction sets of the most prevalent 32-bit and 64-bit modern processors. For each of the x86, x64, 32-bit ARM, and 64-bit ARM processor architectures, the chapter introduced the register set, addressing modes, and instruction categories, and presented a simple but functional assembly language program.

- *Chapter 11, The RISC-V Architecture and Instruction Set,* examined the features of the RISC-V architecture in detail. The chapter introduced the base 32-bit architecture, including the register set, instruction set, and standard extensions to the instruction set. Additional topics included the 64-bit version of the architecture and standard configurations available as commercially produced RISC-V processors. The chapter included a simple RISC-V assembly language program and provided guidance for implementing a RISC-V processor in a low-cost FPGA device.

- *Chapter 12, Processor Virtualization,* introduced concepts associated with processor virtualization, including challenges that virtualization tools must overcome. The techniques used to implement virtualization in modern processor families, including x86, ARM, and RISC-V, were discussed. Several popular virtualization tools were described, and virtualization approaches used in cloud computing environments were presented.

- *Chapter 13, Domain-Specific Computer Architectures* examined some specific computer architectures, including smartphones, personal computers, warehouse-scale cloud-computing environments, and neural networks. The unique processing requirements associated with each of these domains were examined and the tailoring of processor hardware to optimize the trade-off between cost, performance, and power consumption in each case was discussed.

In this chapter, we attempted to gain some perspective on the road ahead for computer architectures. We reviewed the major advances and ongoing trends that have led to the current state of computer design and attempted to extrapolate forward to identify the directions the development of computing system architectures is likely to take in the future. We also examined some potentially disruptive technologies that could alter the path of future computer architectures. To get a tiny glimpse into this future, if you work through the exercises at the end of this chapter, you will develop a quantum computing algorithm and run it on an actual quantum computer, for free!

This chapter also reviewed some suggested approaches for professional development for the computer architect that should lead to a skill set that remains relevant and tolerant of future advances, whatever they may be.

Having completed this chapter, and this book, you will have a good understanding of the evolution of computer architecture design from the earliest days to its current state, and will be familiar with ongoing trends in computer architecture that are likely to indicate future technological directions. You will also be aware of some potentially disruptive technologies that may substantially alter computer architectures in the future. Finally, you will have learned some useful techniques for maintaining a current skill set in the field of computer architecture.

This brings us to the end of the book. I hope you have enjoyed reading it and working through the exercises as much as I have enjoyed writing it and working through the exercises myself.

Exercises

1. Install the Qiskit quantum processor software development framework by following the instructions at `https://qiskit.org/documentation/install.html`. The instructions suggest the installation of the Anaconda (`https://www.anaconda.com/`) data science and machine learning tool set. After installing Anaconda, create a Conda virtual environment named `qisketenv` to contain your work on quantum code and install Qisket in this environment with the command `pip install qiskit`. Make sure that you install the optional visualization dependencies with the `pip install qiskit-terra[visualization]` command.

2. Create a free IBM Quantum Experience account at `https://quantum-computing.ibm.com/`. Locate your IBM Quantum Services API token at `https://quantum-computing.ibm.com/account` and install it into your local environment using the instructions at `https://qiskit.org/documentation/install.html`.

3. Work through the example quantum program at `https://qiskit.org/documentation/tutorials/fundamentals/1_getting_started_with_qiskit.html`. This example creates a quantum circuit containing three qubits that implements a **Greenberger–Horne–Zeilinger (GHZ)** state. The GHZ state exhibits key properties of quantum entanglement. Execute the code in a simulation environment on your computer.

4. Execute the code from *Exercise 3* on an IBM quantum computer.

Answers to Exercises

Chapter 1: Introducing Computer Architecture

Exercise 1

Using your favorite programming language, develop a simulation of a single-digit decimal adder that operates in the same manner as in Babbage's Analytical Engine. First, prompt the user for two digits in the range 0-9: the addend and the accumulator. Display the addend, the accumulator, and the carry, which is initially zero. Perform a series of cycles as follows:

a. If the addend is zero, display the values of the addend, accumulator, and carry and terminate the program.

b. Decrement the addend by one and increment the accumulator by one.

c. If the accumulator incremented from nine to zero, increment the carry.

d. Go back to step a.

Test your code with these sums: 0+0, 0+1, 1+0, 1+2, 5+5, 9+1, and 9+9.

Answer

The Ex__1_single_digit_adder.py Python file contains the adder code:

```python
#!/usr/bin/env python

"""Ex__1_single_digit_adder.py: Answer to Ch 1 Ex 1."""

import sys
```

```python
# Perform one step of the Analytical Engine addition
# operation. a and b are the digits being added, c is the
# carry
def increment_adder(a, b, c):
    a = a - 1          # Decrement addend
    b = (b + 1) % 10 # Increment accum, wrap to 0 if necessary

    if b == 0:         # If accumulator is 0, increment carry
        c = c + 1

    return a, b, c;


# Add two decimal digits passed on the command line.
# The sum is returned as digit2 and the carry is 0 or 1.
def add_digits(digit1, digit2):
    carry = 0

    while digit1 > 0:
        [digit1, digit2, carry] = increment_adder(
        digit1, digit2, carry)

    return digit2, carry
```

The Ex__1_test_single_digit_adder.py file contains the test code:

```python
#!/usr/bin/env python

"""Ex__1_test_single_digit_adder.py: Tests for answer to
chapter 1 exercise 1."""

import unittest
import Ex__1_single_digit_adder

class TestSingleDigitAdder(unittest.TestCase):
    def test_1(self):
```

```
            self.assertEqual(Ex__1_single_digit_adder.add_digits(
            0, 0), (0, 0))

    def test_2(self):
            self.assertEqual(Ex__1_single_digit_adder.add_digits(
            0, 1), (1, 0))

    def test_3(self):
            self.assertEqual(Ex__1_single_digit_adder.add_digits(
            1, 0), (1, 0))

    def test_4(self):
            self.assertEqual(Ex__1_single_digit_adder.add_digits(
            1, 2), (3, 0))

    def test_5(self):
            self.assertEqual(Ex__1_single_digit_adder.add_digits(
            5, 5), (0, 1))

    def test_6(self):
            self.assertEqual(Ex__1_single_digit_adder.add_digits(
            9, 1), (0, 1))

    def test_7(self):
            self.assertEqual(Ex__1_single_digit_adder.add_digits(
            9, 9), (8, 1))


if __name__ == '__main__':
unittest.main()
```

To execute the tests, assuming Python is installed and is in your path, execute the following command:

```
python Ex__1_test_single_digit_adder.py
```

This is the output of a test run:

```
C:\>python Ex__1_test_single_digit_adder.py
.......
----------------------------------------------------------------
--------
Ran 7 tests in 0.001s

OK
```

Exercise 2

1. Create arrays of 40 decimal digits each for the addend, accumulator, and carry. Prompt the user for two decimal integers of up to 40 digits each. Perform the addition digit by digit using the cycles described in *Exercise 1*, and collect the carry output from each digit position in the carry array. After the cycles are complete, insert carries and, where necessary, ripple them across digits to complete the addition operation. Display the results after each cycle and at the end. Test with the same sums as in *Exercise 1* and test 99+1, 999999+1, 49+50, and 50+50.

Answer

The Ex__2_40_digit_adder.py Python file contains the adder code:

```python
#!/usr/bin/env python

"""Ex__2_40_digit_adder.py: Answer to Ch 1 Ex 2."""

import sys
import Ex__1_single_digit_adder

# Add two decimal numbers of up to 40 digits and return the
# sum. Input and output numeric values are represented as
# strings.
def add_40_digits(str1, str2):
    max_digits = 40
```

```
# Convert str1 into a 40 decimal digit value
num1 = [0]*max_digits
for i, c in enumerate(reversed(str1)):
    num1[i] = int(c) - int('0')


# Convert str2 into a 40 decimal digit value
num2 = [0]*max_digits
i = 0
for i, c in enumerate(reversed(str2)):
    num2[i] = int(c) - int('0')
    i = i + 1


# Sum the digits at each position and record the
# carry for each position
sum = [0]*max_digits
carry = [0]*max_digits
for i in range(max_digits):
    (sum[i], carry[i]) = Ex__1_single_digit_adder.\
    add_digits(num1[i], num2[i])


# Ripple the carry values across the digits
for i in range(max_digits-1):
    if (carry[i] == 1):
        sum[i+1] = (sum[i+1] + 1) % 10
        if (sum[i+1] == 0):
            carry[i+1] = 1


# Convert the result into a string with leading zeros
# removed
sum.reverse()
sum_str = "".join(map(str, sum))
sum_str = sum_str.lstrip('0') or '0'
return sum_str
```

396   Answers to Exercises

The `Ex__2_test_40_digit_adder.py` file contains the test code:

```python
#!/usr/bin/env python

"""Ex__2_test_40_digit_adder.py: Tests for answer to
 chapter 1 exercise 2."""

import unittest
import Ex__2_40_digit_adder

class TestSingleDigitAdder(unittest.TestCase):
    def test_1(self):
        self.assertEqual(Ex__2_40_digit_adder.add_40_digits(
        "0", "0"), "0")

    def test_2(self):
        self.assertEqual(Ex__2_40_digit_adder.add_40_digits(
        "0", "1"), "1")

    def test_3(self):
        self.assertEqual(Ex__2_40_digit_adder.add_40_digits(
        "1", "0"), "1")

    def test_4(self):
        self.assertEqual(Ex__2_40_digit_adder.add_40_digits(
        "1", "2"), "3")

    def test_5(self):
        self.assertEqual(Ex__2_40_digit_adder.add_40_digits(
        "5", "5"), "10")

    def test_6(self):
        self.assertEqual(Ex__2_40_digit_adder.add_40_digits(
        "9", "1"), "10")

    def test_7(self):
        self.assertEqual(Ex__2_40_digit_adder.add_40_digits(
```

```
            "9", "9"), "18")

    def test_8(self):
        self.assertEqual(Ex__2_40_digit_adder.add_40_digits(
        "99", "1"), "100")

    def test_9(self):
        self.assertEqual(Ex__2_40_digit_adder.add_40_digits(
        "999999", "1"), "1000000")

    def test_10(self):
        self.assertEqual(Ex__2_40_digit_adder.add_40_digits(
        "49", "50"), "99")

    def test_11(self):
        self.assertEqual(Ex__2_40_digit_adder.add_40_digits(
        "50", "50"), "100")

if __name__ == '__main__':
    unittest.main()
```

To execute the tests, assuming Python is installed and is in your path, execute the following command:

```
python Ex__2_test_40_digit_adder.py
```

This is the output of a test run:

```
C:\>python Ex__2_test_40_digit_adder.py
...........
----------------------------------------------------------------------
Ran 11 tests in 0.002s

OK
```

Exercise 3

Modify the program of *Exercise 2* to implement subtraction of 40-digit decimal values. Perform borrowing as required. Test with 0-0, 1-0, 1000000-1, and 0-1. What is the result for 0-1?

Answer

The `Ex__3_single_digit_subtractor.py` Python file contains the single-digit subtractor code:

```python
#!/usr/bin/env python


"""Ex__3_single_digit_subtractor.py: Answer to Ch 1 Ex 3
(single digit subtractor)."""


import sys


# Perform one step of the Analytical Engine subtraction
# operation. a and b are the digits being subtracted (a - b),
# c is the carry: 0 = borrow, 1 = not borrow
def decrement_subtractor(a, b, c):
    a = (a - 1) % 10 # Decrement left operand, to 9 if wrapped
    b = b - 1        # Decrement accumulator

    if a == 9:        # If accum reached 9, decrement carry
        c = c - 1

    return a, b, c;

# Subtract two decimal digits. The difference is returned as
# digit1 and the carry output is 0 (borrow) or 1 (not borrow).
def subtract_digits(digit1, digit2):
    carry = 1

    while digit2 > 0:
        [digit1, digit2, carry] = decrement_subtractor(
        digit1, digit2, carry)

    return digit1, carry
```

The `Ex__3_test_single_digit_subtractor.py` file contains the test code for the single-digit subtractor:

```python
#!/usr/bin/env python

"""Ex__3_test_single_digit_subtractor.py: Tests for answer
to chapter 1 exercise 3 (tests for single digit
subtractor)."""

import unittest
import Ex__3_single_digit_subtractor

class TestSingleDigitSubtractor(unittest.TestCase):
    def test_1(self):
        self.assertEqual(Ex__3_single_digit_subtractor.
        subtract_digits(0, 0), (0, 1))

    def test_2(self):
        self.assertEqual(Ex__3_single_digit_subtractor.
        subtract_digits(0, 1), (9, 0))

    def test_3(self):
        self.assertEqual(Ex__3_single_digit_subtractor.
        subtract_digits(1, 0), (1, 1))

    def test_4(self):
        self.assertEqual(Ex__3_single_digit_subtractor.
        subtract_digits(1, 2), (9, 0))

    def test_5(self):
        self.assertEqual(Ex__3_single_digit_subtractor.
        subtract_digits(5, 5), (0, 1))

    def test_6(self):
        self.assertEqual(Ex__3_single_digit_subtractor.
        subtract_digits(9, 1), (8, 1))
```

```python
    def test_7(self):
        self.assertEqual(Ex__3_single_digit_subtractor.
        subtract_digits(9, 9), (0, 1))


if __name__ == '__main__':
    unittest.main()
```

The `Ex__3_40_digit_subtractor.py` Python file contains the 40-digit subtractor code:

```python
#!/usr/bin/env python


"""Ex__3_40_digit_subtractor.py: Answer to Ch 1 Ex 3."""

import sys
import Ex__3_single_digit_subtractor


# Subtract two decimal numbers of up to 40 digits and
# return the result. Input and output numeric values are
# represented as strings.
def subtract_40_digits(str1, str2):
    max_digits = 40

    # Convert str1 into a 40 decimal digit value
    num1 = [0]*max_digits
    for i, c in enumerate(reversed(str1)):
        num1[i] = int(c) - int('0')

    # Convert str2 into a 40 decimal digit value
    num2 = [0]*max_digits
    i = 0
    for i, c in enumerate(reversed(str2)):
        num2[i] = int(c) - int('0')
        i = i + 1

    # Subtract the digits at each position and record the
    # carry for each position
```

```
    diff = [0]*max_digits
    carry = [0]*max_digits
    for i in range(max_digits):
        (diff[i], carry[i]) = Ex__3_single_digit_subtractor.\
        subtract_digits(num1[i], num2[i])


    # Ripple the carry values across the digits
    for i in range(max_digits-1):
        if (carry[i] == 0):
            diff[i+1] = (diff[i+1] - 1) % 10
            if (diff[i+1] == 9):
                carry[i+1] = 0


    # Convert the result into a string with leading zeros
    # removed
    diff.reverse()
    diff_str = "".join(map(str, diff))
    diff_str = diff_str.lstrip('0') or '0'
    return diff_str
```

The `Ex__3_test_40_digit_subtractor.py` file contains the test code for the 40-digit subtractor:

```python
#!/usr/bin/env python


"""Ex__3_test_40_digit_subtractor.py: Tests for answer to
chapter 1 exercise 3."""


import unittest
import Ex__3_40_digit_subtractor


class TestSingleDigitSubtractor(unittest.TestCase):
    def test_1(self):
        self.assertEqual(Ex__3_40_digit_subtractor.
        subtract_40_digits("0", "0"), "0")
```

For the `def test_2(self)` file, here is the code:

```
        self.assertEqual(Ex__3_40_digit_subtractor.
        subtract_40_digits("1", "0"), "1")


    def test_3(self):
        self.assertEqual(Ex__3_40_digit_subtractor.
        subtract_40_digits("1000000", "1"), "999999")


    def test_4(self):
        self.assertEqual(Ex__3_40_digit_subtractor.
        subtract_40_digits("0", "1"),
        "9999999999999999999999999999999999999999")


if __name__ == '__main__':
    unittest.main()
```

To execute the tests, assuming Python is installed and is in your path, execute the following commands:

```
python Ex__3_test_single_digit_subtractor.py
python Ex__3_test_40_digit_subtractor.py
```

This is the output of a test run of `Ex__3_test_single_digit_subtractor.py`:

```
C:\>python Ex__3_test_single_digit_subtractor.py
.......
----------------------------------------------------------------
--------
Ran 7 tests in 0.001s


OK
```

This is the output of a test run of `Ex__3_test_40_digit_subtractor.py`:

```
C:\>python Ex__3_test_40_digit_subtractor.py
....
----------------------------------------------------------------
--------
Ran 4 tests in 0.001s


OK
```

Exercise 4

1. 6502 assembly language references data in memory locations using an operand
    value containing the address (without the # character that indicates an immediate
    value). For example, the LDA $00 instruction loads the byte at memory address
    $00 into A. STA $01 stores the byte in A into address $01. Addresses can be any
    value in the range 0 to $FFFF, assuming memory exists at the address and the
    address is not already in use for some other purpose. Using your preferred 6502
    emulator, write 6502 assembly code to store a 16-bit value into addresses $00-$01,
    store a second value into addresses $02-$03, then add the two values and store the
    result in $04-$05. Be sure to propagate any carry between the two bytes. Ignore
    any carry from the 16-bit result. Test with $0000+$0001, $00FF+$0001, and
    $1234+$5678.

Answer

The 6502 assembly file Ex__4_16_bit_addition.asm contains the 16-bit
addition code:

```
; Ex__4_16_bit_addition.asm
; Try running this code at
; https://skilldrick.github.io/easy6502/

; Set up the values to be added
; Remove the appropriate semicolons to select the bytes to add:
; ($0000 + $0001) or ($00FF + $0001) or ($1234 + $5678)

LDA #$00
;LDA #$FF
;LDA #$34
STA $00

LDA #$00
;LDA #$00
;LDA #$12
STA $01

LDA #$01
```

```
;LDA #$01
;LDA #$78
STA $02

LDA #$00
;LDA #$00
;LDA #$56
STA $03

; Add the two 16-bit values
CLC
LDA $00
ADC $02
STA $04

LDA $01
ADC $03
STA $05
```

Try running this code at `https://skilldrick.github.io/easy6502/`.

Exercise 5

Write 6502 assembly code to subtract two 16-bit values in a manner similar to *Exercise 4*. Test with $0001-$0000, $0001-$0001, $0100-$00FF, and $0000-$0001. What is the result for $0000-$0001?

Answer

The 6502 assembly file `Ex__5_16_bit_subtraction.asm` contains the 16-bit subtraction code:

```
; Ex__5_16_bit_subtraction.asm
; Try running this code at
; https://skilldrick.github.io/easy6502/

; Set up the values to be subtracted
; Remove the appropriate semicolons to select the bytes to
; subtract:
```

```
;  ($0001 - $0000) or ($0001 - $0001) or ($0001 - $00FF) or
;  ($0000 - $0001)


LDA #$01
;LDA #$01
;LDA #$01
;LDA #$00
STA $00

LDA #$00
;LDA #$00
;LDA #$00
;LDA #$00
STA $01

LDA #$00
;LDA #$01
;LDA #$FF
;LDA #$01
STA $02

LDA #$00
;LDA #$00
;LDA #$00
;LDA #$00
STA $03

; Subtract the two 16-bit values
SEC
LDA $00
SBC $02
STA $04

LDA $01
SBC $03
STA $05
```

Try running this code at https://skilldrick.github.io/easy6502/.

Exercise 6

Write 6502 assembly code to store two 32-bit integers in addresses $00-03 and $04-$07, then add them, storing the results in $08-$0B. Use a looping construct, including a label and a branch instruction, to iterate over the bytes of the two values to be added. Search the Internet for the details of the 6502 decrement and branch instructions and the use of labels in assembly language. Hint: the 6502 zero-page indexed addressing mode works well in this application.

Answer

The 6502 assembly file Ex__6_32_bit_addition.asm contains the 32-bit addition code:

```
; Ex__6_32_bit_addition.asm
; Try running this code at
; https://skilldrick.github.io/easy6502/


; Set up the values to be added
; Remove the appropriate semicolons to select the bytes to
; add:
; ($00000001 + $00000001) or ($0000FFFF + $00000001) or
; ($FFFFFFFE + $00000001) or ($FFFFFFFF + $00000001)

LDA #$01
;LDA #$FF
;LDA #$FE
;LDA #$FF
STA $00

LDA #$00
;LDA #$FF
;LDA #$FF
;LDA #$FF
STA $01

LDA #$00
;LDA #$00
```

```
;LDA #$FF
;LDA #$FF
STA $02

LDA #$00
;LDA #$00
;LDA #$FF
;LDA #$FF
STA $03

LDA #$01
STA $04

LDA #$00
STA $05
STA $06
STA $07

; Add the two 32-bit values using absolute indexed
; addressing mode
LDX #$00
LDY #$04
CLC

ADD_LOOP:
LDA $00, X
ADC $04, X
STA $08, X
INX
DEY
BNE ADD_LOOP
```

Try running this code at https://skilldrick.github.io/easy6502/.

Chapter 2: Digital Logic

Exercise 1

Rearrange the circuit in *Figure 2.5* to convert the AND gate to a NAND gate. Hint: there is no need to add or remove components.

Answer

Relocate the *R2* resistor and the output signal connection point as follows:

Exercise 2

Create a circuit implementation of an OR gate by modifying the circuit in *Figure 2.5*. Wires, transistors, and resistors can be added as needed.

Answer

The OR gate circuit is as follows:

Exercise 3

Search the Internet for free VHDL development software suites that include a simulator. Get one of these suites, set it up, and build any simple demo projects that come with the suite to ensure it is working properly.

Answer

Some freely available VHDL development suites are as follows:

- Xilinx Vivado Design Suite is available at `https://www.xilinx.com/support/download.html`.

- Intel® Quartus® Prime Software Lite Edition is available at `https://www.intel.com/content/www/us/en/software/programmable/quartus-prime/download.html`.

- The open source GHDL simulator for VHDL is available at `https://github.com/ghdl/ghdl`.

- Mentor ModelSim PE Student Edition is available at `https://www.mentor.com/company/higher_ed/modelsim-student-edition`.

Vivado Design Suite will be used for the examples in this chapter and the following chapters, including installing circuit designs in a low-cost FPGA development board. These steps describe the installation and setup process for Windows 10:

1. Visit `https://www.xilinx.com/support/download.html` and select the web installer for the latest version of Vivado Design Suite for Windows. Be sure to select the full Vivado installer and not an update. During this process, you will need to create a Xilinx account if you do not already have one. Be sure to save your account username and password for later use.

2. Provide the requested information, download the **Windows Self Extracting Web Installer**, and run it. You may need to change your Windows app installation settings to allow the installer to run.

3. You will be asked to log in with your Xilinx account information and accept the license agreements.

4. Select the tool suite you want to install. The examples in this book use Vivado. Select **Vivado** and click **Next**.

5. Select **Vivado HL WebPack** (this is the free version). Click **Next**.

6. Accept the default design tools, devices, and installation options for Vivado HL Webpack. Click **Next**.

7. Accept the default installation directory and other options. Click **Next**.

8. On the **Installation Summary** page, click **Install**. Downloading and installation will take some time. The time required depends on your Internet connection speed. Plan for a few hours.

After the installation completes, follow these steps to build an example project:

1. You should find an icon on your desktop with a name similar to **Vivado 2019.2**. Double-click this icon (and not the icon that says **Vivado HLS**) to start the application.

2. In the Vivado main window, click **Open Example Project**.

3. Click through to the **Select Project Template** screen and select **CPU (HDL)**.

4. Click through and accept the defaults on the following screens and click **Finish** to create the project.

5. On the **Project Manager** page, you'll find the **Sources** panel. Expand the tree listing and double-click some of the files to open them in the editor. Most of the files in this design are in the Verilog hardware design language.

6. Click **Run Synthesis** in the **Project Manager** panel. The **Design Runs** panel will update the status as synthesis proceeds. This may take several minutes.

7. After synthesis completes, a dialog will appear offering to run the implementation. Click **Cancel**.

8. Click **Run Simulation** in the Vivado main dialog **Project Manager** section, then select **Run behavioral simulation**. This may, again, take several minutes.

9. After the simulation completes, you will see a timing diagram in the **Simulation** window showing the simulated CPU signals using the input data provided by the simulation source files.

10. This completes the exercise. You may close Vivado.

Exercise 4

Using your VHDL toolset, implement the 4-bit adder using the code listings presented in this chapter.

Answer

Follow these steps to implement the 4-bit adder:

1. Double-click the **Vivado 2019.2** (or similar) icon to start Vivado.

2. Click **Create Project** in the Vivado main dialog.

3. Click through and accept the default project name and location.

4. Select **RTL Project**, the default project type.

5. On the **Default Part** page, select the **Boards** tab. Type Arty in the search field and select the **Arty A7-35** then click **Next**. If **Arty** does not appear after searching, click **Update Board Repositories** and then search again.

6. Click **Finish** to create the project.

7. Click **Add Sources** in the **Project Manager** panel, select **Add or create design sources**, and add Ex__4_adder4.vhdl and Ex__4_fulladder.vhdl, then click **Finish**.

8. Expand the tree in the **Design Sources** window in the **Project Manager** dialog and locate the two files you added. Double-click each of them and expand the source code window to view the code.

9. Click **Run Synthesis** in the **Project Manager** panel. Leave the options in the **Launch Runs** dialog at their defaults and click **OK**. The **Design Runs** panel will update the status as synthesis proceeds.

10. Wait for the synthesis to complete, then select **View Reports** in the **Synthesis Completed** dialog. Double-click some of the reports produced during the synthesis process. Only the reports that have an icon with a green dot are present.

11. This completes the exercise. You may close Vivado.

Exercise 5

Add test driver code (search the Internet to learn how) to your 4-bit adder to drive it through a limited set of input sets and verify that the outputs are correct.

Answer

Follow these steps to test the 4-bit adder project created in *Exercise 4*:

1. Double-click the **Vivado 2019.2** (or similar) icon to start Vivado.

2. Click **Open Project** in the Vivado main dialog and open the project you created in *Exercise 4*. You will need to select the project filename ending in **.xpr**.

3. Click **Add Sources** in the **Project Manager** panel, select **Add or create simulation sources**, add Ex__5_adder4_testbench.vhdl, and then click **Finish**.

4. Expand the tree in the **Simulation Sources** window in the **Project Manager** dialog and locate the file you added. Double-click the file and expand the source code window to view the code. Observe the six test cases present in the code.

5. Click **Run Simulation** in the Vivado main dialog **Project Manager** section, then select **Run behavioral simulation**.

6. Wait for the simulation to complete, then expand the windows with the timing diagram (probably labeled **Untitled 1**).

7. Use the magnifying glass icons and the window's horizontal scroll bar to view the six test cases in the first 60 **nanoseconds** (**ns**) of execution. Determine if the sum and carry for each addition operation are correct. You can drag the yellow marker to update the information in the **Value** column.

8. This completes the exercise. You may close Vivado.

Exercise 6

Expand the test driver code and verify that the 4-bit adder produces correct results for all possible combinations of inputs.

Answer

Follow these steps to test the 4-bit adder project created in *Exercise 4*:

1. Double-click the Vivado **2019.2** (or similar) icon to start Vivado.

2. Click **Open Project** in the Vivado main dialog and open the project you created in *Exercise 4* and modified in *Exercise 5*. You will need to select the project filename ending in **.xpr**.

3. We're going to replace the test driver code from *Exercise 5* with a different test driver. Expand the tree in the **Simulation Sources** window in the **Project Manager** dialog and locate the module you added in *Exercise 5* (ADDER4_TESTBENCH). Right-click the module name and select **Remove File from Project**, then click **OK** to confirm the removal.

4. Click **Add Sources** in the **Project Manager** panel, select **Add or create simulation sources**, add Ex__6_adder4_fulltestbench.vhdl, and then click **Finish**.

5. Expand the tree in the **Simulation Sources** window in the **Project Manager** dialog and locate the file you added. Double-click the file and expand the source code window to view the code. Observe the loop with 256 test cases in the code.

6. Click **Run Simulation** in the Vivado main dialog **Project Manager** section, then select **Run behavioral simulation**.

7. Wait for the simulation to complete, then expand the windows with the timing diagram (probably labeled **Untitled 1**).

8. Use the magnifying glass icons and the window horizontal scroll bar to view the test cases. *Uh-oh!* The run stops after 1,000 ns, which isn't enough time for all of the tests to execute.

9. Right-click **Simulation** in the **Project Manager** panel, then select **Simulation Settings...**.

10. Click the **Simulation** tab and change the value for xsim.simulate.runtime to 3000ns. Click **OK**.

11. Click the **X** on the **Simulation** window to close the simulation.

12. Re-run the simulation.

13. After expanding and scaling the timing diagram, you will be able to see all 256 test cases. See if the error signal has a value of 1 anywhere along the trace. This would indicate that the adder's output did not match the expected output.

14. This completes the exercise. You may close Vivado.

Chapter 3: Processor Elements

Exercise 1

Consider the addition of two signed 8-bit numbers (that is, numbers in the range -128 to +127) where one operand is positive and the other is negative. Is there any pair of 8-bit numbers of different signs that, when added together, will exceed the range -128 to +127? This would constitute a signed overflow. Note: we're only looking at addition here because, as we've seen, subtraction in the 6502 architecture is the same as addition with the right operand's bits inverted.

Answer

The range of the positive (or non-negative) numbers is 0 to 127. The range of negative numbers is -128 to -1. It is only necessary to consider the extremes of each of these ranges to cover all possibilities:

Sum	Result
0 + -128	-128
127 + -128	-1
0 + -1	-1
127 + -1	126

In the preceding table, we can see that there is no pair of 8-bit numbers of different signs that, when added together, exceeds the range -128 to +127.

Exercise 2

If the answer to *Exercise 1* is *no*, this implies the only way to create a signed overflow is to add two numbers of the same sign. If an overflow occurs, what can you say about the result of performing XOR between the most significant bit of each operand with the most significant bit of the result? In other words, what will be the result of the expressions left(7) XOR result(7) and right(7) XOR result(7)? In these expressions, (7) indicates bit 7, the most significant bit.

Answer

Bit 7 is the sign bit. Since overflow can only occur when both operands are of the same sign, left(7) must equal right(7) when an overflow occurs.

When overflow occurs, the sign of the result differs from the sign of the two operands. This means result(7) differs from bit 7 of both of the operands.

Therefore, left(7) XOR result(7) = 1 and right(7) XOR result(7) = 1 whenever overflow occurs.

Exercise 3

Review the VHDL listing in the *Arithmetic Logic Unit* section in this chapter and determine whether the logic for setting or clearing the V flag is correct for addition and subtraction operations. Check the results of adding 126+1, 127+1, -127+(-1), and -128+(-1).

Answer

The listing of the VHDL implementation of a portion of a 6502-like **Arithmetic Logic Unit (ALU)** in this chapter implements the computation of the overflow flag with the following code:

```
if (((LEFT(7) XOR result8(7)) = '1') AND
    ((right_op(7) XOR result8(7)) = '1')) then -- V flag
  V_OUT <= '1';
else
  V_OUT <= '0';
end if;
```

The following table shows the results of this code for the four test cases in the question:

left	right	left(7)	right(7)	result8(7)	V_OUT	Correct?
126	1	0	0	0	0	Yes
127	1	0	0	1	1	Yes
-127	-1	1	1	1	0	Yes
-128	-1	1	1	0	1	Yes

The logic for setting or clearing the V flag is correct for these test cases.

Exercise 4

When transferring blocks of data over an error-prone transmission medium, it is common to use a **checksum** to determine whether any data bits were lost or corrupted during transmission. The checksum is typically appended to the transferred data record. One checksum algorithm uses these steps:

1. Add all of the bytes in the data record together, retaining only the lowest 8 bits of the sum.

2. The checksum is the two's complement of the 8-bit sum.

3. Append the checksum byte to the data record.

After receiving a data block with the appended checksum, the processor can determine whether the checksum is valid by simply adding all of the bytes in the record, including the checksum, together. The checksum is valid if the lowest 8 bits of the sum are zero. Implement this checksum algorithm using 6502 assembly language. The data bytes begin at the memory location store in addresses $10-$11 and the number of bytes (including the checksum byte) is provided as an input in the X register. Set the A register to 1 if the checksum is valid, and to 0 if it is invalid.

Answer

The Ex__4_checksum_alg.asm file contains the following checksum code:

```
; Ex__4_checksum_alg.asm
; Try running this code at https://skilldrick.github.io/
easy6502/


; Set up the array of bytes to be checksummed
LDA #$01
STA $00

LDA #$72
STA $01

LDA #$93
STA $02

LDA #$F4
```

```
STA $03


LDA #$06 ; This is the checksum byte
STA $04


; Store the address of the data array in $10-$11
LDA #$00
STA $10
STA $11


; Store the number of bytes in X
LDX #5


; Entering the checksum algorithm
; Move X to Y
TXA
TAY


; Compute the checksum
LDA #$00
DEY


LOOP:
CLC
ADC ($10), Y
DEY
BPL LOOP


CMP #$00
BNE ERROR


; The sum is zero: Checksum is correct
LDA #1
JMP DONE


; The sum is nonzero: Checksum is incorrect
```

```
ERROR:
LDA #0

; A contains 1 if checksum is correct, 0 if it is incorrect
DONE:
```

Exercise 5

Make the checksum validation code from *Exercise 4* into a labeled subroutine that can be called with a JSR instruction and that ends with an RTS instruction.

Answer

The Ex__5_checksum_subroutine.asm file implements the checksum algorithm as a subroutine:

```
; Ex__5_checksum_subroutine.asm
; Try running this code at https://skilldrick.github.io/
easy6502/

; Set up the array of bytes to be checksummed
LDA #$01
STA $00
LDA #$72
STA $01
LDA #$93
STA $02
LDA #$F4
STA $03
LDA #$06 ; This is the checksum byte
STA $04

; Store the address of the data array in $10-$11
LDA #$00
STA $10
STA $11
```

```
; Store the number of bytes in X
LDX #5


; Call the checksum calculation subroutine
JSR CALC_CKSUM


; Halt execution
BRK


; ===================================================
; Compute the checksum
CALC_CKSUM:
; Move X to Y
TXA
TAY


LDA #$00
DEY


LOOP:
CLC
ADC ($10), Y
DEY
BPL LOOP


CMP #$00
BNE CKSUM_ERROR


; The sum is zero: Checksum is correct
LDA #1
JMP DONE


; The sum is nonzero: Checksum is incorrect
CKSUM_ERROR:
LDA #0
```

```
; A contains 1 if checksum is correct, 0 if it is incorrect
DONE:
RTS
```

Exercise 6

Write and execute a set of tests to verify the correct operation of the checksum testing subroutine you implemented in *Exercise 4* and *Exercise 5*. What is the shortest block of data your code can perform checksum validation upon? What is the longest block?

Answer

The Ex__6_checksum_tests.asm file implements the following checksum test code:

```
; Ex__6_checksum_tests.asm
; Try running this code at https://skilldrick.github.io/
easy6502/

; After tests complete, A=$AA if success, A=$EE if error
detected

; Store the address of the data array in $10-$11
LDA #$00
STA $10
STA $11


; ================================================
; Test 1: 1 byte; Checksum: 00 Checksum should pass? Yes
LDA #$00
STA $00

; Store the number of bytes in X
LDX #1

; Call the checksum calculation subroutine
JSR CALC_CKSUM

CMP #$01
```

```
BEQ TEST2
JMP ERROR


TEST2:
; ================================================
; Test 2: 1 byte; Checksum: 01 Checksum should pass? No
LDA #$01
STA $00


; Store the number of bytes in X
LDX #1


; Call the checksum calculation subroutine
JSR CALC_CKSUM


CMP #$00
BEQ TEST3
JMP ERROR


TEST3:
; ================================================
; Test 3: 2 bytes: 00 Checksum: 00 Checksum should pass? Yes
LDA #$00
STA $00
STA $01


; Store the number of bytes in X
LDX #2


; Call the checksum calculation subroutine
JSR CALC_CKSUM


CMP #$01
BEQ TEST4
JMP ERROR
```

```
TEST4:
; ================================================
; Test 4: 2 bytes: 00 Checksum: 01 Checksum should pass? No
LDA #$00
STA $00
LDA #$01
STA $01


; Store the number of bytes in X
LDX #2


; Call the checksum calculation subroutine
JSR CALC_CKSUM


CMP #$00
BEQ TEST5
JMP ERROR


TEST5:
; ================================================
; Test 5: 2 bytes: 01 Checksum: 00 Checksum should pass? No
LDA #$01
STA $00
LDA #$00
STA $01


; Store the number of bytes in X
LDX #1


; Call the checksum calculation subroutine
JSR CALC_CKSUM


CMP #$00
BEQ TEST6
JMP ERROR
```

```
TEST6:
; ================================================
; Test 6: 3 bytes: 00 00 Checksum: 00 Checksum should pass? Yes
LDA #$00
STA $00
STA $01
STA $02

; Store the number of bytes in X
LDX #3

; Call the checksum calculation subroutine
JSR CALC_CKSUM

CMP #$01
BEQ TEST7
JMP ERROR

TEST7:
; ================================================
; Test 7: 3 bytes: 00 00 Checksum: 00 Checksum should pass? Yes
LDA #$00
STA $00
STA $01
STA $02

; Store the number of bytes in X
LDX #3

; Call the checksum calculation subroutine
JSR CALC_CKSUM

CMP #$01
BEQ TEST8
JMP ERROR
```

```
TEST8:
; ================================================
; Test 8: 3 bytes: 00 00 Checksum: 01 Checksum should pass? No
LDA #$00
STA $00
LDA #$00
STA $01
LDA #$01
STA $02

; Store the number of bytes in X
LDX #3

; Call the checksum calculation subroutine
JSR CALC_CKSUM

CMP #$00
BEQ TEST9
JMP ERROR

TEST9:
; ================================================
; Test 9: 3 bytes: 00 01 Checksum: FF Checksum should pass? Yes
LDA #$00
STA $00
LDA #$01
STA $01
LDA #$FF
STA $02

; Store the number of bytes in X
LDX #3

; Call the checksum calculation subroutine
JSR CALC_CKSUM
```

```
CMP #$01
BEQ TEST10
JMP ERROR

TEST10:
; ==================================================
; Test 10: 5 bytes: 01 72 93 F4 Checksum: 06 Checksum should
pass? Yes
LDA #$01
STA $00
LDA #$72
STA $01
LDA #$93
STA $02
LDA #$F4
STA $03
LDA #$06  ; This is the checksum byte
STA $04

; Store the number of bytes in X
LDX #5

; Call the checksum calculation subroutine
JSR CALC_CKSUM

CMP #$01
BEQ PASSED

ERROR:
; ==================================================
; Error occurred; Halt execution with $EE in A
LDA #$EE
BRK

PASSED:
; ==================================================
```

```
; All tests passed; Halt execution with $AA in A
LDA #$AA
BRK


; ================================================
; Compute the checksum
CALC_CKSUM:
; Move X to Y
TXA
TAY

LDA #$00
DEY

LOOP:
CLC
ADC ($10), Y
DEY
BPL LOOP

CMP #$00
BNE CKSUM_ERROR

; The sum is zero: Checksum is correct
LDA #1
JMP DONE

; The sum is nonzero: Checksum is incorrect
CKSUM_ERROR:
LDA #0

; A contains 1 if checksum is correct, 0 if it is incorrect
DONE:
RTS
```

The checksum routine works for byte sequences with lengths from 1 to 255 bytes.

Chapter 4: Computer System Components

Exercise 1

Create a circuit implementation of an NAND gate using two CMOS transistor pairs. Unlike NPN transistor gate circuits, no resistors are required for this circuit.

Answer

The diagram for this circuit is as follows:

Exercise 2

A 16-gigabit DRAM integrated circuit has two bank group selection inputs, two bank selection inputs, and 17 row address inputs. How many bits are in each row of a bank in this device?

Answer

The DRAM circuit contains 16 gigabits = 16×2^{30} bits.

The number of address bits is 2 bank group bits + 2 bank bits + 17 row address bits = 21 bits.

The row dimension of each bank is therefore $(16 \times 2^{30}) \div 2^{21} =$ **8,192 bits**.

Chapter 5: Hardware-Software Interface

Exercise 1

Restart your computer and enter the BIOS or UEFI settings. Examine each of the menus available in this environment. Does your computer have a BIOS or does it use UEFI? Does your motherboard support overclocking? When you are finished, be sure to select the option to quit without saving changes unless you are absolutely certain you want to make changes.

Answer

In Windows, you can enter the BIOS/UEFI settings by changing the startup options while Windows is running. To access these settings, perform the following steps:

1. In the Windows search box, type `startup` and select **Change advanced startup options**.

2. Select the **Restart now** button under **Advanced startup**.

3. When asked **Choose an option**, select **Troubleshoot**.

4. On the **Troubleshoot** screen, select **Advanced options**.

5. On the **Advanced options** screen, select **UEFI Firmware Settings**.

6. On the **UEFI Firmware Settings** screen, click the **Restart** button.

7. The system will restart and display the UEFI configuration main screen. Use the left and right arrow keys on the keyboard to move between the screens.

The following is in answer to the questions in this exercise for a specific computer system (an Asus ZenBook UX303LA laptop, in this example):

- Although the messages displayed in the menus use the term "BIOS" frequently, mentions of "EFI applications" and its age indicate it is actually **UEFI**.

- **No overclocking options** are available.

After you've finished examining the UEFI information, exit without saving any changes by following these steps:

1. Move to the **Save & Exit** page.

2. Use the up and down arrow keys to select **Discard Changes and Exit**.

3. Press **Enter**.

4. Select **Yes** and press **Enter** on the **Exit Without Saving** dialog.

5. The system will reboot.

Exercise 2

Run the appropriate command on your computer to display the currently running processes. What is the **process ID (PID)** of the process you are using to run this command?

Answer

In Windows, open a Command Prompt window (type command in the Windows search box to locate the application) and type the tasklist command as follows:

```
C:\>tasklist

Image Name                     PID Session Name        Session#    Mem Usage

==================== ===== ============ ======== =============
System Idle Process              0 Services                   0            8 K
System                           4 Services                   0        9,840 K
Registry                       120 Services                   0       85,324 K
smss.exe                       544 Services                   0          640 K
csrss.exe                      768 Services                   0        4,348 K
wininit.exe                    852 Services                   0        4,912 K
services.exe                   932 Services                   0        8,768 K
lsass.exe                      324 Services                   0       18,160 K
svchost.exe                   1044 Services                   0        2,308 K
svchost.exe                   1068 Services                   0       27,364 K
     .
     .
     .
svchost.exe                  12184 Services                   0        8,544 K
cmd.exe                      16008 Console                    3        3,996 K
conhost.exe                  21712 Console                    3       18,448 K
tasklist.exe                 15488 Console                    3       10,096 K
```

The current process is the one running the tasklist.exe application. The PID of this process is 15488.

Chapter 6: Specialized Computing Domains

Exercise 1

Rate monotonic scheduling (RMS) is an algorithm for assigning thread priorities in preemptive, hard, real-time applications in which threads execute periodically. RMS assigns the highest priority to the thread with the shortest execution period, the next-highest priority to the thread with the next-shortest execution period, and so on. An RMS system is schedulable, meaning all tasks are guaranteed to meet their deadlines (assuming no inter-thread interactions or other activities such as interrupts causing processing delays) if the following condition is met:

$$\sum_{k=1}^{n} \frac{C_i}{T_i} \le n\left(2^{1/n} - 1\right)$$

This formula represents the maximum fraction of available processing time that can be consumed by n threads. In this formula, C_i is the maximum execution time required for thread i, and T_i is the execution period of thread i.

Is the following system composed of three threads schedulable?

Thread	Execution time (C_i), ms	Execution period (T_i), ms
Thread 1	50	100
Thread 2	100	500
Thread 3	120	1,000

Answer

First, evaluate the left side of the RMS formula using the data from the table:

$$\frac{50}{100} + \frac{100}{500} + \frac{120}{1000} = 0.82$$

Then evaluate the right side of the RMS formula:

$$3\left(2^{\frac{1}{3}} - 1\right) = 0.7798$$

Because *0.82* is not less than or equal to *0.7798*, this set of tasks is not schedulable in RMS.

Exercise 2

A commonly used form of the one-dimensional **discrete cosine transform (DCT)** is as follows:

$$X_k = \sum_{n=0}^{N-1} x_n \cos\left[\frac{\pi}{N}\left(n + \frac{1}{2}\right)k\right]$$

In this formula, k, the index of the DCT coefficient, runs from 0 to N-1.

Write a program to compute the DCT of the sequence $x = \{0.5, 0.2, 0.7, -0.6, 0.4\ -0.2, 1.0, -0.3\}$.

The cosine terms in the formula depend only on the indexes n and k, and do not depend on the input data sequence x. This means the cosine terms can be computed one time and stored as constants for later use. Using this as a preparatory step, the computation of each DCT coefficient reduces to a sequence of MAC operations.

This formula represents the unoptimized form of the DCT computation, requiring N^2 iterations of the MAC operation to compute all N DCT coefficients.

Answer

The `Ex__2_dct_formula.py` Python file contains the DCT code:

```python
#!/usr/bin/env python

"""Ex__2_dct_formula.py: Answer to Ch 6 Ex 2."""

import math

# Input vector
x = [0.5, 0.2, 0.7, -0.6, 0.4, -0.2, 1.0, -0.3]

# Compute the DCT coefficients
dct_coef = [[i for i in range(len(x))] for j in range(len(x))]
for n in range(len(x)):
    for k in range(len(x)):
        dct_coef[n][k] = math.cos((math.pi/len(x))*
            (n + 1/2)*k);
```

```
# Compute the DCT
x_dct = [i for i in range(len(x))]
for k in range(len(x)):
    x_dct[k] = 0;
    for n in range(len(x)):
        x_dct[k] += x[n]*dct_coef[n][k];

# Print the results
print('Index', end='')
for i in range(len(x)):
    print("%8d" % i, end='')

print('\nx      ', end='')
for i in range(len(x)):
    print("%8.4f" % x[i], end='')

print('\nDCT(x) ', end='')
for i in range(len(x)):
    print("%8.4f" % x_dct[i], end='')
```

To run the code, assuming Python is installed and is in your path, execute the following command:

```
python Ex__2_dct_formula.py
```

This is the output produced by the program:

```
C:\>Ex__2_dct_formula.py
Index        0      1      2      3      4      5      6      7
x         0.50   0.20   0.70  -0.60   0.40  -0.20   1.00  -0.30
DCT(x)    1.70   0.42   0.64   0.49  -1.20   0.57  -0.49   2.33
```

Exercise 3

The hyperbolic tangent is often used as an activation function in **Artificial Neural Networks (ANNs)**. The hyperbolic tangent function is defined as follows:

$$\tanh(x) = \frac{e^x - e^{-x}}{e^x + e^{-x}}$$

Given a neuron with inputs from three preceding neurons as depicted in *Figure 6.4*, compute the neuron's output with the hyperbolic tangent as the activation function *F(x)* using the following neuron outputs and path weights:

Neuron	Neuron output	Weight
N_1	0.6	0.4
N_2	-0.3	0.8
N_3	0.5	-0.2

Answer

The `Ex__3_activation_func.py` Python file contains the following code:

```python
#!/usr/bin/env python

"""Ex__3_activation_func.py: Answer to Ch 6 Ex 3."""

# Output produced by this program:
# Neuron output = -0.099668

import math

# Neuron signal and weight vectors
neuron = [0.6, -0.3,  0.5]
weight = [0.4,  0.8, -0.2]

sum = 0
for i in range(len(neuron)):
    sum = sum + neuron[i] * weight[i]

output = math.tanh(sum)

# Print the results
print('Neuron output = %8.6f' % output)
```

To run the code, assuming Python is installed and is in your path, execute the following command:

```
python Ex__3_activation_func.py
```

This is the output produced by the program:

```
C:\>Ex__3_activation_func.py
Neuron output = -0.099668
```

Chapter 7: Processor and Memory Architectures

Exercise 1

A 16-bit embedded processor has separate memory regions for code and data. Code is stored in flash memory and modifiable data is stored in RAM. Some data values, such as constants and initial values for RAM data items, are stored in the same flash memory region as the program instructions. RAM and ROM reside in the same address space. Which of the processor architectures discussed in this chapter best describes this processor?

Answer

Because the code and data are located in the same address space, this is a **von Neumann architecture**.

The fact that the code and some data items are stored in ROM and other data items reside in RAM is not relevant to determining the architecture category.

Exercise 2

The processor described in *Exercise 1* has memory security features that prevent executed code from modifying program instruction memory. The processor uses physical addresses to access instructions and data. Does this processor contain an MMU?

Answer

While the protection of memory regions is a feature of MMUs, the presence of memory protection alone does not mean an MMU is in use. *This processor does not contain an MMU.*

MMUs generally perform virtual-to-physical address translation, which does not occur in the processor described here.

Exercise 3

The order of accessing sequential elements in a large data structure can have a measurable impact on processing speed due to factors such as the reuse of TLB entries. Accessing distant array elements in sequence (that is, elements that are not in the same page frame as previously accessed elements) requires frequent soft faults as new TLB entries are loaded and old TLB entries are discarded.

Write a program that creates a two-dimensional array of numbers with a large size, such as 10,000 rows by 10,000 columns. Iterate through the array in column-major order, assigning each element the sum of the row and column indices. Column-major means the column index increments fastest. In other words, the column index increments in the inner loop. Measure precisely how long this procedure takes. Note, you may need to take steps to ensure your programming language does not optimize away the entire calculation if the results from the array are not used later. If may suffice to print one of the array values after the timing is complete, or you may need to do something like sum all the array elements and print that result.

Repeat the process, including the timing, exactly as explained before, except change the inner loop to iterate over the row index and the outer loop to iterate over the column index, making the access sequence row-major.

Since general-purpose computers perform many other tasks while running your code, you may need to perform both procedures a number of times to get a statistically valid result. You might start by running the experiment 10 times and averaging the times for column-major and row-major array access.

Are you able to determine a consistently superior array access method? Which order is fastest on your system using the language you selected? Note that the difference between the column-major and row-major access order may not be dramatic – it might be just a few percent.

Answer

The `Ex__3_row_column_major_order.py` file contains the following Python implementation of a solution to this exercise:

```python
#!/usr/bin/env python


"""Ex__3_row_column_major_order.py: Answer to chapter 7
exercise 3."""


# Typical output from a run of this script:
# Average row-major time    : 16.68 sec
# Average column-major time: 15.94 sec
# Average time difference   : 0.74 sec
# Winner is column-major indexing; It is faster by 4.42%


import time


dim = 10000
matrix = [[0] * dim] * dim


num_passes = 10
row_major_time = 0
col_major_time = 0


for k in range(num_passes):
    print('Pass %d of %d:' % (k+1, num_passes))

    t0 = time.time()
    for i in range(dim):
        for j in range(dim):
            matrix[i][j] = i + j

    t1 = time.time()

    total_time = t1 - t0
    col_major_time = col_major_time + total_time
```

```
    print('  Column-major time to fill array: %.2f sec' %
        total_time)

    t0 = time.time()
    for i in range(dim):
        for j in range(dim):
            matrix[j][i] = i + j

    t1 = time.time()

    total_time = t1 - t0
    row_major_time = row_major_time + total_time
    print('  Row-major time to fill array: %.2f sec' % total_
        time)
    print('')

row_major_average = row_major_time / num_passes
col_major_average = col_major_time / num_passes

if (row_major_average < col_major_average):
    winner = 'row'
    pct_better = 100 * (col_major_average - row_major_average)
        / col_major_average
else:
    winner = 'column'
    pct_better = 100 * (row_major_average - col_major_average)
        / row_major_average

print('Average row-major time    : %.2f sec' % row_major_
    average)
print('Average column-major time: %.2f sec' % col_major_
    average)
print('Average time difference   : %.2f sec' % ((row_major_
    time-col_major_time) / num_passes))
print(('Winner is ' + winner + '-major indexing; It is faster
    by %.2f%%') % pct_better)
```

This program takes a few minutes to run on a Windows PC.

This is the typical output from a run of this program:

```
Average row-major time    : 16.68 sec
Average column-major time: 15.94 sec
Average time difference   : 0.74 sec
Winner is column-major indexing; It is faster by 4.42%
```

Chapter 8: Performance-Enhancing Techniques

Exercise 1

Consider a direct-mapped L1-I cache of 32 KB. Each cache line consists of 64 bytes and the system address space is 4 GB. How many bits are in the cache tag? Which bit numbers (bit 0 is the least significant bit) are they within the address word?

Answer

The cache contains 32,768 bytes with 64 bytes in each line. There are $32,768 \div 64 = 512$ sets in the cache. $512 = 2^9$. The set number is thus 9 bits in length.

Each cache line contains 64 (2^6) bytes, which means the lower 6 bits of each address represent the byte offset within the cache line.

A 4 GB address space requires 32-bit addresses. Subtracting the 9 bits in the set number and the 6 bits in the byte offset from the 32-bit address results in $32 - (9 + 6) = 17$ bits in the cache tag.

The cache tag lies in the 17 most significant bits of the address, so **the range of these bits within a 32-bit address runs from bit 15 to bit 31**.

Exercise 2

Consider an 8-way set-associative L2 instruction and data cache of 256 KB, with 64 bytes in each cache line. How many sets are in this cache?

Answer

The number of lines in the cache is $262,144 \div 64 = 4,096$.

Each set contains 8 lines.

The number of sets = 4,096 lines $\div$ 8 lines per set = **512 sets**.

Exercise 3

A processor has a 4-stage pipeline with maximum delays of 0.8, 0.4, 0.6, and 0.3 nanoseconds in stages 1-4, respectively. If the first stage is replaced with two stages that have maximum delays of 0.5 and 0.3 nanoseconds respectively, how much will the processor clock speed increase in percentage terms?

Answer

The maximum clock speed is determined by the slowest pipeline stage. The slowest stage of the 4-stage pipeline takes 0.8 ns. The maximum clock frequency is $1 \div (0.8 \times 10^{-9}) = 1.25$ GHz.

The 5-stage pipeline has a slowest stage of 0.6 ns. The maximum clock frequency is $1 \div (0.6 \times 10^{-9}) = 1.667$ GHz.

The clock frequency increase resulting from the addition of the pipeline stage is $100 \times (1.667 \times 10^9 - 1.25 \times 10^9) \div (1.25 \times 10^9) = $ **33.3%**.

Chapter 9: Specialized Processor Extensions

Exercise 1

Using a programming language that allows access to the byte representation of floating-point data types (such as C or C++), write a function that accepts a 32-bit single-precision variable as input. Extract the sign, exponent, and mantissa from the bytes of the floating-point variable and display them. Remove the bias term from the exponent before displaying its value and display the mantissa as a decimal number. Test the program with the values 0, -0, 1, -1, 6.674e-11, 1.0e38, 1.0e39, 1.0e-38, and 1.0e-39. The numeric values listed here containing e are using the C/C++ text representation of floating-point numbers. For example, 6.674e-11 means 6.674×10^{-11}.

Answer

The Ex__1_float_format.cpp C++ file contains the code for this exercise:

```
// Ex__1_float_format.cpp


#include <iostream>
#include <cstdint>
```

```cpp
void print_float(float f)
{
    const auto bytes = static_cast<uint8_t*>(
        static_cast<void*>(&f));

    printf(" Float  | %9g |       ", f);

    for (int i = sizeof(float) - 1; i >= 0; i--)
        printf("%02X", bytes[i]);

    printf("      | ");

    const auto sign = bytes[3] >> 7;
    const auto exponent = ((static_cast<uint16_t>(
        bytes[3] & 0x7F) << 8) | bytes[2]) >> 7;
    auto exp_unbiased = exponent - 127;

    uint32_t mantissa = 0;
    for (auto i = 0; i < 3; i++)
        mantissa = (mantissa << 8) | bytes[2 - i];

    mantissa &= 0x7FFFFF; // Clear upper bit

    double mantissa_dec;
    if (exponent == 0) // This is zero or a subnormal number
    {
        mantissa_dec = mantissa /
            static_cast<double>(0x800000);
        exp_unbiased++;
    }
    else
        mantissa_dec = 1.0 + mantissa /
            static_cast<double>(0x800000);

    printf("  %d  |  %4d   | %lf\n", sign,
        exp_unbiased, mantissa_dec);
```

```
}

int main(void)
{
    printf("  Type  |   Number   |          Bytes        "
        "| Sign | Exponent | Mantissa\n");
    printf("  -------|------------|-------------------"
        "|------|----------|---------\n");

    print_float(0);
    print_float(-0); // Minus sign is ignored
    print_float(1);
    print_float(-1);
    print_float(6.674e-11f);
    print_float(1.0e38f);
    //print_float(1.0e39f); // Compile-time error
    print_float(1.0e-38f);
    print_float(1.0e-39f);

    return 0;
}
```

This is the output of the program:

Type	Number	Bytes	Sign	Exponent	Mantissa
Float	0	00000000	0	-126	0.000000
Float	0	00000000	0	-126	0.000000
Float	1	3F800000	0	0	1.000000
Float	-1	BF800000	1	0	1.000000
Float	6.674e-11	2E92C348	0	-34	1.146585

Float 1.175494	1e+38	7E967699	0	126
Float 0.850706	1e-38	006CE3EE	0	-126
Float 0.085071	1e-39	000AE398	0	-126

These are some notes about the results:

- Zero in IEEE 754 can have a positive or negative sign. The zero passed to the `print_float` function in the second row of the table is preceded with a minus sign, but the sign is ignored during the conversion to floating point.

- The value `1.0e39f` is not shown because using it causes a compile-time error: floating constant is out of range.

- Zero is represented as a mantissa of zero and a biased exponent of zero.

- The last two rows contain numbers that cannot be represented with an implicit leading 1 bit because the exponent would underflow. These numbers are called **subnormals** and contain the special biased exponent of 0. Subnormals have reduced precision because not all bits of the mantissa contain meaningful digits.

- Numerically, subnormal floats actually use a biased exponent of 1, which translates to an unbiased exponent of -126.

Exercise 2

Modify the program from *Exercise 1* to also accept a double-precision floating-point variable and print the sign, exponent (with the bias removed), and mantissa from the variable. Test with the same input values as in *Exercise 1*, and also with the values 1.0e308, 1.0e309, and 1.0e-308, 1.0e-309.

Answer

The `Ex__2_double_format.cpp.cpp` C++ file contains the code for this exercise:

```
// Ex__2_double_format.cpp


#include <iostream>
#include <cstdint>

```

```cpp
void print_float(float f)
{
    const auto bytes = static_cast<uint8_t*>(
        static_cast<void*>(&f));

    printf(" Float  | %9g |      ", f);

    for (int i = sizeof(float) - 1; i >= 0; i--)
        printf("%02X", bytes[i]);

    printf("       | ");

    const auto sign = bytes[3] >> 7;
    const auto exponent = ((static_cast<uint16_t>(
        bytes[3] & 0x7F) << 8) | bytes[2]) >> 7;
    auto exp_unbiased = exponent - 127;

    uint32_t mantissa = 0;
    for (auto i = 0; i < 3; i++)
        mantissa = (mantissa << 8) | bytes[2 - i];

    mantissa &= 0x7FFFFF; // Clear upper bit

    double mantissa_dec;
    if (exponent == 0) // This is zero or a subnormal number
    {
        mantissa_dec = mantissa /
            static_cast<double>(0x800000);
        exp_unbiased++;
    }
    else
        mantissa_dec = 1.0 + mantissa /
            static_cast<double>(0x800000);

    printf("  %d  |   %4d   | %lf\n", sign,
        exp_unbiased, mantissa_dec);
```

```cpp
}

void print_double(double d)
{
    const auto bytes = static_cast<uint8_t*>(
        static_cast<void*>(&d));

    printf(" Double | %9g | ", d);

    for (int i = sizeof(double) - 1; i >= 0; i--)
        printf("%02X", bytes[i]);

    printf(" | ");

    const auto sign = bytes[7] >> 7;
    const auto exponent = ((static_cast<uint16_t>(
        bytes[7] & 0x7F) << 8) | bytes[6]) >> 4;
    auto exp_unbiased = exponent - 1023;

    uint64_t mantissa = 0;
    for (auto i = 0; i < 7; i++)
        mantissa = (mantissa << 8) | bytes[6 - i];

    mantissa &= 0xFFFFFFFFFFFFF; // Save the low 52 bits

    double mantissa_dec;
    if (exponent == 0) // This is zero or a subnormal number
    {
        mantissa_dec = mantissa /
            static_cast<double>(0x10000000000000);
        exp_unbiased++;
    }
    else
        mantissa_dec = 1.0 + mantissa /
            static_cast<double>(0x10000000000000);

    printf("  %d  |  %5d  | %lf\n", sign,
        exp_unbiased, mantissa_dec);
```

```
}

int main(void)
{
    printf(" Type   |   Number   |       Bytes      "
        "| Sign | Exponent | Mantissa\n");
    printf(" -------|------------|------------------"
        "|------|----------|---------\n");

    print_float(0);
    print_float(-0); // The minus sign is ignored
    print_float(1);
    print_float(-1);
    print_float(6.674e-11f);
    print_float(1.0e38f);
    //print_float(1.0e39f); // Compile-time error
    print_float(1.0e-38f);
    print_float(1.0e-39f);

    print_double(0);
    print_double(-0); // The minus sign is ignored
    print_double(1);
    print_double(-1);
    print_double(6.674e-11);
    print_double(1.0e38);
    print_double(1.0e39);
    print_double(1.0e-38);
    print_double(1.0e-39);

    print_double(1.0e308);
    //print_double(1.0e309); // Compile-time error
    print_double(1.0e-308);
    print_double(1.0e-309);

    return 0;
}
```

This is the output of the program:

Type | Mantissa	Number	Bytes	Sign	Exponent
Float | 0.000000	0	00000000	0	-126
Float | 0.000000	0	00000000	0	-126
Float | 1.000000	1	3F800000	0	0
Float | 1.000000	-1	BF800000	1	0
Float | 1.146585	6.674e-11	2E92C348	0	-34
Float | 1.175494	1e+38	7E967699	0	126
Float | 0.850706	1e-38	006CE3EE	0	-126
Float | 0.085071	1e-39	000AE398	0	-126
Double | 0.000000	0	0000000000000000	0	-1022
Double | 0.000000	0	0000000000000000	0	-1022
Double | 1.000000	1	3FF0000000000000	0	0
Double | 1.000000	-1	BFF0000000000000	1	0
Double | 1.146584	6.674e-11	3DD25868F4DEAE16	0	-34
Double | 1.175494	1e+38	47D2CED32A16A1B1	0	126
Double | 1.469368	1e+39	48078287F49C4A1D	0	129
Double | 1.701412	1e-38	380B38FB9DAA78E4	0	-127
Double | 1.361129	1e-39	37D5C72FB1552D83	0	-130

Double |	1e+308 |	7FE1CCF385EBC8A0 |	0 |	1023 |
1.112537				
Double |	1e-308 |	000730D67819E8D2 |	0 |	-1022 |
0.449423				
Double |	1e-309 |	0000B8157268FDAF |	0 |	-1022 |
0.044942				

These are some notes about the results:

- Zero in IEEE 754 can have a positive or negative sign. The zero passed to the print_double function in the second row of the table containing the Double type is preceded with a minus sign, but the sign is ignored during the conversion to floating-point.

- The value 1.0e309 is not shown because using it causes a compile-time error: **floating constant is out of range**.

- Zero is represented as a mantissa of zero and a biased exponent of zero.

- The last two rows contain numbers that cannot be represented with an implicit leading 1 bit because the exponent would underflow. These numbers are called subnormals, and contain the special biased exponent of 0. Subnormals have reduced precision because not all bits of the mantissa contain meaningful digits.

- Numerically, subnormal doubles actually use a biased exponent of 1, which translates to an unbiased exponent of -1,022.

Exercise 3

Search the Internet for information about the NXP Semiconductors i.MX RT1060 processor family. Download the product family datasheet and answer the following questions about these processors.

Answer

Introductory information about the i.MX RT1060 processor family is available at https://www.nxp.com/docs/en/nxp/data-sheets/IMXRT1060CEC.pdf.

The complete i.MX RT1060 reference manual is available only after you create an account at https://www.nxp.com.

While logged into your account, search for i.MX RT1060 Processor Reference Manual to locate the reference manual and download it. The filename is IMXRT1060RM.pdf.

Exercise 4

Do the i.MX RT1060 processors support the concept of supervisor-mode instruction execution? Explain your answer.

Answer

Performing a search for `supervisor` in the i.MX RT1060 processor reference manual produces a few hits. However, all of these usages refer to access restrictions related to a particular subsystem, such as the FLEXCAN module.

Supervisor mode in the i.MX RT1060 processor does not operate at the instruction execution level, so *these processors do not implement supervisor mode instruction execution* as described in *Chapter 9, Specialized Processor Extensions.*

Exercise 5

Do the i.MX RT1060 processors support the concept of paged virtual memory? Explain your answer.

Answer

The i.MX RT1060 processors use physical memory addressing with up to 16 memory protection regions. *These processors do not support the concept of paged virtual memory.*

Exercise 6

Do the i.MX RT1060 processors support floating-point operations in hardware? Explain your answer.

Answer

Section 1.3, **Features**, in the reference manual lists the following capability: **Single-precision and double-precision FPU (Floating Point Unit)**.

The **ARM Cortex-M7 Processor Technical Reference Manual**, available at `http://infocenter.arm.com/help/topic/com.arm.doc.ddi0489b/DDI0489B_cortex_m7_trm.pdf` states the FPU provides "*floating-point computation functionality that is compliant with the ANSI/IEEE Std 754-2008, IEEE Standard for Binary Floating-Point Arithmetic, referred to as the IEEE 754 standard.*"

The i.MX RT1060 processors support floating-point operations in hardware.

Exercise 7

What power management features do the i.MX RT1060 processors support?

Answer

Section 12.4 of the reference manual describes the processor power management subsystem. Some of the key features are as follows:

- Separate power domains for the processor, memory, and the remainder of the system.
- Integrated secondary power supplies that support independently powering a variety of subsystems.
- Voltage and clock frequency control enabling **dynamic voltage and frequency scaling (DVFS)**.
- Temperature sensors.
- Voltage sensors.

Exercise 8

What security features do the i.MX RT1060 processors support?

Answer

Chapter 6, Specialized Computing Domains, in the reference manual describes the system security components. Some of the key features are as follows:

- Secure boot, enforcing digital signature verification of an encrypted code image.
- On-chip, one-time programmable ROM for storing security-related information.
- Hardware cryptographic coprocessor supporting the AES-128, SHA-1, and SHA-256 encryption algorithms.
- True random number generator for creating secure cryptographic keys.
- JTAG debug controller with password-enabled secure debug capability.
- Memory interface supporting on-the-fly decryption of encrypted ROM instruction data.

Chapter 10: Modern Processor Architectures and Instruction Sets

Exercise 1

Install the free Visual Studio Community edition, available at `https://visualstudio.microsoft.com/vs/community/`, on a Windows PC. After installation is complete, open the Visual Studio IDE and select **Get Tools and Features...** under the `Tools` menu. Install the **Desktop development with C++** workload.

In the Windows search box in the taskbar, begin typing `x86 Native Tools Command Prompt for VS 2019`. When the app appears in the search menu, select it to open command prompt.

Create a file named `hello_x86.asm` with the content shown in the source listing in the *x86 assembly language* section of this chapter.

Build the program using the command shown in the *The x86 assembly language* section of this chapter and run it. Verify the output **Hello, Computer Architect!** appears on the screen.

Answer

Install Visual Studio Community as described in the question, then install the **Desktop development with C++** workload within Visual Studio Community.

Create your assembly language source file. The `Ex__1_hello_x86.asm` file contains the following example solution to this exercise:

```
.386
.model FLAT,C
.stack 400h

.code
includelib libcmt.lib
includelib legacy_stdio_definitions.lib

extern printf:near
extern exit:near
```

```
public main
main proc
    ; Print the message
    push    offset message
    call    printf

    ; Exit the program with status 0
    push    0
    call    exit
main endp

.data
message db "Hello, Computer Architect!",0

end
```

Open the **x86 Native Tools Command Prompt** for VS 2019 and change to the directory containing your source file.

Build the executable with this command:

```
ml /Fl /Zi /Zd Ex__1_hello_x86.asm
```

This is the output produced by the program:

```
C:\>Ex__1_hello_x86.exe
Hello, Computer Architect!
```

This is the listing file created by the build procedure:

```
Microsoft (R) Macro Assembler Version 14.24.28314.0
01/15/20 18:40:04
Ex__1_hello_x86.asm                              Page 1 - 1


                        .386
                        .model FLAT,C
                        .stack 400h


00000000                .code
```

```
                              includelib libcmt.lib
                              includelib legacy_stdio_definitions.lib


                              extern printf:near
                              extern exit:near


                              public main
00000000                      main proc
                                  ; Print the message
00000000  68 00000000 R           push    offset message
00000005  E8 00000000 E           call    printf


                                  ; Exit the program with status 0
0000000A  6A 00                push    0
0000000C  E8 00000000 E           call    exit
00000011                      main endp


00000000                      .data
00000000  48 65 6C 6C 6F       message db "Hello, Computer
                                          Architect!",0
          2C 20 43 6F 6D
          70 75 74 65 72
          20 41 72 63 68
          69 74 65 63 74
          21 00


                              end
```

```
Microsoft (R) Macro Assembler Version 14.24.28314.0
01/15/20 18:40:04
Ex__1_hello_x86.asm                              Symbols 2 -
1
```

Segments and Groups:

N a m e	Size	Length	Align	Combine Class
FLAT	GROUP			
STACK	32 Bit	00000400	DWord	Stack 'STACK'
_DATA	32 Bit	0000001B	DWord	Public 'DATA'
_TEXT	32 Bit	00000011	DWord	Public 'CODE'

Procedures, parameters, and locals:

N a m e	Type	Value	Attr
main	P Near	00000000	_TEXT
Length= 00000011 Public C			

Symbols:

N a m e	Type	Value	Attr
@CodeSize	Number	00000000h	
@DataSize	Number	00000000h	
@Interface	Number	00000001h	
@Model	Number	00000007h	
@code	Text	_TEXT	
@data	Text	FLAT	
@fardata?	Text	FLAT	
@fardata	Text	FLAT	
@stack	Text	FLAT	
exit	L Near	00000000	FLAT
External C			

```
message  . . . . . . . . . .   Byte    00000000 _DATA
printf . . . . . . . . . . .   L Near           00000000 FLAT
External C
```

```
        0 Warnings
        0 Errors
```

Exercise 2

Write an x86 assembly language program that computes the following expression and prints the result as a hexadecimal number: *[(129 – 66) × (445 + 136)] ÷ 3*. As part of this program, create a callable function to print one byte as two hex digits.

Answer

Create your assembly language source file. The Ex__2_expr_x86.asm file contains the following example solution to this exercise:

```
.386
.model FLAT,C
.stack 400h

.code
includelib libcmt.lib
includelib legacy_stdio_definitions.lib

extern printf:near
extern exit:near

public main
main proc
    ; Print the leading output string
    push    offset msg1
    call    printf

    ; Compute [(129 - 66) * (445 + 136)] / 3
    mov     eax, 129
    sub     eax, 66
```

```
        mov     ebx, 445
        add     ebx, 136
        mul     bx
        mov     bx, 3
        div     bx

        ; Print the most significant byte
        push    eax
        mov     bl, ah
        call    print_byte

        ; Print the least significant byte
        pop     ebx
        call    print_byte

        ; Print the trailing output string
        push    offset msg2
        call    printf

        push    0
        call    exit
main endp

; Pass the byte to be printed in ebx
print_byte proc
        ; x86 function prologue
        push    ebp
        mov     ebp, esp

        ; Use the C library printf function
        and     ebx, 0ffh
        push    ebx
        push    offset fmt_str
        call    printf
```

```
        ; x86 function epilogue
    mov       esp, ebp
    pop       ebp
    ret
print_byte endp


.data
fmt_str db "%02X", 0
msg1        db "[(129 - 66) * (445 + 136)] / 3 = ", 0
msg2        db "h", 9


end
```

Open the **x86 Native Tools Command Prompt** for VS 2019 and change to the directory containing your source file.

Build the executable with this command:

```
ml /Fl /Zi /Zd Ex__1_hello_x86.asm
```

This is the output produced by the program:

```
C:\>Ex__2_expr_x86.exe
[(129 - 66) * (445 + 136)] / 3 = 2FA9h
```

This is the listing file created by the build procedure:

```
Microsoft (R) Macro Assembler Version 14.23.28107.0
01/26/20 20:45:09
Ex__2_expr_x86.asm                                    Page 1 - 1



                    .386
                    .model FLAT,C
                    .stack 400h

00000000            .code
                    includelib libcmt.lib
                    includelib legacy_stdio_definitions.lib
```

```
                              extern printf:near
                              extern exit:near


                              public main
00000000                      main proc
                              ; Print the leading output string
00000000   68 00000005 R         push    offset msg1
00000005   E8 00000000 E         call    printf


                              ; Compute [(129 - 66) * (445 + 136)]
/ 3
0000000A   B8 00000081           mov     eax, 129
0000000F   83 E8 42              sub     eax, 66
00000012   BB 000001BD           mov     ebx, 445
00000017   81 C3 00000088        add     ebx, 136
0000001D   66| F7 E3             mul     bx
00000020   66| BB 0003           mov     bx, 3
00000024   66| F7 F3             div     bx


                              ; Print the most significant byte
00000027   50                    push    eax
00000028   8A DC             mov     bl, ah
0000002A   E8 00000017           call    print_byte


                              ; Print the least significant byte
0000002F   5B                    pop     ebx
00000030   E8 00000011           call    print_byte


                              ; Print the trailing output string
00000035   68 00000027 R         push    offset msg2
0000003A   E8 00000000 E         call    printf


0000003F   6A 00             push    0
00000041   E8 00000000 E         call    exit
00000046                      main endp
```

```
                              ; Pass the byte to be printed in ebx
00000046                      print_byte proc
                              ; x86 function prologue
00000046  55                      push    ebp
00000047  8B EC               mov     ebp, esp

                              ; Use the C library printf function
00000049  81 E3 000000FF          and     ebx, 0ffh
0000004F  53                      push    ebx
00000050  68 00000000 R           push    offset fmt_str
00000055  E8 00000000 E           call    printf

                              ; x86 function epilogue
0000005A  8B E5               mov     esp, ebp
0000005C  5D                      pop     ebp
0000005D  C3                      ret
0000005E                      print_byte endp


00000000                  .data
00000000 25 30 32 58 00    fmt_str db "%02X", 0
00000005 5B 28 31 32 39    msg1    db "[(129 - 66) * (445 +
136)] / 3 = ", 0
         20 2D 20 36 36
         29 20 2A 20 28
         34 34 35 20 2B
         20 31 33 36 29
         5D 20 2F 20 33
         20 3D 20 00
00000027 68 09                    msg2    db "h", 9

                          end
```

Microsoft (R) Macro Assembler Version 14.23.28107.0
01/26/20 20:45:09

```
Ex__2_expr_x86.asm                                    Symbols 2 -
1
```

Segments and Groups:

N a m e	Size	Length	Align Combine Class
FLAT	GROUP		
STACK	32 Bit	00000400	DWord Stack 'STACK'
_DATA	32 Bit	00000029	DWord Public 'DATA'
_TEXT	32 Bit	0000005E	DWord Public 'CODE'

Procedures, parameters, and locals:

N a m e	Type	Value	Attr
main	P Near	00000000	_TEXT Length= 00000046 Public C
print_byte	P Near	00000046	_TEXT Length= 00000018 Public C

Symbols:

N a m e	Type	Value	Attr
@CodeSize	Number	00000000h	
@DataSize	Number	00000000h	
@Interface	Number	00000001h	

@Model	Number	00000007h
@code	Text	_TEXT
@data	Text	FLAT
@fardata?	Text	FLAT
@fardata	Text	FLAT
@stack	Text	FLAT
exit . . . . External C	L Near	00000000 FLAT
fmt_str	Byte	00000000 _DATA
msg1	Byte	00000005 _DATA
msg2	Byte	00000027 _DATA
printf . . . . External C	L Near	00000000 FLAT

```
        0 Warnings
        0 Errors
```

Exercise 3

In the Windows search box in the taskbar, begin typing x64 Native Tools Command Prompt for VS 2019. When the app appears in the search menu, select it to open command prompt.

Create a file named hello_x64.asm with the content shown in the source listing in the *x64 assembly language* section of this chapter.

Build the program using the command shown in the *x64 assembly language* section of this chapter and run it. Verify the output **Hello, Computer Architect!** appears on the screen.

Answer

Create your assembly language source file. The Ex__3_hello_x64.asm file contains the following example solution to this exercise:

```
.code
includelib libcmt.lib
includelib legacy_stdio_definitions.lib

extern printf:near
extern exit:near
```

```
public main
main proc
    ; Reserve stack space
    sub      rsp, 40

    ; Print the message
    lea      rcx, message
    call     printf

    ; Exit the program with status 0
    xor      rcx, rcx
    call     exit
main endp

.data
message db "Hello, Computer Architect!",0

end
```

Open the x64 Native Tools Command Prompt for VS 2019 and change to the directory containing your source file.

Build the executable with this command:

```
ml64 /Fl /Zi /Zd Ex__3_hello_x64.asm
```

This is the output produced by the program:

```
C:\>Ex__3_hello_x64.exe
Hello, Computer Architect!
```

This is the listing file created by the build procedure:

```
Microsoft (R) Macro Assembler (x64) Version 14.24.28314.0
01/15/20 18:44:39
Ex__3_hello_x64.asm              Page 1 - 1



 00000000    .code
```

```
        includelib libcmt.lib
        includelib legacy_stdio_definitions.lib


        extern printf:near
        extern exit:near


    public main
00000000    main proc
        ; Reserve stack space
00000000    48/ 83 EC 28        sub     rsp, 40


        ; Print the message
00000004    48/ 8D 0D       lea     rcx, message
    00000000 R
0000000B    E8 00000000 E       call    printf


        ; Exit the program with status 0
00000010    48/ 33 C9       xor     rcx, rcx
00000013    E8 00000000 E       call    exit
00000018    main endp


00000000    .data
00000000 48 65 6C 6C 6F  message db "Hello, Computer
                            Architect!",0
    2C 20 43 6F 6D
    70 75 74 65 72
    20 41 72 63 68
    69 74 65 63 74
    21 00


    end
```

Microsoft (R) Macro Assembler (x64) Version 14.24.28314.0
01/15/20 18:44:39

```
Ex__3_hello_x64.asm              Symbols 2 - 1



Procedures, parameters, and locals:

                N a m e                 Type      Value     Attr

main . . . . . . . . . . . . . . P     00000000 _TEXT Length=
00000018 Public


Symbols:

                N a m e                 Type      Value     Attr

exit . . . . . . . . . . . . . L       00000000 _TEXT External
message  . . . . . . . . . . . Byte    00000000 _DATA
printf . . . . . . . . . . . . L       00000000 _TEXT External

    0 Warnings
    0 Errors
```

Exercise 4

Write an x64 assembly language program that computes the following expression and prints the result as a hexadecimal number: $[(129 - 66) \times (445 + 136)] \div 3$. As part of this program, create a callable function to print one byte as two hex digits.

Answer

Create your assembly language source file. The Ex__4_expr_x64.asm file contains the following example solution to this exercise:

```
.code
includelib libcmt.lib
includelib legacy_stdio_definitions.lib
```

```
extern printf:near
extern exit:near

public main
main proc
    ; Reserve stack space
    sub     rsp, 40

    ; Print the leading output string
    lea     rcx, msg1
    call    printf

    ; Compute [(129 - 66) * (445 + 136)] / 3
    mov     eax, 129
    sub     eax, 66
    mov     ebx, 445
    add     ebx, 136
    mul     bx
    mov     bx, 3
    div     bx

    ; Print the most significant byte
    push    rax
    mov     bl, ah
    and     ebx, 0ffh
    call    print_byte

    ; Print the least significant byte
    pop     rbx
    and     ebx, 0ffh
    call    print_byte

    ; Print the trailing output string
    lea     rcx, msg2
    call    printf

    ; Exit the program with status 0
```

```
       xor      rcx, rcx
       call     exit
main endp

; Pass the byte to be printed in ebx
print_byte proc
       ; x64 function prologue
       sub      rsp, 40

       ; Use the C library printf function
       mov      rdx, rbx
       lea      rcx, fmt_str
       call     printf

       ; x64 function epilogue
       add      rsp, 40

       ret
print_byte endp

.data
fmt_str db "%02X", 0
msg1    db "[(129 - 66) * (445 + 136)] / 3 = ", 0
msg2    db "h", 9

end
```

Open the **x64 Native Tools Command Prompt for VS 2019** and change to the directory containing your source file.

Build the executable with this command:

```
ml64 /Fl /Zi /Zd Ex__3_hello_x64.asm
```

This is the output produced by the program:

```
C:\>Ex__4_expr_x64.exe
[(129 - 66) * (445 + 136)] / 3 = 2FA9h
```

This is the listing file created by the build procedure:

```
Microsoft (R) Macro Assembler (x64) Version 14.23.28107.0
01/26/20 20:58:00

Ex__4_expr_x64.asm                 Page 1 - 1


  00000000    .code
      includelib libcmt.lib
      includelib legacy_stdio_definitions.lib


      extern printf:near
      extern exit:near


    public main
  00000000    main proc
          ; Reserve stack space
  00000000   48/ 83 EC 28       sub      rsp, 40


          ; Print the leading output string
  00000004   48/ 8D 0D          lea      rcx, msg1
     00000005 R
  0000000B   E8 00000000 E      call     printf


          ; Compute [(129 - 66) * (445 + 136)] / 3
  00000010   B8 00000081        mov      eax, 129
  00000015   83 E8 42           sub      eax, 66
  00000018   BB 000001BD        mov      ebx, 445
  0000001D   81 C3 00000088     add      ebx, 136
  00000023   66| F7 E3          mul      bx
  00000026   66| BB 0003        mov      bx, 3
  0000002A   66| F7 F3          div      bx


          ; Print the most significant byte
  0000002D   50        push     rax
  0000002E   8A DC        mov      bl, ah
  00000030   81 E3 000000FF     and      ebx, 0ffh
```

```
00000036   E8 00000020         call     print_byte


      ; Print the least significant byte
0000003B   5B          pop     rbx
0000003C   81 E3 000000FF      and      ebx, 0ffh
00000042   E8 00000014         call     print_byte


      ; Print the trailing output string
00000047   48/ 8D 0D           lea      rcx, msg2
   00000027 R
0000004E   E8 00000000 E       call     printf


      ; Exit the program with status 0
00000053   48/ 33 C9           xor      rcx, rcx
00000056   E8 00000000 E       call     exit
0000005B   main endp


   ; Pass the byte to be printed in ebx
0000005B   print_byte proc
      ; x64 function prologue
0000005B   48/ 83 EC 28        sub      rsp, 40


      ; Use the C library printf function
0000005F   48/ 8B D3           mov      rdx, rbx
00000062   48/ 8D 0D           lea      rcx, fmt_str
   00000000 R
00000069   E8 00000000 E       call     printf


      ; x64 function epilogue
0000006E   48/ 83 C4 28        add      rsp, 40


00000072   C3          ret
00000073   print_byte endp


00000000   .data
00000000 25 30 32 58 00 fmt_str db "%02X", 0
```

```
 00000005 5B 28 31 32 39 msg1      db "[(129 - 66) * (445 + 136)]
/ 3 = ", 0
      20 2D 20 36 36
      29 20 2A 20 28
      34 34 35 20 2B
      20 31 33 36 29
      5D 20 2F 20 33
      20 3D 20 00
 00000027 68 09    msg2    db "h", 9


      end
```

Microsoft (R) Macro Assembler (x64) Version 14.23.28107.0
01/26/20 20:58:00

Ex__4_expr_x64.asm   Symbols 2 - 1

Procedures, parameters, and locals:

N a m e	Type	Value	Attr
main . . . . P	00000000	_TEXT	Length=
0000005B Public
print_byte . . . . P	0000005B	_TEXT	Length=
00000018 Public

Symbols:

N a m e	Type	Value	Attr
exit L	00000000	_TEXT	External
fmt_str . . . . Byte	00000000	_DATA	
msg1 . . . . Byte	00000005	_DATA	

```
msg2 . . . . . . . . . . . . . . Byte  00000027 _DATA
printf . . . . . . . . . . . . . L    00000000 _TEXT External


      0 Warnings
      0 Errors
```

Exercise 5

Install the free Android Studio IDE, available at `https://developer.android.com/studio/`. After installation is complete, open the Android Studio IDE and select **SDK Manager** under the **Tools** menu. In the **Settings for New Projects** dialog, select the **SDK Tools** tab and check the **NDK** option, which may be called **NDK (Side by side)**. Complete the installation of the NDK (**NDK** means **native development kit**).

Locate the following files under the SDK installation directory (the default location is `%LOCALAPPDATA%\Android`) and add their directories to your PATH environment variable: `arm-linux-androideabi-as.exe` and `adb.exe`. Hint: the following command works for one specific version of Android Studio (your path may vary):

```
set PATH=%PATH%;%LOCALAPPDATA%\Android\Sdk\ndk\20.1.5948944\
toolchains\arm-linux-androideabi-4.9\prebuilt\windows-x86_64\
bin;%LOCALAPPDATA%\Android\Sdk\platform-tools
```

Create a file named `hello_arm.s` with the content shown in the source listing in the *The 32-bit ARM assembly language* section of this chapter.

Build the program using the commands shown in the *The 32-bit ARM assembly language* section of this chapter.

Enable **Developer Options** on an Android phone or tablet. Search the Internet for instructions on how to do this.

Connect your Android device to the computer with a USB cable.

Copy the program executable image to the phone using the commands shown in the **32-bit ARM assembly language** section of this chapter and run the program. Verify that the output **Hello, Computer Architect!** appears on the host computer screen.

Answer

Create your assembly language source file. The `Ex__5_hello_arm.s` file contains the following example solution to this exercise:

```
.text
.global _start


_start:
    // Print the message to file 1 (stdout) with syscall 4
    mov     r0, #1
    ldr     r1, =msg
    mov     r2, #msg_len
    mov     r7, #4
    svc     0


    // Exit the program with syscall 1, returning status 0
    mov     r0, #0
    mov     r7, #1
    svc     0


.data
msg:
    .ascii      "Hello, Computer Architect!"
msg_len = . - msg
```

Build the executable with these commands:

```
arm-linux-androideabi-as -al=Ex__5_hello_arm.lst -o Ex__5_
hello_arm.o Ex__5_hello_arm.s
arm-linux-androideabi-ld -o Ex__5_hello_arm Ex__5_hello_arm.o
```

This is the output produced by copying the program to an Android device and running it:

```
C:\>adb devices
* daemon not running; starting now at tcp:5037
* daemon started successfully
List of devices attached
```

```
9826f541374f4b4a68          device
```

```
C:\>adb push Ex__5_hello_arm /data/local/tmp/Ex__5_hello_arm
Ex__5_hello_arm: 1 file pushed. 0.0 MB/s (868 bytes in 0.059s)
```

```
C:\>adb shell chmod +x /data/local/tmp/Ex__5_hello_arm
C:\>adb shell /data/local/tmp/Ex__5_hello_arm
Hello, Computer Architect!
```

This is the listing file created by the build procedure:

```
ARM GAS   Ex__5_hello_arm.s                     page 1




    1                         .text
    2                         .global _start
    3
    4                    _start:
    5                         // Print the message to file 1
                             //(stdout) with syscall 4
    6 0000 0100A0E3          mov     r0, #1
    7 0004 14109FE5          ldr     r1, =msg
    8 0008 1A20A0E3          mov     r2, #msg_len
    9 000c 0470A0E3          mov     r7, #4
   10 0010 000000EF          svc     0
   11
   12                         // Exit the program with syscall 1,
                             //returning status 0
   13 0014 0000A0E3          mov     r0, #0
   14 0018 0170A0E3          mov     r7, #1
   15 001c 000000EF          svc     0
   16
   17                    .data
   18                    msg:
   19 0000 48656C6C          .ascii      "Hello, Computer
                             Architect!"
   19      6F2C2043
   19      6F6D7075
```

19	74657220
19	41726368
20	msg_len = . - msg

Exercise 6

Write a 32-bit ARM assembly language program that computes the following expression and prints the result as a hexadecimal number: $[(129 - 66) \times (445 + 136)] \div 3$. As part of this program, create a callable function to print one byte as two hex digits.

Answer

Create your assembly language source file. The file Ex__6_expr_arm.s contains for an example solution to this exercise.

```
.text
.global _start


_start:
    // Print the leading output string
    ldr      r1, =msg1
    mov      r2, #msg1_len
    bl       print_string


    // Compute [(129 - 66) * (445 + 136)] / 3
    mov      r0, #129
    sub      r0, r0, #66
    ldr      r1, =#445
    add      r1, r1, #136
    mul      r0, r1, r0
    mov      r1, #3
    udiv     r0, r0, r1


    // Print the upper byte of the result
    push     {r0}
    lsr      r0, r0, #8
```

```
    bl        print_byte

    // Print the lower byte of the result
    pop       {r0}
    bl        print_byte

    // Print the trailng output string
    ldr       r1, =msg2
    mov       r2, #msg2_len
    bl        print_string

    // Exit the program with syscall 1, returning status 0
    mov       r0, #0
    mov       r7, #1
    svc       0

// Print a string; r1=string address, r2=string length
print_string:
    mov       r0, #1
    mov       r7, #4
    svc       0
    mov       pc, lr

// Convert the low 4 bits of r0 to an ascii character in r0
nibble2ascii:
    and       r0, #0xF
    cmp       r0, #10
    addpl     r0, r0, #('A' - 10)
    addmi     r0, r0, #'0'
    mov       pc, lr

// Print a byte in hex
print_byte:
    push      {lr}
    push      {r0}
    lsr       r0, r0, #4
```

```
        bl        nibble2ascii
        ldr       r1, =bytes
        strb      r0, [r1], #1


        pop       {r0}
        bl        nibble2ascii
        strb      r0, [r1]


        ldr       r1, =bytes
        mov       r2, #2
        bl        print_string


        pop       {lr}
        mov       pc, lr


.data
msg1:
        .ascii    "[(129 - 66) * (445 + 136)] / 3 = "
msg1_len = . - msg1


bytes:
        .ascii    "??"


msg2:
        .ascii    "h"
msg2_len = . - msg2
```

Build the executable with these commands:

```
arm-linux-androideabi-as -al=Ex__6_expr_arm.lst -o Ex__6_expr_
arm.o Ex__6_expr_arm.s
arm-linux-androideabi-ld -o Ex__6_expr_arm Ex__6_expr_arm.o
```

This is the output produced by copying the program to an Android device and running it:

```
C:\>adb devices
* daemon not running; starting now at tcp:5037
* daemon started successfully
```

```
List of devices attached
9826f541374f4b4a68          device


C:\>adb push Ex__6_expr_arm /data/local/tmp/Ex__6_expr_arm
Ex__6_expr_arm: 1 file pushed. 0.2 MB/s (1188 bytes in 0.007s)

C:\>adb shell chmod +x /data/local/tmp/Ex__6_expr_arm
C:\>adb shell /data/local/tmp/Ex__6_expr_arm
[(129 - 66) * (445 + 136)] / 3 = 2FA9h
```

This is the listing file created by the build procedure:

```
ARM GAS   Ex__6_expr_arm.s       page 1


 1                      .text
 2                      .global _start
 3
 4                  _start:
 5                      // Print the leading output string
 6 0000 A8109FE5      ldr     r1, =msg1
 7 0004 2120A0E3      mov     r2, #msg1_len
 8 0008 110000EB      bl      print_string
 9
10                      // Compute [(129 - 66) * (445 + 136)] /
                        // 3
11 000c 8100A0E3      mov     r0, #129
12 0010 420040E2      sub     r0, r0, #66
13 0014 98109FE5      ldr     r1, =#445
14 0018 881081E2      add     r1, r1, #136
15 001c 910000E0      mul     r0, r1, r0
16 0020 0310A0E3      mov     r1, #3
17 0024 10F130E7      udiv    r0, r0, r1
18
19                      // Print the upper byte of the result
20 0028 04002DE5      push    {r0}
21 002c 2004A0E1      lsr     r0, r0, #8
22 0030 100000EB      bl      print_byte
```

23				
24			// Print the lower byte of the result	
25	0034	04009DE4	pop	{r0}
26	0038	0E0000EB	bl	print_byte
27				
28			// Print the trailng output string	
29	003c	74109FE5	ldr	r1, =msg2
30	0040	0120A0E3	mov	r2, #msg2_len
31	0044	020000EB	bl	print_string
32				
33			// Exit the program with syscall 1, //returning status 0	
34	0048	0000A0E3	mov	r0, #0
35	004c	0170A0E3	mov	r7, #1
36	0050	000000EF	svc	0
37				
38			// Print a string; r1=string address, //r2=string length	
39			print_string:	
40	0054	0100A0E3	mov	r0, #1
41	0058	0470A0E3	mov	r7, #4
42	005c	000000EF	svc	0
43	0060	0EF0A0E1	mov	pc, lr
44				
45			// Convert the low 4 bits of r0 to an ascii //character in r0	
46			nibble2ascii:	
47	0064	0F0000E2	and	r0, #0xF
48	0068	0A0050E3	cmp	r0, #10
49	006c	37008052	addpl	r0, r0, #('A' - 10)
50	0070	30008042	addmi	r0, r0, #'0'
51	0074	0EF0A0E1	mov	pc, lr
52				
53			// Print a byte in hex	
54			print_byte:	
55	0078	04E02DE5	push	{lr}
56	007c	04002DE5	push	{r0}

```
57 0080 2002A0E1         lsr      r0, r0, #4
```

```
58 0084 F6FFFFEB         bl       nibble2ascii
59 0088 2C109FE5         ldr      r1, =bytes
60 008c 0100C1E4         strb     r0, [r1], #1
61
62 0090 04009DE4         pop      {r0}
63 0094 F2FFFFEB         bl       nibble2ascii
64 0098 0000C1E5         strb     r0, [r1]
65
66 009c 18109FE5         ldr      r1, =bytes
67 00a0 0220A0E3         mov      r2, #2
68 00a4 EAFFFFEB         bl       print_string
69
70 00a8 04E09DE4         pop      {lr}
71 00ac 0EF0A0E1         mov      pc, lr
72
73                       .data
74                 msg1:
75 0000 5B283132              .ascii   "[(129 - 66) * (445 + 136)] / 3
                                        = "
75      39202D20
75      36362920
75      2A202834
75      3435202B
76                 msg1_len = . - msg1
77
78                 bytes:
79 0021 3F3F              .ascii   "??"
80
81                 msg2:
82 0023 68                .ascii   "h"
83                 msg2_len = . - msg2
```

Exercise 7

Locate the following files under the Android SDK installation directory (the default location is %LOCALAPPDATA%\Android) and add their directories to your PATH environment variable: aarch64-linux-android-as.exe and adb.exe. Hint: the following command works for one version of Android Studio (your path may vary):

```
set PATH=%PATH%;%LOCALAPPDATA \Android\sdk\ndk-bundle\
toolchains\arm-linux-androideabi-4.9\prebuilt\windows-x86_64\
bin;%LOCALAPPDATA%\Android\Sdk\platform-tools
```

Create a file named hello_arm64.s with the content shown in the source listing in the *64-bit ARM assembly language* section of this chapter.

Build the program using the commands shown in the *64-bit ARM assembly language* section of this chapter.

Enable **Developer Options** on an Android phone or tablet.

Connect your Android device to the computer with a USB cable.

Copy the program executable image to the phone using the commands shown in the *64-bit ARM assembly language* section of this chapter and run the program. Verify the output **Hello, Computer Architect!** appears on the host computer screen.

Answer

Create your assembly language source file. The Ex__6_expr_arm.s file contains the following example solution to this exercise:

```
.text
.global _start


_start:
    // Print the leading output string
    ldr     r1, =msg1
    mov     r2, #msg1_len
    bl      print_string


    // Compute [(129 - 66) * (445 + 136)] / 3
    mov     r0, #129
```

```
    sub     r0, r0, #66
    ldr     r1, =#445
    add     r1, r1, #136
    mul     r0, r1, r0
    mov     r1, #3
    udiv    r0, r0, r1

    // Print the upper byte of the result
    push    {r0}
    lsr     r0, r0, #8
    bl      print_byte

    // Print the lower byte of the result
    pop     {r0}
    bl      print_byte

    // Print the trailng output string
    ldr     r1, =msg2
    mov     r2, #msg2_len
    bl      print_string

    // Exit the program with syscall 1, returning status 0
    mov     r0, #0
    mov     r7, #1
    svc     0

// Print a string; r1=string address, r2=string length
print_string:
    mov     r0, #1
    mov     r7, #4
    svc     0
    mov     pc, lr

// Convert the low 4 bits of r0 to an ascii character in r0
nibble2ascii:
    and     r0, #0xF
```

```
        cmp     r0, #10
        addpl   r0, r0, #('A' - 10)
        addmi   r0, r0, #'0'
        mov     pc, lr


// Print a byte in hex
print_byte:
        push    {lr}
        push    {r0}
        lsr     r0, r0, #4
        bl      nibble2ascii
        ldr     r1, =bytes
        strb    r0, [r1], #1


        pop     {r0}
        bl      nibble2ascii
        strb    r0, [r1]


        ldr     r1, =bytes
        mov     r2, #2
        bl      print_string


        pop     {lr}
        mov     pc, lr


.data
msg1:
    .ascii  "[(129 - 66) * (445 + 136)] / 3 = "
msg1_len = . - msg1


bytes:
    .ascii  "??"


msg2:
    .ascii  "h"
msg2_len = . - msg2
```

Build the executable with these commands:

```
arm-linux-androideabi-as -al=Ex__6_expr_arm.lst -o Ex__6_expr_
arm.o Ex__6_expr_arm.s
```

```
arm-linux-androideabi-ld -o Ex__6_expr_arm Ex__6_expr_arm.o
```

This is the output produced by copying the program to an Android device and running it:

```
C:\>adb devices
* daemon not running; starting now at tcp:5037
* daemon started successfully
List of devices attached
9826f541374f4b4a68        device


C:\>adb push Ex__6_expr_arm /data/local/tmp/Ex__6_expr_arm
Ex__6_expr_arm: 1 file pushed. 0.2 MB/s (1188 bytes in 0.007s)


C:\>adb shell chmod +x /data/local/tmp/Ex__6_expr_arm
C:\>adb shell /data/local/tmp/Ex__6_expr_arm
[(129 - 66) * (445 + 136)] / 3 = 2FA9h
```

This is the listing file created by the build procedure:

```
ARM GAS   Ex__6_expr_arm.s                     page 1



     1                          .text
     2                          .global _start
     3
     4                  _start:
     5                          // Print the leading output string
     6 0000 A8109FE5           ldr      r1, =msg1
     7 0004 2120A0E3           mov      r2, #msg1_len
     8 0008 110000EB           bl       print_string
     9
    10                          // Compute [(129 - 66) * (445 +
                                //136)] / 3
    11 000c 8100A0E3           mov      r0, #129
    12 0010 420040E2           sub      r0, r0, #66
```

```
13  0014  98109FE5        ldr     r1, =#445
14  0018  881081E2        add     r1, r1, #136
15  001c  910000E0        mul     r0, r1, r0
16  0020  0310A0E3        mov     r1, #3
17  0024  10F130E7        udiv    r0, r0, r1
18

19                        // Print the upper byte of the
                          //result
20  0028  04002DE5        push    {r0}
21  002c  2004A0E1        lsr     r0, r0, #8
22  0030  100000EB        bl      print_byte
23

24                        // Print the lower byte of the
                          //result
25  0034  04009DE4        pop     {r0}
26  0038  0E0000EB        bl      print_byte
27

28                        // Print the trailng output string
29  003c  74109FE5        ldr     r1, =msg2
30  0040  0120A0E3        mov     r2, #msg2_len
31  0044  020000EB        bl      print_string
32

33                        // Exit the program with syscall 1,
                          //returning status 0
34  0048  0000A0E3        mov     r0, #0
35  004c  0170A0E3        mov     r7, #1
36  0050  000000EF        svc     0
37

38                        // Print a string; r1=string address,
                          //r2=string length
39                        print_string:
40  0054  0100A0E3        mov     r0, #1
41  0058  0470A0E3        mov     r7, #4
42  005c  000000EF        svc     0
43  0060  0EF0A0E1        mov     pc, lr
44
```

45			// Convert the low 4 bits of r0 to an //ascii character in r0
46			nibble2ascii:
47	0064	0F0000E2	and r0, #0xF
48	0068	0A0050E3	cmp r0, #10
49	006c	37008052	addpl r0, r0, #('A' - 10)
50	0070	30008042	addmi r0, r0, #'0'
51	0074	0EF0A0E1	mov pc, lr
52			
53			// Print a byte in hex
54			print_byte:
55	0078	04E02DE5	push {lr}
56	007c	04002DE5	push {r0}
57	0080	2002A0E1	lsr r0, r0, #4

ARM GAS   Ex__6_expr_arm.s   page 2

58	0084	F6FFFFEB	bl nibble2ascii
59	0088	2C109FE5	ldr r1, =bytes
60	008c	0100C1E4	strb r0, [r1], #1
61			
62	0090	04009DE4	pop {r0}
63	0094	F2FFFFEB	bl nibble2ascii
64	0098	0000C1E5	strb r0, [r1]
65			
66	009c	18109FE5	ldr r1, =bytes
67	00a0	0220A0E3	mov r2, #2
68	00a4	EAFFFFEB	bl print_string
69			
70	00a8	04E09DE4	pop {lr}
71	00ac	0EF0A0E1	mov pc, lr
72			
73			.data
74			msg1:

75	0000	5B283132	.ascii "[(129 - 66) * (445 + 136)]
			/ 3 = "
75		39202D20	
75		36362920	
75		2A202834	
75		3435202B	
76			msg1_len = . - msg1
77			
78			bytes:
79	0021	3F3F	.ascii "??"
80			
81			msg2:
82	0023	68	.ascii "h"
83			msg2_len = . - msg2

Exercise 8

Write a 64-bit ARM assembly language program that computes the following expression and prints the result as a hexadecimal number: *[(129 – 66) × (445 + 136)] ÷ 3*. As part of this program, create a callable function to print one byte as two hex digits.

Answer

Create your assembly language source file. The Ex__8_expr_arm64.s file contains the following example solution to this exercise:

```
.text
.global _start


_start:
    // Print the leading output string
    ldr     x1, =msg1
    mov     x2, #msg1_len
    bl      print_string


    // Compute [(129 - 66) * (445 + 136)] / 3
    mov     x0, #129
    sub     x0, x0, #66
```

```
        mov     x1, #445
        add     x1, x1, #136
        mul     x0, x1, x0
        mov     x1, #3
        udiv    x0, x0, x1


        // Print the upper byte of the result
        mov     x19, x0
        lsr     x0, x0, #8
        bl      print_byte


        // Print the lower byte of the result
        mov     x0, x19
        bl      print_byte


        // Print the trailng output string
        ldr     x1, =msg2
        mov     x2, #msg2_len
        bl      print_string


        // Exit the program with syscall 93, returning status 0
        mov     x0, #0
        mov     x8, #93
        svc     0


// Print a string; x1=string address, x2=string length
print_string:
        mov     x0, #1
        mov     x8, #64
        svc     0
        ret     x30


// Convert the low 4 bits of x0 to an ascii character in x0
nibble2ascii:
        and     x0, x0, #0xF
        cmp     x0, #10
```

```
        bmi     lt10


        add     x0, x0, #('A' - 10)
        b       done


lt10:
        add     x0, x0, #'0'


done:
        ret     x30


// Print a byte in hex
print_byte:
        mov     x21, x30
        mov     x20, x0
        lsr     x0, x0, #4
        bl      nibble2ascii
        ldr     x1, =bytes
        strb    w0, [x1], #1


        mov     x0, x20
        bl      nibble2ascii
        strb    w0, [x1]


        ldr     x1, =bytes
        mov     x2, #2
        bl      print_string


        mov     x30, x21
        ret     x30


.data
msg1:
        .ascii  "[(129 - 66) * (445 + 136)] / 3 = "
msg1_len = . - msg1
```

```
bytes:
    .ascii   "??"


msg2:
    .ascii   "h"
msg2_len = . - msg2
```

Build the executable with these commands:

```
aarch64-linux-android-as -al=Ex__8_expr_arm64.lst -o Ex__8_
expr_arm64.o Ex__8_expr_arm64.s
aarch64-linux-android-ld -o Ex__8_expr_arm64 Ex__8_expr_arm64.o
```

This is the output produced by copying the program to an Android device and running it:

```
C:\>adb devices
* daemon not running; starting now at tcp:5037
* daemon started successfully
List of devices attached
9826f541374f4b4a68        device


C:\>adb push Ex__8_expr_arm64 /data/local/tmp/Ex__8_expr_arm64
Ex__8_expr_arm64: 1 file pushed. 0.1 MB/s (1592 bytes in
0.015s)


C:\>adb shell chmod +x /data/local/tmp/Ex__8_expr_arm64
C:\>adb shell /data/local/tmp/Ex__8_expr_arm64
[(129 - 66) * (445 + 136)] / 3 = 2FA9h
```

This is the listing file created by the build procedure:

```
AARCH64 GAS   Ex__8_expr_arm64.s                    page 1



      1                        .text
      2                        .global _start
      3
      4                        _start:
      5                            // Print the leading output string
```

6	0000	C1050058	ldr	x1, =msg1
7	0004	220480D2	mov	x2, #msg1_len
8	0008	13000094	bl	print_string
9				
10				// Compute [(129 - 66) * (445 + //136)] / 3
11	000c	201080D2	mov	x0, #129
12	0010	000801D1	sub	x0, x0, #66
13	0014	A13780D2	mov	x1, #445
14	0018	21200291	add	x1, x1, #136
15	001c	207C009B	mul	x0, x1, x0
16	0020	610080D2	mov	x1, #3
17	0024	0008C19A	udiv	x0, x0, x1
18				
19				// Print the upper byte of the //result
20	0028	F30300AA	mov	x19, x0
21	002c	00FC48D3	lsr	x0, x0, #8
22	0030	14000094	bl	print_byte
23				
24				// Print the lower byte of the //result
25	0034	E00313AA	mov	x0, x19
26	0038	12000094	bl	print_byte
27				
28				// Print the trailng output string
29	003c	21040058	ldr	x1, =msg2
30	0040	220080D2	mov	x2, #msg2_len
31	0044	04000094	bl	print_string
32				
33				// Exit the program with syscall 93, //returning status 0
34	0048	000080D2	mov	x0, #0
35	004c	A80B80D2	mov	x8, #93
36	0050	010000D4	svc	0
37				

38		// Print a string; x1=string address, //x2=string length
39		print_string:
40	0054 200080D2	mov x0, #1
41	0058 080880D2	mov x8, #64
42	005c 010000D4	svc 0
43	0060 C0035FD6	ret x30
44		
45		// Convert the low 4 bits of x0 to an //ascii character in x0
46		nibble2ascii:
47	0064 000C4092	and x0, x0, #0xF
48	0068 1F2800F1	cmp x0, #10
49	006c 64000054	bmi lt10
50		
51	0070 00DC0091	add x0, x0, #('A' - 10)
52	0074 02000014	b done
53		
54		lt10:
55	0078 00C00091	add x0, x0, #'0'
56		
57		done:

AARCH64 GAS   Ex__8_expr_arm64.s   page 2

58	007c C0035FD6	ret x30
59		
60		// Print a byte in hex
61		print_byte:
62	0080 F5031EAA	mov x21, x30
63	0084 F40300AA	mov x20, x0
64	0088 00FC44D3	lsr x0, x0, #4

65	008c	F6FFFF97	bl	nibble2ascii
66	0090	C1010058	ldr	x1, =bytes
67	0094	20140038	strb	w0, [x1], #1
68				
69	0098	E00314AA	mov	x0, x20
70	009c	F2FFFF97	bl	nibble2ascii
71	00a0	20000039	strb	w0, [x1]
72				
73	00a4	21010058	ldr	x1, =bytes
74	00a8	420080D2	mov	x2, #2
75	00ac	EAFFFF97	bl	print_string
76				
77	00b0	FE0315AA	mov	x30, x21
78	00b4	C0035FD6	ret	x30
79				
80			.data	
81			msg1:	
82	0000	5B283132	.ascii	"[(129 - 66) * (445 + 136)] / 3 = "
82		39202D20		
82		36362920		
82		2A202834		
82		3435202B		
83			msg1_len = . - msg1	
84				
85			bytes:	
86	0021	3F3F	.ascii	"??"
87				
88			msg2:	
89	0023	68	.ascii	"h"
90			msg2_len = . - msg2	

Chapter 11: The RISC-V Architecture and Instruction Set

Exercise 1

Visit `https://www.sifive.com/boards/` and download **Freedom Studio**. Freedom Studio is an Eclipse IDE-based development suite with a complete set of tools for building an RISC-V application and running it on a hardware RISC-V processor or in the emulation environment included with Freedom Studio. Follow the instructions in the *Freedom Studio User Manual* to complete the installation. Start Freedom Studio and create a new Freedom E SDK project. In the project creation dialog, select `qemu-sifive-u54` as the target (this is a single-core 64-bit RISC-V processor in the RV64GC configuration). Select the `hello` example program and click on the **Finish** button. This will start a build of the example program and the RISC-V emulator. After the build completes, the **Edit Configuration** dialog box will appear. Click on **Debug** to start the program in the emulator debug environment. Single-step through the program and verify that the text **Hello, World!** appears in the console window.

Answer

Install **Freedom Studio** as described. Note that the directory path for your workspace cannot include spaces. Start Freedom Studio.

1. In the **Welcome to SiFive FreedomStudio! Let's Get Started...** dialog, select **I want to create a new Freedom E SDK Project**.

2. In the **Create a Freedom E SDK Project** dialog, select **qemu-sifive-u54** as the target.

3. Select the **hello** example program.

4. Click the **Finish** button.

5. After the build completes, the **Edit Configuration** dialog box will appear.

6. Click **Debug** to start the program in the emulator debug environment.

7. Single-step through the program and verify that the text **Hello, World!** appears in the console window.

Exercise 2

With the project from *Exercise 1* still open, locate the hello.c file in the src folder in the **Project** window. Right-click on the file and rename it to hello.s. Open hello.s in the editor and delete the entire contents. Insert the assembly language program shown in the *RISC-V assembly language* section in this chapter. Perform a clean and then rebuild the project (press *Ctrl + 9* to initiate the clean operation). Select **Debug** under the **Run** menu. Once the debugger starts, open windows to display the hello.s source file, the **Disassembly** window, and the **Registers** window. Expand the **Registers** tree to display the RISC-V processor registers. Single-step through the program and verify the text **Hello, Computer Architect!** appears in the console window.

Answer

With the project from *Exercise 1* still open, locate the hello.c file in the src folder in the **Project** window, then do the following:

1. Right-click on the file and rename it to hello.s.

2. Open hello.s in the editor and delete the entire contents.

3. Insert the assembly language program shown in the *RISC-V assembly language* section in this chapter. This is the assembly code, also available in the Ex__2_ riscv_assembly.s file:

```
.section .text
.global main


main:
    # Reserve stack space and save the return address
    addi    sp, sp, -16
    sd      ra, 0(sp)


    # Print the message using the C library puts function
1:  auipc   a0, %pcrel_hi(msg)
    addi    a0, a0, %pcrel_lo(1b)
    jal     ra, puts


    # Restore the return address and sp, and return to
caller
```

```
        ld        ra, 0(sp)
        addi      sp, sp, 16
        jalr      zero, ra, 0


.section .rodata
msg:
        .asciz "Hello, Computer Architect!\n"
```

4. Perform a clean and then rebuild the project (press *Ctrl* + *9* to initiate the clean operation).

5. Select **Debug** under the **Run** menu.

6. Once the debugger starts, open windows to display the hello.s source file, the **Disassembly** window, and the **Registers** window.

7. Expand the Registers tree to display the RISC-V processor registers.

8. Single-step through the program and verify that the text **Hello, Computer Architect!** appears in the console window.

Exercise 3

Write a RISC-V assembly language program that computes the following expression and prints the result as a hexadecimal number: $[(129 - 66) \times (445 + 136)] \div 3$. As part of this program, create a callable function to print one byte as two hex digits.

Answer

Create a new Freedom Studio project using the same steps as in *Exercise 1* in this chapter. Locate the hello.c file in the src folder in the **Project** window.

1. Right-click on the file and rename it to hello.s.

2. Create your assembly language source code within the hello.s file. The Ex__3_riscv_expr.s file contains the following example solution to this exercise:

```
.section .text
.global main


main:
```

```
# Reserve stack space and save the return address
addi    sp, sp, -16
sd      ra, 0(sp)


# Print the leading output string
la      a0, msg1
jal     ra, puts


# Compute [(129 - 66) * (445 + 136)] / 3
addi    a0, zero, 129
addi    a0, a0, -66
addi    a1, zero, 445
add     a1, a1, 136
mul     a0, a1, a0
addi    a1, zero, 3
divu    a0, a0, a1


# Print the upper byte of the result
sw      a0, 8(sp)
srl     a0, a0, 8
jal     ra, print_byte


# Print the lower byte of the result
lw      a0, 8(sp)
jal     ra, print_byte


# Print the trailng output string
la      a0, msg2
jal     ra, puts


# Restore the return address and sp, and return to
caller
ld      ra, 0(sp)
addi    sp, sp, 16
ret
```

```
# Convert the low 4 bits of a0 to an ascii character in
a0
nibble2ascii:
    # Reserve stack space and save the return address
    addi    sp, sp, -16
    sd      ra, 0(sp)

    and     a0, a0, 0xF
    sltu    t0, a0, 10
    bne     t0, zero, lt10

    add     a0, a0, ('A' - 10)
    j       done

lt10:
    add     a0, a0, '0'

done:
    ld      ra, 0(sp)
    addi    sp, sp, 16
    ret

# Print a byte in hex
print_byte:
    # Reserve stack space and save the return address
    addi    sp, sp, -16
    sd      ra, 0(sp)

    addi    t1, a0, 0
    srl     a0, t1, 4
    jal     ra, nibble2ascii
    la      t3, bytes
    sb      a0, 0(t3)

    addi    a0, t1, 0
    jal     nibble2ascii
```

```
        sb      a0, 1(t3)

        la      a0, bytes
        jal     ra, puts

        ld      ra, 0(sp)
        addi    sp, sp, 16
        ret

.section .data
msg1:
        .asciz  "[(129 - 66) * (445 + 136)] / 3 = "

bytes:
        .asciz  "??"

msg2:
        .asciz  "h"
```

3. Perform a clean and then rebuild the project (press *Ctrl + 9* to initiate the clean operation).

4. Select **Debug** under the **Run** menu.

5. Once the debugger starts, open windows to display the hello.s source file, the **Disassembly** window, and the **Registers** window.

6. Expand the **Registers** tree to display the RISC-V processor registers.

7. Single-step through the program and verify that the text *[(129 - 66) * (445 + 136)] / 3 = 2FA9h* appears in the Console window.

Exercise 4

Program an Arty A7-35T board with a RISC-V processor image. Build and run the hello assembly language program shown in the *RISC-V assembly language* section in this chapter on the RISC-V processor using the Olimex ARM-TINY-USB-H debugger as described in the *Implementing RISC-V in an FPGA* section near the end of this chapter. Verify that the program outputs the text **Hello, Computer Architect!**

Answer

The instructions in this answer are based on information provided at `https://github.com/sifive/freedom`, with some updates to work with more recent versions of libraries. Several of these steps are quite time consuming and the entire process may take several hours:

Steps 1-11 build a RISC-V firmware image in a file named `E300ArtyDevKitFPGAChip.mcs`. If you prefer to skip these steps, you can download this file directly at `https://github.com/PacktPublishing/Modern-Computer-Architecture-and-Organization/blob/master/Chapter11/Answers%20to%20Exercises/src/E300ArtyDevKitFPGAChip.mcs` and continue at step 12.

1. If you already have a Linux system available for this exercise, you can skip to *step 2*. Otherwise, begin by downloading and installing **VirtualBox** from `https://www.virtualbox.org/wiki/Downloads`. Download an operating system image from OSBoxes at `https://www.osboxes.org/virtualbox-images/`. Select the most recent 64-bit Ubuntu VDI image. Follow the instructions at `https://www.osboxes.org/guide/` to set up the **virtual machine** (**VM**) image and get logged in to Linux.

2. Install and license Vivado in the Linux VM. See the solution to *Chapter 2*, *Digital Logic*, *Exercise 3* for Vivado installation instructions for Windows. You should expect some minor differences because you are now installing on Linux.

3. Execute the following commands to update the Linux operating system and install the SiFive RISC-V development kit:

```
sudo apt update
sudo apt upgrade
sudo apt install git
cd ~
git clone https://github.com/sifive/freedom.git
cd freedom
git submodule update --init --recursive
```

4. Install additional required tools:

```
sudo apt-get install autoconf automake autotools-dev curl
libmpc-dev libmpfr-dev libgmp-dev libusb-1.0-0-dev gawk
build-essential bison flex texinfo gperf libtool
patchutils bc zlib1g-dev device-tree-compiler pkg-config
libexpat-dev python wget
sudo apt-get install default-jre
```

5. Build and install **sbt**, the Scala Build Tool:

```
echo "deb https://dl.bintray.com/sbt/debian /" | sudo tee
-a /etc/apt/sources.list.d/sbt.list
sudo apt-key adv --keyserver hkp://keyserver.ubuntu.
com:80 --recv 642AC823
sudo apt-get update
sudo apt-get install sbt
```

6. Build and install **verilator**, a Verilog HDL simulator:

```
sudo apt-get install git make autoconf g++ flex bison
git clone http://git.veripool.org/git/verilator
cd verilator
unset VERILATOR_ROOT
autoconf
./configure
make -j `nproc`
sudo make install
```

7. Install **Scala**, an object-oriented programming language influenced by Java:

```
sudo apt install scala
```

8. Download the RISC-V toolchain from https://www.sifive.com/boards/. Select the **GNU Embedded Toolchain for Ubuntu**. Unzip the file as follows:

```
cd ~
tar xvf Downloads/riscv64-unknown-elf-gcc-8.3.0-
2019.08.0-x86_64-linux-ubuntu14.tar.gz
```

9. Set environment variables for Vivado. Place these commands in your ~/.bashrc file to set them automatically each time you log back in. Use your own directory paths if they are different:

```
export RISCV=/home/osboxes/riscv64-unknown-elf-gcc-8.3.0-
2019.08.0-x86_64-linux-ubuntu14
export PATH=${PATH}:/tools/Xilinx/Vivado/2019.2/bin
```

10. Download the Digilent board files from `https://github.com/Digilent/vivado-boards/archive/master.zip`. Open the ZIP file in the Linux File Manager and navigate to the `/vivado-boards-master/new/board_files/` directory. Copy the entire contents of this directory. Paste the copied contents into `/tools/Xilinx/Vivado/2019.2/data/boards/board_files`.

11. The RISC-V design is programmed in the **Chisel** language. The first `make` command, as follows, compiles the RISC-V chisel code into Verilog HDL. The second `make` command uses Vivado to compile the Verilog into an FPGA binary image. Build the Arty A7-35T RISC-V image with these commands:

```
cd ~/freedom
make -f Makefile.e300artydevkit verilog
sudo ln -s /usr/lib/x86_64-linux-gnu/libtinfo.so.6 /usr/lib/x86_64-linux-gnu/libtinfo.so.5
make -f Makefile.e300artydevkit mcs
```

When this step completes, the output file is located at `~/freedom/builds/e300artydevkit/obj/E300ArtyDevKitFPGAChip.mcs`.

12. Copy the `E300ArtyDevKitFPGAChip.mcs` file to the Windows host. Follow the instructions at `https://www.sifive.com/documentation/freedom-soc/freedom-e300-arty-fpga-dev-kit-getting-started-guide/` to connect the Olimex debugger to the Arty A7 board and flash the `E300ArtyDevKitFPGAChip.mcs` file onto the board.

13. Close Vivado and shut down the Ubuntu VM. Start **Freedom Studio** in your Windows (or Linux) host. Keep the Arty A7 USB cable connected to the host computer and keep the Olimex debugger connected to the host.

14. Select **Create a new Freedom E SDK Software Project** in the **Freedom Studio SiFive Tools** menu. Select **freedom-e310-arty** as the target. Select **hello** as the example program. Click **Finish** to create the project and start a build.

15. After the build completes, a dialog titled **Edit configuration and launch** will appear. Click **Debug** to download the executable image to the Arty A7. If you watch the red LED on the cable side of the Olimex device you should see some flickering as the download progresses.

16. Open the **Windows Device Manager** (type `device` into the Windows search box and select **Device Manager** from the list). Under **Ports (COM & LPT)**, identify the COM port number of the Arty, which will be named **USB Serial Port**.

17. In FreedomStudio, close any COM Console windows that are open.

18. In FreedomStudio, click the icon that looks like a screen to create a new COM Console window. In the **Choose Terminal** field, select **Serial Terminal**. Set the serial port to the port you identified in **Device Manager**. Set the baud rate to 57600. Click **OK** to open the console window.

19. Click the mouse cursor inside the FreedomStudio window containing the C source code. Press *F6* to single-step the C program. The text **Hello, World!** should appear in the console window. This is output from the program running on the RISC-V processor implemented in the Arty A7 FPGA.

Chapter 12: Processor Virtualization

Exercise 1

Download and install the current version of VirtualBox. Download, install, and bring up Ubuntu Linux as a VM within VirtualBox. Connect the guest OS to the Internet using a bridged network adapter. Configure and enable clipboard sharing and file sharing between the Ubuntu guest and your host operating system.

Answer

Perform the following steps:

1. Download the VirtualBox 6.1 (or later version) installer from https://www.virtualbox.org/wiki/Downloads. Be sure to select the version appropriate for your host operating system.

2. Run the VirtualBox installer and accept the default prompts.

3. Download a VirtualBox image of 64-bit Ubuntu Linux. One source for such an image is https://www.osboxes.org/ubuntu/. If the image is in a compressed format, uncompress it. Use 7-zip (https://www.7-zip.org/) if the filename ends with *.7z*. After unzipping, the VirtualBox disk image filename will have the extension *.vdi*.

4. Start VirtualBox Manager and click the **New** icon. Give the new machine a name, such as Ubuntu, select **Linux** as the type, and select **Ubuntu (64-bit)** as the version. Click **Next**.

5. In the **Memory size** dialog, accept the default memory size (or increase it if you prefer).

6. In the **Hard disk** dialog, select **Use an existing virtual hard disk file**. Click the **Browse** button (it looks like a folder), then click the **Add** button in the **Hard disk selector** dialog. Navigate to the `.vdi` file you downloaded and select **Open**. Click **Create** to finish creating the VM.

7. Click the **Settings** icon in VirtualBox. In the **General** section, on the **Advanced** tab, select **Bidirectional** for **Shared Clipboard**.

8. Click **Network**. In the **Adapter 1** tab, select **Bridged Adapter** next to **Attached to:**.

9. Create a folder on the Windows disk named `share` in your `Documents` folder. Click **Shared Folders** in the VirtualBox Manager **Settings** dialog for your Ubuntu VM. Click the icon to add a shared folder (it looks like a folder with a plus on it). Select the `share` folder you just created on the host computer and click **OK**.

10. Click **OK** in the **Settings** dialog to close it.

11. Click the **Start** icon to start the VM. When the Ubuntu system finishes booting, login with the password `osboxes.org`.

12. After login has finished, open a Terminal window by pressing *Ctrl + Alt + T*.

13. In the VM Terminal, create a directory named `share` with the following command:

```
mkdir share
```

14. Enter the following command in the VM Terminal to mount the shared folder:

```
sudo mount -t vboxsf -o rw,uid=1000,gid=1000 share ~/
share
```

Exercise 2

Within the Ubuntu operating system you installed in *Exercise 1*, install VirtualBox and then install and bring up a virtual machine version of FreeDOS. Verify that DOS commands such as `echo Hello World!` and `mem` perform properly in the FreeDOS VM. After completing this exercise, you will have implemented an instance of nested virtualization.

Answer

1. With your Ubuntu VM not running, select the **Settings** icon in the VirtualBox manager for the VM. In the **System** section, under the **Processor** tab, check the box for **Enable Nested VT-x/AMD-V**. You must be running VirtualBox 6.1 or later for this feature to be fully supported. Click **OK** to save the change.

2. Start your Ubuntu VM. Log in to the VM, open a Terminal window, and install VirtualBox in the Ubuntu VM with the following commands:

```
wget -q https://www.virtualbox.org/download/oracle_
vbox_2016.asc -O- | sudo apt-key add -
```
```
sudo add-apt-repository "deb [arch=amd64] http://
download.virtualbox.org/virtualbox/debian $(lsb_release
-cs) contrib"
```
```
sudo apt update && sudo apt install virtualbox-6.1
```

3. Install 7-zip in the Ubuntu VM with this command:

```
sudo apt-get install p7zip-full
```

4. Download a VirtualBox virtual disk image for FreeDOS from `https://www.osboxes.org/freedos/`. Perform the following steps (assuming the downloaded file is in the `~/Downloads` directory, and the FreeDOS image filename is `1-2.7.z`):

```
cd
mkdir 'VirtualBox VMs'
cd 'VirtualBox VMs'
mv ~/Downloads/1-2.7.z .
7z x 1-2.7z
```

5. Start **VirtualBox** with the following command:

```
virtualbox &
```

6. Create a new VM in the **VirtualBox** instance running in the Ubuntu VM. Select the following options:

```
Name: FreeDOS
Type: Other
Version: DOS
```

```
32MB RAM
```

```
Use an existing virtual hard disk file
```

7. Select the VDI file in ~/VirtualBox VMs and complete the VM configuration.

8. Click the **Start** icon in VirtualBox manager to start the FreeDOS VM.

9. After the VM completes booting, execute these commands in the FreeDOS prompt:

```
echo Hello World!
```

```
mem
```

```
dir
```

This screenshot shows the output of the mem command:

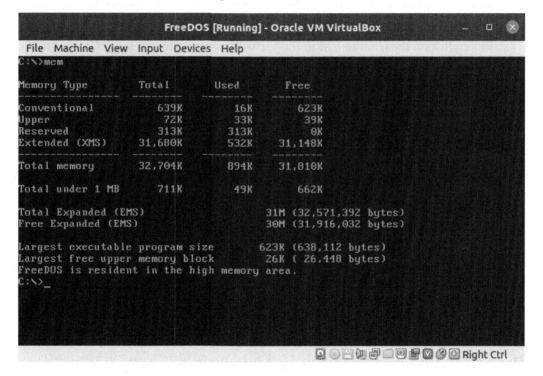

10. When you are finished using FreeDOS, close the VM with the following command in the FreeDOS prompt:

```
shutdown
```

Exercise 3

Create two separate copies of your Ubuntu guest machine in your host system's VirtualBox environment. Configure both Ubuntu guests to connect to the VirtualBox *internal* network. Set up the two machines with compatible IP addresses. Verify that each of the machines can receive a response from the other using the `ping` command. By completing this exercise, you have configured a virtual network within your virtualized environment.

Answer

1. In your host system VirtualBox, open the **Settings** dialog for the Ubuntu VM you set up in *Exercise 1* and select the **Network** settings. Set the **Attached to:** network type to `Internal`, then click **OK**.

2. Right-click on the Ubuntu VM in the VirtualBox manager and select **Clone...** from the context menu. Click **Next** in the **Clone VM** menu. Leave **Full clone** selected and click **Clone**. Wait for the cloning process to complete.

3. Open Command Prompt on your host system and navigate to the installation directory for **VirtualBox**. On Windows, this command takes you to the following default installation location:

    ```
    cd "\Program Files\Oracle\VirtualBox"
    ```

4. Start a DHCP server for the `intnet` VirtualBox network with this command:

    ```
    VBoxManage dhcpserver add --netname intnet --ip
    192.168.10.1 --netmask 255.255.255.0 --lowerip
    192.168.10.100 --upperip 192.168.10.199 --enable
    ```

5. Start both of the VMs. Based on the DHCP server settings recommended in the previous step, the VMs should be assigned the IP addresses `192.168.10.100` and `192.168.10.101`.

6. Log in to one of the running VMs. Click the downward-facing triangle in the upper right corner of the screen. Select **Wired Connected** from the dialog, then click **Wired Settings**.

7. Click the gear icon in the **Wired** section of the **Settings** dialog. The machine's IP address will be displayed. It should be one of the two IP addresses listed in step 5.

8. Open a Terminal window in the VM (press *Ctrl + Alt + T*).

9. Ping the other machine. For example, if this machine's IP address is 192.168.10.100, enter the following command:

```
ping 192.168.10.101
```

You should see a response similar to the following. Press *Ctrl + C* to stop the updates:

```
osboxes@osboxes:~$ ping 192.168.10.101
PING 192.168.10.101 (192.168.10.101) 56(84) bytes of
data.
64 bytes from 192.168.10.101: icmp_seq=1 ttl=64
time=0.372 ms
64 bytes from 192.168.10.101: icmp_seq=2 ttl=64
time=0.268 ms
64 bytes from 192.168.10.101: icmp_seq=3 ttl=64
time=0.437 ms
64 bytes from 192.168.10.101: icmp_seq=4 ttl=64
time=0.299 ms
^C
--- 192.168.10.101 ping statistics ---
4 packets transmitted, 4 received, 0% packet loss, time
3054ms
rtt min/avg/max/mdev = 0.268/0.344/0.437/0.065 ms
osboxes@osboxes:~$
```

10. Log in to the second Ubuntu VM and repeat steps 6-9 to display its IP address and ping the first Ubuntu VM.

Chapter 13: Domain-Specific Computer Architectures

Exercise 1

Draw a block diagram of the computing architecture for a system to measure and report weather data 24 hours a day at 5-minute intervals using SMS text messages. The system is battery powered and relies on solar cells to recharge the battery during daylight hours. Assume the weather instrumentation consumes minimal average power, only requiring full power momentarily during each measurement cycle.

Answer

Based on the performance requirements, a processor capable of entering a very low power state for minutes at a time should be able to operate from a moderately sized battery for days at a time. By only powering weather sensors when necessary to take a measurement, and only powering the cellular transceiver when it is time to transmit data, power usage is minimized.

The following diagram represents one possible configuration for this system:

Exercise 2

For the system of *Exercise 1*, identify a suitable, commercially available processor and list the reasons why that processor is a good choice for this application. Some factors to weigh are cost, processing speed, tolerance for harsh environments, power consumption, and integrated features such as RAM and communication interfaces.

Answer

Perform the following steps:

1. An Internet search for `low-power microprocessor` brings up a selection of processors from manufacturers including STM, Analog Devices, Texas Instruments, Microchip Technology, and several others.

2. A second search for `embedded cellular modem` produces a list of cellular modems suitable for this application. Some of these devices are in the form of a **system-on-module (SoM)**, incorporating the RF modem with a programmable processor core in a single module.

3. The MultiTech Dragonfly Nano SoM (`https://www.multitech.com/brands/multiconnect-dragonfly-nano`) appears to be suitable for this application. This device is available for US$103.95 and integrates an ARM Cortex-M4 processor for hosting user applications. The Dragonfly Nano provides I/O interfaces including a serial UART, USB, I2C, SPI, 9 analog inputs, and up to 29 digital I/O pins. The Cortex-M4 contains 1 MB of flash memory and 128 KB of RAM.

4. The Dragonfly Nano documentation states that when transmitting a small amount of data each day, the device can run for years on two AA-size batteries.

5. The reasons for selecting the Dragonfly Nano for this application are as follows:

- **Cost**: While a price over $US100 is high for a microprocessor board, the integration of the cellular modem directly accomplishes a key system design goal.

- **Low power consumption**: Depending on the power requirements for the weather sensors, a small solar panel combined with a small rechargeable battery should easily satisfy system power requirements.

- **Environmental compatibility**: The temperature range specification for the SoM is -40° to +85° C (-40° to +185° F), which should support operation anywhere in the world. The relative humidity tolerance range (20% to 90% RH, non-condensing) will require installation in a weatherproof enclosure.

- **Processing power**: The SoM contains an `STM32L471QG` 32-bit ARM processor operating at 80 MHz. This processor provides a great deal of capability, including an FPU and dynamic voltage scaling. It is possible to perform extensive preprocessing (filtering, sensor fault detection, and so on) on sensor measurements prior to the transmission of data. The flash and RAM within the device should be more than adequate for the application.

- **Certified solution**: The Dragonfly Nano is certified by the FCC and wireless carriers for use on cellular networks.

- **Development support**: Free development tools and online resources are available at `https://os.mbed.com/platforms/MTS-Dragonfly-Nano/`.

The dashed box in the following diagram indicates the portion of the system implemented by the Dragonfly Nano SoM:

Chapter 14: Future Directions in Computer Architectures

Exercise 1

Install the Qiskit quantum processor software development framework by following the instructions at `https://qiskit.org/documentation/install.html`. The instructions suggest installation of the Anaconda (`https://www.anaconda.com/`) data science and machine learning toolset. After installing Anaconda, create a Conda virtual environment named `qiskitenv` to contain your work on quantum code and install Qiskit in this environment with the `pip install qiskit` command. Be sure to install the optional visualization dependencies with the `pip install qiskit-terra[visualization]` command.

Answer

1. Download the Anaconda installer from `https://www.anaconda.com/distribution/`. Select the Python 3.7 version, in the appropriate 32-bit or 64-bit variant for your host computer.

2. Run the Anaconda installer and accept the defaults. Close the installer after it completes.

3. Start Anaconda from the Windows search box by typing `anaconda` and clicking on **Anaconda prompt** when it appears in the search list. A console window will appear.

4. In the Anaconda prompt, create and activate a virtual environment named `qiskitenv` with the following commands. Install any recommended packages:

```
conda create -n qiskitenv python=3
conda activate qiskitenv
```

5. Install Qiskit and the visualization dependencies with these commands:

```
pip install qiskit
pip install qiskit-terra[visualization]
```

6. This completes the installation.

Exercise 2

Create a free IBM Quantum Experience account at `https://quantum-computing.ibm.com/`. Locate your IBM Quantum Services API token at `https://quantum-computing.ibm.com/account` and install it into your local environment using the instructions at `https://qiskit.org/documentation/install.html`.

Answer

1. Visit `https://quantum-computing.ibm.com/`. If you don't already have an account, click the **Create an IBMid account** link to get started.

2. Once you are logged in, click on the account icon at the top right (it looks like a little person).

3. Locate the **Copy token** button on the screen. Click it to copy your API token to the clipboard.

4. Return to the Anaconda prompt for the `qiskitenv` environment you created in *Exercise 1*.

5. Enter the following commands at the Anaconda prompt to set up your API token. You will need to replace MY_TOKEN with the token you copied to the clipboard in *step 3*:

```
python
import qiskit
from qiskit import IBMQ
IBMQ.save_account('MY_TOKEN')
```

Exercise 3

Work through the example quantum program at `https://qiskit.org/documentation/tutorial/fundamentals/1_getting_started_with_qiskit.html`. This example creates a quantum circuit containing three qubits that implements a **Greenberger–Horne–Zeilinger (GHZ)** state. The GHZ state exhibits key properties of quantum entanglement. Execute the code in a simulation environment on your computer.

Answer

1. Start an Anaconda prompt console. Type `anaconda` in the Windows search box and click on **Anaconda prompt** when it appears in the search list. A console window will appear.

2. Enter the `qiskitenv` environment with this command:

```
conda activate qiskitenv
```

3. Enter the following commands at the Anaconda prompt:

```
python
import numpy as np
from qiskit import *
```

4. Create a quantum circuit containing a three-qubit GHZ state and add measurements for each qubit:

```
circ = QuantumCircuit(3)
# Add an H gate to qubit 0, creating superposition
circ.h(0)
# Add a CX (CNOT) gate. Qubit 0 is control and qubit 1 is
target
circ.cx(0,1)
# Add a CX (CNOT) gate. Qubit 0 is control and qubit 2 is
target
circ.cx(0,2)

# Add a measurement to each of the qubits
meas = QuantumCircuit(3, 3)
meas.barrier(range(3))
```

```
meas.measure(range(3),range(3))
```

```
# Combine the two circuits
qc = circ + meas
```

5. Display the circuit onscreen:

```
qc.draw()
```

The output of this command should appear as follows:

```
>>> qc.draw()
```

```
>>>
```

6. Run the circuit on your computer using the `qasm_simulator` simulator. The `shots` parameter provides a count of the number of times the circuit will be executed to collect statistical results:

```
backend_sim = Aer.get_backend('qasm_simulator')
job_sim = execute(qc, backend_sim, shots=1024)
```

7. Retrieve and display the count of the number of times each bit pattern resulted from a simulation run:

```
result_sim = job_sim.result()
counts_sim = result_sim.get_counts(qc)
counts_sim
```

You should see results similar (but not identical) to these:

```
>>> counts_sim
{'000': 527, '111': 497}
>>>
```

Exercise 4

Execute the code from *Exercise 3* on an IBM quantum computer.

Answer

1. Repeat *steps 1-5* from *Exercise 3* to create the quantum circuit.

2. Import your IBMQ account information and list the available quantum computing providers:

```
from qiskit import IBMQ
IBMQ.load_account()
provider = IBMQ.get_provider(group='open')
provider.backends()
```

3. If you visit the IBM Quantum Experience home page at https://quantum-computing.ibm.com/, you will be able to see the length of the job queues for the available quantum computers. Select a system with sufficient qubits for your circuit and a short job queue. This example assumes the **ibmq_essex** computer is your choice.

4. Add your job to the queue and monitor its status with these commands. The shots parameter provides a count of the number of times the circuit will be executed to collect statistical results:

```
backend = provider.get_backend('ibmq_essex')
from qiskit.tools.monitor import job_monitor
job_exp = execute(qc, backend=backend, shots=1024)
job_monitor(job_exp)
```

After the run completes, you will see the following output line:

```
Job Status: job has successfully run
```

5. After the job completes, retrieve the results with this command:

```
result_exp = job_exp.result()
```

6. Retrieve and display the count of the number of times each bit pattern resulted from a quantum computer run:

```
counts_exp = result_exp.get_counts(qc)
counts_exp
```

Approximately 50% of the time, the output bit string for this circuit should be 000, and the other 50% of the time it should be 111. However, these systems are **noisy, intermediate-scale quantum (NISQ)** computers

7. You should see results similar (but not identical) to these:

```
>>> counts_exp
{'000': 459, '010': 28, '011': 35, '110': 17, '111': 428,
'101': 23, '100': 22, '001': 12}
>>>
```

If the description for this answer isn't clear, see:

https://github.com/PacktPublishing/Modern-Computer-Architecture-and-Organization/blob/master/Chapter14/Answers%20to%20Exercises/Ex__4_run_quantum_computer.md

Other Books You May Enjoy

If you enjoyed this book, you may be interested in these other books by Packt:

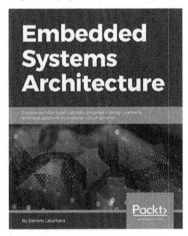

Embedded Systems Architecture

Daniele Lacamera

ISBN: 978-1-78883-250-2

- Participate in the design and definition phase of an embedded product
- Get to grips with writing code for ARM Cortex-M microcontrollers
- Build an embedded development lab and optimize the workflow
- Write memory-safe code
- Understand the architecture behind the communication interfaces
- Understand the design and development patterns for connected and distributed devices in the IoT
- Master multitask parallel execution patterns and real-time operating systems

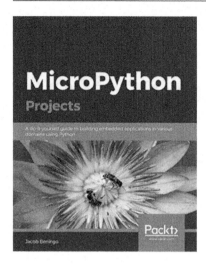

MicroPython Projects

Jacob Beningo

ISBN: 978-1-78995-803-4

- Develop embedded systems using MicroPython
- Build a custom debugging tool to visualize sensor data in real time
- Process and parse GPS and National Marine Electronics Association (NMEA) messages in MicroPython
- Detect objects using machine learning and MicroPython
- Discover how to minimize project costs and reduce development time
- Get to grips with gesture operations and parsing gesture data

Leave a review - let other readers know what you think

Please share your thoughts on this book with others by leaving a review on the site that you bought it from. If you purchased the book from Amazon, please leave us an honest review on this book's Amazon page. This is vital so that other potential readers can see and use your unbiased opinion to make purchasing decisions, we can understand what our customers think about our products, and our authors can see your feedback on the title that they have worked with Packt to create. It will only take a few minutes of your time, but is valuable to other potential customers, our authors, and Packt. Thank you!

Index

U

V

Z